Religion and the Rise of Historicism

W. M. L. de Wette, Jacob Burckhardt, and the Theological Origins of Nineteenth-Century Historical Consciousness

This book offers an interpretation of the rise of secular historical thought in nineteenth-century Europe. Instead of characterizing "historicism" and "secularization" as fundamental breaks with Europe's religious heritage, they are presented as complex cultural permutations with much continuity; for inherited theological patterns of interpreting experience determined to a large degree the conditions, possibilities, and limitations of the forms of historical imagination realizable by nineteenth-century secular intellectuals.

This point is made by examining the thought of the German theologian W. M. L. de Wette (1780–1849) and that of the Swiss-German historian Jacob Burckhardt (1818–97). A theological radical, de Wette disputed orthodox doctrine and practiced historical biblical criticism. The son of a Protestant minister, Burckhardt aspired to become a clergyman and studied theology – until he encountered de Wette at the University of Basel. His studies under de Wette provoked a religious crisis that compelled him to forsake theology for a career in history.

Burckhardt's encounter with de Wette and his decision for history over theology are interpreted as revealing moments in nineteenth-century intellectual history. By examining the encounter, its larger historical context, and the thought of both men, the book demonstrates the centrality of theological concerns and forms of knowledge in the emergence of modern, secular historical consciousness.

*   *   *

Thomas Albert Howard graduated summa cum laude/Phi Beta Kappa from the University of Alabama in 1990. He completed his MA (1992) and PhD (1996) in European intellectual history at the University of Virginia. The recipient of a Deutscher Akademischer Austauschdienst fellowship, Howard conducted research at Freiburg University (and at nearby Basel) in 1994–95. At Valparaiso University (Valparaiso, IN) he held a fellowship in the Lilly Fellows Program in the Humanities and the Arts in 1997–99. Presently Howard is Assistant Professor of History at Gordon College (Wenham, MA). Howard has delivered papers in both Europe and the United States, and has published articles and book reviews in such journals as *The Journal of the History of Ideas*, *Christian Scholar's Review*, *German Studies Review*, *Storia della Storiografia*, *The National Interest*, and *The Journal of Religious History*.

Religion and the Rise of Historicism

W. M. L. de Wette, Jacob Burckhardt, and the Theological Origins of Nineteenth-Century Historical Consciousness

THOMAS ALBERT HOWARD

Gordon College

CAMBRIDGE
UNIVERSITY PRESS

PUBLISHED BY THE PRESS SYNDICATE OF THE UNIVERSITY OF CAMBRIDGE
The Pitt Building, Trumpington Street, Cambridge, United Kingdom

CAMBRIDGE UNIVERSITY PRESS
The Edinburgh Building, Cambridge CB2 2RU, UK   http://www.cup.cam.ac.uk
40 West 20th Street, New York, NY 10011-4211, USA   http://www.cup.org
10 Stamford Road, Oakleigh, Melbourne 3166, Australia
Ruiz de Alarcón 13, 28014, Madrid, Spain

First published 2000

Printed in the United States of America

Typeface Sabon 10/12 pt.   *System* QuarkXPress ™ [BTS]

A catalog record for this book is available from the British Library.

Library of Congress Cataloging in Publication data
Howard, Thomas Albert, 1967–
Religion and the rise of historicism :
W. M. L. de Wette, Jacob Burckhardt, and the theological origins of nineteenth-century
historical consciousness / Thomas Albert Howard.
p.   cm.
Includes bibliographical references and index.
ISBN 0-521-65022-4 (hardcover)
1. Historicism.   2. History (Theology)   3. De Wette, Wilhelm
Martin Leberecht, 1780–1849.   4. Burckhardt, Jacob, 1818–1897.   I. Title.
D16.9.H69   1999
901 – dc21   99-12874
                                                                        CIP

ISBN   0 521 65022 4   Hardback

For Agnes

Contents

Acknowledgments

While working on this project, I have incurred many pleasant debts. Because of a fellowship from the Deutscher Akademischer Austauschdienst (DAAD), I was able to spend a year (1994–95) in Freiburg, Germany, conducting research at the University of Freiburg and at nearby Basel, Switzerland. At Freiburg, I am grateful to Professor Ernst Schulin for inviting me to participate in his seminar and for his insightful comments on my work. At the University of Basel, I profited from discussions with professors Andreas Cesana, Niklaus Peter, Karl Hammer, Ulrich Gäbler, and the late Hans Rudolf Guggisberg. My conversations with these scholars will be fondly remembered.

At the University of Virginia, Allan Megill deserves special recognition for his thoughtful and detailed criticism when this project was still my dissertation. The other members of my committee, H. C. Erik Midelfort, Alon Confino, and James D. Hunter, also contributed valuable suggestions. I deeply appreciate the support and encouragement of Kenneth G. Elzinga; his magnanimity and friendship during my time at Virginia will be long treasured.

I would like to thank Lionel Gossman of Princeton University for his generous correspondence during the early stages of my research. His interest in Jacob Burckhardt and the cultural history of Basel played no small role in kindling my own interest in this project.

At Valparaiso University, where I currently teach, I am grateful for support provided by the Lilly Fellows Program in Humanities and the Arts. The goodwill of its directors, Mark R. Schwehn and Arlin G. Meyer, along with the friendship and humor of Thomas D. Kennedy, Gilbert Meilaender, and David Weber, have made my time at "Valpo" enriching and enjoyable.

After starting research on this project, John Rogerson's biography of de Wette (Sheffield Academic Press, 1992) appeared, to my great profit. Rogerson's impressive research led me to a number of important texts and archival documents. His previous works on the history of biblical criticism, moreover, guided my steps at many points. I would like to recognize a special debt to Rogerson, especially in chapters one and two.

Some previously copyrighted material in chapter five appeared as an article, "Jacob Burckhardt, Religion, and the Historiography of 'Crisis' and 'Transition'," in *The Journal of the History of Ideas*, volume 60 (January 1999): pp. 149–64. I am grateful to the editor of this journal for allowing me to reprint this material here.

For their patience and courtesies, I thank librarians and archivists at Freiburg and Basel. At Basel, I benefited from documents and papers provided by the Basel Staatsarchiv, the University library's Handschriftenabteilung, and the Jacob Burckhardt Stiftung. At Virginia and Valparaiso, I am similarly grateful to the interlibrary loan staffs for handling a number of unusual requests.

Finally, my greatest debt goes to Agnes, whose selfless assistance in editing this manuscript has been remarkable. Her companionship, more importantly, has been and remains an abiding source of adventure and joy, recently supplemented by the arrival of our first child, Elizabeth Rose.

Thomas Albert Howard
Valparaiso, Indiana
July 1998

In the last century men asked of a belief or a story, is it true?
We now ask, how did men come to take it for true?

– Lord John Morley, 1874

Introduction

History, Theology, and Modernity

[A] secular understanding of reality and the social bond is essentially constituted within the religious field, whether it was nurtured by religion's substance or deployed as an expression of one of its fundamental potentialities.
　　　　　　　– Marcel Gauchet, *Désenchantement du monde*

[We] anti-metaphysicians take our fire from the brand kindled by the faith of many centuries.
　　　　　　　– Friedrich Nietzsche, *Also Sprach Zarathustra*

IT IS LARGELY TAKEN FOR GRANTED today that a greater historical sense or historical consciousness is a distinguishing feature of modern Western thought.[1] To a large extent, this heightened sensitivity to history and to the "constructed" character of one's ideas and beliefs – historicism as it is generally called and as I shall call it[2] – first developed among German scholars, in universities and academies, at the end of the eighteenth and beginning of the nineteenth century. At this time, it is said, a secular historical consciousness freed itself from long-standing theological conceptions of history. Present-day intellectual and cultural historians have generally portrayed the process as fundamentally discontinuous: history triumphed over the "theological stranglehold" that it had languished under for centuries; the "modern mind" became historicized, emancipated from traditional, biblical-theological *modi cognoscendi*.[3]

In the present study, I suggest limitations with this view. Instead of charting the liberation of history from theology, I focus on the impact of theology on the development of secular historical thinking. I hope to awaken interest among historians of Europe in the significance of theology, especially German Protestant theology, in the modern period. Particular attention will be devoted to post-Enlightenment epistemological problems confronted by theologians and to problems associated with the application

1

of critical scholarship – *Wissenschaft* – to biblical hermeneutics. The broad cultural ramifications of these distinctively theological problems greatly affected the character of modern historical thought and the shaping of historical studies as an academic enterprise.

Previous studies have examined the impact on historical scholarship of developments at the universities of Göttingen and Halle in the eighteenth century, of activities at various German academies, of the philosophies of Herder and Hegel, of Wilhelm von Humboldt's writings, and of Leopold von Ranke's seminars and methods.[4] Less is known, however, about the role played by theology during the "emancipation" of modern, critical history from traditional, religious patterns of thought. Theology's role is important because of the close relationship between theology and history in German universities before the nineteenth century and because of their relationship of antagonism or indifference ever since. In premodern Europe theology was, after all, the "queen of the sciences," and, as Konrad Jarausch rightly notes, history, like philosophy, was long considered a "handmaiden of theology," an unsung ancillary field (*Hilfswissenschaft*) whose primary purpose was to instruct in the development of dogma and church history and to act as a repository of moral lessons for theologians, law professors, and statesmen.[5]

But history did not remain in its subordinate position. "A gradual reversal of roles" occurred by the nineteenth century, notes Jarausch, from "history as a handmaiden of theology" to history as a "dominant form of humanistic scholarship."[6] At the University of Göttingen in the eighteenth century, such scholars as Johann Christoph Gatterer and August Ludwig von Schlözer, began a melting down of *historia sacra* into secular world history.[7] The tradition of universal history (*Universalgeschichte*), originally based on the four monarchies of the seventh chapter of Daniel and expressed best in the lectures of the Reformation humanist Philip Melanchthon and in Jacques-Bénigne Bossuet's *Discours sur l'historie universelle*, gradually separated itself from theological assumptions and biblical chronology.[8] This process of secularization, which was largely complete by the early nineteenth century, paved the way for history's institutionalization and professionalization. In short, history became an autonomous *Wissenschaft*, and perspectives and methods drawn from history began to affect other areas of inquiry, notably theology and biblical criticism.

Many critics have perceived in the expanded scope of historical thinking pioneered by German scholars nothing less than the nascence of a posttheological worldview coeval with modernity. Friedrich Meinecke, for example, in 1936 famously described historicism as "one of the greatest intellectual revolutions that has ever taken place in Western thought."[9] "Historicism," writes Ninian Smart, "[is] the decisively new element in

2

modern Western thought."[10] But conclusions of this type beg many questions. How did history overcome its ancillary position and achieve such a grand(iose) stature? What explains the fact that history and theology, with respect to *wissenschaftliche* dominance and credibility, more or less switched places in the nineteenth century? Moreover, how does one account for the historicization of theology, a process that was greatly accelerated during this time? And how have the religious and cultural uncertainties generated by a historicized approach to theology affected intellectual conventions and social forms, including academic life, pedagogical theory, personal belief, and the like? Finally, why did such extensive historicization occur at this particular time in European history? In pursuing such questions, I am less concerned with charting the emancipation or triumph of historicism – which, as indicated, much recent scholarship does in a persistently progressivist fashion – than in understanding the cognitive situation of its emergence, its prior rootedness in deep-seated religious *Weltanschauungen*. The German Enlightenment is distinguished, one must remember, by its profoundly religious character: "among thinkers of the German Enlightenment," writes Ernst Cassirer, "the fundamental objective is not the dissolution of religion but its 'transcendental' justification and foundation."[11] Might then a secular historical outlook, born in the wake of the German Enlightenment, retain traces, revealing elisions, hereditary marks that betray significant continuities between premodern-theological and modern-historical ways of thinking? Karl Löwith has pointed out that even outspoken critics of Christianity in the nineteenth century were for the most part theologically educated Protestants.[12]

In this study I use the term *theology* not only narrowly, to describe a disciplinary practice or academic faculty, but also broadly, to denote a manner of regarding the world and human existence that privileges questions of faith, religious truth, transcendence, biblical interpretation, and moral behavior. "In its explicit attempt to come to grips with ultimate values," notes Douglas Cremer, "theological reflection verbalizes concerns that remain unspoken in many other discourses."[13] Indeed, since the Enlightenment, changes and continuities in the vocabularies and epistemologies of theology are crucial sources for illuminating broader cultural developments and problems. Admittedly, changes have been immense: European cultural life has experienced processes of secularization and historicization, whereby religious symbols, theological reflection, and ecclesiastical authority have undergone "disenchantment" (*Entzauberung*), as Max Weber put it, or "detheologization" (*Enttheologisierung*), as certain present-day German critics phrase it.[14] These processes and their attendant "isms" – secularism and historicism – represent valid, however terminologically problematic, attempts to account for fundamental transformations in modern European and Western intellectual life.

Yet there are few wholesale breaks in history: modernity's predominantly secular, historical elite culture bears a complex and profound relationship to its predecessor biblical-theological culture; the latter has exercised extensive and often unrecognized influence on the former. M. H. Abrams noted in his interpretation of nineteenth-century Romanticism that

> we ... remain unaware of the full extent to which characteristic concepts and patterns of ... [nineteenth-century] philosophy and literature are a displaced and reconstituted theology, or else a secularized form of devotional experience. ... [We] readily mistake our hereditary ways of organizing experience for the conditions of reality and the universal forms of thought.[15]

Abrams's words apply to attitudes toward history as well; theological presuppositions and religious attitudes shadowed and shaped nineteenth-century historicist thinking.

Despite secularizing and historicizing tendencies, theology *qua* theology has persisted (albeit with diminished institutional prestige and power) both as an academic discipline and as a general way of thinking, insistent on its own *raison d'être* and sources of legitimation (ecclesiastical tradition, the Bible, religious conviction). Historians concerned with the secularizing novelties of modernity have been reluctant to recognize theology's resilience in the face of criticism. A host of avowedly secular thinkers have been singled out as defining the discourses of modernity – Comte, Marx, Engels, Darwin, Nietzsche, and Freud, inter alia – and theologians and other religiously inclined thinkers normally do not "make the cut."[16] Indeed, historians often know little of such thinkers; and even when recognized, theologians are looked upon condescendingly, as cultural dinosaurs trafficking in dubious realities – God, transcendence, truth, justice, love – that long ago should have been consigned to the realm of the metaphorical and private. Against this tendency I argue that historians overlook modern theological reflection at the expense of both historical accuracy and valuable cultural knowledge.

To be sure, a few names are widely recognized: Friedrich Schleiermacher, Søren Kierkegaard, Ernst Troeltsch, and Karl Barth are examples. Besides the luminaries, however, there are many other neglected figures, no less important (and often more so) in helping one understand the internal dynamics and intellectual presuppositions of a certain period. German-speaking lands in the nineteenth century comprised a virtual hatchery of "important lesser" theologians and biblical critics: H. E. G. Paulus, Gottlob Wilhelm Meyer, Karl Daub, F. C. Baur, K. G. Bretschneider, August Neander, Ernst Hengstenberg, Philipp Konrad Marheinecke, W. M. L. de Wette, Bruno Bauer, F. A. G. Tholuck, Richard Rothe, Albrecht Ritschl, A. E. Biedermann, Julius Wellhausen, and Martin Kähler, among others.

Apart from scholars interested in Left Hegelianism, intellectual historians have not been passionate about examining any of these figures.[17] Moreover, theologians' forays into history – with a few exceptions – rarely go beyond studies of so-called great men and their ideas. Consequently, a significant and influential component of nineteenth-century German culture remains neglected. From a historian's standpoint, this situation is unfortunate because such overlooked and marginal figures are often the ones who best illuminate the problems and tensions of a given epoch.

The present study was prompted by the discovery of an interesting encounter between one of these secondary theologians, Wilhelm Martin Leberecht de Wette (1780–1849), and a young aspirant to the ministry, the historian Jacob Burckhardt (1818–1897). During his years as a theology student at the University of Basel (1837–1839), Burckhardt came into contact with de Wette's radical historical criticism and innovative, non-orthodox theology. Burckhardt, son of Basel's highest ranking Protestant pastor, experienced a shattering crisis of faith as a result. He vowed to be an "honest heretic" (*ehrlicher Ketzer*) – presumably to avoid being a dishonest one – and gave up theology in favor of historical studies. In 1839, he left his hometown for Berlin, where he studied history under some of the greatest names of nineteenth-century German historical scholarship: Leopold von Ranke, J. G. Droysen, Jakob Grimm, and Franz Kugler.

Scholars interested in Burckhardt's development as a historian are often either puzzled by or dismissive of his prior commitment to theology. Yet many eighteenth- and nineteenth-century scholars began in theology. Fifty-six of the ninety-three holders of historical chairs in Germany before 1800 had received theological training. The major nineteenth-century historians – Ranke, Droysen, and Theodor Mommsen, like Burckhardt – all came from pastors' homes and (except for Mommsen) had studied theology before experiencing difficulties and switching over to history.[18] Numerous lesser historians followed the same path. Even better known are the Tübingen seminary experiences that launched the careers of Hegel, Hölderlin, and Schelling. In the second half of the nineteenth century, the best-known case is Nietzsche, a pastor's son, who spent two semesters studying theology at the University of Bonn, during which time he read D. F. Strauss's critical *Das Leben Jesu* and jettisoned theology for a career in philology.[19] Indeed, the pious *Elternhaus* (sometimes also a *Pfarrhaus*) and the *Theologiestudium* – which was often accompanied by a religious crisis or at least by an extreme attenuation of orthodox belief – were nearly routine and profoundly formative experiences for many nineteenth-century, secular, German intellectuals.[20] This has led Thomas Nipperdey to remark that "modern thought in Germany did not coexist or conflict with theology, but dwelled in the long shadows cast by the problems it had set, by the 'totality' it had laid claim to."[21]

In Burckhardt's case, the *Pfarrhaus* and *Theologiestudium* are treated in the secondary literature only cursorily, and then almost always as a perfunctory prelude to the *Geschichtsstudium*, considered to be more important. It was during the *Geschichsstudium* that Burckhardt trained in Ranke's seminar at Berlin and began to develop as a cultural and art historian and Renaissance scholar. While the importance of Burckhardt's seminar training and subsequent historical scholarship cannot be doubted, one cannot dismiss his prior religious upbringing and theological studies as inconsequential prehistory. In reading the young Burckhardt's letters, in examining his upbringing in Basel as the oldest son of a prominent Protestant minister, and in exploring the theology and pedagogy of his main professor, de Wette, I became persuaded that Burckhardt's pre-Berlin, pre-Ranke theological phase was not only interesting for its own sake but was also of crucial importance for understanding the genesis and makeup of his subsequent historical thought. Although Burckhardt abandoned theology, theology did not easily leave him; an abiding Protestant-theological *Weltanschauung* and *Denkweise*, as well as a lingering sense of crisis and religious uncertainty, provide keys for understanding Burckhardt's mature intellectual personality, philosophy of history, and historiography.

The case of Burckhardt also casts light on larger issues in nineteenth-century intellectual history. With respect to the themes of secularization and historicism, I interpret Burckhardt's transition from theology to history as a paradigmatic event in the nineteenth century. His decision to become a "profane" historian rather than a "pious" clergyman, as well as his conscious rejection of his religious heritage in Basel, dramatically illustrate a more pervasive ebbing of religious sensibilities: "the secularization of the European mind in the nineteenth century," as Owen Chadwick once put it.[22] However, I shall also make clear that Burckhardt's negative stance toward his religious-theological heritage was, paradoxically, conditioned by this same heritage. His religious situation before apostatizing determined to a large degree the course and character of his secularization.[23] Commenting on the emergence of "the modern secular personality," Mircea Eliade makes a relevant observation:

> Nonreligious man descends from *homo religiosus*. . . . [H]is formation begins with the situation assumed by his ancestors. . . . [H]e is an inheritor. He cannot utterly abolish the past, since he is himself the product of his past. To acquire a world of his own, he has desacralized the world in which his ancestors lived; but to do so he has been obliged to adopt the opposite of an earlier type of behavior, and that behavior is still emotionally present to him, in one form or another, ready to be reactualized in his deepest being.[24]

Although Eliade's starkly dichotomous "nonreligious man" and "homo religiosus" do not exist except as ideal types, the quoted passage certainly applies to what Burckhardt called his "transitional period" (*Übergangsperiode*), a time of inner struggle during which he consciously sought to distance himself from his religious heritage.[25] In what follows, I shall elaborate on Eliade's point, calling attention to the manifold complexities, tensions, and continuities involved in the secularizing and historicizing of an influential – and, in some respects, exemplary – nineteenth-century personality. On many counts, Burckhardt resembles Eliade's nonreligious man, but I shall argue that the long shadows of theological presuppositions and attitudes, albeit in secularized forms, are ultimately more significant than the radical break that notions of religious crisis and apostasy seem to entail. Deep-seated biblical and theological patterns of ordering and interpreting human experience determined to a large degree the conditions, possibilities, and limits of the historical imagination realizable by Burckhardt.

The catalyst for Burckhardt's religious crisis was the theologian and biblical critic, W. M. L. de Wette. It is an interesting and perhaps revealing irony of nineteenth-century intellectual life that a theology professor unseated the faith of a pastor's son. De Wette's uncompromising critical theology led directly to Burckhardt's apostasy and to his preference for history over theology. "De Wette's system grows in stature every day," a distraught Burckhardt told a friend in 1838, "one simply *must* follow him, there is no alternative; but every day a part of our traditional church doctrine melts away under his hand."[26]

Who was W. M. L. de Wette? A major part of the present study is an attempt to recover de Wette's thought and capture its rootedness in specific late eighteenth- and early nineteenth-century social, intellectual, and cultural contexts. I have chosen to concentrate on de Wette's thought for a number of reasons, all of which work to illuminate the epistemological, cultural, and religious issues at stake during Burckhardt's encounter with de Wette in the late 1830s. Furthermore, an examination of de Wette's thought calls attention to the interrelatedness of many larger themes in nineteenth-century intellectual history: Enlightenment rationalism, liberalism, Romanticism, positivism, and historicism, among others. In short, my treatment of de Wette functions as an individual case study only in a secondary sense; its primary function is as a reference point for elucidating an assortment of consequential changes occurring in early nineteenth-century thought and theology.

Although I have referred to de Wette as a lesser player in the German theological scene, this characterization is really true only from a twentieth-century perspective. In the nineteenth century de Wette was in fact a theological and biblical-critical titan. Even as late as 1910, the *Encyclopaedia Britannica* noted that de Wette's "tendency to free critical inquiry" and his "unfettered mind toward history" had allowed him to "occupy . . . an almost solitary position among German theologians."[27] The present study attempts to reconstruct de Wette's stature in the eyes of his contemporaries; I also suggest reasons for the subsequent eclipse of his legacy.

Most important, however, particularly with respect to Burckhardt's connection with de Wette, is de Wette's implication in what theologians generally describe as the problem of historical knowledge, or what came to be known in the late nineteenth century as the "crisis of historicism." De Wette was one of the earliest pioneers of the historical-critical method of evaluating biblical texts. Drawing from such *Aufklärung* predecessors as J. S. Semler and J. A. Ernesti, de Wette advocated the use of historical-critical insights in religious apologetics and in the assessment of doctrinal truth. Thus, he assisted in the creation of a hermeneutical situation, exemplified later by D. F. Strauss's *Das Leben Jesu* (1835), in which historical criticism was seen as necessarily prior to dogma and in which "the influence of a biblical author's culture over his mind and outlook played a larger role than his conscious intention in the critic's determination of the meaning of his words."[28] Like many Protestant critics, de Wette believed that he was continuing the work of the Reformation, using historical-critical exegesis to discover the true religious kernel of Christianity while discarding accumulated ecclesiastical and cultural dross. As we shall see, he felt that historical-critical knowledge was epistemically separable from the "true spiritual meaning" (*wahre geistige Sinne*); religious apologetics and hermeneutics could and should accompany seemingly faith-threatening criticism. Yet as we shall also see, de Wette's contemporaries did not always understand his sophisticated theoretical stances. Orthodox and pietist camps often rejected his views outright.[29] Even the sophisticated and avowedly secular had problems. Burckhardt found de Wette's criticism true and justified, but deemed his avant-garde religious apologetics unintelligible.[30] Nietzsche's critique of historicism in *Vom Nutzen und Nachteil der Historie für das Leben* includes an excoriating treatment of "the contemporary *theologus liberalis vulgaris*" that would apply to de Wette: Nietzsche derided those who "have resolved it [Christianity] into pure knowledge about Christianity, [which] . . . ceases to live when it is dissected completely, and lives a painful and moribund life when one begins to practice historical dissection upon it."[31]

Indeed, the relationship of historical knowledge to theology and biblical interpretation and the influence that a critical-historical theology and biblical exegesis has exerted on modern culture at large remain among the most important and perplexing aspects of modern European intellectual history. Moreover, the authority dispute between historical *Kritik* and religious truth, felt poignantly by intellectuals in the early nineteenth century, importantly foreshadowed the question of history (or historicity) as it arose in the course of what Martin Heidegger famously interpreted as the dissolution of Europe's metaphysical tradition. The early nineteenth-century crisis of transcendent Christian orthodoxy, which many (e.g., Ranke, Hegel) softened by attributing historical immanence with a religious character,[32] established the conditions for a later, more pervasive crisis of historical thinking – a crisis that entailed the near wholesale disavowal of history's theo/teleological potential. This later period of crisis (roughly 1880s–1920s) in turn created an inclination toward crisis thinking that has permeated modern and postmodern thought ever since.[33] "Once the historical method is applied to Biblical science and church history," wrote Troeltsch, "it is a leaven that alters everything."[34] Such a situation, Troeltsch claimed, threatened Western civilization with the specter of complete cultural relativism. Although one may have philosophical reservations about Troeltsch's conclusion, his words remain relevant. In present-day humanistic discourse, religious truth-claims, as well as truth-claims in general, notes Alister McGrath, remain "condemned to history."[35] Yet the suggestion that all truth-claims are historically conditioned must itself be treated as a historically conditioned insight, reflecting a specific cultural framework, outside of which (either as in the past or in some unknown future time) it may altogether cease to be valid.

My principal aim in this study is to shed light on the relationship between theology and history in the nineteenth century, reconstructing in particular the impact of theological reflection on secular attitudes toward history. But this is not my sole aim. There are a number of subsidiary themes that function alongside and supplement the main line of the account.

In chapter one, I situate de Wette's early theology and biblical criticism in the broader cultural contexts of the late German Enlightenment, early Romanticism, and nineteenth-century historicism. I show that despite de Wette's near anonymity today, he was in fact a major player on the early nineteenth-century German theological scene. Moreover, I make clear that the epistemological basis of de Wette's biblical exegesis was shaped by then current trends in German philosophy; I call attention to the influences of Herder, Kant, and Schelling on him, and I devote particular attention to de Wette's important friendship with the Kantian-influenced philosopher Jakob Friedrich Fries (1773–1843). What made de Wette's exegesis innovative and influential was his unique blending of *Aufklärung* historical-critical traditions in biblical scholarship, Kantian epistemological sensibilities, and the aestheticizing tendencies of early nineteenth-century philosophy – especially the philosophies of Schelling and Fries. De Wette's exegetical/philosophical abilities are best seen in his application of the category of myth to Old Testament interpretation.

In chapter two, I discuss de Wette's theology during his time at the University of Berlin (1810–1819) and the political events that led to his dismissal in 1819. Because of similarities in their theological positions, scholars often assume that de Wette was a disciple of Schleiermacher, who invited de Wette to join him on Berlin's first theological faculty. I demonstrate, however, that de Wette worked out his theological program – expressed best in his 1815 opus, *Über Religion und Theologie* – in conscious opposition to what he called Schleiermacher's "lax mysticism."

Moreover, I discuss the vitriolic debates at the University of Berlin over the nomination to fill J. G. Fichte's chair in philosophy, vacated on Fichte's death in 1814. De Wette sought to bring his friend and fellow Kantian, Fries, to Berlin. De Wette's efforts were opposed by his colleagues and especially by Schleiermacher, who feared the possible Kantian alliance of Fries and de Wette. Ultimately, the opening was filled by Hegel; and Hegel and Schleiermacher became the pacesetters for subsequent theological and philosophical directions. Yet what if the Kantians, de Wette and Fries, had achieved institutional dominance during this crucial period in the making of modern German thought? Might not the late nineteenth-century "back to Kant" movement have received an important foothold much earlier?[36] Examining this interesting scenario calls attention to institutional and circumstantial contingencies often overlooked in "high" intellectual history.

I conclude chapter two by recounting the so-called "persecution of demagogues" (*Demagogenverfolgung*) that resulted in de Wette's dismissal from Berlin in 1819. I emphasize the important and highly politicized role that religious issues played in German public life during the period. De Wette's dismissal, which had the effect of tarnishing his reputation, helps account for the subsequent eclipse of his legacy; it also suggests why de Wette accepted a position in 1822 at humble Basel, regarded at the time as one of Europe's backwater universities.

In chapter three, I turn to the weightiest dilemma of nineteenth-century Christendom: determining the nature of Christ's identity and of New Testament authority in light of the emergence of historical-critical biblical exegesis. The issue was one of the most explosive and divisive of the entire era; it began with Lessing's publication of Reimarus's *Wölfenbüttel Fragmente* (1774–1778) and culminated with Strauss's *Das Leben Jesu* in 1835. De Wette's lifetime corresponded almost precisely with the playing out of this epoch-making theological issue. Significantly, it was de Wette's nonorthodox *Christusbild*, above all other issues, that precipitated Burckhardt's religious crisis in 1838.

I argue in chapter three that de Wette influenced Strauss much more than previous scholarship has acknowledged. De Wette was in fact the leading theorist of the "mythic principle" in biblical interpretation before Strauss. To a large degree, Strauss only synthesized and applied to the Gospel stories approaches that de Wette and earlier scholars had developed in theory and applied to the Old Testament. I situate the biblical exegesis and christo-logical reflections of Strauss and de Wette, moreover, in what both Thomas Nipperdey and Charles McClelland refer to as the "revolution in *Wissenschaft*" that took place in German universities during the early and mid-nineteenth century.[37] Strauss's and de Wette's motivation for research and their scholarly *modus operandi* were conditioned by an institutional imperative that privileged individual discovery and radical novelty. As we shall see, the critical demands of *Wissenschaft* often sharply conflicted with more conservative and orthodox convictions. This is shown clearly, for example, in de Wette's clash with conservative theologians and clergymen upon his arrival in Basel. By analyzing knowledge-faith tensions of the 1830s, I make clear the broader cultural and epistemic conditions in which Burckhardt encountered de Wette at the University of Basel between 1837 and 1839.

In chapter four, I examine the cultural-religious history of Basel in the late eighteenth and early nineteenth centuries, the character of Burckhardt's father's religious convictions, the coming of de Wette to Basel (in 1822), Burckhardt's experiences as a theology student under de Wette, Burck-hardt's religious crisis, and, finally, his decision to leave theology in favor of history. I argue that knowledge of Burckhardt's religious upbringing in Basel and his theological studies there are of crucial importance in under-standing the genesis of his mature historical thinking. As indicated earlier, I emphasize this point because Burckhardt scholars have tended to mini-mize the importance of the *Pfarrhaus* and *Theologiestudium* experiences when discussing his later historical works.

In the final chapter, I draw conclusions about the persistence of theo-logical thinking in Burckhardt's historical imagination. I contend that despite Burckhardt's avowed secularism (he referred to himself as a *Weltkind*, a "child of this world"[38]), his thought in fact retained a pro-nounced premodern character rooted in Basel's conservative, religious culture.[39] This is evident especially with respect to the notion of original sin and its attendant pessimistic conception of "this world." This Augustinian religious residuum in Burckhardt's thought survived the apostasy induced by de Wette's critical scholarship and fostered in Burckhardt an unusual – but now celebrated – cultural pessimism. In making this claim, I argue against critics who see Burckhardt's pessimism as derived from Arthur Schopenhauer or as a *fin-de-siècle* repudiation of modernity, which fore-shadowed a quasi-Nietzschean, late twentieth-century postmodernist atti-tude. Although Burckhardt spurned many of the cultural norms of modern society, his pessimism does not represent a proto-postmodern novelty; rather, it testifies to the endurance of his premodern inheritance – that is, the "world of his father." Expressed most clearly in his lectures, *Über das Studium der Geschichte*,[40] Burckhardt's retention of a form of original sin made him incredulous of the benevolence of human institutions, especially the modern state, and critical of the idea of progress. I argue that in the final analysis Burckhardt's antimodernism and the influence that his antimodernism has recently experienced – call it postmodernism if one will – is best explained as the subtle continuance of a decidedly nonmodern pessimistic theological outlook.

Historicism and Secularization

The primary and subsidiary arguments of this study are nested in two much larger conceptual-historical issues: historicism and secularization. Admittedly, these words do not lend themselves to easy definition; they are truly umbrella terms that attempt to comprehend a range of theoretical and historical complexities. Despite terminological imprecision, these terms help account, however imperfectly, for some of the most fundamental cultural changes in modern European history.

Historicism: "The Last Religion of the Educated"?[41]   In nineteenth-century Germany, historical ways of understanding reality – or historicism (*Historismus*) – triumphed on an unprecedented scale.[42] Although historicism cannot be defined as a strictly German phenomenon, as Friedrich Meinecke attempted to do in his *Die Entstehung des Historismus*,[43] the German experience during the nineteenth century is nonetheless of crucial importance in understanding the historicization of human thought and its far-reaching influence on humanistic discourses in the Western world.[44] Historicism bespeaks a "*Weltanschauung*," observed Karl Mannheim, "which came into being after the religiously determined medieval picture of the world had disintegrated and when the subsequent Enlightenment, with its dominant idea of a supra-temporal Reason, had destroyed itself. . . . Historicism alone . . . provides us with a world view of the same universality as that of the religious world view of the past."[45]

Historicism is not easily defined. Georg Iggers has pointed out that with respect to German scholarship in the nineteenth and twentieth centuries, historicism has had two principal meanings.[46] The first Iggers identifies with a scholarly practice in the nineteenth and to an extent early twentieth century. The representative figures in this understanding of historicism are Barthold Georg Niebuhr, Friedrich August Wolf, Leopold von Ranke, August Böckh, Theodor Mommsen, J. G. Droysen, and Friedrich Meinecke (Meinecke is the only scholar in this group who actually used the term). This conception of historicism may be referred to as classical historicism. Its roots lie in Ranke's rejection of *a priori* Hegelian conceptualizations of history and in Ranke's attendant effort to ground history in *a posteriori* terms – to begin with the particulars of the past and depict them "wie es eigentlich gewesen."[47] This form of historicism, states Iggers, implies a certain epistemological idealism that posits the world as a concrete, meaningful whole. The general meaning of the world may be discovered by historians, but ascertaining the general proceeds by scrutinizing the individual.[48]

A second important meaning of historicism, and the one more relevant to the present study, grew out of the "crisis of historicism" literature of the late nineteenth and early twentieth centuries. Historicism in this sense has come to be identified with relativism and the loss of faith in the values of modern Western culture. Ernst Troeltsch was the key delineator of this conception of historicism. In his *Historismus und seine Probleme* (1922), Troeltsch accepted historicism as a valid scholarly approach to cultural reality, yet believed that the study of history, far from constituting the key to the acquisition of meaning (as in classical historicism), progressively showed the relativity and hence invalidity of the values and beliefs of Western culture. Nonetheless, Troeltsch accepted the conviction that all human ideas and values are historically conditioned and subject to change; he deemed this attitude the dominant and inescapable result of Western thought in the nineteenth and twentieth centuries.[49] "Historical *Wissenschaft*," wrote Troeltsch, "has so fully and thoroughly worked out the genesis of our civilization, and has made all present conditions intelligible by tracing the history of their development, that all thinking is obliged to become in some measure historical. . . . The consequence of this is, of course, a certain relativism, a mental complexity."[50]

In the present study, I am primarily concerned with Troeltsch's understanding of historicism, which I shall call "crisis historicism." I should point out, however, that a strong interrelationship exists between crisis historicism and classical historicism.[51] To a large degree, Troeltsch's acceptance of insights and methods drawn from classical historicism led him to believe that his own field, theology, could no longer postulate ahistorical, eternal verities. Moreover, when Burckhardt experienced a "crisis of historicism" – that is, when he decided that de Wette's historical-critical approach to the Bible had undermined his religious heritage – he turned to classical historicism, while at the University of Berlin, to authorize a new worldview.[52] Simply put, in the 1830s Burckhardt experienced (as an emotional-religious crisis) precisely what Troeltsch described in the 1920s (as an intellectual inevitability).

Besides Iggers, several insightful, recent commentaries on the 1880s–1920s crisis of historicism literature have appeared by Annette Wittkau, Otto Gerhard Oexle, Wolfgang Hardtwig, and Charles R. Bambach.[53] Bambach's book, in particular, has opened up new doors for understanding crisis historicism. For Bambach, the key figure in crisis historicism is not

Troeltsch, but Heidegger (who did not employ the term). By recasting the historicist's epistemological question about the nature of historical knowledge as an ontological question about the meaning of historical existence, Heidegger, Bambach argues, felt he was deconstructing the entire traditional discourse of Western metaphysics since Socrates.[54] Bambach's great merit is to connect the notion of historicism with a much more pervasive understanding of historical crisis that has characterized existentialist, poststructuralist, and postmodern thought in the twentieth century.[55]

Although I applaud Bambach's efforts to relate historicism to broader questions concerning the (il)legitimacy of Western metaphysics, it is important to bear in mind that the 1880s–1920s discussion of the crisis of historicism stemmed from and found its center of gravity in explicitly theological problems; the discussants were, moreover, almost to a man, committed Protestant thinkers, who sensed that the ascendency of historical modes of inquiry threatened to delegitimize their religious convictions and theology as an academic discipline.[56] Thus, strictly speaking, the crisis of historicism bespeaks a complex of theological problems and not philosophical ones, although it is undoubtedly true that the implications of the theological debate were promptly picked up by philosophers and soon ramified into educated culture at large. Although my departure from Bambach is in part a matter of emphasis, it is not only that.

In fact, historicism emerged from long-standing dilemmas internal to theology and biblical exegesis. I stress this point because the 1880s–1920s crisis of historicism is often portrayed as a consequence of importing Rankean modes of historical scholarship into theology.[57] Admittedly, this was often the case, as the example of Troeltsch suggests. However, the cognitive conditions necessary for the emergence of crisis historicism are more properly traced to hermeneutical and epistemological reorientations, internal to Protestant theology, that were rooted in the early modern period and gained prominence during the late eighteenth and early nineteenth centuries – before one can properly speak of the disciplinary autonomy of history. In other words, the category "history" was experienced as a theological and biblical-exegetical problem long before the popularization of the nineteenth century's "historical method."

What is more, in a certain sense one can even speak of historicism as a latent possibility embedded in Christian-influenced cultures. "For [modern] Western historical culture," notes Jörn Rüsen, "it is crucial that Christianity was a genuine historical religion. . . . The divine as the quintessence of meaning (*Inbegriff der Sinnhaftigkeit*) is simultaneously thought of as a metaphysical-suprahistorical totality of world-order and as an innerworldly-historical event."[58] This central paradox of orthodox Christianity has proved continually troublesome to those who have attempted to rationalize it. After all, the paradox is a direct affront to Aristotle's principle of noncontradiction: A is non-A: Christ is both human (historical) and nonhuman (nonhistorical).[59] The issue bedeviled theologians during the Arian controversy: was Christ coeval with God the Father or did God the Father bestow Godhood on a (historical) human being?[60] While the Nicene Creed affirmed the paradox as the benchmark of orthodoxy,[61] the epistemological and hermeneutical dilemmas that provoked the controversy never completely subsided. They reemerged in the modern notion of history as a realm of purely human endeavor (the benchmark of historicism). This conception of history presupposes, however, a prior attenuation of the cultural and epistemic "structures of plausibility" necessary for belief in the transcendent significance of a historical Jesus.[62]

Despite earlier isolated heretics and skeptics, this process of attenuation was only accomplished on a large cultural scale after the question of the nature of divine revelation and of the authority of the Bible were opened to critical, historical inquiry. Admittedly, the precise origins of modern historical criticism of the Bible and historical-critical theology are the subjects of continuing discussion and argument. They owe much to the seventeenth century – for instance, to Spinoza's *Tractatus theologico-politicus*, to the convictions of Socinians that the veracity of scripture should be attested by independent rational judgment rather than dogmatic authority, and to the pioneering critical exegesis of scholars like Hugo Grotius and Richard Simon.[63] But there is no doubt that as a concerted practice, building into a continuing tradition and literature, historical-critical inquiry started in the second half of the eighteenth century, chiefly among German scholars.[64] In short, the historicizing of biblical inquiry – and, in particular, the nascent *Leben-Jesu Forschung* – by German theologians and exegetes bespeaks a cultural-epistemic watershed of the greatest importance.

Thus it is an oversimplification to hold that *Geschichtswissenschaft* emancipated itself from theology, became autonomous, and came to permeate all other forms of thinking. While not categorically disputing this view, I emphasize instead that the historical-critical treatment of the Bible in the late early modern and Enlightenment periods created in large part the preconditions for the emergence of historicism and for the academic independence of secular historiography. "The critical treatment of the Bible," notes Rüsen, "begot a historicizing process." This process in turn has bequeathed to modern, secular elite culture what Rüsen sees as an unsolved structural problem: the impulse toward establishing truth by critical inquiry into sacred texts resulted in diminishing the texts' sacred meaning. Rüsen expresses this as a conflict between meaning (*Sinn*) and method (*Methode*), which he regards as a paradigmatic problem of modernity: "Because of methodological-critical historicization, the holy texts lose their religious meaning. They gain historical contingency and empirical facticity, but only at the expense of a loss of meaning."[65] In the parlance of a medieval exegete, the literal meaning (*sensus litteralis* or *sensus historicus*) in the modern world has come to supplant and stigmatize other once-important determinations of meaning, including the allegorical (*sensus allegoricus*), moral (*sensus moralis*), and mystical (*sensus mysticus*).[66]

The impact of the historical-critical sense on religious faith in the nineteenth century is well known. The existential pathos that characterized such apostates as Ernest Renan, Matthew Arnold, Leslie Stephen, Walter Pater, Thomas Hill Green, Burckhardt, and many others confirms the view that history, according to Franklin L. Baumer, became the "most devastating of all modes of nineteenth-century skepticism."[67] In 1886, the philosopher Henry Sidgwick stated the matter succinctly in the journal *Mind*:

> It seems to me that the historical study of human beliefs in some very important departments of thought – such as ethics, politics, and theology – does tend to be connected with a general skepticism as to the validity of the doctrines studied. . . . [Skepticism] partly tends to result from the historical study, because of the vast and bewildering variety of conflicting beliefs . . . which this study marshals before us. The student's own most fundamental and most cherished convictions seem forced, as it were, to step down from their secure pedestals, and to take their places in the endless line that is marching past. . . . Thus to the historian . . . the whole defiling train of beliefs tends to become something from which he sits apart, every portion of which has lost power to hold his own reason in the grip of true conviction: for peace's sake, he accepts the beliefs that are pressed on him by public opinion in his own age and country; but in his heart he believes in nothing but history.[68]

Yet even belief in history must be sacrificed to history. The conception of history that emerged from post-Enlightenment, elite European culture has no privileged observer status. The inevitability of cultural relativism articulated by Troeltsch and others, moreover, is logically – if not epistemologically – self-destroying: if all truth is culture-specific, so is the truth of cultural relative analysis. Hence it cannot be said to be true. This is certainly not to undervalue the insights of historical analysis but rather to point out that its underlying attitude toward history is, by its own criteria, itself a product of its times, thereby demonstrating the inescapability of its own historical relativity. This contention should raise a significant hesitation concerning the universality and long-term relevance of the modern historicist attitude. Preoccupation with history is not necessarily a permanent feature of the Western intellectual landscape. The significance of historicism may ultimately reflect the formulation of pivotal philosophical problems through a short-lived, one-sided exploitation of an enduring, irreducible tension between structures of knowledge grounded on universal theories of human nature and those grounded on concrete historical experience.[69]

Secularization, Modernity, and Theology.   Historians are confronted with a Janus-like phenomenon when they attempt to interpret the nature of religion in nineteenth-century Europe.[70] On the one hand, the nineteenth century was a time in which religious devotion played a vital role in the social world, especially in education and politics. At the same time, however, the era witnessed unprecedented processes of secularization, chiefly in urban areas and among the intelligentsia.[71] Put differently, the nineteenth century may be closer to the Middle Ages than the present is, but it was certainly not the Middle Ages.

The case of Protestantism is of particular significance. The sociologists Peter L. Berger and James D. Hunter have noted that of all the world religions, Protestantism has confronted modernity more intensely and for a longer time. "In theology," notes Hunter, "the Protestant case is paradigmatic; throughout the nineteenth century and indeed to the present, Protestant theology has attempted to come to grips with secular intellectual thought, the diffusion of secular consciousness among the wider population, and the churches' increasingly limited role in the social world." If one concedes this point, Protestantism's protracted struggle against (and accommodation to) modernity may be exemplary for understanding the theological enterprise generally in the modern world.[72]

In this study, I employ the term "secularization" to refer to a complex of processes in which religion came to lose its authority over other social institutions. Modern Europe, unlike its premodern past, has largely ceased to legitimize the authority of its laws, learning, and social arrangements by appeal to religious sanctions and supernatural endorsement. Social control is increasingly a matter of law rather than of a consensual moral code, and law becomes increasingly technical and decreasingly moral, while effective sanctions are physical and fiscal threats rather than threats or blandishments about an afterlife. Revelation is distrusted as a source of knowledge, and the methodology of modern learning puts a premium on doubt rather than on faith, on critical skepticism rather than on submissive belief in traditional authorities. The erstwhile functions of religion have been superseded: a process of secularization has taken place.[73]

In the context of Protestant culture, the roles of intellectual elites and institutions of learning are of crucial importance for understanding secularization. To a certain extent, the intellectual legacy of the Reformation already carried the seeds of secularization. Not only did the Reformation question ecclesiastical control and diminish sacerdotalism and sacramentalism, but on a cognitive level the importance of independent inquiry into the Bible (*sola scriptura* and *ad fontes*) set the precedent for a later, more pervasive, faith-threatening conception of *Kritik*.[74] Nearly all nineteenth-century liberal German theologians saw themselves not as debunkers of religion but as faithful torchbearers of the Reformation. Schleiermacher claimed that the Reformation had first suggested an "eternal treaty" between living Christian faith and independent scientific research.[75] De Wette praised the Reformation for its "scholarly striving" and legitimized his own criticism because "Protestantism in its first appearance placed historical criticism in the service of genuine faith."[76] The secularizing consequences of nineteenth-century criticism should thus be regarded not as arising outside of Protestantism but rather as profoundly and problematically embedded in it. "Teachers in the Protestant theological faculty," noted Berlin historian Friedrich Paulsen in 1902, "assume a fundamentally different attitude [from their Catholic counterparts]: they do not aim to be servants of the church, but first of all servants of science (*Wissenschaft*), servants of the church only through science (*Wissenschaft*)."[77]

Yet, throughout the nineteenth century, theological faculties of both confessions experienced a general decline in prestige and student interest. The fate of theology in this respect is a telling testimony of secularization. At Protestant universities in Germany, for example, the number of theology students declined from nearly one-third of the student body in 1830 to only 13.6 percent in 1892. Catholic universities witnessed a proportional drop: from 11.4 percent in 1830 to a meager 4.8 percent in 1892.[78] At the University of Berlin, theology professors made up 22 percent of the total professoriate in 1810, but only 4 percent a century later.[79] Considering the previous cultural supremacy of theology in the Middle Ages, its ebbing prestige in modern times – both as a general form of knowledge and as a fixture in university curricula – suggests a truly momentous cultural transformation.[80]

During the nineteenth century there were valiant efforts to reestablish the centrality of theological study. Schleiermacher, for instance, deemed a society without learned clerics unimaginable and consequently sought to reinvigorate the position of theology in the academy. The theological program that he established at the University of Berlin encouraged not only the practice of erudite theological scholarship by the faculty but also the active recruitment of new scholars and teachers and the training of pastors supportive of the liberal and critical approach.[81] De Wette too, after 1822, strove to rejuvenate Basel's theological faculty and curricula. In Great Britain, the conservative clergyman John Henry Newman also worried about the decline of theology in the university. The discourses that comprise his *The Idea of a University* were written with the express intent of demonstrating the centrality of theology to the pursuit of knowledge. "Religious Truth," he argued, is not only a portion, but a condition of general knowledge. To blot it out is nothing short . . . of unraveling the web of University Teaching. It is, according to the Greek proverb, to take the Spring from out of the year; it is to imitate the preposterous proceeding of those tragedians who represented a drama with the omission of its principal part.[82]

But the center did not hold. In German universities, during the course of the nineteenth century, the preeminence of the theological faculty was eclipsed by that of the philosophical faculty,[83] which, incidentally, witnessed an increase in student matriculation from 17.7 percent in 1830 to 26.4 percent by the end of the century. Moreover, the number of chaired professors (*Ordinarien*) in history alone rose from five in 1812 to over one hundred at the turn of the century.[84] Revelation-based claims were increasingly overshadowed by scientific and historical treatments of the social world. In 1902, Berlin historian Paulsen assessed the beleaguered situation of theology in Germany:

But it is more than doubtful whether modern times would give it [theology] that place [of honor among the sciences.] It is now scarcely mentioned in the same breath with the sciences, the peculiar pride of the present day. Numerous representatives of a scientific radicalism are inclined to exclude it all together, or to relegate it to the past. Theology, they assert, is a science of things of which we know nothing. . . . The theological faculty is a bald anachronism. Theological students can scarcely avoid meeting with such or similar opinions.[85]

After World War I, there even arose a movement in Germany to abolish theological study in the university altogether. The theologian Adolf Harnack was the key figure who challenged this view and fought for the continuing legitimacy of theology. Interestingly, Harnack's defense was strongly conditioned by his own cultural-epistemic situation. Instead of defending theology qua theology, Harnack argued that theology should be maintained because of the weight of its historical significance. In Harnack, Peter Berger once noted, theology became "a primarily historical discipline."[86]

Paulsen came to a conclusion similar to Harnack's. That faith existed, Paulsen reasoned, is a "historical fact in human life. . . . And hence historical theology, the study of religion in the light of history, will undoubtedly remain as an important task of scholarship."[87] Paulsen went so far as to suggest that doubts brought on by *Wissenschaft* perhaps might help the aspiring clergyman, so long as they did not lead to apostasy.

The more deeply one has been steeped in doubt himself, the better leader he will be for a world steeped in doubt. But if he remains fixed in doubt, if he does not reach a personal certainty, which impels him to testify and preach, it is better for him to choose another calling while there is still time.[88]

As theology diminished in the university setting, so did the plausibility of worldviews legitimized by religious presuppositions. As Berger has noted, institutions of knowledge in modern societies have played a crucial role in the secularizing process, initiating a general crisis of theology, in which religious institutions and individuals face the problem of "how to keep going in a milieu that no longer takes for granted their definitions of reality."[89] The German scene confirms this picture. "Just as theology has lost the first place among the sciences," noted Paulsen in 1902, "so also has the clerical position forfeited its former position as the chief profession, to which the supervision of all human affairs . . . [was once] trusted."[90]

* * *

While religion became disengaged from certain social and cultural arrangements in the nineteenth century, it also reemerged in other, often unlikely, contexts. This understanding of secularization, which I shall also employ, has been described as the "transposition thesis." One critic defines it as follows:

> Secularization is conceived of as the transposition of beliefs and patterns of behavior from the "religious" to the "secular" sphere. . . . The culmination of this kind of secularization process would be a totally anthropologized religion and a society which had taken over all the functions previously attaching to the religious institutions.[91]

Although it is difficult to detect "pure" transpositions with no admixture of other ideas or experience, some well-known theses have portrayed the spirit of capitalism as a secularized Calvinist ethic, the Marxist vision of the consummation of the revolution as a variant of Jewish-Christian eschatology, and psychotherapy as equivalent to confession and cure of souls.[92]

With respect to nineteenth-century attitudes toward history, Karl Löwith has offered the most compelling application of the secularization-as-transposition thesis. In his influential *Meaning in History: Theological Implications of the Philosophy of History* (1949), Löwith argued that post-Enlightenment historical thinking, with its orientation toward the future and its desire to find immanent solutions to problems of history, would be unthinkable apart from antecedent Jewish and Christian theological conceptions of history – especially eschatological and messianic patterns of thought. Theological thinking, in other words, established the indispensable "forestructure" for modern, secular historical thinking. "We of today,"

Löwith writes, "concerned with . . . progress toward an ultimate goal or at least a 'better world' are still in the line of prophetic and messianic monotheism; we are still Jews and Christians, however little we may think of ourselves in those terms." While premoderns, Löwith adds, focused on the supra-historical events of creation, incarnation, and consummation, "moderns elaborate a philosophy of history by secularizing theological principles and applying them to an ever increasing number of empirical facts."[93] Thus modernity, with its faith in gradual human improvement, is for Löwith "Christian by derivation" but "non-Christian by consequence"; while appropriating the hope and futurism of Christianity, modernity rejects the Christian conception of history as a "realm of sin and death."[94]

As with the transposition thesis in general, Löwith's argument has been subjected to criticism. His foremost critic, Hans Blumenberg, argued in *Die Legitimität der Neuzeit* (1966) that Löwith's idea of transposition does not take into adequate consideration the originality and hence legitimacy of modern, nonreligious attitudes toward history, which Blumenberg characterized as "theoretical curiosity" (scientific investigation) and "human self-assertion" (the primacy of anthropocentric thinking).[95] Löwith's claim, according to Blumenberg, represents only a polemically motivated delegitimation of modernity that operates by claiming that the presuppositions underlying "the modern" are in fact stolen capital, bastardized forms of premodern theological *Weltanschauungen*. Countering Löwith's view, Blumenberg attempts to demonstrate that premodern answers to the mysteries of history and human existence proved unsatisfactory and that modernity's new answers, or "reoccupations" as Blumenberg phrases it, offered fresh and illuminating possibilities unimaginable in the older framework. In place, therefore, of the secularization thesis, Blumenberg proposes instead what can be called the reoccupation argument. In his own words, "What mainly occurred in the process that is interpreted as secularization . . . should be described not as the *transposition* of authentically theological contents into secularized alienation from their origin but rather as the *reoccupation* of answer positions that had become vacant and whose corresponding questions could not be eliminated."[96] In short, the fissuring of Christianity's cultural hegemony in the late early modern period opened up, in Blumenberg's view, a cultural space for the emergence of more compelling solutions to problems posed by history.[97]

Philosophers both, Löwith and Blumenberg operate at a level of abstraction uncomfortable to historians. Still, Löwith's claims are considerably more persuasive from a historian's standpoint. While Blumenberg provides an interesting theoretical defense of the "legitimacy of the modern age," he does an insufficient job of accounting for the historical emergence of "the modern." His analysis relies excessively on the absolute distinction between the categories premodern and modern, resulting in a blindness to continuous elements. Moreover, as Martin Jay has pointed out, "[Blumenberg's] very idea of a discrete epoch needing grounding is modern" and neglectful of "the post-modern . . . crisis of the very concept of legitimacy itself."[98] Indeed, the notion of modernity as a "discrete epoch" emancipated from all previous modes of consciousness does not stand up to rigorous historical scrutiny.[99]

Furthermore, few will deny that centuries of institutionally promulgated Christianity in the West have exerted an enormous influence on the very conditions and limitations of intellectual activity. Modernity, in other words, did not spontaneously spring into existence from outside history. The cultural legacy of Christian-theological ways of thinking and organizing experience must be regarded as an enduring existent in evaluating the putatively novel claims of modernity. Just as much of Christian thought developed from Judaic and Greek ideas and beliefs, so also has modernity developed from Christianity. Perhaps only as we, in the late twentieth century, approach a nebulous nonmodern milieu will the nature of the former antagonism wane and the extent of dependency become clearer. Christianity must be regarded as a pervasive codetermining factor even of a relatively new, secular beginning.[100]

For this reason, I shall argue for the transposition thesis, albeit for a modified or weak version of it.[101] Although Löwith articulated a plausible framework for assessing the cultural transformation to secular modernity, he assumed that transposed theological elements are easily identifiable. They are not. Löwith's argument itself, in my view, also suffers from an insufficient appraisal of the complexity and indeterminacy of historical change. Past elements in his scheme simply transmute into new forms, which in turn are readily recognized by the historical observer as dependent on former realities. While not disputing Löwith's premise, I would supplement his conception of change by appealing to Michel Foucault's notion of genealogy. "Genealogy," Foucault notes, "operates on a field of entangled and confused parchments, on documents that have been scratched over and recopied many times. . . . Genealogy requires patience and a knowledge of . . . the details and accidents that accompany every beginning."[102] "Genealogy," unlike Löwith's sweeping "history of ideas," assumes that the old greatly influences the new, but it resists proposing a rigidly schematic interpretation of this influence. With respect to the secularization thesis, older theological elements certainly may be recognized, but an overly neat theory of transposition is, in the final analysis, an impossible task.

In this study, I shall approximate the transposition argument, appropriating the illumination and understanding it offers; I shall also recognize that its bountiful heuristic potential, alas, has limitations.

CHAPTER ONE

W. M. L. de Wette

Enlightenment, Romanticism, and Biblical Criticism

There we saw the giants, the sons of Anak, and we were in our own sight as grasshoppers, and so we were in their sight.
– American theologian, commenting on his impressions of German academic theology, c. 1835.[1]

IN 1836, AN ARTICLE IN THE Boston Unitarian periodical, *The Christian Examiner*, reported to American readers the scholarly achievements of the University of Berlin founded twenty-six years earlier: "The Berlin University numbers illustrious names among its teachers and professors. Fichte, Schleiermacher, de Wette, and Hegel have laid their honors at her feet. Of these de Wette alone still survives and toils industriously at Basel to heighten the glory that already crowns his days. The exile [from Prussia], though a bold innovator is . . . one of the best critics and ablest writers in Germany."[2]

Hegel, Schleiermacher, and Fichte are names well known to students of nineteenth-century German theology and philosophy, but de Wette is not. This is curious, because de Wette's prominence in the nineteenth century, as both theologian and biblical critic, was great. In New England he was one of the most widely translated German theologians.[3] Theodore Parker, Samuel Osgood, James Freeman Clarke, and Frederick Frothingham were all influenced by de Wette and vigorously defended his views to other New England intellectuals. De Wette was known as one of the least mystical German thinkers, as a stylist with "English pith" and clarity, and as a theologian whose ideas influenced and harmonized with those of Transcendentalism.[4] James Clarke once asked Ralph Waldo Emerson to write an article on Friedrich Schleiermacher, pressing his case by arguing that de Wette held Schleiermacher in high regard.[5]

De Wette's reputation was by no means confined to New England circles. In 1858, Samuel Davidson, a leading biblical critic in England, acclaimed de Wette as the finest biblical scholar of the age.[6] In de Wette's native

Germany, Julius Wellhausen, the most influential Old Testament scholar of the late nineteenth century, remarked that many of his claims could already be glimpsed in de Wette.[7] As a young student at the University of Leipzig, Jacob Burckhardt's teacher at Berlin, Leopold von Ranke, read de Wette with great interest.[8] David Friedrich Strauss and Bruno Bauer drew from de Wette in their critical works on primitive Christianity.[9] Rudolf Otto argued that de Wette and Jakob Friedrich Fries were the most sophisticated Kantian theologians in an era otherwise dominated by Hegelian philosophy.[10] Karl Barth puzzled over de Wette's eclipse from modern theological discussions, suggesting that, given more favorable historical circumstances, de Wette might have rivaled Schleiermacher as the giant of nineteenth-century theology.[11]

Even when his significance was acknowledged, de Wette was not always positively esteemed. From pietist and orthodox perspectives, de Wette's innovative and critical points of view were regarded as subverting traditional doctrine. When de Wette accepted a post at the University of Basel in 1822, for example, he was opposed by pietist citizens and conservative faculty members, and even decried by some as a precursor of the Antichrist.[12]

Today, it is mainly students of the history of Old Testament scholarship who attend to de Wette.[13] I shall argue, however, that de Wette has a much broader historical significance and that understanding his thought in its historical context casts light on a variety of important themes in early nineteenth-century German intellectual and cultural history. Perhaps more than any other major figure, de Wette embodied one of the fundamental tensions of the period – the tension between the wish to preserve the true content of Christianity and the desire to embrace the critical spirit of modern science (*Wissenschaft*).

This tension inclined de Wette to regard religious truth as subjective; he desired, as did many continental and British Romantics, to preserve, or rejuvenate, religious truth by seeking the "infinite in the finite," in nature, history, and, above all, human interiority.[14] For all his Romanticist tendencies, however, de Wette must also be considered a pioneering *Wissenschaftler* in historicizing and scientizing biblical studies. His critical approach to the biblical canon paved the way for many important developments not only in biblical interpretation but also in theology and European religious culture at large.

Romanticism and historicism – the complex, often antagonistic, sometimes complementary, relationship between the two lies at the heart of de Wette's scholarly production. He aspired to ensure the survival of Christianity under the critical conditions of modernity. He wanted well-researched (*wissenschaftlich*) knowledge of biblical texts and of the origins of Christianity. Though these were not unique wishes in his time, de Wette skillfully pursued both of them, with an acute awareness of the epistemological and cultural issues at stake. Always a Kantian sympathizer, he was less concerned with reconciling or mediating between religion and science than with granting them both legitimacy in distinct epistemic spheres. Nonetheless, a post-Kantian Idealist and Romanticist hue undeniably colors the instincts and aspirations of his thought. In short, de Wette, like many of his contemporaries, attempted, in the words of M. H. Abrams, "to salvage the cardinal values of [his] religious heritage, by reconstituting them in a way that would make them intellectually acceptable, as well as emotionally pertinent, for the time being."[15] As de Wette put it in the preface to his novel, *Theodor*, "[I desire] . . . a theology truly scientific, and, at the same time, adapted to warm and inspire the soul."[16]

In what follows, I shall not work through the many complexities and tensions in de Wette's thought from an "internal" theological or biblical-critical point of view. Rather, by calling attention to de Wette's cultural heritage, intellectual predecessors, institutional settings, and biography, I shall place his thought in a wider historical context. From this more external standpoint, however, I shall not neglect to comment on de Wette's principal strategies of biblical interpretation and on his attempt to reconstitute Christian theology in light of the intellectual conditions of modernity.[17]

Weimar, Herder, and the Young De Wette[18]

De Wette was born on 12 January 1780 in Ulla, a small village between Weimar and Erfurt. His Dutch ancestors had embraced Protestantism early in the Reformation and had fled to Saxony in 1523 to escape persecution. His mother, Margathera Dorothea Christiana Schneider, was of local Saxon descent. His father, Johann Augustin (1744–1812), was a respected Lutheran minister in Ulla. De Wette was the second of nine children and the oldest son.[19]

When de Wette was still young, his family moved to Grosskromsdorf, a village near Weimar. Initially, de Wette's father instructed him at home in classical languages. From 1792 to 1796 he attended a school at Büttstadt, seven miles north of Weimar. In 1796 he entered the Gymnasium at Weimar, the superintendent of which was Johann Gottfried von Herder. Adelbert Wiegand indicates that de Wette spent much of his spare time among friends, discussing the works of Herder, Wieland, Goethe, and Schiller, with whom he, in all probability, also had some personal contact.[20] In a letter near the end of his life, de Wette referred to Weimar as his "geistige Vaterstadt."[21]

The affinities between Herder's thought and the mature thought of de Wette are striking, although the precise nature of Herder's early influence on de Wette is largely a matter of speculation. According to classmates, Herder recognized de Wette as an excellent student. Wiegand notes that de Wette read Herder's *Ideen zur Philosophie der Geschichte der Menschheit* (1784) as a teenager. In 1844 de Wette, recalling his impressions of Herder's presence and preaching, wrote that Herder's early influence spared him from "the arid wastelands of theological criticism and rationalism" that de Wette encountered a few years later as a student at the University of Jena.[22] Herder's influence can been seen in many of de Wette's later works. In his *Über Religion und Theologie* (1815), for instance, de Wette praised Herder for arousing scholarly interest in the "divine epic" (*göttliche Epos*), which was "the cultural development of the human race" (*die Bildungsgeschichte des Menschengeschlechts*).[23]

In 1798 de Wette interrupted his studies in Weimar to become the private Greek tutor of a young French émigré. He accompanied the boy's family to Leipzig, Dresden, Nuremberg, Stuttgart, Schaffhausen, Zurich, and finally to Geneva while the family investigated means of moving back to France after the Revolution had died down. During his travels, de Wette was much taken by the art collections in Dresden and by the Rhine Fall at Schaffhausen, and he was astonished by the Swiss Alps and valleys. He also came into indirect contact with the French Revolution by encountering French soldiers in Schaffhausen, Zurich, and Geneva.[24]

Jena, De Wette, and Kantianism

According to John Rogerson, the renowned Old Testament scholar Julius Wellhausen was fond of arguing that biblical criticism operated by and large independently of philosophical concerns. "Philosophy," Wellhausen wrote, "does not precede but follows [biblical criticism], in that it seeks to evaluate and systematize that which it has not itself discovered."[25] Wellhausen's own positivism led him, I believe, to regard his own field as the truly scientific field of discovery and the vaguer field of philosophy as derivative.[26] Yet in the late Enlightenment and early nineteenth century the fate of philosophy and biblical criticism were tied to one another in such an integral fashion that generalizations of Wellhausen's sort do hold true. In the case of the young de Wette, philosophical concerns expressive of the Romantic and Idealist climate exerted considerable influence on de Wette's development as a biblical critic and theologian.[27]

On 21 October 1799, de Wette enrolled as a student at the University of Jena, then the center of the German philosophical world.[28] He remained at Jena until 1807 when he accepted a position as *Dozent* at the University of Heidelberg. Jena was home to an impressive group of scholars who had influenced or who would influence greatly the course of modern German philosophy and theology.[29] Because the university was under the control of several rather liberal patrons – including the courts of Gotha, Coburg, and Weimar – Jena attained a greater climate of freedom of expression than many other universities. This freedom was also in part accomplished through Goethe's earlier influence on the university in the 1770s and 1780s.[30] Such academic freedom was an especially important factor during the politically trying years of the Napoleonic invasions. In philosophy, K. L. Reinhold, J. G. Fichte, J. F. Fries, Schiller, Schelling, and Hegel taught at the university. In theology, J. P. Gabler, H. E. G. Paulus, and J. J. Griesbach were the principal figures.[31]

In the late eighteenth century, Jena was known as the center for the new Kantian philosophy. Influential reviews of Kant's *Metaphysik der Sitten* and *Kritik der reinen Vernunft* appeared in Jena's *Allgemeine Literatur-Zeitung*, founded in 1785 and edited by C. G. Schütz. Much influenced by these reviews, Reinhold further diffused Kantian ideas through a series of letters written in the journal *Merkur*. In 1787, Reinhold became a professor of philosophy at Jena and within seven years (1787–94), helped by Gottlieb Hufeland, a lawyer, and K. C. E. Schmid, a theologian, made the university a stronghold of Kantian philosophy and attracted a wide range of students and professors. In 1794, largely because of his *Versuch einer Kritik aller Offenbarung* (1792), Fichte was selected as Reinhold's successor; but he was forced to leave before de Wette's arrival because of the famous "atheism controversy."[32] In 1798, the twenty-three-year-old Schelling was appointed to a chair in philosophy through the influence of Goethe, who saw in Schelling's philosophy of nature an outlook akin to his own. Finally, Hegel came to this "literary storm," as he described it, as a *Privatdozent* in 1801, completing his *Phänomenologie des Geistes* there in 1806.[33]

Indeed, Jena was a unique and, in retrospect, amazingly influential academic environment. Despite differences in opinion and outlook, scholars at Jena shared important unifying experiences. First, they had all felt the political shock waves emanating from Paris during the 1790s; and their activity, to a certain degree, must be interpreted as a desire to come to terms with the exhilarating but conflict-ridden experience of the French Revolution. Second, they shared problems bequeathed to them by Kant. "Kant is our Moses," wrote the poet Hölderlin in 1799, "he has led us from our Egyptian slumbers into the free, lonely desert of his speculations."[34] Because of the revolutionary political and intellectual period in which Jena intellectuals wrote, Charles Taylor has noted that the central issue for their generation was a complete reexamination of the "nature of human subjectivity and its relation to the world."[35] Similarly, Frederick Beiser has observed that the dominant concern facing many German thinkers at the close of the eighteenth century was the "possibility of epistemology." The legacy of the

Enlightenment rationalism, new aesthetic concerns, and a turbulent political and social climate had made problematic what it meant to have "knowledge of the conditions and limits of knowledge."[36] Such issues ramified into theology and were discussed by de Wette and other theologians of his generation.

At the age of nineteen, de Wette came to Jena two years before Hegel's arrival. Once his philosophical and theological interests had been stimulated, he abandoned his initial intention to study law. In a letter to Karl August Böttinger, a former teacher in Weimar, de Wette wrote that it was only in Jena that "I first began live."[37] And it was indeed the philosophy of Kant – the generation's "Moses" – that prompted de Wette to question his inherited Lutheran faith and awakened him to the promises and problems of critical theology.

In the years preceding de Wette's arrival in Jena, Kant had published two important works on religion: *Religion innerhalb der Grenzen der blossen Vernunft* (1793) and *Der Streit der Fakultäten* (1798). The latter was one of Kant's last works, and its contents were widely discussed and debated at Jena.[38] The crucial issue in its longest section dealt with the question: which faculty – philosophy or theology – should determine the true nature of religion? Kant argued that it should be the exclusive privilege of philosophical theologians (those alert to reason) instead of biblical ones to determine the nature of religious truth. The work offered a critique of theologians who read the Bible from a literal and orthodox perspective. Kant accused them of confusing the statutory elements of ecclesiastical doctrine (which Kant saw as partial and contingent) with the timeless precepts of rational religious truth.[39]

In the work, Kant defines knowledge by dividing it into two parts: awareness of the historical (*historischen Erkenntnis*) and awareness of the purely rational (*reinen Vernunftserkenntnisse*). Within this division, philosophy had the ability to sift the rational from the historical and to establish the rational as superior to (historically conditioned) ecclesiastical truth: "the philosophical faculty can . . . lay claim to any [historical] doctrine in order to test its truth."[40] Truths established from reason were the only necessary truths having universal validity and only a religion derived from reason was considered true.[41]

Kant's conception of religion prioritized morality over miracles, reason over revelation; it sought to show that all human beings had the capacity to do what they ought to do, and that it lay within the possibility of human freedom to perform this duty despite latent tendencies to do otherwise. Although Christianity, in Kant's judgment, was the most developed of religions, this did not mean that philosophy could accept its dogmas based solely on historical revelation, as traditional orthodoxy maintained.[42] Indeed, the emergence of philosophical discernment in Kant's times and the establishment of a religion based on morality constituted for Kant an entire philosophy of history, whose roots lay in Hebrew monotheism. Kant hailed his present views as the necessary triumph of reason over the superstitious, the sectarian, and the statutory.

> The euthanasia (*Euthanasie*) of Judaism is pure moral religion, freed from all the ancient statutory teachings, some of which were bound to be retained in Christianity (as messianic faith). But this division of sects, too, must disappear, leading, at last in spirit, to what we call the conclusion of the great drama of religious change on earth (the restoration of all things), when there will be only one shepherd and one flock.[43]

Although Kant often deployed biblical-orthodox phraseology (often as gestures to keep Prussian censors at bay)[44] to support his positions, he rejected most important traditional doctrines. The Trinity and the Virgin Birth, for instance, he deemed meaningless and epistemologically dubious. Especially worrisome also was the doctrine of the Incarnation. Kant asserted that this doctrine only fostered strife and did not further morality. Kant thus recast Jesus as an exemplar of moral achievement; his Jesus became the "idea of humanity in its full moral perfection."[45] Kant similarly redefined other key theological terms, divesting them of their historical and ecclesiastical meanings and adapting them to fit his religion of reason. In short, the following quotation encapsulates the Kantian position that intrigued de Wette:

> For faith in a merely historical proposition (*bloßen Geschichtsfaß*) is, in itself, dead. . . . [T]his kind of interpretation may not only fail to promote but can hinder the real end of religious teaching – the development of morally better men. . . . The God who speaks through our own (morally practical) reason is an infallible interpreter of His words in the Scriptures, whom everyone can understand. And it is quite impossible for there to be any other accredited interpreter of His words (one, for example, who would interpret them in a historical manner); for religion is a purely rational matter (*eine reine Vernunftsache*).[46]

* * *

To further an understanding of de Wette's encounter with Kantianism at Jena, I shall draw from de Wette's semiautobiographical novel, *Theodor, oder des Zweiflers Weihe: Bildungsgeschichte eines evangelischen Geistlichen*.[47] It is important to keep in mind, however, that de Wette wrote *Theodor* in 1822, some twenty years after the occurrence of the autobiographical elements described in the book. Thus, the book reveals de Wette's reflection on his own theological education. De Wette himself spoke frankly of the book's autobiographical content.[48]

As the title suggests, *Theodor* chronicles the formative education, or *Bildung*, of a Lutheran youth, Theodor, who, at the request of his mother, attends a university to study theology in order to return one day to his native village as a pastor. While at the university, however, Theodor loses his childhood faith under the impact of rationalist biblical exegesis. After much distress, he finds consolation in the lectures on ethics by a certain Kantian philosopher who teaches him to translate his former faith into philosophical abstractions. At first, this ability pleases Theodor immensely, but he soon comes to feel that however satisfying his new rational views may be from an intellectual standpoint, they lack emotional and aesthetic depth.[49] From this point, de Wette leads the young Theodor through various relationships, universities, and philosophies – most of which directly parallel situations in de Wette's own life – until he finally reaches an outlook satisfying both the demands of critical inquiry and emotional/aesthetic depth.

While a student at Jena, de Wette, like Theodor (at an unnamed university in the novel), came under the influence of Kantian philosophy, an influence that would endure throughout de Wette's entire life.[50] Like Theodor, de Wette too received stimulation from Schelling's aesthetic philosophy. Finally, both de Wette and his fictional counterpart find in the views of the philosopher Jakob Friedrich Fries a fitting solution to the perceived tensions between rationalism (Kant), aesthetic philosophy (Schelling), and practical piety (de Wette's Lutheran heritage).

At Jena, immediately before discovering the appeal of Kantianism, de Wette's initial religious doubts were stirred by members of Jena's theological faculty. In his first semester, de Wette attended the lectures on the Gospels by J. J. Griesbach (1745–1812),[51] a man of "clear understanding" who put forward all the "controversial opinions and views of the Gospels ... without decisively choosing one over the other."[52] In *Theodor*, de Wette writes:

> The result of the theological studies of the first year was, in Theodor's case, that his former convictions concerning the origin of Christianity were shattered. The holy atmosphere of glory, which had hitherto surrounded the life of Jesus and the whole evangelical history, disappeared; but instead of satisfactory historical insight, he had acquired only doubt, uncertainty, and incoherence of opinion.[53]

According to another passage, Theodor's first year awakened him to "the present state of the theological world – what new discoveries have been made, what surprising views have been put forward, into what a labyrinth of doubt we have been introduced."[54] The crucial issue, which Griesbach pointed out, were the disagreements among Gospel writers concerning details of Jesus' life.

In de Wette's second year, he attended the lectures of H. E. G. Paulus (1761–1851), an acclaimed deist, and those of a Kantian philosopher of ethics.[55] In the novel, Paulus leads Theodor to doubt the possibility of miracles. The Kantian philosopher, however, whose identity is not given, provides Theodor with a new understanding of religious truth. "A whole new world was opened to him [Theodor]," writes de Wette, "the thought of the independence of reason . . . seized his mind with a mighty power."[56] He learned to translate the doctrines of his youth – conversion, rebirth, grace, the love of God and Christ, and so on – into Kantian philosophical language. These ideas conferred new meaning on the biblical lectures of Paulus and offered Theodor a fresh way of interpreting the relationship between historical doctrines and timeless religious truths. "His Bible interpreter showed him [now] in Christ only the Kantian wise man, who taught, in figurative language and emblems suited to this age what our time can express in clear and pure thoughts."[57]

"So went our friend [Theodor]," de Wette continues, "forward upon the path of doubt. He often felt dizzy when he looked down, from the steep summit which he had reached, into the narrow, quiet valley of his childhood's faith . . . [But] a bold spirit kept up his heart."[58]

Yet this boldness soon ebbed. Although Kant stirred de Wette intellectually, de Wette made clear in both *Theodor* and his theological works that he experienced many misgivings. The initial invigoration produced in him by this new philosophy led to a loss of emotion and beauty in religious matters and to a feeling of estrangement from his childhood piety and from the early aesthetic influence of Herder.[59] "In Kantian philosophy," de Wette noted in his *Über Religion und Theologie* (1815), "one [can] find nothing but morality."[60] In another work, *Eine Idee über das Studium der Theologie* (1801), de Wette lamented the effects of Kantianism in the pulpit and the classroom. Kant's impersonal religion, "devoid of nourishment for the spirit and heart," made one feel abandoned, as if one had been simply thrown into the world.[61]

This feeling of estrangement and theological aridity convinced de Wette to reevaluate his newly staked positions. In *Eine Idee*, de Wette described how his "feelings rose up loudly against his reason" to lead him beyond Kantianism. In *Theodor*, de Wette wrote that "Theodor came to feel himself lonely and deserted with his independent self-sufficing reason, like a child who has been abandoned by its father." Kant's God, Theodor reasons, "who is nothing more than the eternal order of the world, the guarantee of the moral law, can only do what is in itself necessary, and has been ordained from eternity."[62] Kant had sought to exorcise determinism from the universe. Ironically – and in stark opposition to Fichte's popular interpretation of Kant – de Wette came to understand the Kantian conception of God as equally deterministic and dismissive of human agency. Theodor's "heavenly father" and "friend" were "taken away from him."[63]

Despite qualms with Kant, however, the intellectual stimulus of Kantianism on de Wette proved lasting. De Wette could not return to his childhood piety: "our friend [Theodor] did not go back on the path he had entered."[64] Still, Kant remained unconvincing in many areas: religion for de Wette had to be more than what he later criticized as "the arid wastelands of theological criticism and rationalism."[65]

The "Aesthetic Turn": De Wette and Schelling

In the summer semester of 1802, Schelling gave a series of lectures in Jena entitled "Vorlesungen über die Methode des akademischen Studiums" and he followed these in the winter semester with his "Philosophie der Kunst."[66] Along with the works of Friedrich Schiller (1759–1805), Schelling's works generally mark the beginning of a novel preoccupation with the role of aesthetics in philosophy – especially with the notion that "aesthetic unity" might "be active not only in art but in thought itself."[67] During his later Jena years, de Wette turned enthusiastically to Schelling's aesthetic philosophy. In *Theodor*, Schelling's lectures make a great impression on Theodor,[68] who reads Schelling's "Vorlesungen" and although the "Philosophie der Kunst" is not explicitly mentioned, de Wette demonstrates familiarity with its contents based on conversations in the novel between Theodor and a young follower of Schelling named Seebald.[69]

In his "Vorlesungen," Schelling disagreed with Kant's premise in *Der Streit der Fakultäten* of holding philosophy and critical thought as the sole arbiters of the other disciplines.[70] Rather, Schelling argued that all modes of thought, including philosophy, should be seen as manifestations of an overarching transcendent reality – "the Absolute," which in later more orthodox works he identified with God.[71] In Schelling's terminology, philosophy was defined as speculation that enables an observer to see a particular thing in light of the Absolute. Thus, although the natural world may be studied in a purely empirical fashion, the science of nature should see the natural world as an expression of the Absolute, the "true source of all natural knowledge" (*wahre Urquelle aller Erkenntiß der Natur*).[72] Since the Bible and religious traditions constitute parts of the Absolute, they too should be approached with awe. For this reason, Schelling was highly critical of biblical interpretation that exorcised the mysterious from the Bible and took from it only prescriptions for moral behavior.[73]

Schelling assigned art a privileged role in helping the philosopher make sense of and unify human experience. Because the world was generated from "divine imagination" ("an epic composed in the mind of God"), human creative faculties were of utmost importance in the pursuit of truth. Thus, like many of his Romantic contemporaries, Schelling held art as sacred and the aesthetic dimension in human life as preeminent: "The highest stage of reason, in which all ideas are embraced, is the aesthetic. . . . The philosopher is as much in need of aesthetic power as the poet."[74] Importantly, Schelling also placed a great emphasis on the role of myth, noting that "mythology is the necessary condition for and the original substance of all art."[75]

Schelling's system made sense to de Wette at the points where Kantianism and rationalist biblical exegesis had left him frustrated. Instead of being merely a postulate of reason, Schelling's conception of God (the Absolute) became primary for de Wette, and human reason was relegated to only a part of the Absolute – though a part that enabled the individual to perceive the Absolute in the particular.[76] This "view of life," de Wette writes in *Theodor*,

> spread over all nature – of all individual life swallowed up in the universal life, the subsuming (*Verschlingung*) of all finite things in the infinite – suited our friend well, as he recognized here a feeling which had often seized him in the contemplation of nature. He had however always before held it as poetry. But now it was to be taken as science (*Wissenschaft*).[77]

The Christian faith for de Wette ceased to be simply a set of moral precepts as Kant had suggested but something much deeper and emotionally compelling.

Yet despite Schelling's influence, it would be misleading to say that de Wette embraced Schelling's system completely. In the novel, Theodor is bewildered by much of it. He cannot see, for example, how one can derive a system of ethics from it.[78] Further, if history is an expression of the Absolute, of which the individual is part, human beings did not seem to be free moral agents: "The idea of the holy, divine will raised above all change, is lost in this view, and the highest moral aspiration is lost with it."[79] In short, de Wette's Theodor is left basically a Kantian, yet one with strong emotional and aesthetic leanings toward Schelling. Reflecting on his Jena years, de Wette wrote in 1841 that he "was not wholly satisfied with the philosophy of Schelling, for I did not find in it enough of perspicuity or certainty; but . . . I could not attain by my own efforts to any secure or fixed convictions."[80] Nevertheless, Schelling's thought underscored to de Wette the insufficiency of Kant and persuaded him of the necessity of myth and religious mystery. Because of Schelling, de Wette came to esteem aesthetic categories and concluded that they could contribute greatly to theological scholarship. It remained for de Wette to combine aesthetic categories such as art, poetry, and especially myth with his developing skills in biblical exegesis.[81]

De Wette, Myth, and the Old Testament

In *Das Leben Jesu* (1835), D. F. Strauss explained the miracles of Jesus as culturally conditioned "myths" with a hitherto unheard-of skeptical consistency and literary elegance. He argued that historical-critical exegesis must be wholly prior to dogma and that the latter must be based on the former's independent findings. Although Strauss's book caused much commotion and influenced such radicals as Bruno Bauer and Ludwig Feuerbach, its mode of argument was far from novel. Strauss's "definition and use of myth," John Toews rightly notes, grew out of "a well-developed and widespread tradition in German biblical scholarship."[82] In the early nineteenth century, de Wette played a key role in directing this tradition toward a Straussian strain of criticism – a strain that the young Burckhardt would later interpret as inherently destructive of traditional faith. To borrow Thomas Kuhn's well-worn phrase, de Wette's early works on the Old Testament bespeak something of a "paradigm shift" in the myth-interpretation (*Mythenauslegung*) of the Bible.[83] Instead of using "myth" in its eighteenth-century negative sense – that is, as the false and discardable elements in the Bible – de Wette, following the leads of Schelling and Herder, employed myth positively, arguing that the entire Bible, and especially the Pentateuch, represented the mythical worldview of ancient Israel. The Pentateuch was Israel's "national epic," which de Wette likened to the epics of ancient Greece and Rome. As literature (*Dichtung*), the Old Testament was a poor historical source (*Geschichtsquelle*) in de Wette's judgment: "one cannot learn history from it . . . [but] can learn about the spirit and character of the poet."[84]

In chapter three, I make Strauss's debt to de Wette explicit. In what follows, I restrict my focus to the pre-Straussian evolution of the method of myth-interpretation in biblical scholarship, concentrating in particular on de Wette's role in this process. Since the myth question is linked inextricably to the history question in biblical criticism, I also comment on de Wette's attempted solutions to the latter.[85] Throughout, I argue that biblical criticism, far from being a neutral science of detached investigation, is in fact a highly culture-bound, time-conditioned enterprise. The exegetical novelties exhibited in de Wette's early works, for instance, strongly reflect the milieu of early nineteenth-century German Romanticism in general and the influences of Schelling and Herder in particular.

In his dissertation (1805) and *Beiträge zur Einleitung in das Alte Testament* (1806–7), de Wette applied notions of art and myth, as developed in two previously written essays, *Eine Idee über das Studium der Theologie* (1801) and *Aufforderung zum Studium der hebräischen Sprache und Literatur* (1805), to cast doubt on the historical accuracy of the picture of Israel in the Old Testament. While earlier scholars had adumbrated many

34

of de Wette's points, de Wette advanced eighteenth-century radical views to new extremes, offering novel solutions to old problems and quite often posing entirely different questions. As such, de Wette, according to John Rogerson, "inaugurated a new era in critical Old Testament scholarship."[86] De Wette's pioneering efforts, however, are largely unintelligible apart from a brief discussion of his eighteenth-century predecessors.

The most influential German biblical critics in the eighteenth century were called "neologians" (*Neologen*), because of their nontraditional approach to the Bible.[87] Composed of J. S. Semler (1725–91), J. A. Ernesti (1707–81), and J. D. Michaelis (1717–91), among others, these scholars shared the goal of evolving internal and external forms of criticism leading to a historical evaluation of the contents of revelation and dogma, and with a consequent exclusion of doctrines deemed irrational or morally indefensible. Contrary to the stereotype of eighteenth-century thinkers as prehistoricist rationalists, neologians were quite concerned about history as a hermeneutical problem in evaluating biblical texts; they wanted to establish grounds for a rationally criticizable theory of historical revelation while not equating history with the antithesis of an ahistorical, rational, religious truth. Thus, they were less dualistic in their understanding of reason and history than figures such as Hermann Samuel Reimarus, Lessing, or Kant. Nonetheless, their criticism considerably undermined traditional scriptural authority and has led Emmanuel Hirsch to refer to them as the founders of a "truly profane-scientific biblical exegesis."[88]

During the middle decades of the eighteenth century many German biblical commentators began to criticize openly the Reformation tradition of orthodox biblicism. Although the distant causes for this change in attitude have been traced to a variety of factors (e.g., to the philosophies of Spinoza and Wolff and to the early modern biblical criticism of scholars such as Richard Simon, Johannes Cocceius, Hugo Grotius, S. J. Baumgarten, and others),[89] its most immediate source was the introduction of English deism to the continent in the mid-eighteenth century. In 1741, L. J. Schmidt translated Matthew Tindal's *Christianity as Old as Creation*, which, in classic deist fashion, asserted the preeminence of reason over revelation in securing religious truth. Between 1745 and 1782, over twenty works by English deists appeared in German. Reimarus and Lessing, notably, appropriated deist ideas and applied them to the Bible in Reimarus's controversial *Wolfenbüttel Fragmente* published by Lessing between 1774 and 1778.[90]

In his *Abhandlung von freier Untersuchung des Kanons* (Halle, 1771–5), J. S. Semler, the most prolific of the neologians, made two distinctions that became foundational for subsequent biblical hermeneutics. First, he argued that *scriptura sacra continet verbum dei* (The holy Bible contains the Word of God) in contrast to the Protestant commonplace that held *scriptura sacra est verbum dei* (The holy Bible is the Word of God).[91] From Semler's premise, it followed that if the Bible only *contained* the Word of God – instead of actually *being* it – scholars gained a new sense of duty to deliver God's Word from the historical and philological morass of the text. Second, Semler distinguished between two types of biblical understanding: the *sensus literalis* and the *realia*. The *sensus literalis*, which previous Protestant theologians held to be the true sense of scripture, could be reached, in Semler's view, only by a rigorous historical-critical methodology. To discover the inspiration of the scripture, one must look behind the actual text to the *realia* of events, personalities, and historical institutions by a process of historical scientific inquiry.[92] In making these distinctions, Semler felt he was carrying forward the work of the Reformation after an unfortunate interlude of rigid orthodoxy and exegetical stagnation. De Wette regarded himself as following in the footsteps of Semler, whom he described as "the instigator of a revolutionary movement in theology and the church which is still being carried forward."[93]

The deistic distinction between reason and revelation and the neologians' endeavors in historical-critical scholarship bequeathed to scholars of the late eighteenth and early nineteenth century wholly new criteria in epistemology and hermeneutics. Theologians began to raise questions about how one should interpret the Bible, given the fact that traditional canonical authority and divine inspiration had been called into question. Perhaps the most creative and consequential response to such questioning in Old Testament scholarship – and the one most important for understanding de Wette's work – was offered by the so-called mythical school, a group of scholars who pioneered the application of myth in biblical interpretation.

In 1753, the Oxford scholar Robert Lowth (1710–87) delivered a series of lectures, *De sacra poesi Hebraeorum*, in which he approached biblical poetry not from the standpoint of divine inspiration but from its style of expression. In 1786, Lowth's lectures were translated at Göttingen with critical notes by the neologian J. D. Michaelis (1717–91). The Göttingen classicist C. G. Heyne (1729–1812) embraced Lowth's ideas and drew from Lowth's emphasis on poetry to fashion the first known "mythic" interpretation of the Old Testament. Heyne divided myths into historical myths (myths that describe an actual happening) and philosophical myths (myths that attempt to explain the origin of phenomena). Heyne in turn influenced his pupil J. G. Eichhorn (1752–1827), the founder of the mythical school.[94]

The mythical school principally refers to the work of three scholars active in the late eighteenth century: J. G. Eichhorn, J. P. Gabler, and G. L. Bauer.[95] These scholars shared the conviction that the biblical texts were an amalgam of history and myth. They defined as mythical those parts of the

Bible that could not stand up to the rational scrutiny of Enlightenment epistemological presuppositions. Such events as Lot's wife turning into a pillar of salt or God's appearance to Moses in a burning bush were relegated to a mythical status. They felt that through careful scholarship the mythical chaff could be separated from the historical wheat and a truly accurate history of Israel established. Unlike Reimarus, Lessing, and Kant, they still viewed biblical texts as inspired documents. The composition of the Bible, however, reflected the worldview of a "primitive mind" (Eichhorn) or an "oriental mind" (Gabler) unable to recognize the difference between "the fact and the way the fact was perceived."[96] The contribution of their criticism – so these scholars reasoned – was in the newly championed ability to make appropriate epistemological distinctions and supply a natural cause where a biblical author had given only a mythical one.[97]

In light of later criticism, many of the views of the mythical school may seem rather modest. None doubted, for example, Mosaic authorship of the Pentateuch, although they recognized that Moses was perhaps the compiler and editor of several preexisting documents. Moreover, they all believed that the history of Israel as presented in the Old Testament was more or less the real history of Israel – once natural causes had been supplied for supernatural ones. Finally, while "upgrading" the Old Testament to meet contemporary standards, they did not scoff; God, for whatever mysterious reasons, had chosen to reveal himself in what was generally dubbed "the beautiful and simple language of mankind's childhood."[98]

The young de Wette took his scholarly cue from the work of Eichhorn, Gabler, and Bauer. His earliest works are both theological essays: *Eine Idee über das Studium der Theologie* (1801) and *Aufforderung zum Studium der hebräischen Sprache und Literatur* (1805). His first original work of biblical criticism was his dissertation (1805), which was soon followed by his *Beiträge* (1806/07). These works have earned de Wette a prominent place in the history of biblical criticism.[99] Unfortunately, historians of Old Testament scholarship have generally failed to make explicit the relationship between de Wette and the intellectual currents of his day.[100] Although trained disciplinarily as an Old Testament critic, de Wette brought to the field a unique philosophical conception of myth, derived largely from Schelling. In applying this notion of myth to the Bible, de Wette overhauled the exegetical possibilities of the myth category and laid the groundwork for its application as a comprehensive hermeneutical option for making sense of the strange cohesion between the Bible's patently historical characteristics and its radically suprahistorical truth-claims.

De Wette's appreciation of art and myth were already evident in *Eine Idee* and *Aufforderung*. Writing under the influence of Schelling, de Wette addresses "divine art" in *Eine Idee* and notes that since Christ no longer walks the earth, it is primarily art that "bring[s] down to us from heaven the divine in earthly form."[101] Like Schelling, de Wette expanded the aesthetic sense to encompass both nature and human history. Anything, aesthetically perceived served in his view as "a living image of divinity" (*lebendigen Sinnbild der Gottheit*).[102]

In *Aufforderung zum Studium der hebräischen Sprache und Literatur* (1805),[103] de Wette castigated biblical exegetes for treating the Pentateuch as a document written by an ancient historian-like chronicler. De Wette argued instead that the Old Testament is nothing more than a collection of myths and traditions; its authors were completely uninterested in presenting history "as it actually was." "The Hebrew storyteller," writes de Wette, "is not a historian in an actual sense; he is a prophet and seer looking into the past." Such a storyteller presents historical material only to awaken and animate religious concerns:[104] "A complete and thoroughgoing criticism will show that not one of the historical books of the Old Testament has any historical value, and that they all more or less contain myths and traditions; and that we do not have from among any of the books of the Old Testament any real historical witnesses."[105]

While criticizing the historical approach of the mythical school, de Wette importantly did not cast complete doubt on the possibility of historical knowledge. Rather, he claimed that the only method suitable for apprehending historical consciousness in the Old Testament was to approach it in its own terms – which were religious (and patently not historical) ones made accessible to the modern reader through poetry, art, and, above all, myth. He claimed that approaching history in such a matter was not unscientific, but rather the "tiefsten Tiefe der Wissenschaft."[106] Accordingly, he raised this antihistorical conception of Old Testament historical consciousness to a more general scholarly principle and asserted that when handling history, modern theologians should only strive to awaken others to past forms of religious consciousness; they should not worry about pedantic facts. Moreover, since all of human history, according to de Wette, was a revelation of God, the goal of the historical interpreter should be to present the past as an ongoing religious poem. In short, only in aesthetic terms did de Wette deem it possible to understand the changing historical manifestations of the Hebrew religious spirit in the Old Testament.[107]

In his *Dissertatio critica qua a prioribus Deuteronomium pentateuchi libris diversum alias cuiusdam recentioris auctoris opus esse monstratur*,[108] de Wette investigated the book of Deuteronomy following the principles he laid down in the *Aufforderung*. He posited that Deuteronomy represented a religious meditation – not a historical account – and sought to demonstrate that it was written much later than the rest of the Pentateuch. He claimed that his findings refuted the orthodox notion of the Mosaic authorship of the Pentateuch.[109]

For subsequent Old Testament scholarship, the most important part of the *dissertatio* came in a lengthy footnote, in which de Wette suggested that a law book discovered in the temple by Josiah in 622 B.C. (II Kings 22) might have been Deuteronomy or a document on which Deuteronomy was based. De Wette reasoned that the later origins of Deuteronomy made sense because the command to sacrifice at a single sanctuary was unique to Deuteronomy. In Exodus 20:24–25, for example, a multiplicity of altar sites is implied. Deuteronomy also contradicted the behavior of Samuel, Saul, David, and Solomon, who sacrificed wherever necessary without incurring divine disfavor. This practice continued after the completion of the temple by Solomon, until the reign of Josiah, when the law book (perhaps Deuteronomy?) was discovered. Since Deuteronomy reflects the command to sacrifice at a single altar, this would date the book in the seventh century B.C., much later than the rest of the Pentateuch.[110]

De Wette concluded the *dissertatio* by pointing out that the paraphrased verses at the opening of Deuteronomy contradicted earlier passages in the Pentateuch. This demonstrated, according to de Wette, that Deuteronomy might have been written to correct earlier works in light of a new understanding of religion, one that reflected state centralization (in sacrificing practices and in other matters) because of the completed temple in Jerusalem.[111]

Although de Wette was not the first scholar to suggest that important developments in Judaism took place after Moses, his dissertation was later acclaimed because he was the first to hint at a picture of Israel's history that differed markedly from that offered in the Old Testament itself. This innovation was the crucial idea behind his subsequent *Beiträge*, which laid the groundwork for Old Testament criticism in the nineteenth and twentieth centuries.[112] It received classical formulation in the work of Julius Wellhausen.[113] Importantly, unlike his eighteenth-century predecessors (Eichhorn, Gabler, Bauer), de Wette did not expunge the mythological in order to establish the historical. Rather, embracing myth as a positive aesthetic category, much as Schelling did, de Wette concentrated instead on textual problems and inconsistencies. This innovation resulted in the restructuring of the historical question altogether.

In *Beiträge zur Einleitung in das Alte Testament*, de Wette even more decisively broke with previous Old Testament scholars. Eichhorn, Gabler, and Bauer shared two basic principles that de Wette called into question. First, they held to the Mosaic authorship of the Pentateuch based on a *documentary hypothesis* of the various traditions represented in the text of Genesis. This hypothesis held that the different names given for God in Genesis (Elohim and Jehovah) represented different original sources that Moses consulted in composing the Pentateuch. Second, they believed, as indicated earlier, that the Old Testament was indeed a source of reliable historical information. In their view, the stories of Abraham, Isaac, Jacob, and

Moses were all true, but they had been expressed inadequately because they took place in a time that lacked sufficient standards for determining causality.

Along with his contemporary J. S. Vater, de Wette contested the popular documentary hypothesis and put forth instead a *fragmentary hypothesis*. De Wette and Vater argued that Genesis, Exodus, Leviticus, and Numbers were made up of various fragments that had little or no relation to one another. These fragments, written later than the alleged time of Moses, had been collected and compiled hundreds of years after their original composition by an unknown scholar or group of scholars. Vater published in 1805 the third volume of his *Commentar über den Pentateuch*, which, to de Wette's consternation, anticipated his own views in his then unpublished *Beiträge*.[114] Vater's publication, however, prompted de Wette to look elsewhere for originality.

De Wette's path-breaking originality came in his decision to emphasize the conception of myth that he had previously praised in the *Aufforderung*. In doing so, de Wette made a complete break with scholarship that saw the Old Testament as a historical document only in need of "demythologizing." Following his assertions in the *Aufforderung*, de Wette sought to demonstrate that the fragments that made up the Pentateuch, especially the parts that suggested that Moses had introduced the laws and practices of sacrifice, were a composite of myths whose purpose was to express and legitimize the Hebrew religious outlook in the time of the late monarchy. The Pentateuch, like the stories of Homer or Ovid, according to de Wette, was a rich mythological account of Israel's later religious identity and one largely devoid of verifiable factual history.

In the *Beiträge*, de Wette discussed again the mysterious law book discovered in the temple in 622 B.C. during the reign of Josiah (II Kings 22:8–10). He noted that nowhere was it called the book of Moses, that it seemed to be innovative, and that it was in all likelihood a version of what later came to be Deuteronomy. How it was placed in the temple was left open to speculation by de Wette. He did not rule out the possibility that it might have been written by Hilkiah, the high priest.[115] An examination of such books as Ezra and Nehemiah led de Wette to draw the following conclusion: "Until the time of Josiah there is no trace of the existence of the Pentateuch. But after that time, especially after the exile, indications of its existence are most frequent and clear."[116] De Wette's message is straightforward: the discovery of this work, which was likely Deuteronomy, led to the formation of various other fragments into the Pentateuch. Moreover, these fragments were put together, embellished, and even altered in such a way as to reflect the religious identity of Israel during the period of the monarchy.

Throughout the *Beiträge*, de Wette backed his assertion by pointing out various discrepancies between the prescriptions given for religious practices in the Pentateuch and their descriptions in the books of Joshua through Samuel and Kings. He concluded that the Pentateuch can only be understood as a mythological "retro-projection" of views that developed during the monarchy – much later than the time of Moses. De Wette did not deny the existence of Moses or the Hebrew patriarchs, or that Israel undertook an exodus from Egypt. His point is that the question of historicity is not a primary concern, because the stories were composed not to satisfy modern historical curiosity but to express Israel's religious aspirations as a nation. Instead of depicting Abraham as a historical sheik, as constructed by Eichhorn, the fragments, in de Wette's eyes, presented Abraham as a mythologically embellished founder of Israel's sense of national destiny and as an example of Hebrew piety. Instead of the historical Moses, the fragments presented an Aeneas-like hero.[117] "Facts [about many Old Testament personalities]," writes de Wette, "cannot be investigated; one can only observe how they have been narrated."[118]

Thus, de Wette ceased to treat the Pentateuch as a semi-accurate historical account. Instead, as Rogerson notes, he investigated the narrative structure of its "myths" for clues to make sense of Israel's later history; he did this primarily by asking internal, textual questions. Although he cast doubt on the documentary hypothesis, he retained a form of it in two important respects. First, he agreed with a view already extant in Old Testament scholarship that the story of Joseph was attributable to two sources, each representing a self-contained narrative. Second, and more important, de Wette believed that the Pentateuch had a basic framework into which the other fragments had been inserted. The putative framework coincided with Eichhorn's theory of an "Elohim" document.[119] De Wette recognized the presence of this framework, not on the formal grounds of the use of the divine name but on the inner simplicity of the material. This framework constituted the substratum of an epic that expressed the aspirations of Israel as a chosen people. The Pentateuch, in short, described God's promises to provide a land for the Hebrews and to maintain the Abrahamic covenant. Put differently, it was the national story of the Hebrew people, which was refurbished during the monarchy.[120] In de Wette's words, the Pentateuch was "an epic poem, and the poet wishes to be nothing other than a poet, and certainly not a historian."[121] Stressing its poetic dimension, de Wette writes, "In the story of creation our author is obviously not writing historically. He does not give us historical truth, nor even philosophical truth. His presentation is poetic. The days of creation, like the act of creation and the celebration of the first great Sabbath, are products of the Hebrew imagination."[122]

De Wette states that the Pentateuch's value is not lost once the historical facts are called into question; rather, the work assumes a higher meaning:

> Taken as poetry and myth, it appears as a supremely important and rich source for the most important and fruitful observations; and in another sense it is still a most important historical monument (*geschichtliche Denkmal*). It is the product of the religious poetry of the Israelite people that reflects their spirit, way of thought, patriotism, philosophy, and religion.[123]

Although de Wette's scholarship has been disputed on various counts,[124] many aspects of his *Beiträge* became commonplaces of subsequent Old Testament criticism. De Wette was the first scholar to work out a history of Israel radically at variance with the account given in the Old Testament, although one based on careful textual analysis.

Most important, however, de Wette's ideas carried implications far beyond the narrow field of Pentateuch criticism. It is ironic that de Wette targeted history as a category that had limited applicability to biblical interpretation. By history de Wette had in mind the type of criticism practiced by the mythical school – by Eichhorn, Gabler, and Bauer. However, by minimizing the Pentateuch's historical dimension, de Wette suggested a type of historical investigation at another level. De Wette saw the Pentateuch as one might view Virgil's *Aeneid*. Although there is little evidence for the historical veracity of this epic poem, it still offers important information about Roman political sensibilities during the time of Augustus. Likewise, through his appeal to myth, de Wette pointed out that the Pentateuch had (historical) implications for another period, namely that of the later Hebrew monarchy. Other scholars followed de Wette's lead. Indeed, in attempting, through appeals to Romantic notions of poetry and myth, to safeguard the Bible from eighteenth-century rationalist criticism, de Wette in effect laid the groundwork for a radical shift in biblical criticism *toward history*, but history of another kind – namely, the history of the texts themselves and their authors/editors and no longer of the events and the people which the texts narrated. The implications of this shift were worked out by such later scholars as Julius Wellhausen and F. C. Baur and critics of the so-called Tübingen School.[125] Furthermore, the type of investigation that de Wette proposed, as I demonstrate in chapter three, resulted in unsettling cultural and religious repercussions throughout Europe once D. F. Strauss appropriated and applied de Wette's methods in his *Das Leben Jesu*.

Finally, one would be hard pressed to extricate de Wette's biblical-critical concerns and methods from their immersion in broader intellectual and historical currents. Kant prompted de Wette to reject supernatural explanations; Schelling, and perhaps earlier Herder, equipped him with an aesthetic and mythical approach to the Old Testament. Biblical criticism in the early nineteenth century (and today) was not an autonomous field of gradual scientific accretion, but a time-conditioned enterprise predicated on the attitudes and concerns of a specific cultural environment.

De Wette, Jakob Friedrich Fries, and the Epistemology of Theology

While making his name in biblical scholarship, de Wette never forsook his interest in theology. Despite the attraction of Schelling's philosophy, de Wette did not accept it uncritically. In *Theodor*, de Wette intimated that a worldview derived solely from Schelling's aestheticism would lead to confusion, for it would entail the rejection of Kant's persuasive ethical system and epistemology.[126] The vacillation between Schelling and Kant lasted throughout de Wette's years at Jena. It was not until the influence of (and friendship with) J. F. Fries that de Wette came to a satisfying philosophical resolution. In an 1841 letter to James Clarke, de Wette made explicit Fries's influence:

> I was not wholly satisfied with the philosophy of Schelling, for I did not find in it enough perspicuity or certainty; but, as yet, I could not attain by my own efforts to any secure or fixed convictions. Commencing now my theological career, and studying the Old Testament independently, the historical criticism engaged me, and led me, in a measure, to the side of Rationalism. I agreed with some of its negative results. . . . But, as regards the interests more religious, I sought elsewhere for something different, but without attaining anything sure or settled until I met with the philosophy of Fries, which taught me to reconcile understanding and faith in the principle of religious feeling. From this moment I pursued with certainty my course through the freest historical criticism to religious convictions which gave security both to faith and to the existence of the church.[127]

Upon Fries's death in 1843, de Wette wrote a short article of commemoration in which he hailed Fries "as one of the greatest geniuses that the history of philosophy can show. . . . It is already common knowledge that I am completely convinced by his philosophy."[128]

Although Fries taught at Jena when de Wette was a student there, only later in Heidelberg did Fries's influence become pronounced; there the two men began a lasting friendship. Fries had been called to a professorship in philosophy and mathematics at Heidelberg in 1805. De Wette came to Heidelberg's theology department two years later.[129]

The son of devout Herrnhuter pietists, Fries's upbringing manifested itself throughout his life in the religious significance he attributed to emotion.[130] Although convinced by Kant's epistemology, he deemed Kant's rational religion insufficient and set it as his task to redelineate the limitations of reason in order to esteem the nonrational, the emotional, and the intuitive in human experience. For this reason, once at Jena, he found the lectures of Fichte on speculative philosophy highly disturbing. "I listened to Fichte, took notes, then rushed home and wrote rebuttals," Fries later recalled. In 1798 he published an essay "Über das Verhältnis der empirischen Pyschologie zur Metaphysik" in which he argued, *contra* Fichte, that philosophy should set modest tasks; it should be analytical, descriptive, and methodological – not constructive or speculative.[131]

In 1803, Fries published a polemical work, *Reinhold, Fichte, Schelling*, which established his reputation as a Kantian critic of the prevailing Romanticism and speculation in philosophy.[132] Fries was attracted to Schelling after reading his *Ideen zu einer Philosophie der Natur* (1797) because he saw in this work an attempt to justify the role of induction in natural science. Later, however, he became critical of Schelling for confusing methods of criticism with philosophical speculation, which resulted, according to Fries, in "mystery mongering."[133] Shortly after completing *Reinhold, Fichte, Schelling*, in 1805, he was offered a position at the University of Heidelberg, selected over the *Privatdozent* Hegel. Although Fries taught philosophy, physics, and mathematics at Heidelberg, he maintained a strong interest in religion and its relation to other forms of knowledge, especially to the natural sciences. Because of his pietist background and Kantian epistemological leanings, Fries was intent on establishing grounds for faith by limiting the scope of reason. Importantly, this persistent Kantian concern placed Fries at a distance from most of his Romantic and Idealist contemporaries. The former often did not fathom Kant's wholesale separation of religion and nature, while the latter deliberately attempted to reconcile the two.

In 1805, Fries published his threefold approach to reality in a book entitled *Wissen, Glaube, und Ahnung*[134] – a book that greatly influenced de Wette, who applied its insights to theology and biblical interpretation.[135] Following Kant's lead, and in opposition to those devoted to the "pious love of mysticism and other similar sweet temptations," Fries attempted to distinguish three "totally distinct . . . ways in which we consider something to be true." The forms are best regarded as three species – knowledge, belief, and aesthetic sense (*Wissen, Glaube, Ahnung*) – under the rubric of a greater epistemological genus, "cognition" (*Erkenntnis*).[136]

According to Fries, knowing (*Wissen*) was the mode of cognition applicable to the spatiotemporal world and the one most relevant to the natural sciences. He saw the expansion of this form of cognition in the modern world as a threat to religion. In *Wissen, Glaube, Ahnung*, therefore, Fries insisted that knowledge of the natural world had a subjective character: "Nature or the world of the senses, as sum total of the objects of experience, is in no way known as a world of things-in-themselves. Rather it is only the object of our subjectively conditioned manner of mental-representation (*subjectiv bedingten Vorstellungsweise*)."[137] Fries attempted to supersede Kant by grounding knowledge *solely* in a subjective (or what he called a psychological or anthropological) conception of reason: "Every individual stands wondrously alone in his own inward being, as if in his own closed world. Here within the inner world alone the life of reason itself appears to every rational mind. Beginning with it [our inner world] reason projects life . . . [into] the entire material world."[138] In short, Fries radicalized Kant's epistemology in regard to knowledge of the phenomenal world: certainty lies not in any implied connection between subject and object but rather in a coherence within human subjectivity. In attempting to improve upon Kant, Fries required substantial revision of the common understanding of proof. Proof for Fries was a subjective process that could not of itself guarantee the truth of its conclusion – at least, not in the conventional sense of a correspondence with external reality. The knowledge on which proof depended resulted from the purely subjective structure of the human mind and the nonnecessary nature of empirical knowledge. In his understanding of truth, Fries completely eschewed the classical correspondence theory of truth in favor of a conception based on coherence.[139] In doing so, Fries felt that he was continuing a process begun by Kant in order to "win a place for belief" by humbling knowledge. "We succeed in defending the rights of belief (*Rechte des Glaubens*) chiefly by showing that knowledge emerges only subjectively in reason."[140]

In *Wissen, Glaube, Ahnung*, Fries argued that once one becomes conscious of the limitations placed on knowledge, one can guarantee the legitimacy of other forms of attaining certainty. Awareness of the limitations of knowledge (*Wissen*) is the origin of belief (*Glaube*). Fries pointed out that the process of becoming aware of the limits of knowledge does not produce a positive idea of what lies beyond the limits of knowledge. The origin of belief "must remain thoroughly negative, having no positive content other than that of the negation of all negations, of the denial of limitations (*Verneinung der Schranken*)."[141]

But how does belief express itself? If the world of knowing is restricted to space and time, the way to negate this restriction is to think space and time away. The negation of these limitations could be achieved by the idea of a noumenal, infinite reality outside the phenomenal world. A characteristic of the phenomenal world, Fries argued, is its rigid necessity. One can overcome this necessity, however, by positing a realm in which freedom reigns and by recognizing that necessity is absent in the presence of purpose. Both these experiences, according to Fries, were in fact integral to human consciousness: human beings have an ingrained sense of freedom and purpose. But while human beings may postulate a world quite different from the finite world of knowing, Fries conceded that in the final analysis we are unable to *prove* or say anything positive about it.[142] Therefore, Fries argued that the possibility of an infinite, suprasensible world could only be realized through belief. Belief (*Glaube*) originates when one scrutinizes the structure of the mind: when one becomes aware that *Wissen* is limited to the finite world, one also recognizes the peculiar capacity of the mind to postulate an infinite realm outside its own scope:

> Through the logical ideas of infinity (*des Unbeschränkten*) one is able to conceive of something *that* is not appearance and *which* is not subject to the laws of nature. And this idea, which is bound with the original consciousness of reason, is awakened by the knowledge of nature, and is captured in the idea of being-in-itself. This idea is the only speculative basis of belief, and, in accordance with its genesis, must remain thoroughly negative.[143]

Fries's Concept of *Ahnung*

Fries sought to fill in the chasm between knowledge of the finite and faith in the infinite by setting forth the concept of *Ahnung* – a notion destined to became the conceptual leitmotiv of de Wette's theology. Unlike Kant, Fries was not content to make religion into a strictly moral matter. For him, religion was deeply associated with feeling, with the profound sense shared by all people that the finite world is a manifestation of a profounder eternal reality.

Ahnung is a difficult word to translate. Depending on its context, it often comes into English as "intimation," "intuition," "intuitive awareness," "inkling, or "prescience." In both its colloquial and formal usages, it suggests a sense of a reality or truth that remains inexpressible. Although the word "sense" itself would be an appropriate translation in certain settings, *Ahnung* never has the meaning of sense in the sensual connotation of the word (sight, smell, etc.).

In his philosophical lexicon of 1733, the scholar J. G. Walch characterized *Ahnung* as "a sensation that originates from an interior sadness and anxiety that comes from an impending but unknown sense of misfortune." However, Walch also noted that "this sensation arises in the absence of any actual unpleasant object; rather, one feels it even though there is no real sense of danger." In philosophical parlance, the word was later largely divested of its connection with impending misfortune and took on the additional meaning of impending revelation. Simply put, one might speak of it as the (pre)awareness of something without any concrete (empirical) reference to that something. A certain vagueness is integral to its semantic character. Kant spoke of it derogatorily as the "death of all philosophy because it is a vague expectation and hope for a revelation that is only abstractly possible. . . . One can simply see that *Ahnung* is a mental chimera (*Hirngespenst*) because how can one perceive what is not there?" Conversely, F. H. Jacobi attempted to give *Ahnung* philosophical justification, arguing that human beings do not have so much the ability to know what is true as a vague inkling (*Ahnung*) toward the truth.[144]

Despite his loyalty to Kant, Fries made *Ahnung* central to his understanding of human cognition. According to Fries, truth was ultimately a singular phenomenon. Although by distinguishing between *Wissen* and *Glaube* he recognized different modes of understanding, he held that "there is but one [truth] and it must be that the same reality of the eternal is repeated in the finite."[145] Through faith one can become aware of the infinite world, the world of God and eternity, and through knowledge one can know the empirical world. This left Fries with one problem: was there any connection between the infinite and finite? In other words, if truth is unitary, is there a cognitive mode that allows one to infer the eternal from the standpoint of the finite? The formulation of *Ahnung* represents Fries's attempt to answer this question. Fries put the problem as follows:

> We know about the finite in nature; we believe in the eternal. But to our reason this cognition of the finite must finally be one and the same. . . . We look at the finitude of nature, as the appearance of the eternal, and it is only because of the limitations of our finite being and our means of cognition that we are unable to see the eternal as it is in itself. Thus the being of the eternal, which we grasp in belief . . . is really the same being that then appears to us in the finitude of nature. Nature is to us the appearance of the eternal, and so we must recognize the laws of the eternal within the finitude of nature. But which means of laying claim to truth will allow this?[146]

Fries eschewed yoking the eternal only to faith, for faith in relation to knowledge remained for him a purely negative phenomenon. Faith exists only because knowledge has limits, not because faith has knowable content. Therefore, arising from Fries's conviction that truth was unitary and that the eternal subsumes the finite, the eternal at least could be perceived (*die Ewige geahnet*) in the finitude of nature. Fries asserted that a cognition (*Erkenntnis*) of the eternal within the finitude of nature is possible only "through pure feeling."[147]

Fries distinguished sharply between mere sensation and his notion of feeling; he was convinced that the latter had a secure cognitive basis:

Cognition through pure feeling I call *Ahnung*, the eternal in the finite. Only what is particular and finite in nature is an object of our knowing. ... By contrast, for belief's sake we can think about the eternal only through the idea of the non-finite; that is we contemplate the elimination of the limits of finite being for eternal being, without a positive representation of the eternal. All of the ideas through which we gain belief in the higher world order – the ideas of immortality, freedom, and deity – only arise for us because we think away the uncompletability and limitedness from the being of things before our eyes. We have absolutely no positive representation of the eternal, but through the union of knowledge and belief within the same consciousness there arises the conviction that the finite is only an appearance of the eternal. From this conviction arises the feeling of the recognition of the eternal within the finite, a feeling we call *Ahnung*.[148]

Although *Ahnung* in Fries's view was structurally part of human consciousness, it remained an "inexpressible feeling" (*unaussprechliches Gefühl*). It was a conceptual void, "nothing but a feeling, whereby we aesthetically sense (*ahnen*) that higher world in the beauty and sublimity of nature." Fries added that through *Ahnung* the eternal was delivered from its pure negativity: "A positive image of the eternal is thus possible for us only through the relationship of the eternal to the finite, but we can grasp this relationship only in feeling."[149]

Ahnung has an obvious paradoxical character. Fries posited it in order to bridge the gulf between knowledge and faith. Yet he wanted to bridge the two in a manner that left intact the Kantian foundation on which the unavoidable rift (between the finite and the infinite) had been established. In this sense, Fries saw himself as constructing an intellectual basis for the validity of metaphysics and religion and for a conception of the world that viewed nature as an epiphenomenal manifestation of a profounder eternal reality.

Seeing the natural world as a part of the eternal accomplished Fries's epistemological goals. His philosophy gave legitimacy to natural science, which upheld his interests in physics and mathematics. Moreover, it conferred eternal purpose on the natural world. In a chapter in *Wissen, Glaube, Ahnung* entitled "The Teleology of Nature," Fries noted that the theme of "*Ahnung* is one with that of the teleology of nature. For *Ahnung*, nature must be judged as purposeful, and this purposefulness of *Ahnung* is to be related to the idea of the eternal good."[150]

Conclusion

De Wette embraced Fries's philosophy so thoroughly that critics later accused him of following the "spirit" of Fries instead of his own. To these critics, de Wette replied: "Even before I was familiar with him [Fries] and his philosophy, I had arrived at exactly the same standpoint as a result of my own studies and reflection, yet without having built a complete system. ... [In Fries] I only found the scholarly clarity to express what I had achieved on my own."[151] Whether de Wette spoke with complete accuracy here is questionable, because he also referred to Fries as his "leader" (*Führer*) and as someone occupying an "outstanding place in the process of the development of human wisdom" – adulations suggesting that Fries was more than the spokesman for de Wette's preexisting views.[152] Whatever the case, certain tensions in de Wette's early intellectual career made Fries's philosophy attractive. De Wette's divided loyalty between Kant and Schelling especially – poignantly expressed in *Theodor* – was indeed similar to the tension that Fries sought to resolve in *Wissen, Glaube, Ahnung*. In *Theodor*, de Wette wrote of the impact of a certain Professor A (presumably Fries, though de Wette does not mention him by name) on the young Theodor:

> To our friend [Theodor] it was as though by magic that these insights ordered into a beautiful system the scattered fragments of his previous insights and convictions. The gap which he had seen between the systems of Kant and Schelling seemed to him to be bridged. The idealistic or inner view of the world was upheld, but not as the highest or only view. The dependency and limitation of human knowledge was recognized, and the point was identified where it connected with the nature of things and with eternal truth. The teaching of Schelling about the Absolute ... was also to some extent upheld; but the point of view of individual experience was not abandoned.[153]

In short, de Wette found in Fries a kindred spirit and in Friesianism a satisfactory middle ground between Kant and Schelling, a system that maintained the Kantian division between the phenomenon and the noumenon, while making room for the noncritical, the emotional, and the aesthetic.

A Friesian philosophical vocabulary is already noticeable in de Wette's Heidelberg writings, such as his *Beytrag zur Charakteristik des Hebräismus* (1807) and *Commentar über die Psalmen* (1811).[154] But Fries's influences actually became more evident during de Wette's subsequent period at the University of Berlin, when, in his own effort to construct a modern systematic theology, he began to apply Friesian philosophy consistently.[155] For instance, in 1813, he wrote of three types of conviction (*Überzeu-*

gungsarten): "*Glaube* and *Ahnung*, like . . . *Wissen*, find their origins in deduction or their demonstration in human consciousness. God, freedom, and immorality cannot be proven, but can be shown to be necessary ideas in reason (*Vernunft*)."[156] Furthermore, de Wette became persuaded that the events recorded in both the Old and New Testaments could be exposed to the most complete historical criticism without endangering faith because at the most profound epistemic level "the divine government of the world is made known to us through *Ahnung*."[157] This is clearly something that Fries had taught him.

*　　*　　*

In July 1810, Friedrich Schleiermacher, having heard of the young, sophisticated Heidelberg theologian and biblical scholar, invited de Wette to join him on the theology faculty of the recently founded University of Berlin. De Wette accepted. Shortly thereafter, he and his Heidelberg colleague, Philipp Konrad Marheinecke, journeyed to Berlin and joined Schleiermacher, J. G. Fichte, Wilhelm von Humboldt, and a host of other luminaries at what quickly became the most prestigious and influential university in nineteenth-century Europe. In Berlin, de Wette would labor nine productive years, until 1819 when political misfortune befell him.

CHAPTER TWO

De Wette and Schleiermacher at Berlin (1810–1819)

Politics, History, and the Post-Enlightenment Transformation of Theology

If it is true that our religious culture (*Bildung*) rests on history, then our theology must certainly be historical.

– De Wette, *Über Religion und Theologie*

The nineteenth century began with a *tabula rasa* in relation to everything.

– Burckhardt, Letter to Gottfried Kinkel, 13 June 1842

A S MAURICE MANDELBAUM HAS NOTED, the conventional view that hostility prevailed between religion and science in the nineteenth century is often overstated. Although many intellectuals criticized traditional interpretations of Christian doctrines, the vast majority defended the legitimacy of religion in general and celebrated its emotional and aesthetic value. Quite often, attacks on Christian orthodoxy were carried out in the name not of science but of religion itself. Orthodox dogmas were not attacked for "the sake of undercutting religious faith" but rather as "a means of freeing that faith for . . . nobler and more adequate forms in which it could find expression."[1] In their efforts to "free up" religion, many intellectuals repeatedly raised an important question: what is the relationship of traditional Christian orthodoxy to this modern, nondoctrinal understanding of religion? Few theologians were willing to put Christianity on a plane with other world religions (as Ernst Troeltsch did later in the century); but defining Christian belief to guarantee its cultural supremacy, while simultaneously disavowing its orthodox formulation, required unprecedented theological maneuvering.

Because of the dominance of his legacy, Friedrich Schleiermacher is normally associated with the liberal reformulation of Christian belief in the early nineteenth century. Yet his concerns and goals were shared by other thinkers; de Wette wrestled with many of the same theological problems confronting Schleiermacher but often arrived at different solutions. Present-day theologians and intellectual historians have tended to read this period reductively as "the era of Schleiermacher."[2] Although in this chapter I treat de Wette's relationship to Schleiermacher, I also provide a broader consideration of the period, perhaps the most consequential era of theological ferment since the Reformation. I do not regard this period as exclusively Schleiermacher's but rather as a time of complex historical and theological debates, in which a variety of cultural, political, and institutional contingencies contributed to the birth of liberal theology with its far-reaching extra-theological ramifications.

Both de Wette and Schleiermacher operated in a cultural situation still dominated by the influence of the eighteenth century. With respect to theological reflection, the eighteenth-century inheritance principally meant two things. First, it meant having to come to grips with the question of history and particularly with the problems generated by the application of historical-critical methods to biblical texts. Although the "history problem" did not become full blown until the mid-nineteenth century, scholars by the turn of the century had long sensed the threat that history posed to the credibility of religious apologetics.[3] De Wette's solution to this problem, although peculiar in certain respects, was typical in its *a priori* preservation of "the religious view" in the face of seemingly faith-threatening historical criticism. As we shall observe more closely in chapters three and four, de Wette's solution to the "history problem" played no small role in Burckhardt's decision to forsake theology altogether.

Second, and relatedly, both de Wette and Schleiermacher were confronted by the legacy of Kant. Kant not only bequeathed to his successors a critical and negative view of traditional theological concepts, as we saw in chapter one; he also argued for complete separation between the realm of pure or scientific reason and the realm of morality and religion. Most commentators, de Wette and his mentor Fries notwithstanding, perceived this separation as a problem in need of overcoming.[4] In the dominant view, reason and religion must be in harmony in the world at large (as Hegel argued) or, failing that, at least in human consciousness. But de Wette remained fiercely loyal to Kant, and especially to the Kantianism promoted by Fries. Consequently, de Wette persistently defended a theological position that recognized sharp intellectual boundaries – the one between religious truth and critical knowledge being the most important. His adoption of this Kantian, boundary-setting mode of inquiry separated him from Hegel, Schleiermacher, and a host of other synthetic and monistic tendencies in early nineteenth-century German thought.[5]

Theology in the early nineteenth century took place in political and institutional settings. Of crucial importance in this respect was the establishment of the University of Berlin.[6] As a key member of the government's commission to found the university and as its principal theologian, Schleiermacher was consulted in the selection of Berlin's theological faculty, which shortly became one of the most prestigious in Europe. He proposed to the Prussian Minister of the Interior Alexander von Dohna that de Wette and his Heidelberg colleague Philipp Konrad Marheinecke be called to Berlin – de Wette as biblical scholar and Marheinecke as church historian. Schleiermacher and the planning commission placed strong emphasis on choosing professors who might supersede hackneyed rationalism-versus-orthodoxy debates, common in the eighteenth century,[7] and rehabilitate the declining reputation of religion in the academy and in the nation. De Wette's innovative biblical criticism and theology met their criteria, and consequently he received a call to Berlin in 1810.[8]

In Berlin, de Wette was impressively productive. His publications and lectures were numerous. Here he mastered Fries's philosophy and applied it in great detail to his own theological agenda, which achieved virtuoso expression in his *Über Religion und Theologie* (1815). On several occasions, de Wette's views brought him into conflict with Schleiermacher. Although the two eventually arrived at an amicable relationship, their disagreements demonstrate that de Wette was not the mere protégé of Schleiermacher, as has often been assumed.

During the post-1815, conservative Restoration period, de Wette's liberal tendencies, both theologically and politically, made him suspect to Prussian officials as a potential threat to social stability.[9] A tumultuous set of events, culminating in the confiscation of a letter of consolation that de Wette had written to the mother of Karl Sand, murderer of the playwright and publicist August von Kotzebue, resulted in de Wette's dismissal from Berlin in 1819. This event removed him permanently from the capital city's influential academic limelight, forcing him, after three years of unemployment and hardship, to accept a position outside of Prussia at the small and then seemingly insignificant University of Basel, where he would become a major university reformer and, in the 1830s, instruct the young Jacob Burckhardt.

De Wette and Schleiermacher

De Wette and Schleiermacher shared a desire to give theology a respected position in the modern academy. Eighteenth-century rationalism and new aesthetic philosophies had made official church dogma seem provincial and superannuated in the eyes of many "cultured despisers"; theology was losing its status as the "queen of the sciences" and as the principal bearer of the deepest energies of Western culture. Increasingly, students sought careers in the secular fields of law, medicine, and philosophy.[10] The reliability and moral authority of the Bible had come under heavy attack, and the possibility of traditional revelation was in doubt. Furthermore, in Kant's critiques, the natural theology that was a prominent feature of Enlightenment rationalism reached the end of its rope.[11] Admittedly, various pietist movements aroused many to expressions of faith, but they brought forth no intellectually convincing theological vision.

How was a credible theology possible? What did it mean to speak of the truth of theology or the nature of religion? And what, after all, was the church? These questions provided grounds for the often parallel lines of inquiry pursued by de Wette and Schleiermacher. They also provided grounds for disagreement, which assumed at times an institutional and strongly personal dimension. Admittedly, de Wette earlier had read Schleiermacher enthusiastically, but Fries alone remained de Wette's principal mentor. De Wette regarded Schleiermacher's theology as vague and even accused him in a letter to Fries of propounding a "lax mysticism" (*laxe Mysticismus*) harmful to Berlin's theology students.[12]

The anonymous publication of Schleiermacher's *Über Religion, Reden an die Gebildeten unter ihren Verächtern* (1799) has generally been regarded as the beginning of a new theological era, dividing the old theology – the "biblical-Reformation heritage" to use Emil Brunner's phrase[13] – from the new theology, the liberal or cultural Protestantism (*Kulturprotestantismus*) of the nineteenth century.[14] In the words of Karl Barth, Schleiermacher was "the great Niagara Falls" to which the theology of two centuries was inexorably drawn.[15]

It is a mistake, however, to attribute such thorough inevitability to Schleiermacher's views. The mistake obscures many historical contingencies. Among other things, it obscures the historical relation between the theologies of Schleiermacher and of de Wette. I shall demonstrate that, far from being merely a follower or disciple of Schleiermacher, de Wette was in fact Schleiermacher's rival and competed with him to establish the content of a new theological vision. The many similarities between the two men reflect shared generational sensibilities and not the dependence of de Wette on Schleiermacher. Furthermore, despite Schleiermacher's undisputed prominence in theology as we understand it today, for contemporaries his meaning was not immediately clear. De Wette's accusation of "mysticism" applies here. After reading Schleiermacher's *Reden*, Friedrich Schlegel was puzzled at where the author's "center" was.[16] Wilhelm Dilthey, Schleiermacher's first biographer, argued that his subject's intellectual vagueness could be rightly interpreted only if one proceeded biographically.[17]

Like Fries, Schleiermacher grew up and received his initial education in a pietist, Herrnhuter community. His later leitmotiv – religion as feeling (*Gefühl*) – seems obviously connected to these formative years. After encountering the philosophy of Kant and other *Aufklärung* thinkers at the

University of Halle, he experienced a profound religious crisis, which he reported to his father in an anguished letter in January 1787: "Alas, dearest father, if you believe that without this faith no one can attain to salvation in the next world, nor to tranquillity in this . . . then pray to God to grant it to me, for to me it is now lost."[18] After a period of estrangement from his father he eventually regained his faith, became a minister, served in the small villages of Drossen and Stolp and at the Charité Hospital in Berlin. He began his teaching career at the University of Halle in 1804. Following Prussia's defeat by Napoleon in 1806, he moved to Berlin, where he spent the rest of his life. In 1809 he became pastor of Trinity Church and, in 1810, professor of theology at the University of Berlin.[19]

Upon his return to faith, Schleiermacher proclaimed the now famous statement: "I have become a pietist (*Herrnhuter*) again – only of a higher order." He refused to follow Kant in basing religion on moral criteria alone. Religion must be grounded in feeling and in the consciousness and traditions of the Christian Church;[20] the putative conflict between historical religion and natural religion must be ended and simplistic categories like "supernaturalism" and "rationalism" must be dismissed. To accomplish such aims, Schleiermacher had to make theology acceptable outside the confines of believing communities. Theological statements, in his view, must not conflict with other, nontheological claims to truth. Accordingly, he described the ideal of the devout theology student as one in whom "both religious interest and scientific spirit in the highest degree . . . [are] balance[d] for theory and practice alike."[21] In his *Sendschreiben an Dr. Lücke*, Schleiermacher declared it his goal (which he compared to that of the Reformation) to "create an eternal covenant between the living Christian faith and an independent and freely working science, a covenant by the terms of which science is not hindered and faith not excluded."[22]

Schleiermacher's tendency to "mediate" between the claims of science and religion has led to the accepted usage of the term "mediating theology" (*Vermittlungstheologie*) to describe his general intellectual stance. Schleiermacher came to the conclusion that neither the aims of religion nor those of science were advanced so long as they remained in separate spheres. To the contrary, he wanted religion informed by science and vice versa. This reconciliation of spheres was no mere academic endeavor, for he believed that everything was held together by a single purpose: to equip learned leaders for the church. Without this practical goal, theology would collapse and its truths be scattered throughout other parts of the academy. To these ends – the reconciliation of religion and science and the instruction of future church leaders – Schleiermacher labored in his *Kurze Darstellung des theologischen Studiums* (1810), in which he defined the Christian church as a "becoming" (*ein Werdendes*), a body in the process of constant change, whose present must be considered as the product of the past and as the germ of the future.[23] The church cannot retreat from contemporary scientific developments nor can it abandon its own traditions because of them. In short, there must be steady, complex dialogue. From such a premise, Schleiermacher worked out his conception of theology, his definition of religion, and his ideas concerning the role of the church.[24]

De Wette rightly assumed that Schleiermacher was responsible for his call to Berlin.[25] After arriving in the capital city, he, like many contemporaries, puzzled over Schleiermacher's theology. In a long letter to Fries, he expressed his frank opinion:

> Schleiermacher holds that Christianity is something that unfolds in time as a unity that allows development. [It is] a basic disposition of the religious spirit, which is made conscious to the understanding in various ways according to different periods of time (. . . *eine Grundstimmung des religiösen Gemüthes, welche nur verschieden nach veschiedener Zeitbildung zur Selbstverständigung gebracht wird*). This understanding is then transient, the disposition permanent. Therefore, we are Christians when we possess this disposition. We can therefore dispense with that which belongs to various past periods, including pre-Christian ones. In such a way, we undo the knot at which our theologians so pitifully labor. They see biblical and other Christian dogmas no longer as relevant to us, because our knowledge has developed further. Therefore, they try to go around them or to make them mean something different, which is to say, they seek to substitute appropriate ideas for inappropriate ones. Schleiermacher would say [to them]: Let go of the dogmas and hold onto only the underlying ideas; that is, we should free the ideas from the dead body, so that, God willing, they will form into another one. The latter cannot be done easily, but is achieved most readily when they [the ideas] are grasped purely and re-presented purely. This is done scientifically in dogma and then – and this is difficult and requires an aesthetic presentation – in preaching and in the catechism. [However] I prefer to point to the religious ideas in the Bible and in doing so present the true basis (*Grundnorm*) of Christianity. But I want to show by philosophical criticism that the dogmas are nothing (*nichtig*).[26]

Two major differences between Schleiermacher and de Wette emerge from de Wette's summary. First, Schleiermacher's willingness to minimize the importance of past expressions of faith conflicted with de Wette's high esteem of the past. Since de Wette was teaching the Old Testament at the time, he would have found Schleiermacher's dismissal of pre-Christian views especially problematic. It also seems likely that de Wette saw parallels between Schleiermacher and the mythical school. Just as the latter had advocated discarding problematic narratives in order to recover the Bible's historical fundament, so Schleiermacher suggested that all forms of

Christian doctrine – biblical and extrabiblical – should be dissolved in order to arrive at the underlying idea.[27] But this begged prior questions for de Wette, such as how this procedure was to be accomplished and what epistemological criteria were to be used.

De Wette underscored his disagreements with Schleiermacher in *Theodor*.[28] His character Theodor is much taken by Schleiermacher's *Reden*, which he reads several times through. Theodor is particularly struck by Schleiermacher's distinction between religion as something original and unconscious in the heart and religion as something one becomes conscious of and attempts to express in a system of opinions.[29] In another effort to summarize Schleiermacher, de Wette wrote:

> The union of the finite and infinite Schleiermacher calls religion. He places this in the feeling, religious science in the intellect, and morality in the active powers. Knowledge and action are both elevated out of those depths of feeling where the finite and the infinite mysteriously blend together. . . . Knowledge and action result invariably from our desire to unite ourselves with the universe through the medium of some particular object.[30]

In Schleiermacher's view, knowledge and action represent attempts to achieve harmony with the universe by dealing with isolated dimensions of it; they are concerned with single aspects of the world, whereas religion is an apprehension of the world as a whole. On this point, de Wette resisted Schleiermacher. He judged Schleiermacher's definition of religion to have driven a wedge between religion and moral action because religious experience, in de Wette's view, *should* be the principal motivating factor in moral practice, and he could not see how religion (as Schleiermacher defined it) led to the empowerment of the will.[31] Theodor "did not clearly see the relation of [Schleiermacher's] religious feeling to the feeling which excites the will and which he recognized as the source of the moral law."[32]

Where de Wette judged Schleiermacher obscure, he judged Fries lucid and practical. Fries defined the reality apprehended by religion as conferring unity and purpose on human experience.[33] In *Theodor*, de Wette has Professor A (Fries) underscore Theodor's own criticisms. Professor A says that Schleiermacher states that the object of religion is the infinite, the universe, the soul of the world, but he never moves beyond these abstractions. In Fries's judgment, religion was the eternal unity and adaptation of things, where science and morality operate together in harmony.[34]

As Rogerson notes, de Wette also criticized Schleiermacher for contradicting himself. He interpreted Schleiermacher as holding that religion was a matter of reflection (*Betrachtung*), which de Wette saw as a matter of understanding (*Verstand*), not of feeling (*Gefühl*) as Schleiermacher held. In *Theodor*, Professor A defends Schleiermacher on this point and says that *reflection* may not in this case be related to understanding. But de Wette's point is clear. Schleiermacher's terms were often ambiguous. This is also true of Schleiermacher's use of the term "concept" (*Begriff*) to describe how religious experience is presented to consciousness. De Wette maintained that religion is primarily a matter of *Glaube* and *Ahnung*, and held that anyone who thinks feeling (*Gefühl*) can be apprehended by concepts (*Begriffe*) blurs important terminological distinctions.[35]

Finally, de Wette held that Schleiermacher did not treat aesthetics sufficiently. A chapter in *Theodor* ends with Professor A exhorting the young Theodor to attend his upcoming lectures so that he might learn that "Schleiermacher in his *Reden* does not notice art sufficiently, and has taken too narrow a view of the expression of religion, and of religious fellowship. Aesthetic symbols are the surest and highest way of expressing religion."[36]

*   *   *

The rivalry between de Wette and Schleiermacher was not confined to theological disagreement. It also manifested itself in more personal and practical matters. For example, de Wette conveyed to their mutual friend Friedrich Lücke that by preaching sermons, Schleiermacher was guilty of hypocrisy, for de Wette viewed the roles of professor and preacher as incompatible. To satisfy the sensibilities of lay listeners, a preacher, de Wette told Lücke, will inevitably compromise his absolute commitment to truth.[37] In Schleiermacher's view, however, religion naturally expressed itself in the establishment of a community, and he accordingly held that his role as preacher was importantly linked to his professorial duties.[38] De Wette, who did not attend public services in Berlin until 1817, was content to relegate the social organization of the church primarily to state officials and felt that it was the theologian's obligation only to establish the cognitive truth of religion.[39]

In 1816, tensions between de Wette and Schleiermacher became pronounced during discussions concerning the filling of a chair in philosophy. After the death of Fichte in January 1814, the university senate, with Schleiermacher serving as rector, met and decided to petition the government for the establishment of two replacement chairs, one in speculative philosophy, the other in practical philosophy.[40] For the former position, the senate proposed Hegel, Schelling, and G. H. von Schubert as possible candidates. Judging the situation as an occasion to bring Fries from Heidelberg to Berlin, de Wette nominated Fries for both chairs.[41] Although the senate refused to consider Fries for the chair of speculative philosophy, he became the leading candidate for the chair of practical philosophy. However, in the meantime, the Prussian government decided to authorize only the position for speculative philosophy.[42]

Upset by this decision, de Wette expressed his dismay in a memorandum to the government, in which he protested against the philosophies of the candidates who had won out over Fries. He asserted that the philosophies of Hegel and Schelling may be dismissed by the simple fact that they were "philosophers of nature" (*Naturphilosophen*).

> This philosophy has become suspect to all prudent thinkers. . . . I am a theologian, and it would seem only proper that a philosophy be judged according to whether it promotes or detracts from proper religious con- viction. . . . I believe that an inner accord, in spirit and in essence, must take place between Christian faith and true philosophy . . . [However] these ideas [i.e., those of the Christian faith] are not found in the philos- ophy of nature.[43]

Further, de Wette charged that von Schubert was practically a philosopher of the occult, having written on dreams and astrology. If the university were filling a "chair in mystical physics," de Wette complained, then von Schubert would be their man. The debates that followed in the theology department were rancorous.[44] In the end, de Wette failed to bring Fries to Berlin. Schleiermacher cast the deciding vote: for von Schubert and against Fries.[45] Hegel, however, wound up getting the chair in 1818.

The failure to bring Fries to Berlin and the increasing popularity of Schleiermacher's lectures among the students led de Wette to concede that Schleiermacher had achieved the upper hand: "Since the students [now] prefer his esoteric thought (*Gnosis*) to my criticism (*Kritik*), then let it be," he wrote bitterly to Fries.[46] The fact that Schleiermacher cast his vote for von Schubert seems to have been an intentional rebuff of de Wette.[47] It appears that Schleiermacher thought that an alliance between Fries and de Wette would result in the eclipse of his own views and sphere of influence. This point raises an important issue suggested by Rudolf Otto: was there anything necessary about the fact that Schleiermacher and Hegel became the dominant points of reference for developments in German theology and philosophy in the early nineteenth century? What developments might have followed if Fries, instead of Hegel, had come to Berlin and if neither Fries nor de Wette had been ostracized politically after 1819? After all, the intel- lectual authority and prestige of a chair at Berlin was not a matter of secondary importance.[48]

Despite academic conflicts, an understanding – or at least a mutual respect – began to develop between de Wette and Schleiermacher after 1815. At the root of this change was the new mood in politics brought about by Napoleon's defeat. Increasingly, de Wette and Schleiermacher found themselves bedfellows, perceived together as questionable liberals as new conservative and pietistic political forces gained ground in Prussia.[49] Schleiermacher initiated their new understanding by dedicating to de Wette his *Kritische Versuch über die Schriften Lukas* in April 1817. Presumably he did this to give de Wette a vote of confidence among the pietists at the royal court and among other faculty members.[50] Although Schleiermacher made clear the "recognized difference of our views," he praised de Wette for his commitment to scholarship and for "his wonderful sense of truth and his earnest and strict theological character."[51] He went on to write of the difficulty of a theologian's calling and of the complex nature of truth: "There is a general truth, in which all humans have a part, because God is no father of lies; and no one can deny the share that others have of it [truth] without accusing him simultaneously of madness."[52] Although Schleiermacher desired peace with de Wette, he also wanted to make clear, as this passage suggests, that the two were by no means in theological accord. To several friends, Schleiermacher even felt the need to defend his decision to dedicate a work to Wette. To Ludwig Blanc, he wrote that de Wette "is openly radical (*neologisch*), but he is a serious, profound, truth-loving man."[53] To Joachim Christian Gaß, he argued that his dedication was justified because of de Wette's ill-treatment from Prussian officials, but added that "whoever misunderstands me and perceives me to be a supporter of de Wette must be very prejudiced."[54]

De Wette responded to Schleiermacher's gesture by dedicating to him the second edition of his *Biblische Dogmatik Alten und Neuen Testaments* in May 1818. Despite recognized differences, de Wette declared that in the important things he and Schleiermacher were in "complete agreement."[55] Other steps of reconciliation were also under way. In 1817, Lücke persuaded de Wette to hear Schleiermacher preach at Trinity Church; afterward, de Wette became a regular attendee and modified his own views of the church.[56] De Wette was careful to justify his reconciliation with Schleiermacher to Fries: "You will have heard of my peace with Schleiermacher and of his dedication to me," he noted. He also explained to Fries the practical benefits of such a reconciliation – a widening of his own sphere of influence attested by the fact that several Schleiermacher devotees had begun to attend his lectures on dogmatics.[57]

In evaluating de Wette's relationship with Schleiermacher, I would like to raise several further issues. First, although their personal reconciliation did have genuine results, it is important to note – based on its timing and on the cautious phrasing of their dedications – that it stemmed largely from political motives. The conservatism of Prussian court elites during this time posed a grave threat to non-orthodox theologians. Although only de Wette was actually dismissed, Schleiermacher too was regarded with suspicion and investigated on several occasions.[58] Second, because of Schleiermacher's subsequent fame and de Wette's eclipse, and because of the similarities in their theological systems, accounts of de Wette often assume that Schleiermacher was a major influence on him. This was patently not the case.

Although Schleiermacher was the older of the two, they were antagonistic peers. Similarities between their thought should be attributed primarily to their shared historical context; de Wette was not Schleiermacher's apprentice. Last, their interaction and dissimilar legacies should call attention to the institutional contingencies often overlooked in "high" intellectual history. To return to the question posed by Otto, what if de Wette and Fries had achieved institutional hegemony at this crucial period in the making of modern German thought? I would suggest that a form of Kantianism, to which both de Wette and Fries adhered, and which was overshadowed by Hegelian and Romantic sensibilities until their revival in the "back to Kant" movement of late nineteenth century,[59] would have achieved an institutional foothold much earlier and perhaps altered the entire tenor of early nineteenth-century German theology and philosophy. I would not go as far as Otto, who felt that de Wette was wrongly overshadowed by Schleiermacher. I shall argue, however, that the rise of Schleiermacher's thought to dominance – and by extension the rise of Hegel's too – was not as inevitable as Barth's metaphor of a rushing waterfall suggests.

Defining Religion and Theology

Despite de Wette's rapprochement with Schleiermacher and despite surface similarities in their work, de Wette's theology differed considerably from that of his more prominent colleague. Indeed, many of de Wette's publications at Berlin were deliberate reactions against Schleiermacher's "lax mysticism." Equipped with the philosophy of Fries as expressed in *Wissen, Glaube, Ahnung* (1805), de Wette felt that it was in his power to establish a secure basis for the validity of religious truth while also upholding advances in historical and scientific knowledge. Moreover, he designed his theology to provide a way beyond the stalemated debates between rationalism and orthodoxy. By no means however did he want to bring about a reconciliation – neither between religion and science nor between rationalism and orthodoxy. He deemed religion and science as having incommensurable epistemological criteria and he thought that both sides in the rationalism/orthodoxy conflict were ridden with weak logic and emotional excess. In short, he attempted to pioneer a fresh theological vision, which he expressed in *Über Religion und Theologie* (1815), the linchpin and clearest expression of his theology.[60] For the purposes of the present study, this work is significant because it also concisely expresses de Wette's conception of history and his understanding of the relationship between historical and theological ways of knowing. As such, the work helps define de Wette's thought within a widespread, post-Revolution trend toward historicist thinking – a trend beginning in the eighteenth century, but one that became notably more self-conscious in the first decades of the nineteenth century.

At the beginning of *Über Religion und Theologie*, de Wette distinguishes between "the various forms of human certainty" (*die verschiedenen Ueberzeugungsweisen, deren der Mensch fähig ist*).[61] Drawing from Fries, he identifies three forms of certainty: knowing (*Wissen*), belief (*Glaube*), and aesthetic sense (*Ahnung*).

De Wette concentrates at first on *Wissen*, judging it the form of certainty subject to contemporary over- and misapplication. He states that this is the most common form of certainty and that it is derived from the senses and from experience. He divides it into three subcategories: the historical, the mathematical, and the philosophical. First, "all historical truth," he writes, "is derived from one's own perception or from reports of believable sources, and if this is not the case, we must concede that all we have is plausibility or supposition." Second, *Wissen* has a mathematical component, because it is concerned with space and time, size, content, and number. This aspect has a fundamental relation to the historical, because the notion of chronology and sequence provides grounds for historical inquiry. De Wette thus writes of the historical-mathematical dimension of human thought, which allows one to ascertain the general and the necessary, cause and effect, rules, and broader patterns of unity.[62] To the historical-mathematical he adds the philosophical component, which is one's subjective capacity to establish "coherence" (*Zusammenhang*) among heterogeneous sensory experiences. De Wette, ever the Kantian, is quick to point out that this coherence is not an external connection (*nicht mit der äusseren Verbindung*) but rather an internal one (*eine innere*). Of *Wissen*, therefore, he writes:

> Thus we have discovered a third cognition (*Erkenntniss*), the rational or philosophical stemming from concepts, by which the historical-mathematical is completed and lifted, with unity and necessity, to a fullness of experience. These three types of cognition make up human knowledge (*Wissen*) in the realm of the sensory; or, we may say, it is the first type of human certainty. . . . The common characteristic of this type of certainty is that it always focuses on the world in space and time – to finite, limited and contingent (*bedingte*) relations, which we see, even with all our efforts after unity and wholeness, only in fragments.[63]

Yet when one reaches the limits of measuring the world and describing its functions in terms of laws, one still has not explained its purpose. For this reason, de Wette posits a second way of gaining certainty, faith or *Glaube*. Here de Wette bases his argument on the conviction that human free will transcends the deterministic forces of nature.[64] This conviction, which he believes is intrinsic to human nature, "leads us to the point where *Wissen* ceases and a higher level begins."[65] Following Kant and Fries, this "higher level" is the basis of *Glaube*, the guarantor of human free will, the existence of God, and the immortality of the soul.

> The human spirit discovers its limits and humbles itself before what stands above it, which it cannot recognize and cannot grasp. Only through *Glaube* can it raise itself to such heights.[66]

What, de Wette asks, should one make of the contradiction between awareness derived from *Wissen* and that derived from *Glaube*? How can one believe in God, freedom, and immortality when these things do not appear to exist in the sensory world? To answer this question, de Wette turns to the Friesian principle of *Ahnung*. *Ahnung* allows one to experience an inkling of the world beyond *Wissen* through the very things that *Wissen* itself claims knowledge of. For instance, one can perceive a tree by quantifying all its dimensions; but only when one simply regards its beauty and its "purposive purposelessness," to borrow a phrase from Kant, is transcendence experienced. In de Wette's words,

> In the beauty and sublimity of nature and in the spiritual lives of humans, the religious *Ahnung* comes across as a manifestation of true being and of the eternal purpose of things. From the lovely flower to the sublime view of a glacier, from the laughing infant to great souls like Cato and Christ, nature and spirit proclaim to us the truth and reality of eternal ideas. . . . Indeed, there are holy moments in which we glimpse in the world a reflection of the divine glory itself, the traces of the eternal power and goodness, whether in the great spectacles of nature or in the mighty processes of destiny.[67]

In short, de Wette rebuts the view that *Wissen* is the most important form of gaining certainty. Rather, each mode of knowing has its allocated place; one cannot be held in higher regard than the other because each conveys certainty (*Gewissheit*), although the relative clarity (*Klarheit*) or comprehensibility (*Auffassungsbarkeit*) varies in human consciousness. Still, de Wette reasons that perhaps *Wissen* is overrated, since it only comprehends appearances, while *Glaube* and *Ahnung* testify to "the true nature of things."[68]

In one of the initial sections of *Über Religion und Theologie* entitled "The Idea of Religion," de Wette notes that religious conviction clearly belongs in the realms of *Glaube* and *Ahnung* – not *Wissen* – because religion does not lend itself to analysis in terms dictated by the categories of time and space. He refers to religion as a matter of our interior being and not of the physical world. He approvingly mentions Kant's doctrine of the subjectivity of the categories of time and space, and the asserts that the vicissitudes of this life – that is, of the world of forms – are not human beings' final destiny. We can transcend time and space by limiting their domain to *Wissen*, which de Wette associates with the "natural outlook" (*natürliche Ansicht*). However, in religious matters the "ideal view" (*ideale Ansicht*) is more important.

De Wette discusses the many mistakes made by those who attempt to grasp religious phenomena solely from the standpoint of *Wissen*. For example, the idea of an immortal soul becomes problematic when one wants to know its nature. The immortality of a material soul is nonsensical, in de Wette's view, and although people commonly imagine immortal life as the continuation of this life into eternity, he suggests that in this case the subject matter clearly demonstrates the limitations of human *Wissen*.[69]

De Wette distinguishes his notion of an ideal view from Schelling's "Absolute," the idea that the world and God are related ideas and that God should be thought of as that which encompasses all reality in its diversity and unity. De Wette labels this the "pantheistic view" and condemns it: "Such a God is made up only of parts, and since this synthesis must continue into infinity, one cannot say that such a God is, but only that he [continually] is becoming."[70] Moreover, he claims that this view leads to the error of "making the world into a god or, even worse, in transmuting God into the world."[71]

De Wette expands his polemic against Schelling to a criticism of various contemporary trends in theology and philosophy. He lampoons what he calls the "new wisdom" of the philosophers and states that philosophical speculation does not serve Christianity when it wanders too far from traditional modes of thinking. What do new terms for God accomplish, he asks rhetorically, that old terms – God, Lord, Father – do not already do? Combatively, de Wette writes,

> We think of God most properly when we think of him as the ultimate origin (*Ursache*) of all things and as the absolute ground of the eternal world order, and thus place him above the world. This is in fact what is done in biblical and popular ideas of the creator and law-giver of the world, and speculation needs to do no more than add philosophical clarity. . . . The anthropomorphisms of the Old Testament are more suitable to speculation than any philosophical refinements.[72]

Here, one sees de Wette, the biblical scholar, protecting this field against the likes of Schleiermacher, Schelling, and other "philosophical" intruders, whose redefinitions of God had only led in de Wette's judgment to unnecessary jargon.[73]

Since religion for de Wette was primarily a matter of faith and not strictly of knowing, he attempts to give a more precise account of the nature of faith. Like Schleiermacher, he describes religion as a matter of feeling (*Gefühl*), but he subdivides this broad term into three distinctly aesthetic categories. The first category is "inspiration" (*Begeisterung*), according to which one apprehends the eternal in nature and in the noble deeds of human history. The second aesthetic idea, "resignation" (*Resignation*), provides the proper perspective on the conflict between good and evil in the world; it helps one understand human worth amid the vicissitudes of history. At root, this idea bespeaks de Wette's Lutheran heritage: we must simply accept our impotence and God's omnipotence in human events. This submission in turn accomplishes reconciliation with God and permits one to be united with eternity despite "the contradictory nature of things" (*Zweck-widrigkeit*) in the world of appearances.[74] The last aesthetic idea, "worship" (*Andacht*), is also a form of the contemplation of the sublime in life and nature. Worship allows one to apprehend the eternal goodness that directs human destiny.[75] It transmutes all reality into a spiritual experience:

> The world as well as our own interiority will become a temple of God. The hieroglyphs of nature and history develop, for pious beholders, into living, clear pictures of the eternal. Just as the Cherub in the Old Testament, made up of lion, bull, eagle, and man, indicated the presence of the divine majesty, so will the whole of nature and especially humanity and its history become a symbol and witness to God and his creative life-giving spirit.[76]

*   *   *

De Wette's epistemological and aesthetic considerations in the first sections of *Über Religion und Theologie* set the stage for him in the later sections to address the problem of history. Here, he discusses religion in general and Christianity in particular as world-historical phenomena. But more important for our purposes, he discourses on the nature of contemporary historical inquiry and its problematic effects on the attainment of theological certainty. Because of the perceived menace that history posed to faith, I stress that de Wette permitted his own historical *Kritik*, which later precipitated Burckhardt's religious doubts, only because he felt that it had been adequately justified in his theological-epistemological system. In other words, de Wette thought that radical criticism of sacred texts could proceed, but only once one recognized that criticism's epistemic range was limited to *Wissen*; it could not encroach on the religiously more important categories of *Glaube* and *Ahnung*. As we shall see in later chapters, Burckhardt accepted de Wette's *Kritik* but rejected the conception of historical knowledge and the underlying theology of history that must (in de Wette's judgment) accompany it.

In *Über Religion und Theologie*, de Wette likens the history of religion to a growing child. In both cases, maturity is measured by the ability to reflect self-consciously on one's condition. Accordingly, de Wette holds that the modern world, because it provided conditions conducive to critical reflection, demonstrates a religious outlook superior to earlier periods.[77]

De Wette praises ancient Hebrew religion for laying the foundations of a disciplined ethical monotheism. He celebrates Israel's conception of its own history and destiny; this was no arbitrary religion in his eyes, but one based on the interactions of a *specific* deity with *his* nation. Although de Wette criticizes the Hebrews on many counts, he admires the post-exilic prophets and contrasts their inspired words to the dogmatism of the established elites. In de Wette's eyes, the Babylonian exile was the nadir of Judaism, for during this time foreign myths, arid theological speculation, and the exalting of the Old Testament to literal truth (*Buchstaben des Gesetzes*) supplanted the positive elements in early Judaism and the prophets.[78]

De Wette characterizes Christ and early Christianity as elements of restoration and completion. Christ developed all the pure religious tendencies in the prophets to their fullest degree and thus expressed a religion grounded "in spirit and in truth." In the person of Christ, de Wette contends, "we see the human spirit for the first time in world history fully conscious of itself and of its high worth; here we see the human spirit, learning to feel itself to be the son of God."[79] Furthermore, de Wette asserts that Christ provided for all humanity – not just for the Jews – a dignified model (*hohe Vorbild*) that subsequent generations should strive to emulate.[80]

Unfortunately, the Middle Ages extinguished the true religion of early Christianity and instituted a priestly despotism, in which Christianity reverted to a form of Judaism (*Rückfall zum Judenthum*). The medieval papacy was even worse than legalistic Judaism in de Wette's eyes, because "priests set themselves up as judges of human deeds, acquitting and condemning, not simply for this world, but for all eternity."[81] De Wette also criticizes medieval Christendom for its excessive sensuality and for adulterating the truths of Christ with heathen religious instincts. He summarizes the Middle Ages as a time of "Christian paganism."[82]

Yet once lit, the fire of truth cannot be completely extinguished. The Protestant Reformation inaugurated the "third great moment in the history of the freeing of the religious spirit" (*Befreiungsgeschichte des religiösen Geistes*) – the other two great moments being Mosaic monotheism and early Christianity.[83] In de Wette's view, the two great principles that the Reformers of the sixteenth century awakened were a love for truth and a spirit of independence, both of which had languished under medieval superstition and papal authority. De Wette moreover lauds the Reformation for its scholarly (*wissenschaftlich*) character and for its endeavors to depict history accurately. Whereas the traditions of the Catholic church were grounded in superstition and human caprice, the Reformation found legitimation in "the pursuit of scholarship": "And so the great lie [of the papacy] was exposed. This accomplishment was only possible through historical inquiry, and thus we see that Protestantism in its first appearance placed historical criticism in the service of genuine faith."[84]

Despite de Wette's praise for the Reformation, he concedes that several factors led to the decline of its initial zeal. First, the Reformer's high esteem of biblical texts led to the erroneous deification of the text itself: Luther's principle of *sola scriptura*, when not handled properly, could be taken too far, "for Christ did not say that the written word (*die Schrift*) of his apostles should lead us to truth, but rather that the divine spirit (*göttliche Geist*) should; and this divine spirit resides in the human spirit (*im menschlichen Gemüth*) alone."[85] Second, likening Calvin to a dam that blocks the flow of truth, de Wette harshly criticizes the Geneva Reformer's politics and ecclesiology, arguing that at root they contain the same truth-stifling principles as the Catholic Church. Finally, de Wette notes that even his cherished Lutheran tradition ossified over time into pedantry and scholasticism.[86]

In de Wette's view, however, the middle of the eighteenth century witnessed another "great moment" in the development of Protestantism – a moment from whose energy de Wette himself drew strength and attempted to advance. The driving force behind the new quest for truth was biblical criticism, especially as espoused by J. S. Semler and J. A. Ernesti. In de Wette's eyes, nothing less than a revolution in theological thinking was under way:

> The doctrines of the canon and of the inspired word of God, and with it the whole edifice of Protestant dogma, was violently shaken, and the old prejudices inherited from Catholicism brought into the open. The Bible, along with other ancient authors, was submitted to well-tried interpretive principles and accordingly placed in a more human, historical light; and a completely historical research into early Christianity was begun.[87]

De Wette emphasizes the pivotal role that criticism of the doctrines of revelation and inspiration had recently played. He states that such doctrines were after all only the offspring of superstition and dogmatic craftiness (*dogmatische Spitzfindigkeit*) and that the time was at hand when all such dubious doctrines would be discarded since "all human knowledge was undergoing a new revision."[88]

Consistent with his philosophical presuppositions, de Wette is quick to point out that the revolution underway was predominantly a matter of *Wissen* and thus open to misunderstanding. Therefore, he pauses to warn that the Kantian solution – that is, turning religion into purely a matter of ethics – was misguided and led to cold and narrow religious convictions. To the contrary, de Wette proclaims that a living, warm religious life *can* accompany historical criticism, so long as one realizes that religion transcends human *Wissen* and belongs more properly to faith (*Glaube*). In de Wette's view, confusing these categories would lead either to rationalism or to superstition and dogmatism. The former was the choice of many critics, the latter of orthodox and pietist theologians. In de Wette's opinion, however, both options were false, because the criteria for making decisions were derived from *Wissen* alone. De Wette did not want to mediate between these two false paths; rather, he desired to dismantle the conflict altogether by revamping the epistemological framework in which the erroneous modes of thinking had developed. He held this as the only proper, however difficult, task for contemporary theology. In a passage in which he relates his theological vision to a conception of history, de Wette writes:

> Only in oppositions and extremes does the history of human knowledge (*Bildung*) move, and we can only hope that eventually the right middle will be maintained. Great and wonderful events and cataclysms have now brought the world to worship and to inspiration. One feels the emptiness of the past and the eternal validity and . . . strength of pious faith. Everyone searches and strives for a new, higher religious life. But clarity of consciousness has not arrived yet, and the conflicting views and efforts are well known. Many want to return wholly to the old, others want to create something new. A solidly formed, agreed-upon theology eludes us.[89]

De Wette felt that he – and not Schleiermacher – was the man to define the theological direction of the future. Thus he asks what in fact were the basic ideas and spirit of a true Protestant theology and how are they to be developed? The role of theology in its most basic terms, in his view, was to make clear the nature of true religion. There could only be one type of theology, and that was a Christian one, because the Christian faith (read: modern German Protestantism) was the most perfect and spiritual religion, having developed and learned from all previous religious standpoints.

De Wette claims that the task of theology should not be confused with depicting eternal Truth objectively (*objectiv*). This is a task far beyond human abilities. Rather, theology is to present only what it saw from an anthropological standpoint and to seek in history what human beings, according to the laws of their inner nature, necessarily know, believe, and aesthetically intuit (*wissen, glauben, ahnen*). Theology should also not aspire to present a new science, because it only helps "illumine the religious ideas that are already in us."[90]

The category of history in de Wette's eyes posed the greatest challenge for theological advancement. If a true theology was to exist, it had to come to terms with modern historical consciousness and modern historical methods of inquiry; theology must proceed historically and not dogmatically, as Schleiermacher would have it.[91] De Wette identifies and comments on two categories in which he claims almost all contemporary theologians fit. Either they had become unbelieving skeptics and rigid systematizers or mystics. In de Wette's eyes both positions result in a misleading understanding of the nature and purpose of historical knowledge.

> We have seen how important history is for our religious life. Without viewing it in a correct, healthy context (*richtigen gesunden Zusammenhang*), one will inevitably err or take a false path. All theology, which is not anthropologically grounded, will come up short in the manner in which it handles history. Whoever does not recognize and heed religious ideas will only find opinions and delusions in the history of religion.[92]

Skeptics reject religion outright because it cannot be proven, while mystics alter history and make it mean only what corresponds to their nebulous ideas. An authentic critical theology avoids both mistakes and conducts serious historical criticism while maintaining the capacity to take the given materials of history, extract their living and spiritual essence (*das Lebendige und Geistige*), and gain strong nourishment (*kräftige Nahrung*) from them.[93] This is the theological core of de Wette's solution to history, which Burckhardt later contemned, feeling instead that criticism, in the final analysis, led only to the tragic erosion of religious verities.

In 1815, de Wette feared that preachers throughout Germany were hindering theological progress among the people by appealing to tradition, orthodoxy, and biblical literalism.[94] In *Über Religion und Theologie*, de Wette thus accuses such preachers of conflating historical and/or biblical events with religious truth. In attempting to refute their position, de Wette employs two metaphors. First, he likens history to a great chain of events (*Kette von Begebenheiten*) in which each moment stands in necessary and sequential relation to the others. One cannot ignore intermediate developments – such as the development of historical-critical methods – and return to a precritical interpretation of the Bible, because what comes later forms an invaluable part of the overall development of truth. "Could the divinity of a book," he asks condescendingly, "really depend on the name of its author?"

Second, de Wette speaks of Christian history as a great stream with Christ as its source. Although Christ began the process, further developments were left to later generations. By focusing excessively on Christ, the orthodox camp had misunderstood what Christ had hoped to accomplish and distorted the true nature of religion. "If one wants to search out and follow the flow of a stream, then one would not remain standing at the source [i.e., Christ]."[95] But this in de Wette's eyes was exactly what orthodox theologians were doing.

In the final sections of *Über Religion und Theologie* de Wette reiterates his notion that historical events have religious significance not because of their factual quality (as demonstrated through *Wissen*) but because of their symbolic quality perceived through faith. Accordingly, theology can overcome the problem of history when, relying on *Glaube* and *Ahnung*, the theologian interprets history symbolically:

> Every history is symbolic, which is to say an expression and image of the human spirit and its deeds. There is hardly a part of history that does not contain meaning for the higher spiritual life of men. . . . However, the most ideal meaning belongs to the history of religion, because it is almost completely in the realm of the ideal and, as it were, is a pure testament to the highest spiritual activity of men.[96]

For this reason, de Wette had little sympathy with the orthodox theologians, who insisted on proving the historical veracity of miracles. Interestingly, de Wette likens their mistake to the errors made by rationalists and skeptics. Both camps had reduced their epistemological criteria to *Wissen* alone.

Yet for the pious, critical theologian, de Wette argues that history must be interpreted using more rigorous epistemological criteria. He thus refers to historical events as "symbolic," "ideal," "aesthetic-ideal," "ideal-symbolic," and "aesthetic-symbolic." With these terms, which he employs rather interchangeably, de Wette seeks to transform the contemporary epistemological framework and establish the legitimacy of alternate modes of knowing – that is, *Glaube* and *Ahnung* – that had been overshadowed by the contemporary ascendency of *Wissen*. He deems the triumph of *Wissen* as especially problematic, moreover, since *Wissen* seeks to understand the particular while what is more important in religious matters is the general. "In *Ahnung*," he thus asserts, "we apply the general idea to the particular of appearance." While accepting historical criticism, the theologian should still be able to extract "the aesthetic, ideal form" (*ästhetisch, idealen Gestalt*)[97] from particular historical events and arrive at "a purely symbolic meaning" (*bloss eine symbolische Bedeutung*).[98]

De Wette concludes *Über Religion und Theologie* on a bold note, stating that this work demonstrates that "the aesthetic ideal view of religion and the symbolic treatment of history and doctrine have necessary application to the religious nature of men and to the spirit and historical development of Christianity." He suggests that the acceptance of his ideas will lead to a "beautiful and stimulating transformation of the the church" (*schönen lebendigen Umgestaltung des Kirchenwesens*). If his positions are truly Christian and timely, he ends, then truth itself will bear them out; otherwise, his work should rightly be judged idiosyncratic and wrong.[99]

Dismissal from Berlin

Sweeping historical changes were afoot in Prussia that made de Wette's innovative theological views and their anticonservative political implications seem increasingly suspect.[100] In 1815, the year de Wette published *Über Religion und Theologie*, Napoleon was finally defeated at Waterloo. The Congress of Vienna met to assess the new situation and to restore elements of pre-Revolution stability. What emerged in central Europe was a confederation of thirty-nine independent states known as the German Confederation or *Bund*. Prussia – with its territory greatly expanded – and the Austrian Habsburg monarchy were its largest and most influential members. The confederation would form the basis of central European stability for the next fifty years.[101]

Responses to the new political order were conditioned by an (at least partial) acceptance of the ideals of the French Revolution and a widespread concern for the future of German national identity. The struggles and emotions associated with the 1813 War of Liberation, in which the Napoleonic yoke was finally thrown off, became the fountainhead for the quickening of German national consciousness. However, the exact meaning of new political ideals and opportunities was not clear and responses varied widely. In fact, many intellectuals who had once supported the Revolution took a decisively moderate, even pessimistic, turn. Hegel, for instance, an enthusiast for both the Revolution and Napoleon, told a friend in 1819 that "I am just fifty years old, and have lived most of my life in these eternally restless times of fear and hope, and I have hoped that sometimes these fears and hopes might cease. But now I see that they will go on forever, indeed in moments of depression I think they will grow worse." Despite the 1815 settlement, politicians in Berlin and Vienna also had misgivings about the political future of Europe. Metternich once remarked, "My most secret thought is that old Europe is at the beginning of the end. Determined to go down with it, I will know how to do my duty. Elsewhere the new Europe is still taking shape. Between beginning and end there will be chaos."[102]

Yet in many sectors of society the ideals of the French Revolution thrived. German university students saw the defeat of Napoleon as an opportunity to assert their own brand of nationalist identity and to transform the German *Länder* into a nation based on the principles of freedom of expression and representative government. The institutional expression of these ideas was the *Burschenschaft* movement, a group of students dedicated to patriotism and democracy, formed first at the University of Jena in June 1815. Although small at first, this group soon grew to 650 members; within a few months affiliated groups were established at other universities. The great public expression of the movement came at the Wartburg festival in

October 1817, held to celebrate the allies' victory over Napoleon at Leipzig and the tercentenary of the Reformation. Here students proclaimed the freedom of the nation from foreign domination and the freedom of thought from doctrinaire restraints. They gathered at the castle where Luther translated the Bible into the vernacular and listened to speeches celebrating freedom and German nationhood.[103] A few professors cast their lot with the students and delivered fiery political speeches. One of them was J. F. Fries, who had recently moved to Jena from Heidelberg. Fries's actions at the Wartburg festival ultimately cost him his reputation and he was suspended from teaching because of his seditious activity.[104]

In these politically trying times, de Wette too was ousted from German academic life. And though his dismissal ultimately came on political grounds, he had become suspect as a theological radical long beforehand. At no time since the Reformation had theological and political agendas been so closely intertwined in German intellectual life. As during the Reformation, political ideas and attitudes became associated with religious creeds. The government could no longer idly observe theological debates as mere "parsons' quarrels" (*Pfaffengezänk*) as it had done under monarchical absolutism during the seventeenth and eighteenth centuries. Because theology professors continued to play a crucial role in clerical personnel recruitment – by training, examining, and recommending candidates for key church and bureaucratic positions – increased attention of government officials was given to the creed and political sympathies of prospective appointees to the universities, and the government's policy favored those who could be expected to support the conservative policies of the Restoration.[105]

The reforms in Prussia from the time of its defeat by Napoleon in 1806 until 1819 have been memorably described by Otto Hintze as the substitution of "bureaucratic monarchy" for "absolute monarchy."[106] The process of creating a bureaucratic elite in Prussia gave an opportunity for the landed aristocracy to exercise greater control over the affairs of Prussia; these aristocrats were often closely connected with pietism and they desired that their religious convictions influence public life. Their policies of university regulation stood in stark contrast to the Enlightenment-influenced policies of Friedrich II, who had allowed theological rationalism to flourish in Prussian universities. Influential pietist aristocrats wanted to reverse rationalist trends; they emphasized the sinfulness of human nature, the cultivation of piety, and the experience of salvation. In short, pietism – which had hitherto been a nonpolitical factor – began to play a counterrevolutionary role and found itself allied with Lutheran and aristocratic elements of society in opposition to the "ideas of 1789." This period in German history – the "Awakening" or *Erweckungsbewegung* – was a time in which religion became the dominating force behind a political campaign to undo the French Revolution and to eradicate the perceived godless effects of the

Enlightenment.[107] Understandably, de Wette's non-orthodox theological program and biblical criticism were found unacceptable by the new pietist elites.

Two of the most influential pietist aristocrats were Georg Heinrich Ludwig Nicolovius (1767–1839) and Baron Hans Ernst von Kottwitz (1757–1831). In 1810, Nicolovius had become director of the newly established *Kultusabteilung* in the Ministry of the Interior and he steered it in a decisively pietist direction. Nicolovius saw theology not as a scholarly discipline but as a matter of faith and a process of acquiring the hidden wisdom of God. While one of his protégés, Franz Claudius, was studying theology in Berlin, Nicolovius expressed concern that the "cold theological wind" of de Wette and other Berlin professors would damage Claudius's "real theology."[108]

Nicolovius's ideas were shared by Kottwitz, a Silesian nobleman and landowner who had moved to Berlin in 1807 and founded his so-called Berlin circle, which during the 1810s and 1820s became a leading center of pietism. Kottwitz used his influence to promote a political alliance between "awakened" aristocrats and conservative clergymen. Joined by Nicolovius, August Neander, a newly hired pietist theologian at Berlin,[109] and several others, Kottwitz successfully lobbied for the government in 1817 to reestablish the long-defunct University of Wittenburg as a pietist seminary to train conservative clergymen and teachers. In the eyes of its supporters, the seminary would provide an alternative to the universities and would create a crop of young men to serve as "fighters for God against the *Zeitgeist*." Once the seminary was established, the government even provided several scholarships, whose recipients were commissioned to "struggle against the dragon's seed (*Drachensaat*) of rationalism in their future positions."[110]

De Wette believed that this seminary would promote a narrow religious view and he decided to oppose it. In 1817, he spearheaded a protest among liberal theologians to challenge Kottwitz's proposal. De Wette and his associates sent a memorandum to the government that called attention to the dangers of establishing such a seminary. "Sooner or later," the memo stated, "the institution will turn into a stronghold of one-sidedness and narrowness of outlook, hardly worthy to be established as a memorial to the noble and great Luther in the very place where he lived and taught."[111] This was a direct confrontation with Prussia's new political elite.

A year earlier, in 1816, another pietist aristocrat, Count Christian Friedrich von Stolberg-Wernigerode, had complained to the Ministry of the Interior of "blasphemous utterances of several theologians" and requested that they resign their posts. One of his chief targets was de Wette, whose critical works on the Old Testament, *Lehrbuch*, and *Commentatio de morte Jesu Christi expiatoria* were cited as examples of the dangerous influence of impious theologians. Although the reply on behalf of the king expressed his majesty's resolve not to interfere with the university's affairs, the letter said that, because of the Count's complaint, commissions were being set up to help the church put its house in order.[112]

Schleiermacher, whose status was also in question at the time, mentioned in a letter a "cabinet order" in which "the king has noted with great anguish that in our and in other universities wrong teachings are being spread, and that the minister should remove the false teachers (*Irrlehrer*) immediately."[113] For a number of years Schleiermacher feared that he too might suffer the fate that eventually befell de Wette.[114] It was also at this time that Schleiermacher dedicated his critical work on the Gospel of Luke to de Wette in an effort, not just to offer public support to de Wette, but also to promote awareness of the necessity of tolerance and freedom of inquiry within the academy. Significantly, Schleiermacher felt the need to justify his dedication in several letters to friends; he made it clear that he was advocating tolerance and not de Wette's views per se.[115]

De Wette's dismissal from the university came finally on political rather than on theological grounds. In autumn of 1818, de Wette had accompanied his stepson Karl Beck, the son of his second wife by a previous marriage, on a trip to visit family members near Heidelberg.[116] Along the way he stopped to meet his friend Fries in Jena, where he was introduced to a young theology student named Karl Ludwig Sand, an activist in the *Burschenschaft* movement at Jena. De Wette expressed admiration for Sand's political convictions. He also visited Sand's family.[117]

On 23 March 1819, Sand stabbed to death the popular playwright and reactionary publicist August von Kotzebue in Mannheim. Kotzebue was regarded among students in the *Burschenschaften* as a Russian agent and traitor, and his murder was seen as an expression of loyalty to the fatherland. The deed, Sand reasoned, would bring him immortality for advancing the *Burschenschaft* conception of freedom and German unity. "Thank you, God, for the victory," he cried out as he drove a second dagger into his own body.[118] His suicide attempt failed, however, and he later stood trial and was executed by Prussian authorities. Despite feeble efforts to turn Sand into a political hero, his deed was soon viewed with horror and disgust across the political spectrum.

State ministers in both Berlin and Vienna took action quickly to thwart similar acts of radicalism. On 1 August 1919, Metternich met with the Prussian King Friedrich Wilhelm III at Teplitz and secured his cooperation before calling a larger conclave at Karlsbad, where representatives of the German states met and drew up the infamous Karlsbad decrees, which were later ratified by all the German states. The first decree called for close supervision of the universities throughout the Confederation: governments should ensure that no teacher misused his authority "by spreading harmful ideas that would subvert public peace and order and undermine the foundations of the existing states." Should a subversive teacher be dismissed from one university he could not be hired by another. A second decree called for tighter regulation of the press through the creation of a central commission given the power of censorship. Finally, the so-called *Untersuchungsgesetz* established a federal bureau of investigation to handle "revolutionary agitation."[119]

Conservative clergymen also reacted strongly to Kotzebue's assassination. The Potsdam Court preacher and State Council member, Ruhlemann Friedrich Eylert (1770–1852), a former rationalist who had converted to Lutheran orthodoxy, delivered a passionate sermon at the military chapel in Potsdam. He condemned all opposition to the "Prussian system" as political treason and spiritual blasphemy. More than any one person, his fiery sermons incited the waves of political witch-hunts (*Demagogenverfolgung*) that followed.[120]

De Wette's liberal theological tendencies, his recent interaction with Sand, and his well-known devotion to Fries (whose activity at the *Wartburgfest* had been widely condemned) made him suspect in the eyes of the government. Even before the Karlsbad decrees were issued, a full investigation of de Wette was under way. On 12 July, de Wette's publisher's house was searched and on 13 July, de Wette himself was summoned to explain why he had attended a meeting convened by a young radical named Hans Rudolph von Plehwe (1794–1835).[121] At this time, de Wette was accused of no wrongdoing, but a thorough search of his writings and interviews with his students continued. One student, David Ulrich, mentioned that de Wette had referred to the Kotzebue murder in a lecture.[122] When asked about this, de Wette replied that he had done so, but only in a scholarly and nonpartisan manner. De Wette wrote a letter of complaint to Karl von Altenstein, the minister responsible for the universities, protesting his treatment.[123] The whole ordeal began to unnerve de Wette. In a letter to Fries, who was also under interrogation, de Wette wrote that "I . . . have been taken in on account of Plehwe's Monday discussion group, which I visited once. It is regarded as a political society. It disgusts me to write further of these things."[124]

De Wette's fate was sealed when investigators discovered a letter of consolation he had written to the mother of the assassin Sand. In the letter de Wette states explicitly that he would never advise murder, but he notes that Sand should be admired for acting from political conviction.

The error is excusable and to some extent even removed by the firmness and integrity of conviction; and passion is sanctified (*geheiligt*) by the good source from which it flows. I am resolutely convinced that this was the case with your pious and upright son. He was certain about his cause, he believed that it was right for him to do it, and thus he did what was right. Each has to act according to his best conviction.[125]

What is more, de Wette even called Sand's action "a beautiful sign of the times" (*ein schönes Zeichen der Zeit*).[126]

Minister von Altenstein interrogated de Wette about the letter on 29 August 1819. De Wette attempted to justify his actions on theological grounds, arguing that he could not condemn Sand categorically, because Christ had commanded "judge not lest you be judged" and that even the worst of sinners might find grace in the hands of God. At the time, however, strong pressures were placed on the government to dismiss de Wette. Both Bishop Eylert and the pietist circle around Baron von Kottwitz made clear their disapproval of de Wette.[127] Eylert argued in a letter presented to the king by the Police Minister Wittgenstein that there would be no problem if de Wette's ideas existed only "in the realm of speculation and dry representation," but events had shown that they "deeply and destructively affect actual life."[128]

The official cabinet order of dismissal was issued on 30 September 1819 and received by de Wette on 2 October. Several colleagues at Berlin made vain appeals on de Wette's behalf for the decision to be reversed. On 16 October, de Wette himself addressed a long appeal to the king, in which he pleaded for his case to be evaluated by his public statements, not by his private correspondence. He also asked the king to consider the hardship that the dismissal would place on his family, because within the Confederation de Wette presumably would not be allowed to teach elsewhere.[129] Memoranda of support were also submitted by the senate and the faculty of theology at Berlin. But the king refused to give de Wette a hearing. Near the end of October 1819, de Wette was forced to leave what he called Berlin's "inspiring and cultured community."[130]

Conclusion

On 2 November 1819, de Wette arrived in Weimar, his childhood haunt and "geistige Vaterstadt." Here he would spent the next three years. He relocated his wife and children near Heidelberg with relatives who had the financial resources to compensate for his unemployment. "It is hard, very hard," he wrote Schleiermacher, "how am I supposed to find words to describe the feeling of anguish that pervades me?"[131]

The next three years were trying times for de Wette. Without work, he traveled and tried his hand at literature, producing among other works his novel *Theodor*.[132] Finally, through an unusual set of circumstances, in 1822 he was offered and accepted a teaching position at the University of Basel.[133]

But away from Prussia's leading university, de Wette's potential for influence was dramatically curtailed. Basel was not Berlin. The Sand affair had sullied de Wette's name throughout the German-speaking lands. De Wette's chair at Berlin was later given to the conservative theologian, E. W. Hengstenberg.[134] Hegel, whose influence was soon to reach enormous proportions, stated that the Prussian government was fully justified in its actions toward de Wette.[135] And finally, in 1824, Prussia issued a decree that forbade its young men from studying at the Swiss "nest of dema-gogues" – that is, the University of Basel.[136]

CHAPTER THREE

De Wette, D. F. Strauss, and the New *Christusbild*

The greatest achievement of German theology is the critical
investigation of the life of Jesus. What it has accomplished here
has laid down the conditions and determined the course of the
religious thinking of the future.

– Albert Schweitzer, *Geschichte der
Leben-Jesu-Forschung*

History is an abyss in which Christianity has been catapulted
quite against its will.

– Franz Overbeck, *Christentum und Kultur*

THE CONTROVERSY FOLLOWING THE PUBLICATION of David
Friedrich Strauss's *Das Leben Jesu* (1835) has come to signify the
beginning of a radical new phase of theological modernity. This "inspired
book," as Strauss once called it, had much influence on the Left Hegelians,
and through them on Karl Marx.[1] Yet despite its perceived novelty, the ideas
it embodied were far from new; Strauss's path was prepared by many late
Aufklärung biblical scholars whose critical endeavors challenged the
supremacy of traditional literal and figural readings of the Bible characteristic of Protestant scholarship since the Reformation.[2] As is well known, the
Enlightenment among German intellectuals was not predominantly an
antireligious or anti-Christian phenomenon. On the contrary, *Aufklärung*
thinkers earnestly desired to reformulate Christian doctrine and biblical
hermeneutical principles to give Christianity a more secure rational basis
and assure its survival in the modern world.

In eighteenth-century German theological scholarship, rational truth was
held to possess such qualities as necessity, eternity, and universality.[3] For
this reason, historically mediated truth was increasingly regarded as a contradiction in terms. One finds this sentiment already forcefully stated in
Spinoza's influential dictum that knowledge of God "should be derived

from general ideas, in themselves certain and known, so that the truth of a historical narrative is very far from being a necessary requisite for our attaining our highest good."[4] Implicit in such a view is the conviction that truths about God are timeless and cannot be derived from events or later records of events and, therefore, it is an *a priori* impossibility to obtain knowledge about God from putative historical occurrences, such as those recorded about Jesus of Nazareth in the Gospels.[5] As Lessing put it, "The Christian traditions must be explained by the inner truth of Christianity, and no written traditions can give it that inner truth, if it does not itself possess it."[6]

The distinction between (ahistorical) "truth" and (historical) "event" became a commonplace among German scholars in the later decades of the eighteenth century. The distinction laid the foundation for a number of significant, intertwined developments in hermeneutics, epistemology, and christology in the first half of the nineteenth century, when the problem of explaining the identity of Jesus Christ vis-à-vis the historical Gospels' accounts of his life attracted some of the sharpest minds of the time. As Claude Welch notes, "The most interesting theological endeavors of the period all found their point of departure or their center of gravity in the question of Christ."[7] Although the topic was not new, the christological problem was uniquely crystallized in Strauss's *Das Leben Jesu* and in the ensuing religious and political controversies this notorious book aroused.

De Wette's New Testament criticism and his views on the identity of Christ were integrally connected to pre-Straussian developments in the late Enlightenment and early nineteenth century. His work contributed greatly to the pool of ideas available among theologians and biblical scholars. Moreover, his views reflected many of the recurring motifs and theological moods of his generation. Because of their self-conscious modernity, de Wette and many of his contemporaries felt an obligation to criticize and restate the essence of Christ's nature, which in their eyes still languished under the uncritical dogmatic formulations of the early Church.[8]

Ultimately, de Wette stopped short of the radically anti-orthodox solution offered by Strauss. Nonetheless, the tools of criticism that Strauss employed, and that led him to question both orthodox and Hegelian formulations of Christian belief, had already been developed by de Wette. Indeed, on most important issues, de Wette directly influenced Strauss; Strauss made the debt clear in the prefaces and introductions to the various editions of *Das Leben Jesu*, in which he repeatedly praised de Wette for his path-breaking scholarship.[9] Most important, Strauss's debt to de Wette can be seen in the parallels between their conceptions of myth. De Wette applied the mythic principle largely but not exclusively to the Old Testament and only indirectly to the person of Jesus Christ; Strauss applied it exclusively to the New Testament and directly to the person of Jesus Christ.[10] Finally, when the theological world – including Strauss's former mentor F. C. Baur[11] – turned against him for his excess of negative criticism, de Wette called Strauss's work "clear and logical" and praised him for finally demonstrating that Hegelian philosophy was inconsistent with Christian faith.[12] Of course, de Wette also voiced reservations about Strauss's negative version of Christianity, but in the critical assumptions on which Strauss's view rested, de Wette and Strauss were of one mind.

Aufklärung Antecedents

Although christological endeavors before the Enlightenment were by no means static and uninteresting, the eighteenth century witnessed a cognitive crisis[13] that led to a reorientation in the way that difficulties were approached and arguments constructed. The reorientation had two principal foci. First, *Aufklärung* theologians often found themselves battling against the assertion of Protestant orthodoxy that because of original sin, the human intellect was blinded so that it could not fathom the mind of God, and the will was perverted so that it could not function as an autonomous moral agent. Opposition to this doctrine was common in England, France, and the German-speaking lands. German theologians, however, were unique in opposing it not merely in the name of an abstract moral perfection but also with a deft theological sophistication. For example, one theologian argued that the doctrine of original sin had roots in the heresy of Manichaeism and thus represented an anachronism with which modern reason could finally dispense.[14] Second, the preeminent status granted to (ahistorical) reason led many *Aufklärung* thinkers to doubt the claims of history altogether. Lessing captured this view precisely in what is regarded as one of the most characteristic statements of the *Aufklärung*: "The accidental truths of history (*zufällige Geschichtswahrheiten*) can never become the proof of necessary truths of reason (*notwendige Vernunftswahrheiten*)."[15]

A widespread result of the ebbing of pre-Enlightenment epistemic conditions among intellectuals was the problematization of the traditional, orthodox view of a salvific Christ who mediates between God and man – a view in which Christ paradoxically occupies both a transcendent and a historical dimension. The questioning of this accepted model paved the way for new forays into christological understanding. A dominant trend was to opt for what theologians speak of as an exemplarist or moral theory of Atonement, in which Christ is understood as a fully human teacher in his lifetime and as a supreme example of self-giving in his death. A slight variation on this theme was to see Christ as a morally perfect man who fully realized the potential of every rational, ethical individual.

Overall, there was a pronounced inclination to see Christ's function as enabling: he demonstrated what is possible and his example inspires others to attain the moral heights that he reached. In this view, Christianity became an essentially ethical preoccupation, concerned with promoting a moral character modeled on the "founder of Christianity." This approach characterized many of the writings of the neologians, such as Semler, Ernesti, and Michaelis, from 1760 to 1780.[16] As we saw in chapter one, these scholars attempted to work out methods of biblical criticism by which a historical reevaluation of dogma might proceed; their ultimate aim was the exclusion of doctrines that did not comply with the criteria of universal reason. Nevertheless, neologians quite often maintained the idea of a revelation and spoke of Christ in quasi-incarnational terms, where Christ as the Logos essentially came to mean that eternal spiritual truths may be observed in tangible forms. Neologians "retained the *concept* of divine revelation, while subjecting its *content* to historical criticism."[17]

The *Aufklärung* attempt to reinterpret Christ according to the dictates of reason succeeded in the sense that it set a consequential philosophical precedent. Yet despite the efforts of neologians and other critics, a persistent biblical-hermeneutical problem was left unsolved: how could the supernaturalism of orthodoxy be eliminated (philosophically) when the New Testament itself in unapologetically ordinary and realistic prose presented a transcendent understanding of Christ?[18] Hans Frei has called attention to the fact that epistemological assumptions among most late eighteenth-century German theologians made the notion of Christ as an actual deity philosophically untenable. However, this widespread conclusion did not coincide with any agreed-upon, hermeneutical principle for making sense of the relationship between the religious meaning (or religious truth) of New Testament narratives and the history-likeness of their presentation. Scholars widely agreed that the Bible, especially the Gospel accounts of Christ (because of a conflation, in tone as well as emphasis, of the mundane and the extramundane), could not be placed in the same genre as other ancient stories in which gods, supernatural entities, and miraculous events appeared.[19] Hans Frei has stated the problem as follows:

A realistic or history-like (though not necessarily historical) element is a feature, as obvious as it is important, of many of the narratives that went into the making of Christian belief. It is a feature that can be highlighted by the appropriate analytical procedure . . . in contrast to the element itself. It is fascinating that the realistic character of the crucial biblical stories was actually acknowledged and agreed upon by most of the

significant eighteenth-century commentators. But since the precritical analytic or interpretive procedures for isolating it had irretrievably broken
down in the opinion of most commentators, this specifically realistic characteristic, though acknowledged by all hands to be there, finally came to
be ignored, or – even more fascinating – its presence or distinctiveness
came to be denied for lack of method to isolate it.[20]

However, within the situation Frei describes, there was one notable exception: Hermann Samuel Reimarus (1694–1768). More than any single figure,
Reimarus brought the rationalist presuppositions of the *Aufklärung* to bear
on the important biblical narratives and offered a radical (and later
influential) alternative interpretation.

In his enormous *Apologie oder Schutzschrift für die vernünftigen
Verehrer Gottes*,[21] parts of which were published by Lessing in the *Wolfenbüttel Fragmente* (1774–8), Reimarus applied the *Aufklärung* distinction
between reason and history to the Bible with a consistency hitherto unseen.
For Reimarus, the concept of revelation was wholly untenable, since, in his
view, the historical character of revelation was inconsistent with the universal and necessary character of rational truth. Furthermore, if truth was
granted to humanity at a certain point in history, it necessarily followed,
he argued, that people who lived before that point were denied this truth.
Thus, historically mediated knowledge of God must be regarded as a
contradiction.

Such is the epistemic foundation on which *Von dem Zwecke Jesu und
seine Jünger*, the last and most important of the fragments published by
Lessing, rested. Reimarus argued that Jesus' ideas and language about God
were those of a Jewish apocalyptic visionary, with a purely limited temporal reference and relevance. He accepted the late Jewish expectation of a
Messiah who would deliver his people not from sin but from Roman domination and believed that God would act to help his cause. Jesus' cry on the
cross thus reflected his final disillusionment and sense of failure. The notion
of a spiritual redemption was a later invention of his disciples to compensate for the difficulty posed by Jesus' death. Further, Reimarus argued that
the resurrection story was a fraud. Passages in the New Testament that did
not harmonize with the image of Christ as a political visionary should be
seen as fraudulent interpolations by the early church. Reimarus thus pioneered the distinction between the historical Jesus and subsequent attempts
to divinize him by his followers. The actual Jesus, in Reimarus's view, was
merely an earnest fanatic, who knew nothing of his ability to forgive sins
or redeem humanity.[22]

Lessing's publication of Reimarus's work resulted in a storm of controversy and a widespread rejection of Reimarus's views. However, the separation between the so-called Jesus of history and the "Christ of faith" had

been made decisively. From this premise the important questions that animated subsequent christological inquiry arose. In the words of Schweitzer, Reimarus represented the first "really historical mind" "wholly concerned with facts," and his work was "one of the greatest events in the history of criticism."[23] In the words of Alister McGrath, Reimarus almost single-handedly inaugurated a "new era in christological reflection."[24]

Lessing's own theological views were quickened by Reimarus and were developed in several works. The hero in *Nathan der Weise* (1779) represents a pure, tolerant religiosity independent of historical revelation. Lessing also undertook his own study of the Gospels in *Neue Hypothese über die Evangelisten als blosse menschliche Geschichtsschreiber betrachtet* (1788), in which he elaborated on Reimarus's ideas, arguing that Christian traditions must be understood by the inner truth of Christianity and that no written tradition can provide that truth if it does not itself possess it.[25] Lessing was vehemently criticized and his writings were banned in his native Brunswick. Hamburg's Lutheran pastor Johann Melchior Goeze (1717–86) became his most vocal opponent, accusing Lessing not just of blasphemy but of threatening the very foundations of political and social stability.

Toward the end of the eighteenth century, Kant's critiques sought to check the reign of reason; however, Kant's conception of Christ differed little if at all from those of his deist and rationalist predecessors.[26] Moreover, in the eyes of many commentators, Kant's criticism, instead of establishing a place for faith, only resulted in strengthening reason; for how could reason be faulted when it possessed the capability to recognize its own limits? Such an observation led Heinrich Heine, in an allusion to the beheading of Louis XVI in 1793, to refer to Kant's work as theism's 21st of January. Speaking for many of his generation, Heine asserted that Kant's *Kritik* was the "day" on which the personal God of the biblical tradition was eliminated from German thought; he asked: "Do you hear the little hand bell ringing? Kneel down. They are bringing the sacraments to a dying god."[27]

Insofar as they represent attempts to cope with the problem of christology, the mediating theology of Schleiermacher and the speculative philosophy of Hegel were by far the most influential early nineteenth-century efforts to overcome the dichotomy between reason and history set down by Reimarus and Lessing.[28] Schleiermacher, who spoke of having "companionship with Jesus" in his youth, more than any other theologian influenced by the *Aufklärung*, was able to effect – at least in his language – a strong tie with traditional views. Theologians speak of Schleiermacher's "Second Adam Christology," in which Christ is viewed as the completion of the creation of man and the embodiment of a new possibility of human existence that also can be essentially shared (in dependence on him) by his

followers. However, for Schleiermacher, present-day Christian consciousness as mediated by the church, and not the historical manifestation of a
transcendent Christ, was where christological reflection properly began.
Christ was not God inserted into history at only one point; rather, Christ
actualized for the first time what is most true in human consciousness in
general. "As an individual historical being," Schleiermacher wrote, "he
[Christ] must have been at the same time ideal (*urbildlich*); that is, the
ideal must have become fully historical in him, and his every historical
moment must at the same time have carried in it the ideal."[29] Schleiermacher relied heavily on the Johannine notion of "Logos" in his emphasis on
what he saw as Christ's archetypal nature (*Urbildlichkeit*).[30] Strauss succinctly defined Schleiermacher's conception of Christ as only a "postulate
of the Christian experience."[31] Both Strauss and F. C. Baur criticized
Schleiermacher's Christ as a purely dogmatic assertion devoid of critical
investigation.[32]

Hegel saw Christ (the principle of the ideal) as immanent in human
reason. Significantly, Hegel did not deny the importance of an actual, historical Jesus, but on the contrary emphasized the necessity, possibility, and
actuality of the incarnation of God in a single person on the basis of his
anthropology of divine-human union. The ideal unity of God and man is
demonstrated through the appearance (*Erscheinung*) of God in the world.
Hegel's famous distinction between *Vorstellung* (representation) and *Begriff*
(concept) permitted him to criticize specific forms of revelation without
undermining their ultimate philosophical content. For Hegel, *Vorstellungen*
were speculatively deficient apprehensions of God in sensuously mediated
images (e.g., the Gospel accounts), while *Begriffe* were the elevation of
Vorstellungen to mature philosophical expression.[33] As John Toews has
pointed out, a desire to "upgrade" the Gospels to mature philosophical
expression lies at the heart of Hegel's project.[34] In Hegel, Lessing's statement is reversed: the (seemingly) accidental truths of history are actually
the necessary truths of reason: "God governs the world: the content of His
governance, the fulfillment of His plan, is world history."[35]

Schleiermacher and Hegel differed on many points, but both placed the
christological problem at the center of their projects.[36] They sought to define
Christ's nature so as to overcome the either/or predicament articulated by
Reimarus and Lessing.[37] Eschewing historical-critical questions, their goals
were accomplished dogmatically and philosophically by equating the identity of Christ with present, subjective human qualities – Christian experience for Schleiermacher, human reason for Hegel. In both cases, the
structure of present human consciousness rather than the authority (or lack
of it) of ancient texts was the primary reference point for making christological statements. Indeed, human consciousness itself could, they held,
convey knowledge of the divine, and the divine (represented in Christ)

84

accordingly became an integral aspect of human consciousness. As Toews notes,

> Hegel and Schleiermacher . . . rejected the dualism of man and God, the immanent and the transcendent, embodied in the traditional teachings of orthodox Christianity. The reconciliation of finite and infinite being, of the individual self and the absolute, *was conceived as the fulfillment, rather than the transcendence, of human experience in the world, as an experiential reality in the here and now.* For Schleiermacher the incarnation of the infinite in the finite was revealed in the religious feeling. . . . Hegel claimed that man could achieve a satisfactory and completely transparent identity with the absolute only in the activity of speculative thought. Both, however, viewed their own conceptions of ontological identity as the fulfillment of the redemption of Christian history.[38]

Schleiermacher and Hegel eliminated the traditional need for apologetics and for doctrinal definitions of the nature of Christ. They also averted the embarrassing equation of Christianity with the perpetuation of centuries-long fraud, which Reimarus's criticisms had suggested. Finally, they provided sophisticated circumlocutions for rendering unproblematic the history-likeness of the New Testament.

But their solutions did not hold. The problem of the New Testament descriptions of Christ, broached by Reimarus, reemerged forcefully in theological discussions of the 1830s. Thinkers as diverse as de Wette, Strauss, F. C. Baur, Bruno Bauer, Ludwig Feuerbach, Søren Kierkegaard, and F. D. Maurice concluded that the synthetic solutions of Schleiermacher and Hegel ignored the crucial hermeneutical question of Christ and history. Their syntheses needed either to be rethought or, more often, simply discarded. As Toews puts it, "Hegelian converts revealed the tenuous and ambiguous character of his reconciliations and the historically relative experiential validity and thus therapeutic power of his 'truth.'"[39] Similar criticisms were directed against Schleiermacher and his devotees.[40]

Hegel died in 1831, Schleiermacher in 1834. The criticisms of their work that followed, effected especially by the Left Hegelians, constitute one of the most dramatic and important phases of modern European intellectual history.[41] The first and most important of these criticisms was Strauss's *Das Leben Jesu*. Although the work stemmed from Hegelian concerns, its content reflected the insights and vocabulary of biblical scholars of de Wette's generation. Through its impact on Bruno Bauer and Ludwig Feuerbach and through them on Marx, this book not only became a symbol of the political left in Germany but arguably changed the course of world history.[42] Intellectual historians and political theorists have been often fascinated by the political and social consequences of biblical-critical debates in the 1830s but they generally fail to probe very deeply into the scholarly

idiom of these debates or into the origins of the theological and hermeneutical issues animating them.

For this reason, it is important to reflect on the theological scene in the
1830s without allowing one's view to be dominated by an after-the-fact
reductive narrative: Strauss led to Feuerbach, Feuerbach to Marx, Marx
to . . . To be sure, Strauss was a major figure in the period, shaping public
discourse and religious consciousness; however, *Das Leben Jesu* was no
out-of-the-blue scholarly innovation and its notoriety is best understood as
an act of scholarship that more than any other cultural production of the
time, made transparent many preexisting intellectual tensions – between
faith and knowledge, religion and philosophy, or, more fully stated, between
the worldview of traditional Christianity appropriated in faith and
expressed in symbolic forms, and the world of "modern consciousness"
acquired through experience and reason and expressed as scientific and historical knowledge.[43] De Wette was no minor player in these controversies
– neither before nor after Strauss's book. In de Wette's biblical criticism,
in its effect on Strauss, in his influence on generations of theology students
at Berlin and Basel, and in his many scholarly writings, one observes a
mind engaged in the same tensions that Strauss brought forcefully to public
attention.

In the rest of this chapter, I pursue several issues. First, what was de
Wette's christology, what connection did it have to German Idealism, and
what was its place in the controversies of the 1830s? Second, what was de
Wette's position in relation to Strauss and vice versa? Third, with de Wette
and Strauss in mind, how does one explain the theological milieu of the
1830s without reading the period solely from the standpoint of events and
ideas that came afterwards? Finally, how does one account for the many
religious crises, including Burckhardt's, and indeed for the general crisis of
transcendent Christian orthodoxy that occurred during this period?[44]

De Wette's Christology

Dissatisfied with the strict rationalist epistemology of the eighteenth-century
mythical school (Eichhorn, Gabler, Bauer), de Wette pioneered a new notion
of myth, which, once adopted by Strauss and applied consistently to the
Gospels, would lead to wholly negative results.[45] As indicated in chapter
one, the mythical school employed the mythic principle to reduce the fab-
ulous to the natural and thus to establish the historical accuracy of the Old
Testament. They argued radically and frankly about the stories in Genesis,
but maintained a diplomatic reticence concerning the Gospel stories.[46] De
Wette criticized their use of myth, arguing instead that myth should be
understood simply as spontaneous religious and poetic expression whose

relation to possible historical events was not only elusive but, more important, irrelevant to the religious content of the Old Testament. Significantly, de Wette stated that his revised notion of myth was applicable to the New Testament accounts of Christ, although he recognized that this involved more complex theological problems. Nonetheless, he believed that a rigorous philological and historical criticism of the crucial Gospel narratives could proceed, so long as the "religious view" (*religiöse Ansicht*) of Christ had been cognitively liberated from a necessary relationship with historical knowledge.[47]

To accomplish such a cognitive liberation, de Wette sought to establish Christ's religious meaning in symbolic terms, a task that he legitimized through the epistemological-aesthetic category of *Ahnung*, discussed in chapters one and two. Christ was the symbol of a cosmic, divine-human reconciliation. In contradistinction to his notion of "symbol," de Wette employed the term "myth" to describe the stories about Christ "as they appear before us" (*wie sie vor uns liegt*) in the Gospels. These myths originated from the collective religious consciousness of the early Christians and their particular cultural situation.[48] In a passage anticipating Strauss, de Wette noted already in 1815 that "no other option is left for us than to view the Gospel stories . . . as the mythical view of a time after the origins of Christianity. The stories are certainly historical documents, not for primitive Christianity, but for a later period."[49] Thus de Wette employed "symbol" in a theological sense to prevent Christ's identity from being reduced to historical criteria alone; he employed "myth" in a biblical-critical sense to denote the picture of Christ in the Gospels and the historically discernable worldview of those who produced it.[50] Historical inquiry into the latter was possible, although Christ's ultimate identity, symbolically understood, remained religiously true, shrouded in impenetrable mystery beyond questions of historicity.

In his early *Beiträge zur Einleitung in das Alte Testament* of 1806 and 1807, de Wette had already recognized that the mythic principle was applicable to the New Testament. In one passage, where he muses about how later generations of Hebrew priests viewed the miraculous stories of the Pentateuch, de Wette states that regardless of the ultimate historical truth-content of the stories, the priests' faith remained itself true "even when the object of faith is not true." Directly after this, de Wette adds that his inquiry "is important because it can be extended to the myths of the New Testament, which without a doubt are not unimportant to us [today]."[51]

De Wette's first attempt to wrestle directly with the problem of the identity of Christ came in his Latin *Commentatio de morte Jesu Christi expiatoria* (1813), which appeared shortly after his arrival in Berlin. Although de Wette was by then familiar with Fries's work, the *Commentatio* does not reflect the strictly applied Friesian epistemology characteristic of his later works. Rather, the *Commentatio* stemmed more from de Wette's Old Testament interests. Neither the Old Testament nor Judaism, de Wette argued, nor even Jesus himself – when viewed in the Judaic context in which he lived – knew or taught that the coming Messiah would die an atoning death. Rather, the doctrine of Atonement was fabricated by the early church, and thus should not be accepted uncritically. Its significance resided in its "symbolic sense" (*sensu symbolica*) through which the devout individual could attain a sense of reconciliation with God.[52]

The *Commentatio* represents de Wette's formal dismissal of the accepted christology of Protestant orthodoxy. Although not a virtuoso piece of theology, the work nonetheless contained the critical premises on which de Wette's mature christology would be based. In subsequent university lectures and publications, de Wette worked out a conception of Christ in great detail. He attended very carefully to the arguments of conservative orthodox/pietist theologians and to those of their rationalist antagonists. For this reason, he almost always expressed his christological positions with reference to a perceived Scylla–Charybdis theological situation. A true christology was possible, he maintained, only by locating the meaning of the identity of Jesus Christ in a purely aesthetic-epistemic dimension; this would provide a refuge from both the biblical-literalist and the "Straussian" mistake of submitting all religious controversy to historical-epistemic criteria alone.[53]

It is difficult to present de Wette's christology without ambiguity. De Wette's preferred terms – "symbol," "myth," "ideal," "mystery" – are often nebulous. A partial explanation for the difficulty is that his conceptual lodestar, *Ahnung* – a term that essentially means apprehending the non-apprehensible[54] – does not readily yield a vocabulary to explain its mysterious workings. To compound the problem, moreover, once in Basel, de Wette accepted preaching and public speaking engagements. By doing so, in a reversal of his earlier Berlin views, he gradually arrived at the conviction that the interests of Christian truth were not served by confusing lay audiences with sophisticated theological speculation. He therefore chose phrases that had common ground with orthodox views; he spoke of the nature of Christ simply as mysterious (*geheimnisvoll*). His more candid positions were reserved for university lectures and publications.[55] But even in an academic context, de Wette left many points open to conflicting interpretations.

In christological matters, de Wette remained fully committed to the underlying Kantianism of Fries's categories, which forbade rapprochement between *Wissen*, *Ahnung*, and *Glaube*. Yet de Wette's ambiguous phraseology attests to the difficulty he had as a biblical critic wrestling with the Christ-history problem. For this reason, the category of "mystery" became almost a necessary refuge. It should be added that the Hegelian-derived dialectical precision of Strauss's *Das Leben Jesu* was wholly absent in de Wette, although both men shared similar tensions. For de Wette, when the demands of biblical-critical inquiry pointed only to negative results, *Ahnung* provided an epistemic "out" and upheld faith. Strauss, on the other hand, began from the conviction – inspired by Hegel – that a full reconciliation between faith and knowledge was possible. But, as *Das Leben Jesu* attests, knowledge, which in this case meant the demands of historical-critical inquiry, ultimately became the dominant and devouring partner in the rec-onciliation process.

Thus, the aesthetic category of *Ahnung* provides the key to de Wette's christology. In his *Lehrbuch der christlichen Dogmatik* (1813) de Wette cites Reimarus approvingly and argues that Jesus foretold his death, but did not speak of a resurrection.[56] Biblical passages that suggest an atoning, risen Christ should be interpreted as interpolations by the early Church. In stark contrast to Reimarus, however, de Wette refuses to see Christ as a deluded political aspirant. Rather, Christ, in his "true spiritual sense" (*wahre geistige Sinne*), was a beautiful and perfect example of humanity in complete obedience to God.[57] De Wette rejects the traditional idea of revelation taken in an objective or positive sense and instead appeals to *Ahnung*. Christ himself lived a thoroughly natural and historical life, but a person of faith could aesthetically perceive a divine quality in his behavior and teachings. The relationship between the human and the divine could not be expressed in doctrinal formulations that rested on nonaesthetic con-cepts (*Begriffe*).[58]

Additionally, de Wette argues that the doctrine of atonement – the view that Christ bore the guilt of human sin to fulfill the demands of Old Tes-tament law – arose only after Christ's death: "The Atonement cannot be proven based on Jesus' statements. His death is only raised to such impor-tance by the apostles."[59] That a historical Jesus suffered and died a blame-less death, de Wette accepts. However, Jesus' death should be understood in aesthetic terms. De Wette invokes his aesthetic subcategory of resigna-tion (*Resignation*): Christ's death was a beautiful example of virtue and sub-mission to the will of God.[60]

In *Über Religion und Theologie* (1815), de Wette reiterates that the reli-gious meaning of the Gospels does not depend on their historical veracity, but he does note that they involve more complex historical problems than does the Pentateuch. Unlike the Pentateuch, the Gospel accounts have clearer historical origins, which careful research can illuminate. However, he quickly points out difficulties inherent in the Gospels: their disagree-ments, their lack of completeness, dubious miracles, and so on.[61] Histori-cal research is a laudable goal, he states – and he himself would devote a considerable part of his later life to writing a massive commentary on the New Testament[62] – but one should not confuse historical-critical inquiry, worthwhile in its own sphere, with the "inner" (*innere*) understanding of the text, which is possible whether or not the events in the Gospel narratives had been "correctly and faithfully" recorded.[63]

The eternal ideas embedded in the Gospels, not the temporal details of the story, were what was essential for the "religious outlook."[64] In regard to the resurrection, de Wette writes that a "miraculous element remains even if we do not believe that Christ actually lived again."[65] Further, when one envisions the crucified Christ, this should not call a historical event or dogma to mind; rather one should see "an image of humanity purified by self-sacrifice."[66] As such, Christ represents the "instigator (*Urheber*) of a spiritual metamorphosis (*geistige Umwandlung*), not just for his nation, but for all of humanity."[67]

Finally, in accordance with his aesthetic approach, de Wette refers to Christ's life as a living epic and breaks it down according to the three subcategories of *Ahnung*:[68] one may therefore see in Christ's life an example of inspiration (*Begeisterung*), while his suffering and death testify to resignation (*Resignation*), which elicits worship (*Andacht*) from the devoted Christian.

On 17 December 1817, de Wette wrote a letter to Fries, commenting on the implication of Fries's philosophy for a christocentric treatise on ethics that he planned to write:

> You get the greatest praise from me because you have given me the key to the treatment of a Christian ethics which, as I hope, will astonish the world. . . . [I] at last have been able to find and hold fast the standpoint of revelation, albeit in agreement with your teaching. . . . Christ is for me the anticipation of educated reason (*Verstandesbildung*) that has brought about the whole modern period; he is the first free point from which our free life has developed. I work out my Christian morality from the unmediated aesthetic view of Christ. . . . Thus my ethics is thoroughly theological . . . [and] thoroughly philosophical.[69]

De Wette's *Christliche Sittenlehre*, dedicated to Fries, appeared shortly after he wrote this letter.[70] In the *Sittenlehre*, de Wette accepts the life of Christ as "a positive revelation," graspable in faith through *Ahnung*, but one that also had mysteriously entered the historical process. The beautiful in the life of Jesus was simultaneously the moral. Christ demonstrated a type of love so purified of egotistical concerns that he provided for all human beings a model of freedom and altruism. Thus, Christ manifests within the finitude of human history an excellence of humanity otherwise grasped only by critical thought and reflection. In this way, de Wette felt that his interpretation of Christ had unified theology and philosophy.[71] Additionally, Christ's death was necessary, for it "purified and transfigured his humanity and so completed the divine revelation."[72]

De Wette maintained the christological position worked out in the *Sittenlehre* and *Über Religion und Theologie* throughout his life. His stance combined a fundamentally aesthetic approach with one that held Christ to have had a real, however mysterious, relation to history. The connection between Christ and history should be thought of in symbolic not literal terms. De Wette believed that something was indeed miraculous about Christ, but he insisted that this emanated from Christ's aesthetic and ethical character and not, as the orthodox and pietists held, from a divine abrogation of the laws of nature and the entry of a God-man into human history.

De Wette returned to the problem of Christ and history in many subsequent works, always insisting on the religious necessity of seeing Christ in symbolic terms. One of the clearest formulations of "symbol" appears in *Theodor*:

> Everything purely human, in whatever historical connection it may appear, is an image of universal humanity. So also is the life and death of Jesus, in which we see the universal history of man. In a large view of human history, what is it except a continued sacrifice, which humanity offers of itself and all it possesses for the sake of purification and sanctification. All its works pass away with the years; states crumble, peoples pass away. . . . Only the living spirit of humanity goes forward with creative energy over the ruins, creates out of them new forms, or finds for itself new spheres of action and activity.[73]

At one point, Theodor proclaims that Christ is the "archetype of humanity," in which "human nature has endured all its sorrows." Christ's life was a microcosm in which the lengthier drama of humanity's sufferings and search for religious truth was mysteriously demonstrated in advance, and from which later generations could draw inspiration in order to extend and purify the Christian faith.

Relying on his sharp distinction between the symbolic importance of Christ and the mythic portrayal of him in the Gospels, de Wette felt that it was the duty of *Wissenschaft* to analyze historically the personality of Christ and the miracles attributed to him. Here de Wette saw three possibilities. The first he called the "dogmatic view," in which the belief in miracles and textual inspiration was maintained. The second he called the "pseudo-critical" or the "pseudo-pragmatic." Typified by his teacher at Jena, the deist H. E. G. Paulus, this view, according to de Wette, was a form of unbelief, which, through arbitrary explanations, reduced all miracles to bizarre physical occurrences. Third, there was the cautious historical option, which earnestly sought historical evidence, but was content to leave alone that which did not lend itself to final certainty: "recent biblical criticism has . . . proposed to itself an aim that does not belong to it. It seeks for pure historical clearness and certainty, where there can, of course, only be a certain holy darkness (*heiliges Dunkel*)."[74] Although a determined critic, De Wette accepted this "holy darkness," into which the human mind could not penetrate. The tentativeness of his views, compared to those of Strauss, suggests that he remained true to this belief.

De Wette, German Idealism, and the Persistence of Figural Interpretation

De Wette's decision to cling to Kant and Fries instead of turning to Hegel distinguishes him from many of the major theologians and biblical critics at work in the third and fourth decades of the nineteenth century.[75] However, in one important respect de Wette, too, reflects a "Hegelian" generational tendency, found also in Schleiermacher, but characteristic of a broad spectrum of thinkers classifiable as German metaphysical idealists.[76] Namely, one finds among idealists an inclination to interpret the identity of Jesus Christ by locating his significance, not in the transcendence of human consciousness, but in the notion that an individual known as Jesus Christ somehow became an indispensable, exemplary expression of all human consciousness, one who embodied the experience of human nature and instigated a cultural process to inspire and improve humanity – beginning with the European peoples. In a word, Christ became a symbol to legitimize nineteenth-century interpretations of the "essence" of Christianity. Such a view reflects the common idealist tendency to give Christianity a solid "subjectivist" epistemological footing in compensation for perceived losses to empiricism (especially that of Hume) of the eighteenth century. Importantly, idealist reconstructors of Christianity, almost to a man, saw *their* conception of Christ as *the* necessary divine-human union, one that represented the fulfillment of the redemptive promise of Christian faith and the culminating comprehension of Christian history; one might call this an "actualized eschatology."[77]

Although Christ became a symbol, an archetype, or a figure for many idealists, the legitimacy of traditional, figural interpretation as applied to the Old and New Testaments had fallen on hard times. Hans Frei has pointed out that one of the most consequential changes in late eighteenth-century German biblical hermeneutics was the near decimation of the legitimacy of figural interpretation.[78] Frei refers to a type of interpretation among pre-*Aufklärung* Protestant critics that viewed events in the Old Testament – from the *protoevangelium* in Genesis through the later prophets[79] – as prefigurations of, or veiled references to, the life and death of Jesus Christ. Of course, Old Testament happenings also had "ostensivehistorical referents" in the eyes of Protestant interpreters, but the more important spiritual meaning resided in the fact that they prefigured Christ. During the *Aufklärung* and shortly afterward, this mode of interpretation lost credibility among non-orthodox, non-pietist theologians. Figuration was widely criticized as imposing a false dogmatic unity on unrelated texts and events.[80]

Building on Frei's notion of the decline of figural interpretation, but developing it in a somewhat different direction, I would suggest that figural interpretation did not simply perish and give way to historical criticism – where the historical reference became the sole criterion of the meaning of biblical texts;[81] rather, it briefly survived, although in a displaced and transmuted form. Instead of the Old Testament prefiguring Christ (the discredited view), Christ himself came to prefigure, or legitimize, various forms of Christian cultural awareness and/or Christian philosophical systems that emerged in the early nineteenth century. Christ was symbolically or typologically invoked to establish the authority of a number of idealist reworkings of traditional, revelation-based Christianity.[82] In short, Christ became "shadow" to the "substance" of idealist systems.

A fierce opponent of figural interpretation in regard to the Old Testament,[83] de Wette nonetheless reenacted a form of figuration in his theology. This is most clear, as attested by many of the passages cited earlier concerning his christology, in de Wette's assertion that the meaning of Christ did not reside in the person of Christ per se, but in Christ interpreted as an emblematic individual of the larger story of humanity. Thus, symbolically understood, as de Wette told Fries, Christ anticipated the "educated understanding that has brought about the whole modern period."[84] In the life and death of Jesus, de Wette's fictional ego in *Theodor* notes, "we see the universal history of man."[85]

This argument applies, *mutatis mutandis*, to Schleiermacher, Hegel, and even, to a lesser extent, to Strauss before the thorough materialism of his later years.[86] In different forms, but nonetheless in forms that bear a family resemblance, Christ came to *stand for* something wholly outside of and after his particular space-time Palestinian existence. He became a legitimizing metaphor for a later development of Christianity. Just as precritical New Testament scholars sought legitimation of Christ's claims in the Old Testament, so de Wette, Schleiermacher, and Hegel sought legitimation for their own reconstructions by establishing, through a definite shadow-substance pattern of figural interpretation, a teleological narrative from Christ, through early Christianity and the Protestant Reformation, climaxing in their own cultural productions.[87] In Schleiermacher, Christ was the necessary "Urbild" for modern Christian community and consciousness; for Hegel, Christ was the representational precursor of religious truth that reached intellectual maturity only in Hegel's system;[88] and for de Wette,

Christ was an aesthetic symbol for the totality of human dignity and suffering.

In each case, a thoroughgoing subjectivism and an extrabiblical interpretive leniency existed that would have been unimaginable to pre-Enlightenment, pre-idealist critics. However, none was willing to question outright the often tenuous relationship between the Jesus of the New Testament texts and the form of modern Christian consciousness that they wanted actualized. This is why they opted to see the historical existence of Jesus Christ in quasi-figural terms. In doing so, they reenacted an ancient pattern of figural interpretation, which, when applied to the symbolic references to Christ in the Old Testament, had been condemned by practically all non-pietist, non-orthodox theologians as a bad historical argument or an arbitrary allegorizing of texts in the service of dogma.[89]

Strauss on de Wette; de Wette on Strauss

In an 1832 letter to his friend Christian Märklin, Strauss sketched for the first time the ideas that would form the core of *Das Leben Jesu*.[90] Commenting on the theological situation of his day, Strauss noted that

> the discussion now takes place between . . . crude supernaturalism and . . . crude rationalism and both the combatants are equally justified, since rationalism in the critical form is right, as is supernaturalism in the dogmatic form to which it holds fast. But now out of the crude rationalism evolves the refined rationalism of de Wette, which is prepared to allow the fact – indeed every fact – to disappear, while at the same time retaining it as the symbol of a dogmatic idea.

In Strauss's eyes, de Wette was on the right track, but he still lacked an understanding of *Wissenschaft* freed from eighteenth-century rationalism: "Like all rationalism, [de Wette's theology] . . . does not have the concept of spirit (*Geist*), which belongs to science (*Wissenschaft*) alone. . . . It is science now . . . which sees in the life of Jesus the consciousness which the Church has of the human spirit objectified as divine spirit." Strauss closed the letter by stating that his aim was a "perilous task," but that he could not "alter it; in some way or another the material must come out of me. . . . For the present we will commend it to God who will somehow open a door for us."[91]

Because of Strauss's ties to Hegel and his influence on the Left Hegelians, an oversimple philosophical narrative often inhibits an accurate appraisal of Strauss's ideas. To be sure, as the cited passage suggests, Strauss was indebted to Hegel on certain counts; however, as a biblical-critical work adhering to the mythic principle, *Das Leben Jesu* does not have Hegelian origins but arose from critical innovations and hermeneutical controversies among biblical scholars.[92] The introduction to *Das Leben Jesu*, "Development of the Mythical Point of View in Relation to the Gospel Stories," hardly mentions Hegel but is replete with reference to biblical critics like Paulus, Eichhorn, Gabler, and de Wette. In this rather self-aggrandizing introduction, Strauss attributes a key role to de Wette, regarding him no longer as a "refined rationalist" but as the theorist of myth who most completely had broken from eighteenth-century rationalism.

At the beginning of the introduction, Strauss makes clear that the pivotal development that allowed for his own views was the critique of the rationalist use of myth that had taken place in the early nineteenth century. Similar to de Wette, Strauss criticizes eighteenth-century scholars for their treatment of miracles as "drapery which needs only to be drawn aside in order to disclose the pure historic form."[93] He then notes that it was principally de Wette and J. S. Vater "who controverted this [rationalist] opinion [and] . . . contributed to establish[ing] the mythical view of the sacred histories." Between the two, de Wette was the more radical:

> The natural mode of explanation was still more decidedly opposed by de Wette than by Vater. He advocated the mythical interpretation of a large proportion of the Old Testament histories. In order to test the historical credibility of a narrative, he says, we must ascertain the intention of the narrator. If the intention be not to satisfy the natural thirst for historical truth by a simple narration of the facts, but rather to delight or touch the feelings, to illustrate some philosophical or religious truth, then his narrative has no pretension to historical validity.[94]

Strauss adds that de Wette saw the narrators of Old Testament stories more as poets than historians, but not as poets in a subjective sense. Such a poet draws inspiration from himself. De Wette, on the contrary, had in mind a poet that draws inspiration "objectively, as enveloped by and depending on poetry external to himself." Strauss alludes here to the inherited traditions and beliefs that shape a nation, prompting its people to "feel" their history and interpret it in predetermined cultural patterns:

> Tradition, says de Wette, is uncritical and partial; its tendency is not historical, but rather patriotic and poetical. And since the patriotic sentiment is gratified by all that flatters national pride, the more splendid, the more honorable, the more wonderful the narrative, the more acceptable it is; and where tradition has left any blanks, imagination at once steps in and fills them.

Thus, in Strauss's view, de Wette had abandoned the attempt to establish a factual basis for Old Testament miracles. What de Wette left was only poetry, expressing the collective traditional consciousness of a people.

We are solely dependent on those accounts which we cannot recognize as purely historical. They contain no criterion by which to distinguish between the true and the false; both are promiscuously blended, and set forth as of equal dignity. According to de Wette, *the whole natural mode of explanation is set aside by the principle that the only means of acquaintance with history is the narrative which we possess concerning it, and that beyond this narrative the historian cannot go.*[95]

Strauss concludes that "the natural explanation, by its own unnaturalness, ever brings us back to the mythical"; he praises "de Wette's bold and thorough application of the mythical view" and his "strict opposition to the notion of the possibility of arriving at any certainty." Strauss notes that de Wette has given rise to "much controversy," but he nevertheless wants to push forward and apply de Wette's principles of Pentateuch criticism to the Gospels.[96] Unlike the Pentateuch, however, which testified to the mentality of a nation, the Gospels, in Strauss's judgment, were a "product of the particular mental tendency of a certain community" – namely the early Christians.[97] Strauss puzzles at why previous scholars had not made this claim; he is oddly silent concerning de Wette's views on the Gospels, even though de Wette *had* suggested this claim in *Über Religion und Theologie*, which Strauss had read.[98]

In the preface to the first edition of *Das Leben Jesu*, Strauss argues that his "new mythical point of view" would "substitute a new mode of considering the life of Jesus, in the place of the antiquated systems of supernaturalism and naturalism." He deems all previous attempts inadequate and asserts that *Wissenschaft* does not rest satisfied with half-measures. Therefore, "the appearance of a work like the present," he claims, "is not only justifiable, but even necessary," for in his judgment it was high time to decide conclusively "whether in fact, and to what extent, the ground on which we stand in the Gospels is historical."[99] Strauss of course denies the Gospels any historical ground. The mythical worldview of the Gospel narrators, their traditions, religious sensibilities, and expectations rendered genuine historical knowledge impossible. Strauss does not deny that historical events may lie behind the myths, but the narratives themselves are not to be regarded as historical formulations. Thus, Christianity cannot be traced to one individual. This conclusion, he claims, should effect an "internal liberation" from history and allow Christianity – finally – to be constructed on purely philosophical grounds. In Hegelian terms, Strauss severed the "representations" (*Vorstellungen*) from the more important "concepts" (*Begriffe*). The severance, however, was less dependent on Hegel's philosophy than on Strauss's appropriation of a pre-Hegelian exegetical tradition of myth interpretation, transformed by de Wette at the beginning of the century, and applied by Strauss directly and consistently to the Gospels.

Contemporaries reacted to Strauss's book with almost wholesale condemnation. As one commentator has noted, *Das Leben Jesu* was "thrown like a fire-bomb into the tinder-dry pietistic forest of Württemberg."[100] But not only pietists were alarmed: Strauss's book triggered critical responses from practically every theological outlook in Europe – orthodox, rationalist, and Hegelian alike. The book cost Strauss his teaching position at the University of Tübingen and in 1839 it cost him another at Zurich. De Wette was unique among established biblical critics in his positive reaction to Strauss.[101] De Wette not only recognized the legitimacy of Strauss's work but actually praised it, expressing his views candidly in the introduction to his *Erklärung des Evangeliums Matthäi*, which appeared in 1836.

Strauss was quick to recognize the importance of de Wette's reaction. In the preface to the second edition of *Das Leben Jesu* (1836), while scoffing at criticisms from others, Strauss notes that de Wette's *Erklärung* "appeared recently, to my special delight." Here was a work, he writes "in which I find my efforts on many points appreciated by an old master of biblical criticism in such a way to compensate for the derogatory judgments of so many others." Strauss even adds that "from the pages of a work such as de Wette's I have taken note of some rather blatant errors and contradictions on my part and insofar as it was possible and I could agree, I have already corrected my work in a few places according to his pointers."[102]

With little hope of a new professorship and facing ostracism from the church and fellow theologians, Strauss decided to compromise his radicalism in the third edition of *Das Leben Jesu*. He accomplished this by softening his views on the authenticity of the Gospel of John.[103] Strauss attributes his moderation to a closer reading of de Wette and August Neander. "The changes offered by this new edition are all more or less related to the fact that a renewed study of the Fourth Gospel, on the basis of de Wette's commentary and Neander's *Leben Jesu Christi*, has made me again doubtful of my earlier doubt concerning the authenticity and credibility of this Gospel."[104] Strauss adds, however, that his change of opinion came with equivocation: "It is not that I have become convinced of its authenticity, merely that I am no longer certain of its inauthenticity."

Strauss's moderation was short-lived; he returned to his negative conclusions in the fourth edition of *Das Leben Jesu*. It is important to note, however, that the issues at stake in Strauss's concession in the third edition reflect a broader controversy about the nature of the Gospel of John, which had major implications for the future of christology and Gospel criticism. The Gospel of John was not only the touchstone of Schleiermacher's whole christology,[105] but was also regarded as a more sophisticated "spiritual"

Gospel, which practically all eighteenth-century commentators turned to when casting doubt on the miracles found in the more "bodily" Synoptic Gospels. Indeed, the fourth Gospel represented the account of a less problematic eyewitness from whom more abstract, philosophical christological positions – independent of "bodily" miracles – could be constructed.[106] To doubt John's reliability, therefore, meant to locate *all* the important accounts of Christ in the religious outlook of a period removed from the actual time of Jesus.

K. G. Bretschneider, in 1820, was the first major nineteenth-century critic to come out against John's authenticity.[107] The outpouring of criticism that he received, especially from Schleiermacher, led him to confess that his book was mistaken. De Wette, however, came to Bretschneider's defense, arguing modestly that "the acceptance of the authenticity of this Gospel has not been raised beyond all doubt." Strauss's moderation in the third edition of *Das Leben Jesu*, as Strauss himself indicated, was in part derived from de Wette's ambiguity and not from a genuine acceptance of the fourth Gospel. Importantly, therefore, before Strauss, de Wette and Bretschneider (who recanted) were the only major critics to tolerate the possibility of the inauthenticity of John and to accept the theological consequences thereof. De Wette never came to a wholly unambiguous position on the question of the fourth Gospel.[108]

*   *   *

Although de Wette lamented the theological uproar caused by Strauss's book, he nonetheless esteemed the work and expressed gratitude that Strauss had shown "that the Hegelian philosophy is inconsistent with Christian faith, as it does not recognize the religious department of life, and knows nothing of faith."[109] In certain respects, de Wette shared much with the opinions of those who formed the Hegelian Left in the late 1830s. Both de Wette and the Hegelian Left understood Strauss's accomplishment as the rejection of Hegelian Christianity.[110] Yet unlike the more radical Left Hegelians, de Wette was disinclined to equate God consciousness wholly with human consciousness and arrive at the radical anti-Christian humanism of Bruno Bauer or Ludwig Feuerbach. De Wette, like Feuerbach, held that religious experience was subjectively validating, but de Wette, unlike Feuerbach, held that one's subjectivity validated a real God, not the divinity of one's own consciousness.[111] Furthermore, unlike Bauer, Ruge, Feuerbach, Vischer, and others, de Wette believed that the question of divinity was independent of historical criticism; the divine could be grasped only subjectively according to the principle of *Ahnung*, which equated history with symbol. To the end of his life, de Wette never wearied in his conviction that this Friesian concept could insulate the content of Christianity from historical criticism.

98

De Wette articulated his views on Strauss in his *Erklärung des Evangeliums Matthäi* (1836).[112] Because this work appeared the year after Strauss's, de Wette felt obliged to make his position concerning Strauss clear. In the preface, de Wette agreed with Strauss's view that the Synoptic Gospels bespoke an earlier tradition, subject to variation and employed differently by the three evangelists. He acknowledged, with Strauss, that the Synoptic Gospels could not be harmonized and that differences played a larger role than similarities. He agreed that miracles could not be explained from the natural point of view (*natürliche Ansicht*) as rationalist theologians sought to do. Whether the belief in miracles of the early Christians should be ours was a question that de Wette felt could be answered only (a) on the basis of historical criticism, in which area there could be no agreement; (b) from a metaphysical standpoint, where again there could be no agreement; (c) out of different religious convictions. On this last point, de Wette suggested that he, not Strauss, had the right solution: "Whatever one's views on miracles may be, the factor that could bring them together is the ideal-symbolic meaning (*ideal-symbolische Bedeutung*) of miracles, to which I have repeatedly drawn attention, without wanting to claim that the miracle stories have been woven together simply out of ideas [the view of Strauss]."[113]

Overall, he viewed Strauss's conclusions as too negative: "I believe that those who have freed themselves from the fear of criticism (*Unkritik*) and the arbitrariness of the so-called orthodox, but who have preserved the true historical belief, can achieve better results." He defined "true historical belief" as "a sound thoroughly moral faith, which on the basis of the historical church community, holds fast to the fact that the spirit, which has become the life-principle of the modern world, had its beginnings in the person of Christ."[114] De Wette ended his preface by warning young theologians not to return to orthodoxy in fear of Strauss's criticism. In de Wette's eyes, fear was not warranted because "Christianity as the essence of life can never become extinct." Rather, like a "hieroglyph written by God himself (*von Gott selbst geschriebene Hieroglyphe*), it [the Christian faith] will always be subject to (*erfahren*) new and freer explanations, and, one hopes, not simply from understanding (*Verstande*), which often results in profanation, but rather from a deeper reflection (*Sinne*) informed by intuition, creativity, inspiration, and piety."[115]

De Wette returned to the "Strauss problem" in his *Kurze Erklärung des Evangeliums und der Briefe Johannis* (1837).[116] In it he rejected outright Strauss's claim to have written a "presuppositionless" criticism of the Gospels.[117] Against Strauss he argued that criticism must always rely on a search for sure facts and confidence in certain basic principles. De Wette conceded that Strauss had seriously called into questioned the reliability of John's Gospel and had thus created a very unsettled situation, although de

Wette noted that he himself had not come to a firm decision. Documents besides the Gospels, such as those of St. Paul, Josephus, or Tacitus, are not helpful in establishing authenticity, although they do establish certain inviolable limits.[118] Consequently, by default, one has to rely on general principles.[119]

De Wette's main general principle was to regard Jesus as the founder of Christianity. His role as founder was demonstrated by the existence of the Church and by Christian history, as well as by the knowledge that great movements are often begun by unusually gifted individuals. Second, de Wette reasoned that Jesus must have impressed on his disciples the need for harmony between the divine and the human, and must have lived out this conviction in his life. That Jesus had an inspiring affect on his disciples is indisputable. Belief in his deity, therefore, could have been inferred from Jesus' perception of himself as a pioneer of a new way of life and as the founder of a new religious community.[120] Finally, in de Wette's view the "fact of the resurrection" (*Tatsache der Auferstehung*), although the most important point of Christian faith, should be regarded simply as a "mystery" (*Geheimnis*), for its historical content lay in complete darkness.

De Wette criticized those who made historical knowledge prior to faith: "I see in this fervor for the historical (*historischen Eifer*) a large prejudice and a dangerous mistake. People seek after something they cannot attain and are not supposed to attain, and in the process they lose sight of what is most important." None of the apostles had such a clear, retrospective, historical view of Jesus, de Wette reasoned; therefore, "how is it that we, who stand so far from the mysterious origins of Christianity, make so much of a historical knowledge about those beginnings?"[121] Characteristically, de Wette made an appeal for the symbolic mode of handling the Gospels' relationship to history. He saw symbolic treatment as the only option that avoided both the harmonizing of the Gospels by orthodox theologians and the negative criticism of rationalists, with whom he here categorized Strauss. De Wette concluded by asking what it benefits ordinary Christians anyway to confuse them with historical scholarship; for the truth of the Gospel resides as much in the "Christian heart" as it does in history. If one recognizes this, "then doubt will not triumph."[122]

The 1830s: An Extraordinary Theological Situation

Although Strauss was certainly a dominant figure, Protestant theological culture during the 1830s is not reducible to Strauss alone. The period is best considered as a mosaic of several different theological, epistemic, and cultural stances, which, though complex, lend themselves to some general observations. Making these observations will not only help define de Wette's stance within a broader context but will also provide a historical framework for elucidating the conditions of theological scholarship during Jacob Burckhardt's *Theologiestudium* (1837–9), when he encountered de Wette at the University of Basel, gave up theology for history as a career, and ultimately rejected orthodox Christianity altogether.

Specifically, I articulate three historiographical and conceptual issues that illuminate the nature of theological knowledge in the 1830s. First, one must cast doubt on the lingering "great man" image of Strauss, the view that he single-handedly revolutionized, for better or worse, theology and biblical criticism in Germany. Rather, Strauss was a complex – but by no means inevitable – mirror of the time, who clarified – but by no means resolved – certain christological and epistemological tensions, especially the problematic relationship between faith and knowledge, which had been around at least since the time of Reimarus. Second, and related to the first point, I contextualize the faith-knowledge tension within what both Thomas Nipperdey and Charles E. McClelland speak of as the institutional "revolution" of the concept and practice of *Wissenschaft* in the first part of the nineteenth century.[123] De Wette, Strauss, and their contemporaries worked out theological stances within a particular academic milieu with its particular intellectual imperatives. Finally, as important as institutional frameworks are in shaping knowledge, I argue that the religious issues at play had considerable intellectual autonomy, best approached by employing the philosophical distinctions between a "correspondence" and "coherence" theory of truth. Neither theologians nor laypeople viewed their ideas as a matter of opinion or as mere "cultural constructs." Rather, they held deepseated convictions and believed that the confrontation between *Wissenschaft* and faith, felt poignantly in the 1830s, was epochal in nature, having profound implications not just for the "private religious life" but for the very survival of Christianity. Consequently, how one thought of the pursuit of truth in religious matters was not something understood as relative to one's sociocultural situation, as one might assume today. Yet the difficulties broached in securing religious truth during this turbulent decade of theologizing gradually led in some important cases, such as Burckhardt's, to the threshold of a distinctly modern cultural relativism.

* * *

Theologians of various stripes have attributed a certain inevitability to the appearance of Strauss's *Das Leben Jesu* in 1835. Although critical of Strauss, Hans Frei has argued that Strauss represented the decisive climax of eighteenth-century criticism by his reduction of the meaning of the Gospels to a historical understanding of its authors' intentions.[124] William Neil, more sympathetic to Strauss, noted that Strauss was *the* figure who finally cut the Gordian knot between rationalism and orthodoxy and "change[d] the entire direction of New Testament study for the rest of the century."[125]

But ascribing inevitability to Strauss obscures the view held of him by his contemporaries, who tended to judge Strauss in light of a shared heritage going back to the biblical-critical and epistemological controversies of the *Aufklärung*. Significantly, most major commentators did not see *Das Leben Jesu* as an original work or as the beginning of a new era, but rather as a telling reflection of the existing theological situation. A few years after its publication, F. C. Baur at Tübingen wrote:

> If there is any book which is constructed as much as possible only on the work of predecessors, which simply summarizes conclusions from a string of various investigations long ago conducted by so many others, which merely, but consistently, draws the last conclusions from premises about which one had already been agreed, then it is the Straussian *Das Leben Jesu*. . . . It was as if in this book a mirror had been held up to the inner selves of all theologians. They had only one choice – either to acknowledge that they also had already taken the path of the critic who was now in such bad odor and that they could scarcely do anything other than continue with him on the same way, or else, to deny their former freer convictions and surrender unconditionally to the ecclesiastical orthodoxy.[126]

Similarly, Friedrich Vischer claimed in 1838 that the publication of *Das Leben Jesu* made Strauss one of those "representative men" who crystalize the collective consciousness of their generation.[127] E. W. Hengstenberg, de Wette's replacement at Berlin, wrote in the conservative *Evangelische Kirchenzeitung* that "Strauss has done nothing more than bring the spirit of the age to consciousness of itself and of the necessary consequences that proceed from its essential character."[128] Strauss himself also recognized that his views were not pioneering. When dismissed from the Tübingen seminary, he stated to the director of studies that the views expressed in his book were "not merely the notions of one individual, but the conclusions of a whole direction of theological scholarship."[129] Abandoned by his peers, Strauss complained of being "vexed by my isolated position and annoyed with my friends that now, when the situation becomes serious, they suddenly leave the cart standing which for so long we all pulled together."[130]

Strauss's notoriety thus came not from the innovative character of his ideas, but from his clarifying – and to a degree perhaps simplifying – and forcing an either/or dilemma out of a widespread but muddled tension between the high culture claims of *Wissenschaft*, expressed in philosophical abstractions, and those of traditional faith, expressed in the cultivation of piety and obedience to traditional ecclesiastical formulations of dogma. To be sure, it is a fine distinction to make between Strauss and what Strauss came to represent upon publication of *Das Leben Jesu*. But it was decisively the latter that stirred religious emotions and inspired such controversy.

The controversies that ensued were indeed of major proportions. Theological leaders throughout Germany engaged in a polemical warfare of a magnitude rivaling the period after the Reformation. In many ways the 1830s were even more dramatic, because Christianity itself – and not simply the question of which form of Christianity – was taken as one of the main points under discussion. Further, the conflict was by no means confined to elite circles. Educated laypeople and average parishioners also became engaged in the knowledge–faith dilemma of their time. Horton Harris rightly remarks that "not only in the theological seminaries did the book produce a great sensation and continuing controversy over the problems which it raised, but [also] in every church, in every town, in an age when the church [still] formed the central position in the lives of the majority of the populace."[131]

* * *

The second quarter of the nineteenth century witnessed an unprecedented increase in the pursuit and prestige of *Wissenschaft*. German research and German university teaching rose during this time to the pinnacle of esteem. The founding of the University of Berlin and the attendant ideals of Humboldt, Fichte, Schleiermacher, and others were a catalyst in this process, for practically all German-speaking universities quickly adopted the "Berlin model."[132] Indeed, scholars felt a new, nonclerical sense of "calling" – "*Wissenschaft* for the sake of *Wissenshaft*," as Max Weber would later describe it.[133]

The development of the new ideal of *Wissenschaft*, deeply rooted in neo-humanist ideas and in quasi-Romantic notions of the power of human intelligence and creativity, had two principal characteristics: (1) the elevation of scholarly work to a form of moral obligation, and (2) a belief in the insufficiency of past forms of knowledge, and confidence in the individual scholar to improve and create new knowledge. In regard to the first point, Nipperdey writes of a new "Wissenschaftsglaube" or "Wissenschaftsreligion" among the educated: "*Wissenschaft* became even the new measure for the question of meaning in life and happiness; the path of *Wissenschaft* became the path to truth, freedom, and humanity."[134] "The ever expanding scope of truth . . . [and] the accumulation of knowledge was raised to the highest moral duty and became one of the highest forms of human existence, even something holy, a piece of immortality; it became the dominating passion, which disciplined the rest of one's life ascetically."[135] McClelland writes that

> scholars in Germany . . . were convinced that the knowledge of their predecessors was superficial at best, and that bold acts of intelligence and will by the single scholar could uncover the profound secrets of the human world and the universe beyond. One is hard pressed to find any eighteenth-century professors who took research as seriously and passionately as many of the great discoverers and writers of the 1830s onward.[136]

The new ideal of *Wissenschaft* was borne out in exemplary fashion among theologians and biblical critics such as de Wette and Strauss. De Wette emphasized repeatedly that since faith was independent of knowledge, then "Unwissenschaftlichkeit" testified not only to a lack of scholarly nerve, but to a mistaken understanding of the nature of faith.[137] Similarly, Strauss, anticipating critical reactions to his book, wrote that if the theologically timid "regard this absence of presuppositions from his work as unchristian, he regards the believing presuppositions of theirs as unscientific (*unwissenschaftlich*)."[138] De Wette and Strauss were not exceptional cases: bold acts of theological intelligence abounded in mid-nineteenth century. F. C. Baur at Tübingen; Friedrich Lücke and August Neander at Berlin; Karl Ullmann and F. A. G. Tholuck at Halle; Karl August von Hase at Jena; Julius Müller at Marburg, among many others were, regardless of theological differences, "driven by this new passion to *discover* and . . . to communicate their discoveries to others."[139] As the editors put it in the preface to the inaugural volume of Berlin's *Theologische Zeitschrift* (1819): "We insist only on seriousness, profundity, clarity, and liveliness – with one word *Wissenschaftlichkeit*; and we promise to take great pains to accomplish the highest possible impartiality and versatility, although each [scholar] in his own work will remain tenaciously faithful to his own presuppositions and convictions."[140]

*   *   *

However important new institutional and scholarly imperatives may have been in shaping theology, the discussants at the time were by and large unconcerned with what many today might assume to be the socially dependent character of knowledge. Theologians saw themselves as pursuing truth, pure and simple. Their goal was to depict the world and God's relation to it in terms that reflected how things really were, even if this meant engaging in a rarefied scholarly idiom and disturbing the theologically timid. In this respect, mid-nineteenth-century debates are justifiably viewed as an autonomous realm of discourse and thus are best approached with an eye toward shedding light on the underlying intellectual presuppositions of the time. The most dominant of these presuppositions was straightforward: the desire to formulate a *true* theology based on a *true* christology. The philosophical distinctions between a "correspondence" and a "coherence" theory of truth offer considerable conceptual clarity to illuminate the complex theological tensions of the 1830s.[141] Although I refer principally to de Wette and to Strauss, the application of this distinction could be extended to the majority of theologians active during the period.

As Frederick Gregory notes, the correspondence theory of truth is perhaps the oldest theory of truth, owing its most common understanding to Aristotle. Truth consists of some form of correspondence between the world of thought and the world of things or between mind and matter. Nature is "out there," completely independent of the mind that attempts to know it. To establish the truth of an assertion about the world, one must show a correlation between the rational categories about which the assertion is made and the apprehension of nature given in experience.[142] This must be done apart from one's own prejudices and beliefs. As the Dutch physiologist Jacob Moleschott wrote in 1867, "The scientist does not give in to the belief that he has created the law; he feels in his innermost being that the facts imposed it on him."[143]

The correspondence theory of truth requires one to assume that what the mind conceives about the world is ontologically real. As both Karl Popper and Hilary Putnam have noted, it is a theory for the realist, since it allows one to speak of a reality apart from the theory and the theorist conceptualizing it. It entails, in other words, a strong metaphysical claim: stating the truth is nothing less than establishing what actually exists. Accurate knowledge of nature is simultaneously the truth of nature.[144]

Although this understanding of truth was not new in the nineteenth century, the role of empirical verification, stemming from the Scientific Revolution, expanded its importance to every domain of knowledge. As Gregory notes, for nineteenth-century adherents of this view emphasis was placed on the "discovery of the unknown, conformity to nature's authority, the determining role of fact, and reason's incredible power to copy nature."[145] As indicated earlier, belief in such notions formed the basis of the revolution of *Wissenschaft* in the German universities. Leopold von Ranke's famous dictum of writing history *wie es eigentlich geswesen* represented not only a historiographical agenda but a widely felt scholarly mood. Strauss, too, epitomized this view when he wrote in *Das Leben Jesu* that a true historical account can never be at odds with the "known and universal laws that govern the course of events."[146]

The coherence theory of truth, on the other hand, received its most forceful expression in Kant's writings and in those of Kant's followers like Fichte and Fries. Precisely because of the metaphysical claim that the truth of nature lies beyond the realm of knowledge, a Kantian cannot measure truth by professing to establish a correspondence between thought and things in the manner described above. Facts do not impose themselves on us; rather humans' preexisting mental features and dispositions (which in Kant's view are ahistorical) determine what is reasonable and true.[147] De Wette's mentor, Fries, summed up the type of truth that he felt Kant had made possible:

> We cannot, as is usually done, speak of truth as opposed to error by saying that the truth is the correspondence of representation with its object. We can only say that the truth of a judgment is its correspondence with the immediate cognition of reason in which it is grounded. . . . I call this truth the inner . . . cognition, because we concern ourselves in this idea only with the unification of all our cognitions into a system of reason.[148]

Hermann Lotze, an admirer of Fries, made this notion even more precise, when he distinguished "between truths which are valid and things which exist."[149]

Although philosophers today recognize several versions of the coherence view, each has its roots in German idealism's attempt to escape the skepticism to which a thoroughgoing empiricism seemed to lead. Moreover, all variations have in common the view that the truth of a proposition consists not in the correspondence between the proposition and a reality outside the mind, but in the proposition's harmonious fit within a preexisting scheme of belief. As Ralph Walker writes, "The coherence theorist holds that for a proposition to be true is for it to cohere with a certain system of beliefs. It is not just that it is true if and only if it coheres with that system; it is that the coherence, and nothing else, is what its truth consists in."[150]

In making statements in the mid-nineteenth century about the truth of Christ, it is helpful to view German theologians as profoundly divided by these two versions of truth. Was the nature of Christ to be found in propositions that Christ was true only insofar as his nature corresponded to a putative objective historical reality governed by immutable natural laws? Or, was Christ's truth located in the rational structures and/or religious requirements of human beings? If both types of truth are valid, as theologians have often claimed over the years, then what is their relationship to one another? And finally, if they both contained parts of truth, what criteria could one deploy to isolate these parts and determine their relationship with one another?

Strauss's initial Hegelian desire to preserve the philosophical content of Christianity would make him a likely candidate for the coherence view. However, a form of the correspondence view, stemming from his naturalist presuppositions and his eighteenth-century rationalist heritage, became the dominating epistemological determinant in his outlook. This view can already be observed in his earliest edition of *Das Leben Jesu*; and it became fully evident in the complete positivism and anti-Christian humanism of his later years. There are certain inviolable laws in nature and history, Strauss proclaimed, and "the absolute cause never disturbs the chain of secondary causes by single arbitrary acts of interposition, but rather manifests itself in the production of the aggregate of finite causalities, and of their reciprocal actions."[151] In his *Der alte und der neue Glaube* (1872) even this vague "absolute cause" was jettisoned, as was all Christian truth. For Strauss, the final ground for truth became "nothing other than that which we call the modern world-view, the laboriously attained result of continued scientific and historical research, in contrast to Christian theology."[152]

De Wette, on the other hand, was more representative of the epistemological tensions of the time, for he never made an either/or situation out of the seemingly rival claims of Christian theology (coherence) and of modern historical and scientific investigation (correspondence). Rather, he set rigid boundaries between them. For this reason, he did not attempt a complete reconciliation of faith and reason, as did Schleiermacher, Hegel, and Strauss. For de Wette, establishing the truth of Christianity depended on one's ability not to synthesize different forms of truth but rather to recognize their fundamental incommensurability. Such a recognition is reflected in de Wette's attempt to allow for absolute authoritative jurisdiction within the boundaries of disparate epistemic spheres. Historical inquiry, for example, is necessarily confined within the boundaries of knowing (*Wissen*). *Wissen* legitimized de Wette's own radical criticism and reflects a correspondence theory of truth. On the other hand, deeper theological truths are strictly matters of faith (*Glaube*), as apprehended through *Ahnung*. This mode allowed de Wette to embrace and systematize the Christian message; it also reflects his simultaneous adherence to a coherence theory of truth. Christian intellectual maturity, in de Wette's system, thus required the disciplining of the mind to accept the legitimacy, necessity, and inviolability of boundaries between different modes of determining truth.[153]

Conclusion

De Wette recognized that his system would demand a certain mental tension, and he knew that the publication of Strauss's *Das Leben Jesu* did not bode well for the acceptance of this required tension. In some cases, Strauss's unrelenting criticism had prompted a return to orthodoxy among young theological trainees; in others it had led to outright atheism. De Wette regretted the *Unwissenschaftlichkeit* of the orthodox and the lack of faith of the atheists. Consequently, he took it upon himself to promote a form of theological damage control. This is most evident in a preface written to Friedrich Lücke's small polemical book, *Dr. Strauss und die Züricher Kirche: eine Stimme aus Norddeutschland* (1839), published shortly after citizens of Zurich had rejected Strauss's appointment at their university on the grounds of his infidelity.[154] De Wette lamented the fact that Strauss had polarized public debate and provoked suspicion about the importance of *Wissenschaft* to Christian theology. He pled therefore for young theology students, since they will be the future "curators of theological learning" (*die Pfleger der theologischen Wissenschaft*), to avoid passionate involvement in the issues aroused by Strauss and not to be driven away from *Wissenschaft* by the tide of popular disapproval. In fact, de Wette claimed that it was the duty and privilege of all future clergymen to make the achievements of *Wissenschaft* acceptable to laypeople:

> The true mediation between it (*Wissenschaft*) and the church should happen through the clergy, who stand in the middle of the issue, and who should turn out students from universities and seminaries like freshly-minted coins derived from pure gold. It is true that such gold is not always offered in theological lecture halls [these days]; however, whoever has achieved the ability to think independently can . . . find it.[155]

De Wette held it as the greatest need of the church that young scholarly servants arise and lead Christians in a true understanding of knowledge and faith; he therefore ended the preface praying that God would raise up such workers.

Indeed, the theological instruction of the young became a burning concern in the 1830s, not just for theologians like de Wette but for all concerned parties. "The collision with *Wissenschaft*," notes Nipperdey, unraveled more than a few pious young people and led parents, preachers, and townspeople alike to occupy themselves with the problematic relationship between traditional piety and modern critical scholarship.[156] In numerous inaugural and rectorial addresses at the University of Basel, for example, scholars dealt with the issue, seeking a pedagogical balance or at least a workable truce. In 1836, de Wette's conservative colleague Johannes Tobias Beck implored the "theological youngsters" (*theologische Jünglichen*) at Basel to realize the "holy, serious calling of theology today" but be warned against the many "dangerous crags" along the way.[157]

De Wette's own role in the controversies of the time, in the opinion of colleagues in Germany and of the citizens of Basel, was a thorny issue. He was viewed with a mixture of awe and suspicion, praised for his erudition and sincerity but widely criticized for beliefs inconsistent with strict orthodoxy. Jacob Burckhardt's father, Jakob Burckhardt (Sr.), for example, then minister of children's education at Basel's city cathedral, praised de Wette in a letter for his commitment to "unprejudiced truth"; but he also voiced a note of fatherly prescience: "But by no means do our theology students [in Basel] have it easy, because learning (*Wissenschaft*) and faith are so far apart from one another. In the interior of the student, this must eventually lead to an internal contradiction, which can endanger their spiritual lives."[158]

CHAPTER FOUR

Basel, Burckhardt, and de Wette

> Once upon a time I studied theology . . . with the greatest
> interest, and then found I did not have the faith required for
> the pulpit, and thereupon transferred over to history.
>   – Burckhardt, Letter to Friedrich von Preen,
>   7 July 1878[1]

A S A T H E O L O G Y S T U D E N T at the University of Basel (1837–9),
Jacob Burckhardt encountered the thought of de Wette. Burckhardt
embraced wholeheartedly de Wette's *esprit critique*, but soon came to question his reconstruction of Christian belief. Deeming it unintelligible on
many points, Burckhardt vowed to be an "honest heretic" (*ehrlicher Ketzer*)
instead.[2] Indeed, the encounter with de Wette unsettled the young Burckhardt to such an extent that he experienced an intellectual and emotional
"crisis" (his word) of faith, gave up theology altogether, and resolved to
pursue historical studies at the University of Berlin. Significantly, his decision against theology was made at about the time that his father (Jakob
Burckhardt, Sr.) was elected *Antistes*, the highest ecclesiastical office in
Basel, at the city cathedral.[3] That this formative theological experience
has received scant attention from Burckhardt scholars is at first glance
curious.[4]

The omission can be partly explained, however, by three historical
factors. First, Burckhardt's importance as a historical thinker was recognized belatedly,[5] long after de Wette and his early nineteenth-century concerns had been driven from the theological limelight by bigger names –
Schleiermacher, Strauss, and Julius Wellhausen in particular. Second, when
the importance of Burckhardt's thought was recognized, it was done so at
a time when the political events of the twentieth century and an inquiry
into their origins so overshadowed other concerns that Burckhardt became
interesting primarily for his *Kulturgeschichte* and its implicit contempt for
state power as a healthy alternative to the state-aggrandizing orientation of

Prussian historiography. Last, the omission of Burckhardt's theological roots in Basel can be explained by the prominence and international reputation of his teachers at the University of Berlin – Leopold von Ranke, J. G. Droysen, Franz Kugler, August Boeckh, and Jakob Grimm, among others. Such acclaimed professors have made Burckhardt's final studies in Berlin (rather than his early years in humble Basel) seem the appropriate place to inquire into the origins of his mature historical thought.[6]

However, I argue that Burckhardt's prior theology studies and his encounter with de Wette in Basel – an encounter that took place at a time when the city was ecclesiastically presided over by Burckhardt's own father – is the proper entry point for understanding the genesis of Burckhardt's historical mind. Significantly, it was against de Wette that one first hears Burckhardt's criticisms of liberal theology and of secular, quasi-theistic philosophies of history – criticisms that foreshadow his later, well-known critique of Hegelian philosophy. Although Burckhardt's politics and his work as a cultural historian are relevant to my concerns, my focus is on a decisively theological element in Burckhardt's historical thought, deeply rooted in his native Basel, in his encounter with de Wette, and in his rejection of Christianity and resolve to be an "honest heretic."[7] The implication, of course, is that Burckhardt regarded de Wette, Hegel, and others as dishonest modernizers, who vitiated Christian orthodoxy (the faith of his father) while attempting to upgrade it. For this reason, Burckhardt has been regarded as a prescient voice by neo-orthodox theologians and by other intellectuals critical of modernity.[8]

Burckhardt's transition to history did not entail a wholesale break with theological concerns. Residual elements of his religious sensibilities and theological training appear throughout his subsequent historical writings. At the same time, however, this transition is also indicative of a more pervasive shift in German and European educated thought in the nineteenth century – a shift from ahistorical, theological ways of thinking to ones that became increasingly historical. Indeed, the question of historicism and its relation to theological *modi cognoscendi* lies at the heart of Burckhardt's intellectual development; one can see in his transition to history a complex frustration with theological problems indigenous to the German Enlightenment and especially with the struggle between *Wissenschaft* and faith, which was often waged most fiercely in christology.

In this chapter, I explore the nature of Burckhardt's theological studies, his encounter with de Wette, and his decision to leave theology in favor of history. However, before addressing these issues, I must pursue several important prior questions. First, since Burckhardt broke with the "Basler orthodoxy"[9] of his father, what was the nature of Basel's religious milieu in the first part of the nineteenth century and, specifically, what was the religious character of Burckhardt's own father, who, incidentally, was an amateur historian and had also as a young man studied briefly under de Wette in Heidelberg? Second, how did a theological radical like de Wette wind up in Basel to begin with? Before de Wette's arrival, the University of Basel was regarded as one of the most conservative theological outposts in Europe.

"Pious Basel"[10]

The *Ancien Régime* in Europe did not wane in a geographically uniform fashion; certain repositories of nostalgia were able to resist for quite some time the sweeping forces of social and cultural modernization.[11] During the late eighteenth and early nineteenth century, Basel emerged as one of the most entrenched centers of anti-Enlightenment religiosity in Europe.[12] A peculiar geographical location, combined with a proudly defended heritage of Reformation humanism, eighteenth-century pietism, and a long-standing, native tradition of cultural conservatism gave the city of Burckhardt's upbringing a unique and almost wholly skeptical attitude toward the phenomena of dechristianization and secularization emanating from other universities and urban centers in Europe. In short, Basel was neither Paris nor northern Germany, and neither the shrill anticlericalism of Voltaire, d'Alembert, and D'Holbach nor the sophisticated rationalism of Wolff and Kant found many adherents in this pious, patrician city-republic on the Rhine.[13]

In part, Basel's conservatism grew out of its geographical situation in the corner of three countries (*Das Dreiländereck*).[14] As a border city nestled between France, Germany, and the rest of Switzerland, Basel has vigilantly struggled to maintain its own identity against the intentions of hostile and greedy neighbors, be they Habsburgs, Bourbons, or Bonapartes. Although, for defensive purposes, Basel joined the Swiss Confederation in 1501, the city's inhabitants until late in the nineteenth century chose to regard their "Vaterstadt" as an autonomous republic within the confederation. Even early in the twentieth century, elderly inhabitants would speak of "going to Switzerland" when leaving their city for one of the other cantons. The "national" in Basel's newspaper, the *Nationalzeitung*, referred to Basel, not to Switzerland. Furthermore, the majority of Basel's small population – which reached 20,000 only during the middle of the nineteenth century – remained within the old medieval wall until 1850, when it was finally taken down.[15] Such dogged *Kantönligeist* at one of the major cultural crossroads of Europe gave Baslers a rather distinct preservationist instinct. As one commentator has noted, the view of the world of the nineteenth-century Basler was not "the dominating view of the hero and conqueror [i.e., of France or Prussia]; but the cautious, questioning, mistrustful view of the prosaic anti-hero among giants whose dangerous games threaten his livelihood and his very existence."[16] This observation has been applied to Basel's civic institutions, but it perhaps even more accurately describes the preoccupation of Basel's church and university elites with their religious heritage and their desire to protect it against the threats of *philosophes*, *Neologen*, and *Aufklärer* alike.

Throughout the eighteenth and early nineteenth centuries, Basel's educated citizenry strove to preserve the accomplishments of their religious past, especially the "Basilea Reformata." The symbolic significance of the ecumenical Council of Basel (1431–49); the founding of the University of Basel by the humanist pope Aeneas Silvius Piccolomini (Pius II) in 1460, the first and only university for nearly three hundred years in what was to become modern Switzerland; the establishment of a printing industry, headed by Johannes Froben (1460–1527); the emergence of Basel as a humanist center of learning and piety, which attracted such figures as Erasmus, Sebastian Franck, Wolfgang Fabritius Capito, Johannes Oecolampadius, Conrad Pellican, and Sebastian Castellio; and the peaceful introduction of Protestantism to Basel, which began in 1529 and was consolidated with the Basel Confession in 1534[17] – all contributed to the creation of a very powerful religious legacy that was idealized and invoked in the eighteenth and nineteenth century in antagonistic response to the perceived threat of "modern scientific consciousness."[18] Importantly, Basel's earlier flowering of humanism never experienced a pagan stage, nor was it dominated by national interests.[19] From the beginning, its main interest was directed toward the sources of Christianity: learning was idealized, not in the Promethean sense of *Wissenschaft*, but rather as the modest handmaiden of Christian truth and ethical character formation.[20]

The ideal of Christian learning in Basel did not vanish in the seventeenth and eighteenth centuries, although the sixteenth century was certainly its golden period.[21] One extremely influential later figure – from whom Burckhardt's father would draw inspiration – should be mentioned: Samuel Werenfels (1657–1740) and his "moderate orthodoxy" (*gemilderte Orthodoxie*) or "rational orthodoxy" (*vernünftige Orthodoxie*).[22] With Erasmus as his model, Werenfels strove in numerous sermons, lectures, and publications to bring the truths of the Gospel into harmony with humanist learning and practical wisdom – to create "ad maiorum simplicitatem unitatemque." He even claimed that if learning was submitted to the Gospel one could learn from Voltaire without doubting the Basel Confession.[23] Werenfels initiated a serious study of biblical hermeneutics at Basel, but warned against over-interpretation.[24] He maintained that reason and revelation only appeared in conflict from a human perspective, and that the true religious life was not found in intellectual wrangling but in a "praxis pietatis," which emphasized "tolerantia, caritas, pax et sanctitas."[25] During his lifetime, Werenfels advocated the unification of the divided Protestant churches.[26]

Werenfels was by no means an anomaly among eighteenth-century Basel theologians. His plea for a "praxis Christianismi" was adopted by such figures as Hieronymous Burckhardt (1680–1737), Jacob Christoph Iselin (1681–1737), Johann Ludwig Frey (1682–1759), Johann Jakob Grynäus (1705–44), Jakob Christoph Beck (1711–85), Emanuel Ryhiner (1695–1792), Hans Balthasar Burckhardt (1710–92), Johann Wernhard Herzog (1726–1815), Jakob Meyer (1741–1813), Emanuel Merian (1765–1829) and Johann Rudolf Buxtorf (1747–1831). Practically all these men were native Baslers, but they were far from being provincial. All were polyglots in ancient and modern languages; each had spent time abroad – usually in Paris, Lyons, Geneva, and various German universities.[27] Hans Balthasar Burckhardt had sat, if skeptically, at the feet of Christian Wolff in Marburg before returning home to condemn his teacher.[28] Following Werenfels, these men advocated theological moderation and tolerance; but some doctrines were unnegotiable. A collective condemnation of the radical biblical critic in their midst, J. J. Wettstein (1693–1754), demonstrated that certain issues – in this case the doctrine of revelation and the inspiration of the canon – were by no means open to free interpretation. Truth should be kept to the essentials, but these essentials should be vigilantly upheld.[29]

Intellectual circles in Basel claimed their Reformation heritage and its continued relevance, especially the humanist synthesis between learning and faith, to a degree that put them largely at odds with more dominant theological trends. The church historian and de Wette's later colleague at Basel, Karl Rudolf Hagenbach, himself a Basler and an instructor of the young Jacob Burckhardt, noted with exasperation of his native city that "during the second half of the eighteenth century, Basel was hardly disturbed by the great developments in German theology. The whole *Sturm und Drang* period of rationalism in its various phases passed by the Basel church and university like a storm, which was only observed from a distance." "Neither Semler's criticism of the canon," noted Hagenbach further, "nor Kant's *Kritik der reinen Vernunft* unsettled [these theologians] from their self-satisfied allegiance to their fathers' glorious past."[30]

*　　*　　*

When pietism emerged in Basel in the mid-eighteenth century, it found sympathetic allies among university and church elites. The persistence of an ideal of "praxis pietatis" in the theological faculty resonated with many pietist emphases. By the end of the eighteenth century the alliance between church, university, and pietist pastors transformed Basel into an intellectual and missionary center of a revitalized Christian faith – what the historian

Paul Burckhardt has called a "Widerstandzentrum" against the Enlightenment.[31] Jacob Burckhardt's father, his grandfather, and many of his uncles were closely connected with this renewal of religious life and its vocal skepticism of secularizing trends in the late eighteenth and early nineteenth centuries.[32]

The so-called father of pietism in Basel was the Muttenz[33] pastor Hieronymus d'Annoni (1697–1770), who in his student years at the University of Basel had been influenced by Werenfels's moderate orthodoxy.[34] On a series of trips through Germany and Switzerland, d'Annoni encountered pietist-revival pastors and their supra-confessional, emotional expression of Christian faith. His resolution to join their ranks soon led to his own preaching of the pietist message of forgiveness, salvation, and love. His sermons in Muttenz drew large crowds from nearby Basel and prompted a religious "awakening" among the people.[35] Burckhardt's grandfather, Johann Rudolf Burckhardt, heard d'Annoni preach and later commented that "when I was fifteen years old I was stirred and awakened (*erweckt*) by his sermons and moved to pay heed to the one necessary thing."[36]

A second strand of pietism was introduced to Basel by the Herrnhuter community from northern Germany. In 1738, several emissaries from the pious community of Count Nikolaus von Zinzendorf (1700–60) arrived in the city preaching emotionally charged sermons.[37] A Herrnhuter *Brüdergemeinde* was formed, which soon numbered 500 members. Zinzendorf himself visited Basel on three occasions and formed a close friendship with d'Annoni.[38] Upon the death of Werenfels, Zinzendorf presented to the devout of Basel a long poem, in which he called Werenfels the "great Gamaliel" of modern Christendom and the University of Basel his "school of understanding."[39]

Although some separatists among the pietists ran afoul of Basel's public authorities, the ecclesiastical and academic establishment on the whole welcomed the new religious enthusiasm.[40] The event which brought d'Annoni's followers, the Herrnhuter community, university theologians, and the confessional church together was the founding of the German Christian Society (*Deutsche Christentumsgesellschaft*) in 1780.[41] The founder, the Augsburg theologian Johann August Urlsperger (1728–1806), left his theology post in Augsburg in 1776 and set out to establish a society to promote a "pure doctrine and true godliness."[42] Such a society was needed, he reasoned, to fight the godless effects of rationalism on the youths of Germany and Switzerland.[43] He judged Basel the best place to base the Society, because

the people in Basel have already proclaimed the good news for so long that they have gathered others to them. They have spared neither effort nor cost to improve their [spiritual] establishment. Moreover, they have upright men from all walks of life, who, with their prosperity, have the superior ability and desire to support this cause; and they live in a place of freedom, where the fewest hindrances will block their efforts.[44]

The Society began humbly enough with a private gathering of Urlsperger and several supportive Baslers – the theology professor, Johann Wernhard Herzog; the businessman Wilhelm Brenner; two young men, Georg David Schild and Jakob Friedrich Liesching; and two local pastors, Jakob Friedrich Meyenrock and Johann Rudolf Burckhardt, Jacob Burckhardt's grandfather.[45] The Christian pedagogy, the missionary activities, and the daughter organizations that ultimately arose from this group had far-reaching effects not only in Basel but throughout German-speaking Europe and beyond.[46] Already in 1784, the Society was perceived by the *Aufklärer* newspaper, the *Berlinischen Monatsschrift*, as a hindrance to free thought and it was condemned for its narrow-mindedness: "This spirit of antipathy against different ways of thinking shows that this institute is a true Protestant form of Jesuitism."[47]

Despite opposition from abroad, the activities of the *Christentumsgesellschaft* enjoyed widespread support in Basel. Its most important center was in St. Peters, the church that Johann Rudolf Burckhardt pastored for fifty-four years.[48] The Society's ideals also enjoyed acceptance among theology professors, especially from Johann Wernhard Herzog, whose interest in establishing ties between Basel's religious present and past can be seen in his massive *Athenae Rauricae*, a study of Basel's *Gelehrten* from the Reformation to his own day, and in a work on Erasmus.[49] Moreover, *Antistes* Emmanuel Merian, Hieronymous Falkeisen, and later Burckhardt's father, Jakob Burckhardt, faithfully supported the work of the Society. That such an expression of pietist religiosity enjoyed strong ecclesiastical and academic cooperation was rare, perhaps even unique, and set Basel apart from practically all other learning centers in Europe at the time. In this respect, the church historian Paul Wernle writes of "Basel's peculiarity" and claims that Basel "until the end of the [eighteenth] century and afterwards must be called a center of the Old Faith. It was the hub of the German Christian Society, which everywhere led the fight against rationalism in Switzerland and Germany for preserving the Old Faith."[50]

It would be an error simply to dismiss the religious elite in Basel as idiosyncratic anachronisms, wholly out of step with the "really" important intellectual currents of their time. To be sure, they were not "enlightened" men, looking to classical antiquity for models of knowledge and society and finding in Christian history only an "adversary worthy of their hostility."[51] Nonetheless, they were learned men, keenly aware of secular criticisms of the church, which they obviously perceived as a threat. It was for precisely this reason that they reclaimed a local Christian history to serve as a bulwark against the "Sapere-aude" ethos of German philosophy and its theological expression, rationalism, and against the *philosophes'* equation of supernatural Christianity with superstition. Thus, they turned to Basel's own legacy of Christian humanism to find a "useful past," with which to cultivate a sense of intellectual moderation, an ability to recognize the limits of human understanding in this world.

Not surprisingly, Basel's religious elite were dismayed, even horrified, at the terrors of the French Revolution and the Napoleonic period, and they tended to see the bloodshed and threat of Jacobinism as divine judgment on Enlightenment hubris. To a man, they opposed the Helvetic imposition in Basel (1798–1803) and strove to restore their native political and religious institutions afterward.[52] In the opinion of many, the Enlightenment had led to theories about society and human nature that oversimplified reality and did not adequately take divine agency into account. In a letter discussing Jacobinism to his son Johann, a medical student at Göttingen, Burckhardt's grandfather reflected this point of view precisely. In a tone comparable to Edmund Burke, J. R. Burckhardt wrote that "only a deep knowledge of history, human nature and practical experience [can] protect us so that we are not easily deceived by a beautiful system and then gladly relinquish the governance of the world from the wisdom of God."[53]

Many of J. R. Burckhardt's contemporaries were concerned that practical, pious wisdom was under attack in the modern world. To safeguard their worldview, they called for a restored understanding of the divine limitations placed on human thought. They wanted to curb the trend, stemming from the French Revolution, to reshape society with "beautiful systems."[54] That changing society *ipso facto* meant improvement was in many respects unthinkable to these men, accustomed as they were to religious sensibilities unsympathetic to the progressive ideologies of the Enlightenment. "For the power of sin and imperfection is so strong in us," read their cherished Basel Confession, "that reason cannot follow what it knows nor can the mind kindle a divine spark and fan it."[55] Jacobinism, Burckhardt's grandfather commented, "certainly looks wonderful in theory, but its practice shows where it leads."[56]

De Wette and the Theological Scene in Basel

Lecturing during the second half of the nineteenth century, the theology professor K. R. Hagenbach told his audience that de Wette's calling to Basel "was not only epoch-making for Basel's church and university, but also for the rest of Switzerland."[57] Indeed, the fact that such a modernizing theologian – advocating a very explicit and unorthodox "system" – wound up in "pious Basel" and became the most influential, albeit controversial, university professor in the city in the first part of the nineteenth century merits investigation. In the judgment of later liberals like Hagenbach, by gaining de Wette, Basel had procured for the first time a theologian bearing the latest philosophical and critical skills of the *Aufklärung*. De Wette's reputation, moreover, was associated with such learned German scholars as Herder, Kant, Schelling, Fries, Gabler, Paulus, and Schleiermacher. It is no surprise, then, that reactions to de Wette among Baslers varied from curiosity and quiet acceptance to deep consternation. Several upset pietists even regarded him as a precursor of the Anti-Christ.[58]

The theological faculty in Basel had been reorganized in 1818, but the chair in practical theology remained vacant because of funding shortages, its duties being temporarily executed by part-time help from local pastors and other faculty members.[59] The idea of nominating de Wette was initially put forward by Alexander Stein (1789–1833), a pastor in Sachsenhausen near Frankfurt and a former student of de Wette at Heidelberg. Aware of the vacancy in Basel, Stein wrote to his friend Karl Rudolpf Wolleb (1789–1866), pastor of the St. Elizabeth Church in Basel, suggesting that Basel had the opportunity to bring "the most learned living German theologian" to their university.[60] Wolleb conveyed the matter to *Bürgermeister* Johann H. Wieland (1758–1838), who also served as chancellor of the university. Wieland encouraged Wolleb to find out through Stein if de Wette actually had "true Christian theological views" and would accept the post despite a poor salary.[61] Stein wrote de Wette and received the reply that "any teaching position would be invaluable to me, so that I could overlook the small pay. I feel the loss of my activity as a teacher painfully. I would gladly accept the post in Basel if it is offered to me."[62] Stein conveyed the good news to Wolleb and also sent a copy of a letter of de Wette's to give evidence of his "true Christian theological views."[63]

In the meantime, Wolleb had been in contact with Wieland and other officials at the university. References were sought from de Wette's former colleagues at Heidelberg, including professors Creuzer, Daub, and Schwarz.[64] Each responded approvingly, testifying to de Wette's warm character, scholarly skills, and "very religious and Christian way of thinking."[65] Daub mentioned that de Wette's earlier removal to Berlin was felt as a tremendous loss at Heidelberg.[66] On 28 July 1821, a special committee of the university (the *Kuratel*) requested that the city's Education Committee (*Erziehungsrat*) appoint de Wette.[67]

Basel's theological faculty and conservative clergy, however, received news of the appointment and began to form an organized opposition against the more liberal Wieland and his associates. On 8 August, the theological faculty members, Johann Rudolf Buxtorf (1747–1831), Emanuel Merian (1765–1829), and Simon La Roche (1786–1861), along with the church *Antistes*, Hieronymous Falkeisen (1758–1838), disputed de Wette's orthodoxy, basing their argument on selected passages from de Wette's *Christliche Sittenlehre, Commentatio de morte Jesu Christi expiatoria, Lehrbuch der christlichen Dogmatik*, and his Old and New Testament Introductions.[68] These objections were then passed on to three referees, Pastor Wolleb, Johann Jakob Fäsch (1752–1832), and Rudolf Hanhardt (1780–1856), rector of Basel's *Pädagogium*. Here the matter stood for the rest of 1821.[69] On 17 January 1822, however, the Education Committee decided by a narrow eight votes to six to appoint de Wette; the decision was ratified two days later by the City Council (*Kleiner Rat*).[70] The liberal *Bürgermeister* Wieland expressed his preference for de Wette's theology over that of "our present guardians of piety."[71]

Immediately, however, Buxtorf, Merian, La Roche, and Falkeisen submitted a written protest to Wieland, claiming that de Wette's appointment was of utmost concern to the "church of the fatherland" (i.e., the church of Basel), because his views "endangered the highest points of church doctrine and stood against its basic principles." They asserted that their cause was not just about the person of de Wette; rather, there was "one decisive question": "whether rationalism or supernaturalism is to govern us, or in other words whether reason (*Vernunft*) is to be regarded as the highest judge in the things of faith or if the Bible is [to remain] the supreme foundation of faith (*oberster Erkenntnis-Grund des Glaubens*)?"[72] The city refused to rescind the decision, however, and de Wette was admitted to Basel, despite opposition from the head of Basel's church (Falkeisen) and from all his future colleagues in the theology department.

Aware of antagonism in Basel and reluctant to leave Weimar, de Wette nevertheless accepted the offer.[73] He arrived with his family on 3 May 1822, greeted by *Bürgermeister* Wieland and several members of the university. His presence would soon lead to the wholesale transformation of the theology department; he also reshaped the makeup of the university at large. Serving as rector five times, he ceaselessly strove to turn Basel into a center of *Wissenschaft* "in the German fashion" (*nach deutscher Art*).[74] His efforts to upgrade the theology department and university met persistent opposition on religious grounds from native Baslers. In the end, however, he found enough allies and generated sufficient trust to accomplish his aims and to reconstitute for himself the sphere of influence that he had sorely missed since his dismissal from Berlin.

De Wette's first two public speaking engagements in Basel gave him a needed boost among the citizens and paved the way for their gradual toleration of his theological outlook.[75] The first was a lecture given to various faculty members. In it he expressed gratitude to the people of Basel for the opportunity to teach again. In an effort to allay skepticism about his critical theology, he noted that "faith, above all inquiry and knowledge, is the

119

highest thing in Christianity and the final source of all truth." However, he also noted that the Bible, like Christ himself, "has a human and a divine aspect. It is the source of all divine truth, but it is conveyed in human language and with human forms of representation. Therefore, it is simultaneously a matter of historical research and of faith."[76]

Pastor Wolleb invited de Wette to speak a second time. De Wette accepted and on 26 May 1822 he preached a sermon at St. Elizabeth's church entitled "Von der Prüfung der Geister" based on I John 4: 1–3. Beginning with the Pentecost of Acts 2, de Wette commented on the spirit of Christ and its transmission through the ages. He especially praised the Reformation and its creeds, but added that all formulations of faith ultimately have the "characteristic of human incompleteness, because they were brought into being by the requirements of the time (*Bedürfniß der Zeiten*), and are the work of men." The true criterion of the spirit of Christ, he concluded, is the free spirit of inquiry exercised by those who believe in Christ. Such individuals will necessarily work toward harmony with one another.[77]

The sermon, which makes no reference to Christ in atoning terms, nevertheless had the effect of convincing the audience of de Wette's sincerity and thereby assuring him a tolerated niche in Basel's tighly knit religious community. Of crucial importance was the reaction of the prominent professor of French, Alexandre Vinet (1797–1847). Formerly a leading opponent of de Wette, Vinet became convinced of de Wette's sincerity, began to attend his lectures in exegetical theology, and subsequently made efforts to win Basel's approval for the new professor by translating a copy of de Wette's first sermon into French. "His doctrine has not always been the same," Vinet wrote to a friend, "[but] he has searched for the truth in good faith and has progressively found it."[78] Through Vinet's influence, many city officials and members of the more liberal legal and medical faculties came to back de Wette.[79]

Having secured a modicum of acceptance, de Wette launched an attempt to reform the theological faculty, which he deemed drastically behind the times, despite the earlier university reforms of 1818. His two colleagues, Buxtorf and Merian, both approaching retirement, were contemptuous of his goals.[80] Despite protests, they were unable to thwart de Wette, who also enjoyed the backing of university chancellor and *Bürgermeister* Wieland. A 15 December 1822 faculty meeting considered a proposal from de Wette for a four-year curriculum for theology students, the years being divided respectively into exegetical, historical, systematic, and practical theology. This plan was ultimately accepted and remained in practice for the next twenty-five years.[81]

De Wette was particularly concerned about the lack of historical instruction in the old curriculum. To remedy this, he designed three obligatory courses for first- and second-year students: "History and Antiquity of the Hebrews," "Church History" (*Kirchengeschichte*), and "The History of Dogma" (*Dogmengeschichte*). He also petitioned the Education Committee to hire an official Church historian. At first, de Wette advocated for this position a former colleague at Heidelberg, Karl Ullmann (1796–1865), but his suggestion was rejected.[82] De Wette then successfully secured the appointment of Karl Rudolf Hagenbach as a part-time lecturer. A native Basler, Hagenbach had studied theology in Berlin and was sympathetic to de Wette's desire to improve the standards of *Wissenschaft* at Basel.[83] With the retirement of Buxtorf in 1828 and the death of Merian in 1829, de Wette and Hagenbach became the sole members of the theology faculty. To fill Merian's chair, the Education Committee decided to elevate Hagenbach to Professor Ordinarius, despite the objections of many who felt he was the mere echo of de Wette. Two young *Dozenten* were also hired at this time.[84]

Although he enjoyed initial institutional success, throughout the 1820s and 1830s de Wette still faced strong opposition from orthodox and pietist circles in Basel. The young E. W. Hengstenberg, who was later appointed to de Wette's chair in Berlin, noted after a trip to Basel in 1823 that the people of Basel consider de Wette "a thorn in the flesh. They claim he is not a Christian, as many told me directly, and they seek ways to malign him."[85] De Wette's most vocal critic was Christian Friedrich Spittler (1782–1867), founder of the *Basler Mission* and the first secretary of the German Christian Society.[86] Extremely conservative and pietist in his views, Spittler condemned de Wette's lectures as "heathen" and forbade students at the Mission to attend them. In 1823, Spittler and several others gathered objectionable statements from de Wette's publications and circulated them among the people of Basel.[87] In 1825, de Wette received from this same group a formal call to renounce the blasphemous utterances of his works. In an accompanying letter, Spittler urged de Wette to consider those for whom the Bible was the chief authority of faith and to think about how parents felt about their children, adrift in a "sea of uncertain opinions and systems," and not to deny them their true anchor of faith.[88] In a reply to Spittler, de Wette defended his views and rebuked Spittler for circulating passages of his *Commentatio de morte Jesu Christi* in German, because de Wette claimed they were written for theological experts and could easily be misunderstood.[89] Spittler replied that de Wette stood on weak ground dividing expert and nonexpert Christians; Luther, Spittler asserted, had done away with that division.[90]

The period of the *Basler Wirren* of 1830–33 brought de Wette again into conflict with Basel's conservative Christians. The *Wirren* (or "troubles") refer to the period in Basel's history when landowners in the countryside, inspired by the Paris July Revolution of 1830, rebelled against the city government. The *Land* dwellers felt that they were underrepresented in the government in relation to their numbers and their tax burden. They also resented supporting the university, given that they derived little benefit from it. Their grievances were brought before the City Council, but on 18 October 1830 the Council decided against lowering taxes. On 4 January 1831 the landowners, backed by a small army, responded by bringing an ultimatum to the city, demanding a more representative government. Again the Council refused. Skirmishes soon broke out. Periodic fighting continued until 3 August 1833, when the country actually defeated the city. Shortly thereafter, the Swiss Confederation intervened and divided the canton politically into *Basel-Land* and *Basel-Stadt*.[91]

These events bore upon de Wette, because the *Wirren* precipitated in the city an apocalyptic mood among many of the pietists, who felt that God must be judging their city for wrongdoing. In August 1833, *Der graue Mann*, a locally circulated journal, blamed the university for the *Wirren* because of its "rebellion against the heavenly sovereignty of Jesus Christ." The reason given was that the university had provided refuge to enemies of the public order who had fled from Prussia (de Wette was obviously intended). Basel had thus shared in the sins of others. Moreover, these so-called martyrs to the cause of freedom in north Germany were becoming intellectual despots in Basel and were thus responsible for the present blood and murder.[92] De Wette and Carl Gustav G. Jung (1794–1864),[93] his colleague in the medical faculty, attempted to sue the editor, E. J. G. de Valenti, for libel; however, their case was rejected by the court and they even had costs awarded against them.[94] De Wette published an account of the affair in an attempt to clear his and the university's name.[95] Overall, the accusation in *Der graue Mann*, the landowner rebellion, and, earlier, the Spittler affair, had the effect of inciting much public skepticism against the University of Basel and the Prussian "heretics" it supported.

Opposition to the university also had an outside source. In 1829–30, many cantons had agitated for the establishment of a single university for Switzerland and for the closure of all others. De Wette had defended the existence of the University of Basel. However, two Basler professors had sided with the opposition – Wilhelm Snell (1789–1851), professor of law, and Ignaz Paul Vital Troxler (1780–1866), professor of philosophy. Troxler was rector of the university at the time and attempted to sway citizens and students to his opinion. Again, pietist disapproval of de Wette and taxpayer disaffection in the countryside tilted large segments of the populace toward Troxler's camp; after all, was not the university a drain on public expenditure and a haven for suspect theologians? Ultimately, however, nothing came of Troxler's efforts. The actual fate of the university was decided by the 1833 settlement negotiated by the Swiss Confederation, in which *Basel-Stadt* was given full custody of the university and forced to pay the countryside 331,451 francs in compensation.[96] The near defunct university now faced an acute funding crisis as well as continued opposition from the city's pietists. Among others, Professor Alexandre Vinet feared that the university would be forced out of operation.[97] De Wette too had written to a friend, "The termination of the university is to be feared."[98]

De Wette's fears prompted him to work for the university's preservation; for such efforts he was elected rector in 1834. His rectorial address of 1834 stands out all the more when one considers its immediate historical background. "Einige Betrachtungen über den Geist unserer Zeit" was delivered by de Wette on 12 September 1834. In it de Wette condemned the effects of rationalism and materialism in contemporary intellectual and political life, and contrasted them to the spirit of "genuine *Wissenschaftlichkeit*," which alone had the power to animate university and civic life.[99] He called for the people of Basel to be intellectually and spiritually awakened, and made clear that the survival of the university was not only imperative for Basel, but for the good of humanity. He claimed this out of love for

> ... [the] high meaning of *Wissenschaft* and the enthusiasm I carry for it, which filled my soul from an early age to adulthood and shall fill it beyond. I would venture to say this out of love for Basel and out of a clear knowledge of her needs. Also, I would venture to express again today that the question concerning the continuance and reestablishment of our university is truly a vital question for Basel.[100]

De Wette observed further that Basel had the potential to become a "bastion of *Wissenschaft*, where the holy flame of truth is kept," a university that would spread light throughout the world and would become the first university "in the German sense" (*im deutschen Sinne*) in Switzerland.[101] To this end, he committed himself and encouraged others to follow in order that the university not come to an end.

And indeed it did not. "Just the opposite," according to Andreas Staehelin: largely because of de Wette's efforts, the university began to thrive and came to be "supported ideally and materially by the citizenry as never before in the history of the city."[102] The work that de Wette had begun in the 1820s survived the *Wirren* and gradually led to the regeneration of the university, which later in the century would host such luminaries as Franz Overbeck, Friedrich Nietzsche, Jakob Bachofen, Wilhelm Dilthey, and, of course, Jacob Burckhardt. "This regeneration," observed Edgar Bonjour, "was above all tied with the character of one man: Wilhelm Martin Leberecht de Wette."[103]

In short, through his efforts in the 1820s and 1830s, de Wette succeeded in establishing the ideal of *Wissenschaft* at the University of Basel. Moreover, what he had previously hoped to accomplish on a large scale in Berlin – namely, instigate the "transformation of the essence of the church"[104] as he put it in *Über Religion und Theologie* – was on a smaller scale realized in the theological curriculum at Basel. Theology there would no longer rest on Basel's idealized Reformation heritage but on the critical premises of post-Kantian modernity. Indeed, in less than two decades after his arrival, de Wette had turned Basel, a backwater among European universities, into a fledgling center of *Wissenschaft* "im deutschen Sinne."

The *Aufklärung* had come, belatedly, to Basel.

Jakob Burckhardt, the Elder (*Antistes*)

On 4 June 1818, Jacob Burckhardt was baptized into Christendom at Basel's city cathedral. A proud and hopeful family attended the event. His mother had written earlier to a friend: "May his heavenly father be pleased to register him in the Book of Life." Burckhardt's father also rejoiced, glad to oversee this important event in the Christian upbringing of his first son.[105]

Considering Burckhardt's later disavowal of the faith of his father, the relationship between the two is undoubtedly worthy of exploration. Regrettably, its precise nature remains a mystery on account of Burckhardt's decision after his father's death to destroy most of their correspondence.[106] Because of the dearth of evidence, Werner Kaegi has warned against overdramatizing a conflict between father and son.[107] I too am persuaded that no major conflict took place. Yet there are too many dangling issues to let the matter simply rest.[108] Despite the absence of an overt emotional conflict, there were nonetheless dramatic differences between the two men's understanding of Christian faith and its relationship to the modern world. Burckhardt's father, like his own pietist father (J. R. Burckhardt), believed that recent political and social events in Europe as well as the spread of modern scientific consciousness threatened the very heart of the Christian (specifically the Basler Protestant) understanding of God, society, and human beings. For Burckhardt's father, this secular threat occasioned a return to a Protestant theology based on apostolic confessions and the Bible as well as a recovery of the local humanist legacies of Erasmus and Werenfels.[109] In short, he turned to a humanist, orthodox, and highly pastoral theological vision to ward off the perceived threat of modernity. His traditional stance stood in sharp contrast to de Wette's innovative critical and aesthetic positions. It would be the fate of the young Jacob Burckhardt to experience the tension between the world of his father and the *Wissenschaftlichkeit* of de Wette.

Interestingly, some twenty years before his son encountered de Wette, Jakob Burckhardt (Jacob's father) briefly encountered de Wette's teachings as a theology student at Heidelberg, where de Wette was then a lecturer.

124

Dismayed by de Wette's critical treatment of the Bible, Jakob Burckhardt reported home to his father:

> De Wette gives the introductory lecture on the Old Testament. He takes an approach which is all his own. For example, he asserts that the Pentateuch is not by Moses and that the texts of Solomon are not by Solomon. Moses, David, Solomon are collective names, to which one ascribes everything found written in their spirit. Despite all this, [de Wette still claims] they are not unauthentic. He asserts that Jonah is a didactic fairy tale.[110]

Skeptical of the young de Wette, Jakob Burckhardt turned to a more kindred spirit in the theologian Karl Daub, who, "is the crown of the theological faculty," he noted to his father, "[and] has . . . true orthodox faith, i.e., he believes that Jesus came into the world in order to save sinners."[111] He soon ceased attending de Wette's lectures altogether, in order to concentrate on courses more congenial to his own pietist and orthodox heritage.[112]

Jakob Burckhardt completed his theological studies at Heidelberg with a strong desire to become a pastor like his father; he was especially interested in theological pedagogy.[113] In 1810, he returned to Basel, married, and later procured a pastorship at a small church in Lausen. In 1816 he was elected to the position of *Obersthelfer*, or archdeacon, at the Basel cathedral, where his principal assignment was the instruction of the young. Importantly: during Jacob Burckhardt's entire youth, his father was in charge of Sunday morning children's services as well as special *Hauskinderlehre* in his home during the week.[114]

Jakob Burckhardt viewed his work as a contribution to undoing the regrettable period of the Helvetic Republic, which had attempted to separate church and state in Basel and, in the opinion of many, had introduced a dangerous godlessness among the youth. Indeed, the city's conservative clergy despised the Helvetic imposition and after its full burden was removed in 1815, clergymen labored to purge the city of its legacy.[115] The commemoration of the Reformation in 1819 was designed especially for this purpose; it attempted to reanimate Basel's traditional church life by fostering an atmosphere of continuity with the original church-state settlement of the Reformation.[116]

For this occasion, Jakob Burckhardt penned a short book, *Kurze Geschichte der Reformation in Basel*, complete with a picture of the city's reformer Oecolampadius on the title page and a preface written by the *Antistes*, Hieronymus Falkeisen. It was written explicitly for the "edification" (*Erbauung*) of the citizens of Basel, encouraging them to remain true to apostolic teachings.[117] In brief, Jakob Burckhardt attempted in this work to demonstrate that Basel played no minor role in the Reformation movement of the sixteenth century; he mentioned the attempted church reforms at the medieval Council of Basel, he showed the importance of the printing industry in the city, and he lauded the writings of Erasmus. The book's main protagonist, however, is the reformer, Oecolampadius, whose humanist erudition and mediating theological behavior led to Basel's peaceful acceptance of the Reformation in 1529. "Oecolampadius," the senior Burckhardt wrote, "was the guardian angel, through which God then protected and blessed our country and city. May his spirit live in the heart of each Basler as long as his grave is within our city walls."[118]

On 10 January 1819, Jakob Burckhardt gave a special sermon for children on the meaning of the Reformation in Basel. Citing reformers' writings and biblical passages as evidence, he spoke of the Reformation as a "work of God" and invoked the city's reformers as models of piety and learning. He admonished the children to "make the period of your youth count, for you [too] will be responsible before your conscience, before the fatherland, and before God." He urged the children to dispel any "vile gossip" among townspeople who might think of them as "impious, lazy, and rebellious." Rather, they should make a "covenant with God" and strive to become "pious, obedient, moral, and industrious."[119]

The senior Burckhardt's most far-reaching accomplishment as *Obersthelfer* was the drafting of a new catechism for the young. *Lehrbuch des christlichen Religionsunterrichtes für die Kirchen des Kantons Basel, Zum Gebrauch für die Kinderlehre und für den Confirmationsunterricht* was published and put into use in 1832.[120] The cover page includes a passage from the New Testament book II Timothy, in which Paul exhorts his spiritual protégé Timothy to "follow the pattern of the sound words you have heard from me, in faith and love which are in Christ Jesus; guard the truth that has been entrusted to you by the Holy Spirit who dwells within us."[121]

Karl Barth has called Jakob Burckhardt's catechism a classic example of "Basler orthodoxy" – a moderate orthodoxy written in the spirit of Samuel Werenfels.[122] Kaegi described it as a "confrontation with the powers of the times," in which one can see the "old protestant Republic in its purity."[123] The catechism consists of three parts: a doctrine of faith (*Glaubenslehre*), a doctrine of ethics (*Sittenlehre*), and a doctrine of salvation (*Lehre von den Mitteln des Heils*). In a short preface, *Antistes* Falkeisen made clear that Burckhardt's catechism was the appropriate antidote against these "present, sad times" where, more than before, "unbelief and lack of restraint" characterized the young people.[124] The catechism was completed when Jacob Burckhardt was fifteen years old, and there could hardly be a document more revealing of his father's religious character, not to mention of Burckhardt's own early religious instruction. The young Burckhardt would surely have known most of the catechism by heart.[125]

In regard to Burckhardt's religious upbringing, two aspects of the catechism are of crucial importance. The first is its strong emphasis on the idea of original sin. In the section entitled, "Von dem Sündenfalle," a question reads: "What makes up original sin (*Erbsünde*)?" "That I by nature," the young catechists would respond, "am inclined to sin; as the Scripture says: every thought and action of the human heart is evil from childhood on." "Did this disobedience of the first parents affect only them?" goes another question. "No," respond the children, "rather as through one person, sin came into the world, and death through sin, so death spread to all people because all have sinned."[126]

The catechism does not reflect the notion of total depravity after associated with strict Calvinism. Question 103 reads: "Did original sin destroy the good design of humans?" Answer given: "No, there are still traces of the image of God to be seen."[127] Other question-answer sets echo this notion, speaking of humankind as the crown of creation, endowed with free will, designed as children of God to enjoy eternal life. For all this, however, the catechism is clear on the point that any goodness attributable to human beings derives solely from the fact that they were originally "created in the image of God."[128] Apart from God, all goodness is ultimately subject to corruption.[129]

Second, the catechism speaks of Christ as the incarnate Son of God and the redeemer of fallen humanity – the *sine qua non* of traditional Protestant orthodoxy. In the section "Von Jesu Christo, dem Sohn Gottes, unserem Erlöser," question 149 reads: "Why is he called Jesus, that is a savior?" Answer: "Because he came into the world to seek and save that which was lost." Further, Jesus was no mere envoy from God; he was simultaneously God and man, the "only begotten of the father . . . [in whom] lives incarnate the complete fullness of divinity."[130]

Antistes Falkeisen saw the catechism as a major triumph against the "present, sad times." The senior Burckhardt's clerical peers and the cathedral congregation also admired the diligent work of the *Obersthelfer* on behalf of the children of Basel. Thus widely esteemed, Jakob Burckhardt was chosen Falkeisen's successor upon the latter's death in 1838. In this year, the senior Burckhardt became the seventeenth *Antistes* of Basel's Reformed church, the first of whom was none other than the reformer Oecolampadius.[131] He became, in other words, the single most important leader of the Protestant church community in Basel, the "supervisor (*Vorsteher*) of all the clergymen of the Reformed church in our section of the canton" and the "leading pastor of the [city's] cathedral."[132]

On Sunday 25 November 1838, with I Timothy 3:1 as his text,[133] Jakob Burckhardt delivered his inaugural sermon, in which he recognized the many joys, responsibilities, but also potential abuses that came with a high clerical position. The new *Antistes* expressed deep gratitude for his listeners' trust in him and vowed to remain a worthy " 'under-shepherd' of the head shepherd, Jesus Christ."[134] "My family and I desire to serve the Lord," he proclaimed, for "such a household is not just an encouragement in itself, but also a blessing for the people of God."[135] He ended the sermon with a prayer, asking God to discipline him like a son if he went astray, but "teach me," he prayed, "that I may also teach others, lead me that I may also lead others."[136]

Jakob Burckhardt faithfully executed his office for twenty years until his death in 1858. He was the last *Antistes* to be buried in the cathedral's courtyard. Besides overseeing the needs of the church, he found time for a number of intellectual hobbies: coin collecting, writing amateur historical essays, and traveling were among his favorites. Apart from the early death of his first wife (Jacob Burckhardt's mother) in 1830, his family relations were idyllic.[137]

As the oldest son, Jacob Burckhardt had a special place in his father's affections. The most revealing document of their early relationship is an 1832 New Year's letter from Burckhardt. Written in Greek, presumably to impress his father with the progress of his language skills, the young Burckhardt wrote:

> I wish you happiness, health, long life, and joy without end. Forgive me, father, and please don't think of my frequent and large mistakes. . . . Almighty God will send me the strength that I need, so that I can be better this year than in the one before. I just want to thank you immensely for all that you have given me – all that I ever needed. Every day you have given me something new. May God almighty give you his divine protection – this I wish for you.[138]

Several early letters express similar sentiments. However, again, detailed knowledge of their relationship, especially their mature relationship, is inaccessible because Burckhardt destroyed their post-1838 correspondence.

By most standards Burckhardt's father would not classify as an "intellectual." However, he was far from being a parochial pastor (as most commentators on Burckhardt assume) and his influence on Burckhardt's early outlook was presumably great. His studies at Heidelberg and his pastorship in Basel brought him into contact (often antagonistically) with many contemporary intellectual developments. Like others, he viewed de Wette's coming to Basel with trepidation, referring to de Wette in one letter – perhaps with his Heidelberg experience in mind – bluntly as an "enemy."[139] Simultaneously, however, he expressed admiration for de Wette's writings and was disturbed by the pietists' tendency to condemn him outright. "Sometimes we must learn truth from our enemies," he wrote to a friend, summing up his position on the matter.[140] When Schleiermacher visited de

Wette in Basel in 1830, the senior Burckhardt, then *Obersthelfer*, was invited to a dinner with "the greatest teachers of German theology," he recalled in a letter afterward.[141]

Despite his guarded attitude toward de Wette, Burckhardt's father had much respect for *Wissenschaft*, and frequently used the term. However, his understanding of its practice had more in common with sixteenth-century humanism than with the Kantian concerns, critical methods, and research spirit characteristic of the German Enlightenment. For this reason, he openly regretted in 1829 the fact that modern *Wissenschaft* and faith were so far apart and he felt their division posed dangers for theology students. Nevertheless, he expressed a belief in the "progress of *Wissenschaft*" and felt, presumably with his son in mind, that God would soon raise up a learned "fighter for the evangelical point of view."[142]

Perhaps the best description of *Antistes* Burckhardt was given by his nephew, J. J. Oeri, who described his uncle as "a catechist of God's grace, a born evangelist of the young, neither rationalist nor pietist, but simply and thoroughly a Bible-believing Christian (*Bibelchrist*), knowledgeable in both history and art, and all-around well-educated."[143]

Burckhardt's *Theologiestudium*

"With every breath of fresh air, *Wissenschaft* lays bare the disintegration of the Church as an inner fact, and hastens it as an external one," Burckhardt (the younger) wrote in 1844 to his friend, the theologian Willibald Beyschlag.[144] A few months later, to Gottfried Kinkel, he stated: "That Christianity has its great ages behind it is as evident to me as the fact that twice two is four . . . [and] I am really sorry for the present restorers (*Restauratoren*)."[145] Burckhardt wrote these letters after completing his historical studies at the University of Berlin. He had given up the study of theology with de Wette in Basel some four years earlier, convinced that critical theology, by exposing the mythic nature of early Christianity, had more or less put itself out of business.

Burckhardt's "Übergang zur Geschichtswissenschaft," as he described it, was undoubtedly the most consequential decision of his early years. The letters in his correspondence concerning the religious crisis that led to this decision are among the most revealing documents of his private life – before the onset, in his later years, of his characteristic irony, his reticence about personal religious matters, and a desire to "live *par distance* from other clever people."[146]

For our purposes, it is of no small importance that Burckhardt's decision for history over theology was precipitated by a confrontation with intellectual conditions ascendent in late-*Aufklärung* theology and biblical criticism, which confronted him in the person of de Wette. The young Burckhardt, catechized in the humanist "Basler orthodoxy" of his father, collided head-on with one of the most sophisticated biblical critics and theological "restorers" of post-Kantian German Protestantism. The collision proved to have far-reaching ramifications in Burckhardt's later intellectual development, especially (as I argue in chapter five) in setting in motion a skeptical, reactionary pattern against theological liberalism and philosophical modernity and in shaping his own epistemological and anthropological convictions.

Burckhardt's transition from theology to history should not be characterized simply as a private, temperamental choice – that is, he did not just switch fields. At issue for him was the very legitimacy of a Christiantheological outlook and the knowledge about the world it presupposed. Viewed in this light, his "Übergang" exemplifies a more pervasive shift among nineteenth-century intellectuals from allegiance to the beliefs of orthodox Christianity to the weakening, and often outright disavowal, of the possibility of faith through historicization and relativization.[147] Burckhardt's early *Auseinandersetzung* with Christian faith and liberal theology offers a window into a constellation of mid-nineteenth-century intellectual energies and moods, which encouraged the young Burckhardt to restrict his understanding of human existence to its culturally or historically graspable dimensions and, accordingly, to distance himself from modern, speculative theological and philosophical modes of thought. In de Wette's terms, Burckhardt erred by expanding the epistemological authority of *Wissen* at the expense of *Glaube* and *Ahnung*. Similar to de Wette's fictional Theodor, Burckhardt thus found himself on the slippery slope of doubt. But unlike Theodor, Burckhardt's doubt stemmed less from eighteenth-century rationalism than from the flux of nineteenth-century historicism transmitted to him in de Wette's biblical criticism.

*   *   *

The initial "historicist turn" in Burckhardt's thinking occurred in his first semester at the University of Basel. De Wette's lobbying for a church historian affected Burckhardt directly, for it was in the lectures on *Kirchengeschichte* and *Dogmengeschichte*, given by de Wette's "echo," K. R. Hagenbach, that Burckhardt first experienced a thorough historical (and *wissenschaftlich*) treatment of Christianity. Unlike de Wette, however, Hagenbach was no theological original and besides the historical stimulus of his lectures he seems to have had no disturbing effect on Burckhardt.[148] The lectures covered major aspects of Christianity in Europe from the apostolic period through the *Aufklärung*, with an emphasis on doctrinal changes, heresies, and important theological personalities.[149] Burckhardt's

130

Nachschriften to these lectures are among the most detailed of his entire *Theologiestudium.*[150]

In the Winter semester of 1837–8, Burckhardt recorded in his notes that "the church is a religious community, which has its roots in the *historical* Jesus of Nazareth; it is an *historically-given* appearance. . . . The church is not simply a concept derived from pure abstraction." Elsewhere he noted that "church history rests on (*ruht auf*) world history."[151] Viewing "sacred history" from the standpoint of "world history" was Hagenbach's principal challenge to his students at Basel, and Burckhardt's notes clearly reflect this. Toward the end of his life, in a conversation with the theologian Arnold von Salis, Burckhardt held up Hagenbach as a model church historian, noting that "church history can only be properly written from a secular point of view."[152]

Admittedly, from lecture notes alone it is impossible to establish the complete extent of Burckhardt's encounter with Hagenbach. However, it is indisputable that these lectures were the first in which the young Burckhardt encountered a systematic, historical-critical presentation of the background of his own religious convictions. All the more impressive to Burckhardt would have been the knowledge that Hagenbach himself was a Basler, albeit one whose Berlin theology degree had invested him with the authority of German *Wissenschaft.* In short, Hagenbach's lectures were a far cry from the celebratory Reformation history and edifying sermons of Burckhardt's father.[153]

By far, however, the encounter with de Wette and its far-reaching consequences remain the central point in assessing Burckhardt's intellectual development as a theology student. Burckhardt's biographer Werner Kaegi has observed that de Wette is the "crucial question" of Burckhardt's theological studies and that his influence on the young Burckhardt appears "extraordinary."[154]

Besides tutorials in homiletics, Burckhardt took the following courses from de Wette: the book of Acts during the winter semester of 1837–8; Romans, Proverbs, and dogmatics during the summer semester of 1838; I and II Corinthians and de Wette's *Glaubenslehre* during the winter semester of 1838–9; and Isaiah during the summer semester of 1839. Burckhardt would have been exposed to de Wette's historical-critical exegesis and to his speculative theology – the latter especially in the course on dogmatics and in the *Glaubenslehre.*[155]

In a letter of 28 August 1838, Burckhardt first conveyed his reaction to de Wette to his friend Johannes Riggenbach (1818–90), who was then studying theology in Berlin.[156] "In my eyes, Burckhardt wrote,

> de Wette's system grows in stature every day; one simply *must* follow him, there is no alternative; but every day a part of our traditional church doc-

trine melts away under his hand. Today, finally, I realized that he regards the birth of Christ simply as a myth – and that I do too. And I shuddered as a number of reasons struck me why this almost *must* be so.[157] [Burckhardt's emphasis]

Moreover, Burckhardt indicated that de Wette was no lone radical voice but that his views, unlike the orthodox counter-reaction in theology, were in line with the "tremendous advance in theology of the last and present century."[158]

Burckhardt became certain that the "tremendous advance in theology," mediated to him through de Wette, had rendered a devastating criticism of revelation-based Protestant orthodoxy, the faith of his youth. Significantly, he experienced this neither as a liberation from ideology (à la Marx's reading of Strauss, Bauer, and Feuerbach) nor as the unmasking of an illusion leading to nihilism (à la Nietzsche's reading of Strauss). Burckhardt's response was profoundly ambivalent – in large part because of his identity as "filius Antistitis," as Hagenbach once referred to him.[159] A combination of deep-seated local religious and emotional factors tempered Burckhardt's confrontation with de Wette's application of myth criticism to the person of Christ. In the act of accepting de Wette's criticism, Burckhardt became puzzled: while he was persuaded by the authority of de Wette's *Wissenschaftlichkeit*, he was also extremely uncertain of the condition and future of his own religious standpoint. One can even detect a trace of wistfulness:

> For the moment I cannot look the ruins of my former convictions in the face. De Wette is certainly on guard against getting too deeply involved in the conclusions of his arguments, and I can only follow his example in not merely demolishing (*bloß einreißt*), but also in rebuilding (*wieder aufbaut*), but the result is less reassuring than what has been destroyed.[160]

Although Burckhardt never wavered in accepting de Wette's criticism, he did soon become skeptical of de Wette's efforts at theological "rebuilding." In a subsequent letter to Riggenbach, Burckhardt complained that on many points de Wette was "eternally as dark as night" and that de Wette's Christian doctrine at root consisted "of all the old stuff trotted out in unintelligible terms (*unverständlichen Worten*), and as a result [it] sometimes looks new. De Wette's only real strength seems to be criticism."[161]

Burckhardt's vacillation between an acceptance of de Wette's criticism on one hand and an increasing skepticism of de Wette's theological reconstruction on the other remained constant during the remainder of Burckhardt's theological studies. Like de Wette, Burckhardt became critical (even contemptuous) of orthodox and pietist reactions in theology, deeming them timid retreats from theological progress.

Cases of desperate pietism (*Desperationspietisten*) are common enough in the pulpit and in the lecture room; people are often intolerant because they fear that a new religious idea might sound like a clap of thunder in their conscience and wake them from their sleep. . . . What a comfortable time the orthodox have! They deafen one another mutually and enjoy universal recognition and inward peace simultaneously. Of course anyone who determines to set his mind to rest will have no trouble in doing so. I simply cannot make up my mind to do it.[162]

Burckhardt also complained to Riggenbach about the present "miserable juste-milieu between supernaturalism and rationalism," citing the *Dozent* J. J. Staehelin as a "terrible example of the positions theologians sometimes reach trying to be enlightened and orthodox at the same time."[163]

Burckhardt did not achieve "inward peace"; rather he vowed to remain an "honest heretic" and in a letter to the Freiburg historian Heinrich Schreiber described his condition as "apostasy."[164] He also confessed experiencing periods of "crisis," during which he brooded in what he called his "theological lumber room" (*theologische Rumpelkammer*).[165] Burckhardt made his condition known to no one, apart from a select group of correspondents. Along with Riggenbach, he confided in Alois Emanuel Biedermann (1819–85) and Friedrich von Tschudi (1820–86), both theology students at Basel. Nearly a year after his decision to embrace de Wette's *Kritik*, Burckhardt wrote von Tschudi that he had been "living in a state of great inner uncertainty regarding the highest questions of life." "Do not blame me," he continued,

for not admitting the fact, for I hardly admitted it to myself and drove away each crisis with violent distractions, sometimes of a studious order, at other times in society. I had a whole army of figures in reserve with which to distract my imagination from the ever more pressing problem of my condition, of my relation to God and the world. And now here I am grubbing about in the ruins of my former view of life, trying to discover what is still usable in the old foundations. . . . Abyss after abyss opens at my feet.[166]

No letters exist from Burckhardt to Alois Emanuel Biedermann, who became Switzerland's most renowned Hegelian theologian in the mid-nineteenth century.[167] This is unfortunate because statements in other letters suggest that Burckhardt's early relationship with Biedermann was among his closest.[168] Thus, it is all the more significant that their friendship came apart over theological issues. After his studies in Basel, Biedermann too studied in Berlin; however, he continued in theology. He soon came under the spell of the Hegelian system – referring to Hegel once as the greatest individual since Jesus Christ – and also referred to himself as an "enthusiastic Straussian."[169] Accordingly, he sided with the liberal faction in Zurich's "Strauss affair" of 1839. Biedermann's optimistic belief in the future of liberal theology and his radicalism in favor of Strauss did not sit well with Burckhardt.[170] "Biedermann and I have become alien to one another," he wrote von Tschudi in 1839;[171] and a few months later he noted that "things remain tense with Biedermann. Those from Zurich, here in Berlin like everywhere, are . . . full of philosophical hot-air (*philosophischen Schwadronierens*)."[172] The political commotion surrounding Strauss gave Burckhardt deep misgivings about the future of theology. "What happened in Zurich," Burckhardt commented to Schreiber, "reminded me again of how dangerous and sinful it would be, in times such as these, when the position of the Church is so unsettled, to dedicate one's life to theology without the clearest inner call."[173]

Burckhardt never found an "inner call." "There is no revelation, that I know," he wrote to Riggenbach, expressing a desire to "leave dogma and revelation on one side" and devote himself only to the historical aspect of theology.[174] Ultimately however, history alone became his new life's dedication. "Next autumn, it has now been decided," he wrote in May of 1839, "I go to Berlin; but I am thankful to say that it is now quite clear to me that I shall not make theology, nor indeed find in it, my life's work."[175]

* * *

Kaegi interpreted Burckhardt's reticence on matters of faith and family as a mere matter of temperament and claimed that much continuity existed between Burckhardt, his father, and their common humanist, orthodox heritage in Basel.[176] I shall argue, however, that such continuity is largely a fiction, and that Burckhardt's crisis (a crisis, not simply a religious mutation in which the "deeper essence of Christianity" was maintained) caused a major rift between Burckhardt's religious orientation and that of the tightly knit, congregational, catechetical world of his father, and the pious, humanist sensibilities that his father and generations of Basel's elites had cultivated.

On 29 May 1839, Burckhardt told von Tschudi that he would conduct him to "the most secret chamber of my being," (*die geheimsten Gewölbe meines Innern*). Thereafter, Burckhardt wrote:

> My family knows, or at any rate suspects, the changing of my religious convictions. I told you once about my eldest, married sister; in her goodness she is the living image of my mother, who lived and died a saint. Not long ago I argued somewhat fierily with her in favor of freedom of belief, though one ought never to do so with women, because, unlike us, they

cannot fight with the weapons of learning, so that we only cause them grief.[177]

Upset by the change in her brother's religious views, but afraid to confront him directly, Louise Burckhardt apparently wrote a letter to her younger brother. Referring to this letter, Burckhardt wrote von Tschudi:

> She begs me to recollect my mother's words: to cherish my father's life; she conjures me by my father's health to alter the course of my life. "O, do not be cheated of your childlike faith, they will give you nothing, absolutely nothing, in return." She tells me how my mother prayed with us as children, how once, when I was not a year old and dangerously ill, she fell on her knees, and that she is now praying for her children before the eternal God.[178]

Burckhardt pleaded with his sister not to tell their father about his religious change. "You think I should communicate also to my father the changing of my religious and moral views," Burckhardt wrote Louise, "but I prefer to show it to him by *facts and life* on my returning, and I hope you do not conceive [sic] me! I beg you say to him *nothing*! if you love me."[179]

In September 1839, Burckhardt wrote Schreiber that "my public appearance did something to make my apostasy more acceptable to my father, and that was my principal object. He has now been able to take a certain pride in me, though at bottom it doesn't mean much (*im Grunde nicht viel besagen will*)."[180] Although Burckhardt's meaning here is rather cryptic, one senses that at least some "serious discussion" took place between father and son. Indeed, Burckhardt must have conferred with his father concerning his inability to remain on the clerical track and his desire to pursue history. In all likelihood this conversation took place before 10 April 1839, for on this date Burckhardt wrote Riggenbach telling him that he had talked to his father and "wanted to relay to him everything face to face when he came to Berlin."[181] Burckhardt added: "Say nothing to any soul about this!" When Burckhardt's father was elected *Antistes*, Burckhardt noted (again rather cryptically) to Schreiber that "the dreaded has happened. . . . My father has been chosen as the chief pastor."[182]

One can only imagine the young Burckhardt on 25 November 1838, the day of his father's inaugural address as *Antistes*. He would have sat among the congregation, among his family – a self-proclaimed apostate, an "honest heretic." "Our traditional Doctrine melts away under his [de Wette's] hand," Burckhardt had written Riggenbach just three months before this scene. New theological convictions had rendered, in Burckhardt's eyes, the world of his father as a historical anachronism.

Conclusion

It is little wonder that irony has become the category of choice for describing Burckhardt's intellectual personality.[183] Burckhardt never outwardly rebelled against the conservative Christian order of his upbringing; instead, he came to endure (even enjoy) the "Philistine facade" he later adopted as a teacher in Basel.[184] Moreover, unlike his more infamous colleague, Nietzsche, Burckhardt's rejection of orthodox Christianity assumed a very cautious, stoic cast, isolated largely in his private person.

Burckhardt's decisions with respect to belief and career represent a significant moment in the ascendency of historicism as a worldview in the middle decades of the nineteenth century. To be sure, there *was* tension between the world of the son and the world of the father – however unclear the emotional conflict between actual father and son may have been. That Burckhardt, the twenty-year-old "filius Antistitis," felt compelled to leave the restrictive pious community of Basel and take up history in Berlin – to find in it his new "calling"[185] – was something he later regarded as the watershed of his early years.[186] His "inner uncerainity" and *wissenschaftlich* convictions persuaded him that intellectual honesty could be found neither in the pious outlooks of his clerical forebears nor in the future of modern theology, as practiced by the likes of de Wette and Strauss. "The most prudent thing a negative theologian can do is to change over to another faculty," he reasoned in a letter to Beyschlag in 1844, "So much was clear to me when I gave up theology."[187] The same year, when Bruno Bauer was considered for a chair in theology at the University of Bonn, Burckhardt commented:

> People like him ought to be honest enough to keep their distance from *sancta theologia*. But what, for example, would be the position regarding the appointment of an honest history teacher with no ties whatsoever to the Church? . . . I will, for once, say straight out what so many *viri doctissimi* think and dare not express: from our point of view Christianity has entered the realm of purely human periods of history (*rein menschlichen Geschichtsepochen*).[188]

CHAPTER FIVE

History without Centaurs

Our task, in lieu of all wishing, is to free ourselves as much as
possible from foolish joys and fears and to apply ourselves
above all to the understanding of historical development.
– Burckhardt, *Historische Fragmente*

The philosophy of history is a centaur.
– Burckhardt, *Über das Studium der Geschichte*

FRANZ OVERBECK (1837–1905), PROFESSOR of theology and church
history and colleague of both Burckhardt and Nietzsche at the University of Basel, once commented that Burckhardt's work as a historian had
its "deepest roots" in a desire to overcome prejudices inherited from Christianity.[1] Overbeck praised Burckhardt for his "amazingly unbiased point of
view" even though "his education and entire upbringing were so strongly
stamped by Christian influence."[2] In the present chapter I show that one of
Burckhardt's principal aims as a historical thinker was indeed to distance
himself from his own Christian past by constructing a "profane" history of
the emergence and decline of Christianity in Europe.[3] However, unlike
Overbeck, I argue that despite Burckhardt's avowed secularism, a strong
theological undercurrent persisted in his thought.

The undercurrent was not the characteristic nineteenth-century historical optimism, often regarded as the secularization of Christianity's eschatological content.[4] On the contrary, what one sees in Burckhardt is nearly
the opposite: a deep-seated historical and cultural pessimism inherited from
the idea of original sin.[5] The character of Burckhardt's early religious life
is exhibited not only in the relationship with his father, discussed earlier,
and in his catechetical training but also in the pronounced spiritual sensitivity of his youthful poems and sketches, in which two prominent medieval
motifs recur: the Last Judgment and Basel's famous "dance of death"
(*Totentanz*).[6] The spirit of Basel's dance of death, an irreducible belief in

evil and human limitations in this world, resided in Burckhardt's thought long after he made the transition from apostate theology student to accomplished secular historian.

Scholars often note that Burckhardt's cultural pessimism made him an anomaly among nineteenth-century historians and philosophers of history. In a century when progressive, evolutionary models of history reigned supreme, Burckhardt maintained that "progress . . . is intrinsically ridiculous, for greed and desire know no limits; one will always encounter a dissatisfied humanity."[7] Concerning Hegelian philosophy, Burckhardt warned his students that "this bold assumption of a world plan leads to fallacies because it starts out from false premises."[8] Similarly, Burckhardt doubted Rousseau's "moral dream," the "assumption that all men are by nature good."[9]

Although out of place in his own century, Burckhardt's legacy has found a home in ours. I would even suggest that what Ranke has come to represent for the foundations of modern political historiography, Burckhardt has become for more recent cultural history, with its anti- or postmodern tendencies. His lack of system, his characteristic irony, his zeal for knowledge but willingness to voice epistemological shortcomings, and his preference for culture over politics have earned Burckhardt a near hagiographical status in the eyes of historians, philosophers, and others in Europe and America since the mid-twentieth century.[10] Jörn Rüsen, for instance, has celebrated Burckhardt's moderate postmodernism, which, unlike the radical postmodernism of Nietzsche, should be "used as an historical mirror in which we can see what is wrong with our time."[11] Other critics have thought similarly; all agree that Burckhardt somehow transcended his time and became precociously critical of modernity.[12]

Yet neither postmodernism nor Burckhardt benefits from the yoking. A less presentist and more judicious historical evaluation of Burckhardt proceeds by suspending the postmodernism question. Without forgetting Burckhardt's posthumous fortunes, I employ instead premodern criteria – and specifically premodern theological criteria – to evaluate the formation of Burckhardt's historical thought. Such an evaluation is accomplished by rethinking the possible long-term implications of Burckhardt's religious upbringing and his encounter with modern liberal theology.

As shown in chapter four, the encounter with de Wette profoundly disturbed Burckhardt, forcing him to confront his situation: he could neither return to orthodoxy nor accept de Wette's liberal Protestantism.[13] As we have seen, Burckhardt sought to escape his predicament by not choosing between them and by turning instead to historical studies as his new "calling."[14] Yet the theological unrest never completely dissipated; Burckhardt retained an inclination to think in categories and language derived from the biblical-cultural heritage of "pious Basel." His vow to remain an "honest heretic" even suggests a residual allegiance to his childhood faith – a faith no longer held, but one whose deep-seated presence revealed itself in Burckhardt's refusal to allow any compensatory teleological vision of history to fill its absence. The ruins of his faith, ramifying throughout his subsequent career, furnished him with an incredulity toward the optimizing tendencies and the epistemological confidence characteristic of Rankean, Hegelian, Comtean, and Marxian approaches to history alike – in a word, to the very foundations of modern historical thinking. Burckhardt's post- or antimodernism is curiously accounted for by the inertia of his premodernism.

Viewed in this light, Burckhardt's secularism presents a problem. As noted, there is the view that Enlightenment and post-Enlightenment philosophies of history – especially the German tradition of *Universalgeschichte* – are transposed, secular versions of preexisting Christian eschatological ideas. As the legatee of millennial expectation, modern secular historical consciousness – so goes the argument – inherited a "grand vision" of the waxing power of knowledge and progress over human affairs.[15] This version of secularization has been stated forcefully by many critics, including Karl Löwith, M. H. Abrams, Carl Becker, Ronald S. Crane, and Ernest L. Tuveson.[16]

Even a casual glance at Burckhardt's thought reveals that little historical optimism accompanied him after his religious crisis and therefore the model cited earlier would seem inapplicable in his case. But what if one were to seek other elements of Christian belief, besides eschatology, in transposed, secularized forms? After all, Christianity cannot be reduced to its eschatology. An equally important aspect of Christianity (especially in its orthodox Protestant expression) is its thorough pessimism concerning the things of this world. This profound pessimism toward a sinful, rebellious creation must be viewed alongside millennial expectation if one is to understand the premodern Christian sentiment expressed in, say, the Basel Confession (1534), in Burckhardt's father's catechism, or in artistic renderings of the Last Judgment and dance of death.

Those secularization theorists who interpret modern historical consciousness as a transposition of Christian eschatology rarely seek out the transposed whereabouts of original sin. This is understandable given the generally optimistic character of most influential philosophies of history in the late eighteenth and nineteenth centuries. One need think only of Condorcet's belief in the "limitless perfectibility of the human species,"[17] of Comte's positivist vision, or of the *Universalgeschichte* of German Romantics.[18] In de Wette's eyes, as we have seen, history was redeemed and hence capable of being positively appraised through *Ahnung*. Ranke and Hegel saw history, respectively, as the "holy hieroglyphs" of God and as the inevitable march of the World-Spirit.[19] In short, the idea of "this world" as sin, misery, and death – a vale of tears, a *Jammertal* – witnessed extreme attenuation among most of the influential bearers of modern high culture.[20] To be sure, I do not mean that the doctrine of original sin was completely extinguished or that secular thinkers did not take the problem of evil seriously. Moreover, Christian thinkers like Kierkegaard, Dostoevsky, or John Henry Newman, as well as the Catholic Church, never saw original sin as an anachronism. Yet in Burckhardt's genuinely unusual case, the persistence of a metamorphosed form of original sin (i.e., cultural pessimism), minus both redemptive hope and progressive optimism, outlived his secularization and became the most distinctive and insightful feature in his mature historical thinking.[21]

Melancholy, Meaning, and the Formation of a Historicist Personality

The shaping of Burckhardt's historical consciousness may be described as the superimposition of historicist thinking on an unsettled religious mind. Once at the University of Berlin, Burckhardt zealously turned to history to find solace and direction for what he described as "the pressing problem of my condition (*Bestimmung*), of my relation to God and the world."[22] In 1840, he wrote Heinrich Schreiber exuberantly, describing the "enormous expansion of [historical] scholarship" found in Berlin's lecture halls: "I had loved history on hearsay, and here it was appearing before me in gigantic proportions. . . . Now I am firmly resolved to devote my life to it, perhaps at the cost of a happy home life; from now on no further hesitation shall disturb my resolve."[23] Burckhardt discovered in the study of history what he soon described as his new "calling" (*Beruf*).[24]

Burckhardt did not slacken in his determination. From his student days in Berlin and Bonn (1839–43)[25] until his death, historical learning and scholarship forged a link between self and world and provided a means for self-transformation and self-justification. The early and mid-1840s were the crucial years for the fashioning of his new historicist personality.[26] At Berlin, he came into direct contact with the greatest names of German historical scholarship: Leopold von Ranke, August Böckh, J. G. Droysen, Franz Kugler, Heinrich von Sybel, and Jakob Grimm.[27] Moreover, Hegel's legacy still animated debate in nearly all of Berlin's faculties; the relationship between philosophy and history had never been closer or more controversial; and the religious issues associated with Hegelianism were also much discussed. It was during this intellectually stimulating period that Burckhardt first articulated his own conception of the character of historical knowledge. Also at this time, his religious crisis remained a burning personal issue: he was torn between a deep skepticism toward the claims of both orthodox and liberal Christianity on the one hand, and longing for religious meaning on the other.[28] The combination of this inner conflict with the intellectual stimuli at Berlin is crucial for understanding the germination of Burckhardt's conception of historical knowledge.[29]

The relationship between historical scholarship and religious meaning has been exceedingly complex and antagonistic in the modern period. The rise of scholarly methods has often resulted in the marginalization of questions pertaining to faith and meaning.[30] "Modern scholarly practice is the specifically god-foreign power," noted Max Weber in articulating his famous "disenchantment" thesis.[31] Historical scholarship seeks to explain the world critically; faith seeks to behold the world devotionally. And despite the best efforts of de Wette or Kant to keep them separate, they often remain muddled in human consciousness, claiming authority to the same dimension of human existence: the experience of time and the attendant desire to interpret one's experience as meaningful. Burckhardt's statements during his Berlin years reflect this tension; they also attest to a strong desire to overcome it by establishing for himself a semi-religious sense of calling in the very pursuit of historical knowledge.[32]

Two fundamental presuppositions may be observed in the young Burckhardt. First, despite his rejection of Christianity, he believed that the world displayed meaning; there existed for him a noumenal reality, a "providence" (*Vorsehung*) as he phrased it, that stands above or in the world (or both – he is not clear) and confers meaning on human affairs. Second, Burckhardt believed that historical knowledge is of absolute importance; much more than natural knowledge, the pursuit of historical or cultural knowledge constitutes a goal demanding one's highest commitment. Realizing these two articles of belief, however, proved difficult for Burckhardt; there is much uncertainty, melancholy, and conflict in Burckhardt's early letters. He struggled to express a coherent worldview and confessed having to resort to "a dreadfully inadequate philosophical vocabulary."[33]

Burckhardt's religious crisis and his subsequent move to Berlin initially plunged him into a state of depression. From Berlin he wrote frequently of his "melancholy sadness."[34] "Berlin is my Patmos and more than one book shall make my belly bitter," he told Schreiber in 1839.[35] To Beyschlag he noted, "I am an exile and shall always look upon myself as one in Berlin. . . . I suffer great distress in this sandy desert!"[36] An unusual mixture of religious and artistic melancholy characterize his utterances: when Burckhardt describes his "inward anguish" (*Anfechtung*) and his "storm-swept mind" one hears both the distant echo of Luther's spiritual turmoil and the tapering ethos of an earlier nineteenth-century Romanticism.[37] Burckhardt makes clear in his letters that unresolved religious issues had left his mind fragmented beyond the aid of any theological or philosophical "system," a term he came to regard with much skepticism.[38]

141

Burckhardt held on to the idea of providence, however, and asserted that altruism should be one's highest duty. He referred to these beliefs as his "home-made little system" and described them in a letter to Riggenbach:

> The end which Providence has set before mankind is the conquest of selfishness and the sacrifice of the individual for the sake of the universal. Hence man's most necessary attribute is resignation; each hour preaches abnegation, and our dearest wishes remain unfulfilled. . . . On no count must he [the individual] grumble at mankind, or withdraw from life; he must hold out to the end.

Burckhardt added a personal note of extreme *Weltschmerz*: "[Yet] I would exchange my life against never having been, at any moment, and, were it possible, return to the womb. . . . I see that the aim of life is to bear existence as best one can, and to try to do as much as possible for others."[39]

Although convinced by the negative results of modern theology and biblical criticism, Burckhardt never celebrated the critique of traditional Christianity. He held that Christianity's demise would lead to an enormous sense of spiritual loss. Consequently, there is a strong nostalgic element in his early reflections; images of ruins and rebuilding recur as means of expressing his spiritual state. Attempting to console his sister, for example, about changes in his religious views, he wrote:

> So let us build a new home out of shattered dreams and ruins of all sorts, like the Roman vine-grower building his *vigna* out of old marble friezes and broken columns! Perhaps you may even be surprised from time to time by my carefree view of life, but believe me, my faith in an eternal providence stands as firm as a rock. Providence is not mere blind fate. . . . This belief will never again desert me, however my view of religions and confessions may be modified.[40]

But a lingering *Weltschmerz* prevented Burckhardt from resting in providence. "It seems to me at times as though I were Faust, full to overflowing with yearning," he noted in one letter.[41] Like the images of ruins, allusions to Goethe and *Faust* abound in Burckhardt's 1840s correspondence. Burckhardt himself later referred to this time as his "Faust period." Like many German-speaking youths, Burckhardt had been deeply affected by Goethe's poem.[42] In 1855, he noted to Albert Brenner, a young student, that Brenner's "Faust-fever" reminded him of a similar epoch in his own life:

> It is the certain, inescapable fate of the educated youth of Germany at a certain age to dig down and explore *Faust*, and you are in the process of fulfilling that destiny. The old gentleman would be deeply hurt if one were to discover *fixed dogmas* in Faust! . . . The best minds have all had to follow the same path, because they sought for solid truths; the

poem attracted them, drew them deep down into its subterranean and supernatural paths, and left them at long last no *truths*, but a purified *impulse toward the truth*, such as preoccupation with spiritual matters ought to evoke.[43]

The *Weltschmerz*, the Faust fever, the lack of "fixed dogmas" but "purified impulse toward the truth" reflect Burckhardt's attitude in the early 1840s. An overflowing religiosity contended with a resolute skepticism in his inner life during the period that he sought to assume his new calling. He directed these uncertainties into an intense preoccupation with history, hoping to find solutions to the problems of selfhood, calling, and meaning, which had earlier been rendered uncertain by de Wette's critical theology. In one very revealing letter to his friend von Tschudi, Burckhardt wrote:

> I feel that I ought to keep silent a long time. Had I but emerged from skepticism, in itself a great step, I could speak from my heart, as you have the right to do. At the same time there are other demons to overcome; to state it succinctly: a totally secular point of view in seeing and doing everything (*eine völlige Verweltlichung in der Anschauungsweise wie in der Behandlungsweise aller Dinge*). One remedy (*Heilmittel*) against this I have found in my main subject, history, which was the first shock that unseated my fatalism and the view of life I had based upon it.[44]

Burckhardt turned to history as a "Heilmittel," which means remedy or cure, but also contains the German root word for redemption and salvation.[45]

Burckhardt gradually transmuted his religious uncertainty into scholarly labor and a quest for historical truths. In March 1840 he reported to von Tschudi that his religious doubts had abated because of the "exceptionally distracting character of my work"; he also noted that "the philosophy of history is [now] daily in my thoughts." Responding to von Tschudi's praise of some poems that Burckhardt had sent him, Burckhardt wrote:

> My poetry, for which you prophesied fair weather, is in great danger of being sent packing now that I have found the height of poetry in history itself. There was a time when I looked upon the play of fantasy as the highest requirement of poetry; but since I must esteem the development of spiritual states, or, quite simply, inner states as such, higher still, I now find satisfaction in history itself (*Befriedigung schon in der Geschichte*).[46]

"My entire historical work," Burckhardt told Willibald Beyschlag in June 1842, "springs from an enormous thirst to behold the world (*Anschauung*)."[47]

A particular understanding of history informed Burckhardt's new calling in its nascent stages: his turn to history reflects predominantly an *a posteriori* (historical) appreciation of the individual rather than an idealist *a priori* (philosophical) preoccupation with the general or the speculative.[48] Indeed, Burckhardt's earlier misgivings about de Wette's speculative theology remained with him, resurfacing strongly in his encounters with Hegelians and with F. W. J. Schelling, who came to Berlin in 1841.[49] Burckhardt's negative response to idealism at Berlin is intriguing because it has been argued that without overtly embracing Hegel, Burckhardt nonetheless maintained a lifelong debt to a Hegelian conception of history.[50] I do not dispute that Burckhardt appropriated certain aspects of a Hegelian vocabulary, but even in his initial encounter with Hegelianism (and with other idealist views), Burckhardt questioned its fundamental premise: the validity of *a priori* concepts for interpreting the historical process.[51]

Burckhardt's first misgivings about Hegelianism actually arose before he arrived in Berlin, when he judged his friends, Biedermann and Riggenbach, to have succumbed to the temptation of the "World-Spirit." In a letter to von Tschudi in 1839, Burckhardt told his friend, who was already in Berlin, that when he arrived they would get together for a *tête-à-tête* without Biedermann and Riggenbach and would speak to one another "not in the bombastic Hegelian dialect, but rather in sincere words from the heart."[52] Burckhardt personally encountered Hegelians in the spring semester of 1840. He wrote to von Tschudi of several lectures that he had attended on the philosophy of history; "unfortunately," he complained, "they are all [given] by *Dozenten* and what is more they are almost all by post-Hegelians, whom I do not understand."[53]

Despite his early misgivings about Hegel, Burckhardt undeniably appropriated some Hegelian language. In 1842, he noted to Karl Fresenius, a philosophy student, that "the highest conception of the history of mankind, the development of the spirit to freedom, has become my leading conviction, and consequently my studies cannot be untrue to me, cannot let me down, and must remain my good genius all through my life."[54] Yet he was quite aware of the origins of such a sentiment and confessed in the same letter that he was perhaps "unconsciously led by certain tendencies in modern philosophy." "The *facta* of history" remained his primary concern and he thus bid Fresenius to grant him the right to "experience and feel history on *this lower level*, instead of understanding it from the standpoint of first principles."[55]

Indeed, Burckhardt often described himself in his 1840s correspondence as not possessing a philosophical mind capable of speculation (*Speculation*) but only a historical one capable of perception (*Anschauung*): "My surrogate is perception. . . . I cling by nature to the concrete, to visible nature, and to history."[56] More fully:

Historical perception issues from the impression we receive from sources. What I build up historically is not the result of criticism and speculation, but on the contrary, of imagination, which fills up the gaps of perception. . . . Accordingly I simply don't believe in an *a priori* standpoint; that is a matter for the World Spirit, not for men of history (*Geschichtsmenschen*).[57]

Additionally, he noted to Fresenius that he sought the "correlative [to speculation] in history": "Do not misunderstand me. . . . I do not regard it [history] romantically or fantastically, all which is quite worthless, but as a wonderful process of chrysalis-like transformations (*wundersamen Prozeß von Verpuppungen*)."[58]

The theologically tinged philosophy of Schelling offended Burckhardt even more than Hegelianism. He visited several lectures by Schelling and summed up his experience quite humorously to his friend Gottfried Kinkel in Bonn:

I attended his lectures a couple of times as an outsider during the most turgid of dogmatic discussions, and explained it all to myself as follows: Schelling is a Gnostic in the proper sense of the word, like Basilides. Hence all that is sinister, monstrous, formless in this part of his doctrine. I thought that at any moment some monstrous Asiatic God on twelve legs would come waddling in and with twelve arms take six hats off six heads. Little by little even the Berlin students will not be able to put up with his frightful half-nonsensical, intuitional, contemplational form of expression. It is awful to have to listen to long historical explanations and discussions of the destiny of Messias, epically drawn out, complicated and entirely formless. Anyone who can love Schelling's Christ must have a large heart.[59]

Although Burckhardt lampooned Schelling's Christ, the christological question nonetheless had remained troublesome for him ever since his encounter with de Wette. Willibald Beyschlag, who studied theology under Neander at Berlin, queried Burckhardt about the matter on several occasions and received the following response:

Had I lived when Jesus of Nazareth walked the countryside of Judaea – I should have followed Him and should have allowed pride and arrogance to vanish in love of Him. . . . But eighteen centuries separates our [religious] longing (*Sehnsucht*) from him, and it is only when I am alone and in moments of melancholy longing that a majestic image appears before my soul and consoles me, the image of the Greatest of Men. As God, Christ is a matter of indifference to me – what can one make of Him in the Trinity? As man He is the light of my soul, because He is the most *beautiful* figure in world history. Call that religion who likes. . . . I make no claim to call it religion.[60]

Various matters – De Wette's criticism, Bruno Bauer's appointment at Bonn, the Strauss affair in Zurich,[61] Schelling's lectures, the Hegelians at Berlin – finally led Burckhardt to conclude that Christianity had reached the end of its rope. "That Christianity has its great ages behind it," he wrote in 1845, "is as evident to me as the fact that twice two is four; in what way its eternal content (*ewiger Gehalt*) is to be saved in new forms, history will instruct us in due course. But I am really sorry for the present restorers (*jetzigen Restauratoren*)."[62] Consequently, Burckhardt told Kinkel that he "had broken with the Church forever, from quite personal motives, because I quite literally can't make sense of it . . . [T]he Church has lost all power over me, as over so many others." Burckhardt held out hope that a "spontaneous, personal perhaps undenominational religion" might arise one day; but for the foreseeable future he predicted only "the coming *mêlée* between the Church and the intelligentsia" and a "period of disintegration (*Auflösungsperiode*)."[63]

What Burckhardt meant by the "ewiger Gehalt" of Christianity is unclear. At times, he wrote of a vague otherworldly reality, a higher providence, independent of human consciousness. More often, however, he seems to have regarded the religious impulse as a purely human phenomenon. For example, he noted in 1844 that Christianity "has brought up the nations morally, and given them strength and independence to reconcile themselves from now on, not with God, but inwardly, *with their own consciences*."[64] Unlike such contemporaries as Comte or Marx, Burckhardt never professed a dogmatic atheism. Religion remained for him a fundamental human reality, an "expression of human nature's eternal and indestructible metaphysical need," as he put it in his lectures.[65] Yet despite its "ewiger Gehalt," Christianity, in Burckhardt's view, had entered "the realm of purely human periods of history." The "enchantment" of the Christian message – its symbolic expression in sacraments, art, architecture, and the like – lost their religious authority over Burckhardt. At the same time, however, Christianity's "symbolic universe" remained for him a sublime and inspiring ruin long after he had decided against the validity of its dogmatic content.[66]

In a long, moving letter to his sister, he narrated a scene that subtly but poignantly expresses the historicization and aestheticization of his religious views. After recounting various travels through Germany, he described an experience at the cathedral of Fulda. He wrote that after observing the tomb of St. Bonifacius and the cathedral altar he discovered that he could experience no inner stirring (*Regung*) but instead "only a historical form of worship (*bloß historische Verehrung*)."[67] "Art," Burckhardt stated years later, "is the most arrant traitor of all, first because it profanes the substance of religion, that is, it robs men of their faculty for more profound worship, putting eyes and ears in its place, and substituting figures for feelings, which are only transiently deepened by them." But he also revealingly noted that art is an "ally of religion, and in the most surprising circumstances refuses to be driven from the temple. It represents religion for the educated . . . even when the religious spirit has died."[68]

History and the Secular in Antiquity and the Renaissance

The historicization of Burckhardt's thinking in the 1840s led him to religious skepticism, but not to contempt for religion. Throughout his life, he recognized the power of religious ideas and made clear on several occasions that without a "transcendent urge" (*überweltliches Wollen*) individuals had neither a defense against the "whole power and money racket" of modern civilization nor a source for sublime art.[69] Yet he was deeply puzzled by his own religious situation, which he interpreted as emblematic of the critical spirit of Europe's intelligentsia. He came to hold that his personal "transitional period" reflected a fundamental shift in European religious consciousness, the outcome of which remained unknown.[70] For the time being, however, historical knowing offered considerable consolation: new possibilities of understanding and meaning and a way of thinking that allowed him to transcend prejudices inherited from his religious past.

Burckhardt's religious skepticism and his affirmation of historical knowing came together in his first major book, *Die Zeit Constantins des Grossen* (1853). Finished several years after the completion of his Berlin studies during a lectureship at the University of Basel, the book sought to demonstrate that the emergence of Christianity in Europe could be given a purely secular interpretation. Covering a crucial period of religious change, the book has manifest biographical roots in Burckhardt's own "transitional period" during the 1840s. In fact, the terms "Übergangsperiode" or "Übergangszeit," which Burckhardt used to describe his inner state after his religious crisis, are the same terms used to describe the period under discussion in his *Constantin*.[71] The idea of devoting a book to the subject grew out of Burckhardt's friendship with the controversial theologian and preacher, Gottfried Kinkel (1815–83).[72]

Burckhardt and Kinkel became close friends during the summer semester of 1841, which Burckhardt spent doing research at the University of Bonn, where Kinkel taught. The center of their interaction was a literary club, the *Maikäferbund*, a group of creative spirits who convened to enjoy one another's literary and musical skills. At the time, Kinkel was a well-known lecturer in theology and church history at the university; his most popular course was entitled "the history of paganism," which Burckhardt found extremely interesting.[73] The course represented the outline of a book Kinkel intended to write about the first three centuries after Christ, analyzing "pagan" political and intellectual developments during the time in which Christianity had become a "historical necessity."[74] Kinkel and Burckhardt shared the conviction that, like late Roman antiquity, their own period was one of religious crisis and transition. But they interpreted the present as the reverse of antiquity: Christianity was receding, being displaced by an inchoate neo-paganism, which had been made possible by critical theology and by the natural philosophies of Goethe and other modern poets.[75] Burckhardt esteemed Kinkel's work on paganism as a major contribution to contemporary understanding and regarded its eventual completion as the "most decisive step" in Kinkel's life. As a result, Burckhardt became increasingly frustrated with Kinkel's dalliance in highly politicized theological issues. "Drop theological discussions," he rebuked Kinkel on one occasion, "where you won't come across a single green twig." "History," he advised, "[unlike theology] will remain faithful to you."[76]

Kinkel had been trained as a theologian and pastor, but like Strauss, de Wette, and others he had taken a critical, non-orthodox stance. A Rhinelander and a Protestant, Kinkel's political sympathies lay with the predominantly Catholic, anti-Prussian population on the Rhine. His controversial theological and political views brought him into conflict with public authorities on several occasions. In 1844, Kinkel's decision to marry a woman who was divorced and Catholic cost him his preaching career and nearly his teaching position as well. The situation was eased by his wife's becoming Protestant and by Kinkel's forced relocation to the philosophy faculty. To Burckhardt's consternation, Kinkel sided with the Republican cause in 1848; after taking part in several uprisings, Kinkel joined the revolution in the Palatinate, where he was wounded and taken prisoner. He was given the death sentence, but this was later commuted to life imprisonment. After several months imprisonment, his release was arranged and he and his wife fled to England. He never completed his book on the history of paganism.[77]

Even more than Kinkel, Burckhardt was convinced that the origins of Christianity in Europe were wholly explicable in historical terms and that the Christian faith had no privileged claim to truth, contrary to what the orthodox held. Burckhardt expressed his contempt for such "loathsome orthodoxy" on several occasions to Kinkel.[78] In 1845, for instance, he wrote that

> [When] those people [the orthodox] have made a *decision to will* to believe ... then nothing one can say is any good. Have the gentlemen really forgotten their Church history so completely? Do they no longer know that every faith, so long as it was entitled to the dominion of the world, came upon men as a power (*Gewalt*)?[79]

148

Thus, what Kinkel labeled "the reverse-situation of our days," the conflict in antiquity between paganism and Christianity, Burckhardt chose as his first major endeavor of historical inquiry.[80] Judged in the light of Burckhardt's later works, *Constantin* appears anomalous and isolated; on closer inspection, however, one sees that it was deeply rooted in Burckhardt's youthful religious personality.[81]

Despite his personal religious skepticism, the prospect of Christian orthodoxy's disintegration in modern times represented for Burckhardt a historically earth-shattering event and one that deeply affected his intellectual and psychological makeup. "Great and tragic experience," Burckhardt would later write, "ripens the mind and gives it a new standard, a more independent judgment of life on earth. If it had not been for the collapse of the Roman Empire . . . St. Augustine's *City of God* would not have become such a great and independent book."[82] As did Augustine's great work, Burckhardt's *Constantin* grew out of a perceived "great and tragic experience." In his attempt to comprehend *secularization* in his own times, Burckhardt turned to the Christian *sacralization* of history in late antiquity. Applying newly acquired skills of historical inquiry, he sought to interpret the nascence of Christian orthodoxy – using Kinkel's exact phrase – as a product of "historical necessity."[83]

To accomplish such an aim, Burckhardt attempted, as Overbeck later put it, to "execute [his] task as a historian completely without recourse to Christianity."[84] In *Constantin*, Burckhardt accordingly ceded "edifying" historiography to theologians: "No one can begrudge the present work because its viewpoint is not that of edification (*Erbaulichkeit*) which a scholar like Neander, for example, may properly adopt."[85] He urged his readers to leave aside all "Christian feelings of sinfulness and humility, of which the ancient world was not capable."[86] Finally, Burckhardt criticized Eusebius's hagiographical treatment of Constantine and accused Eusebius of being "the first thoroughly dishonest historian of antiquity."[87]

Burckhardt's secular criteria led him to reevaluate the reigns of emperors Diocletian and Constantine. From a traditional religious perspective, Diocletian was regularly treated unfavorably because of the persecutions against Christians during his reign. Constantine, on the other hand, came off in glowing, providential terms because of his conversion to Christianity and his leadership in the period of early Church Councils. Burckhardt attempted to call both views into question. The arch-persecutor, Diocletian, received a favorable interpretation: "If we are not prejudiced . . . by the Christian persecutions and by [subsequent Christian] distortions and exaggerations . . . [then] the traits of the great ruler assume a quite different aspect."[88] Instead, Burckhardt thus focused on Diocletian's political craftiness.

With regard to Constantine, Burckhardt consciously avoided the conventional scholarly debate about the authenticity of his faith; he depicted the emperor solely as a cunning egoist, willing to manipulate religious energies for political goals.[89] Burckhardt noted with regret that no "reasonable pagan" had written on Constantine and stated that if one had, then "the odious hypocrisy which disfigures his character would disappear." Burckhardt lamented "the glimmer of edification [that] still clings to Constantine" and declared that "this last glimmer must also vanish."[90] In his summary interpretation of Constantine, he strove to remove the glimmer himself:

> In a genius driven without surcease by ambition and lust for power there can be no question of Christianity and paganism, of conscious religiosity or irreligiosity; such a man is essentially unreligious, even if he pictures himself standing in the midst of the churchly community. Holiness he understands only as a reminiscence or as a superstitious vagary. Moments of inward reflection, which for a religious man are in the nature of worship, he consumes in a different sort of fire.[91]

Burckhardt regarded Christianity – as he regarded all historical phenomena – as strictly a "power," successful on account of a favorable confluence of contingent factors. Importantly, however, he did not reject the role of religious motives, whether Christian or pagan, in his interpretation. Although he historicized the institutional success of Christianity as epiphenomenal to power politics, he thought that the appeal of Christianity belonged to the realm of religious consciousness – albeit a very historicized understanding of such a consciousness. He argued that Christianity had arisen because of religious conditions "internal to paganism": "the essential content of late pagan beliefs was directly analogous to Christianity. The aim of existence was no longer limited to life on earth and to its pleasures and destiny, but was extended to the beyond, even to union with the deity." Further, he noted that "the disintegration of paganism as such was generally favorable to Christianity . . . [and] the individual symptoms of disintegration involved a presage (*Vorahnung*) of Christianity and an approach to it."[92] "The influence of Christianity" on declining paganism, as he put it in the preface, seemed to be rated too highly by other scholars and thus Burckhardt "preferred to explain the relevant phenomena as due to an *internal development in paganism itself.*"[93]

Yet the "polytheist madness" of the pagan scene could not compete with Christianity, for Christianity had radically simplified the situation and provided a divine world order and an all-embracing system of moral purpose: "Christianity was bound to conquer in the end because it provided answers which were incomparably simpler, and which were articulated in an impressive and convincing whole, to all the questions for which the period of ferment was so deeply concerned to find solutions."[94] For all his histori-

cizing, Burckhardt nonetheless expressed wonder at the wholesale transformation brought about by the new religion: "despite the exceptions which
historical criticism may justly take . . . [the triumph of Christianity was]
nevertheless a historical spectacle of the greatest magnitude."[95]

But Burckhardt stopped short of celebrating this spectacle. For practical
diplomatic reasons, he refused to castigate the Christian message per se and
instead focused his lament on Christianity's ascent to "world power."
"Christianity," he asserted, "grows alien to its essence when it is made into
law for those born instead of for those reborn."[96] Still, he regretted the
waning of paganism:

> Anyone who has encountered classical antiquity, if only in its twilight,
> feels that with beauty and freedom there departed also the genuine
> antique life, the better part of the national genius, and that the rhetoriz-
> ing orthodoxy which was left to the Greek world can only be regarded
> as a lifeless precipitate of a once wonderful totality of being.[97]

The monuments of antiquity, he continued, "the pure harmony of archi-
tectural forms, the untrammeled grandeur of the images of the gods, uttered
a language that was no longer wholly intelligible to the [new Christian]
spirit of this age."[98]

In his art guide to Italy, the *Cicerone*, published shortly after *Constantin*, Burckhardt continued to bemoan the decline of paganism. In his eyes
the new Christian religion had resulted in the suppression of aesthetic creativity: "the [Christian] artist no longer invents; he has only to reproduce
what the Church has discovered for him. For a time art still keeps up the
joyous spirit inherited from ancient times. . . . But gradually it sinks back
at last into mere mechanical repetition." The loss of creativity entailed the
extinguishing of a more abstract principle of individuality, which Burckhardt cherished in the pagan world (and which he saw reborn in the Renaissance): "It is astonishing to observe this complete dying out of individual
character, which is gradually supplanted by uniform type, similar in every
detail. We have to compare it [early Christian art] with the art of ancient
unprogressive nations (Egyptians, Chinese, etc.) to conceive how form could
be subjected to an uniform traditional law."[99] In the final analysis, the
period of the Church triumphant with its quest for orthodoxy – the orthodox heritage of Burckhardt's own immediate past – presented for the young
historian "a picture of the saddest devolution (*traurigsten Ausartung*). . . .
For the sake of orthodox dogma, it [the period of Church councils] suffered the inward man to be famished, and, itself demoralized, it completely
forfeited its higher moral effect upon the individual."[100]

Constantin appeared in 1853. Today most readers would scarcely take
offense at – and would even expect – a secular and largely political mode
of argument. Yet given Burckhardt's personal religious situation in the mid-

nineteenth century, it is important to observe just how self-consciously and deliberately he sought to justify and execute his secular historiographical program. The implications of his approach were not overlooked by conservative theologians. In the *Zeitschrift für lutherische Theologie*, for example, one reviewer criticized Burckhardt's book for its "dishonest disinterestedness" and judged it as a sign of the "ailments of modern historiography." "We have seen," the reviewer concluded, "a striking example of where this modern historiography can lead, over which abysses it now stands."[101] One can only wonder what *Antistes* Burckhardt thought of his son's first historical achievement.

*　*　*

The biographical issues animating Burckhardt's *Constantin* also laid the groundwork for many important aspects of his subsequent scholarship. His next great work, *Die Kultur der Renaissance in Italien*, has rightly been judged a sequel to *Constantin*.[102] Where *Constantin* deals with the twilight of ancient pagan individualism, the better-known *Renaissance* addresses the dawning of a semi-pagan, albeit distinctly modern, individualism, reborn from the Middle Ages, that time of "faith, illusion and childish prepossession."[103] Both books deal with "transitional periods"; both depict times of religious unrest (*Gärungszeiten*) brought on by "historical necessity,"[104] and both derive their profundity of insight from Burckhardt's own religious crisis and his subsequent "historicist turn." As Overbeck observed, "what Burckhardt did in his *Constantin*, he also did in his *Renaissance*; yes, this is what he sought to do in his own life."[105]

Burckhardt himself was acutely aware of the autobiographical roots of his *Renaissance*, commenting candidly in the first famous paragraph that "subjective judgment and feeling" were inseparable from the book's production.[106] In 1860, he told Heinrich Schreiber that the book was "altogether a wild plant dependent upon nothing whatever already existing;"[107] to another friend he commented that the work arose "from sheer inner necessity."[108] "A great historical subject," he advised a younger historian some years after finishing the book, "should cohere sympathetically and mysteriously to the author's innermost being."[109]

Parallels between Burckhardt's life and the themes of his *Renaissance* have not gone unnoticed, but observations of this sort have been almost exclusively geared to political and cultural considerations, and have rarely risen above unsupported generalizations and allusive suggestions.[110] Yet it is above all the religious dimension of Burckhardt's identity and thought – his own religious background, "crisis," and "transition" to skepticism and historical inquiry – that most clearly manifests itself in the structure of the *Renaissance*. Burckhardt's description of the "irreligious" and "individually developed" "modern educated men" of Renaissance civilization –

152

however historically accurate his picture may be – bears strong witness to Burckhardt's own experiences (vis-à-vis religion and theology) and to his historicized, secularized state of mind. Put differently, Burckhardt "found" writ large in the Renaissance the prototype of his own nineteenth-century apostasy and transition from being a pastor's son, which entailed primarily a religious, communal identity in Basel, to being the skeptical, individualist humanist-aesthete of his later years.

Not accidentally, Burckhardt titled the last – and hence presumably important – chapter of the *Renaissance* "Morality and Religion." Various subdivisions of the chapter bear such revealing headings as "The Necessity of Subjectivity," "Worldliness of the Spirit," "Beginnings of Criticism of the Sacred," "Fatalism and the Humanists," "The Complete Shattering of Faith," "Religious Confusion and the General Spirit of Doubt," and "The Waning of Christian Doctrine."[111] In this final chapter, more explicitly than anywhere else in the book, Burckhardt fused his leitmotifs of individualism and the revival of antiquity with the distinctly modern question of secularization.[112] The Renaissance, in his view, was the first period to produce a distinctly modern, secular, learned individual not bound by traditional religious sanctions. Although some scholars had tentatively anticipated his point, Burckhardt was the first historian who rigorously (and imaginatively) joined the ideas of Renaissance, modernity, and secularization to the Italian scene and produced one of the most durable and influential theses of modern historical scholarship. Like his forebears Pierre Bayle and Voltaire, Burckhardt expressed great admiration for the new secular elite; yet his admiration often gave way to misgivings and doubts. In the end, his response was deeply ambivalent: he admired but simultaneously evinced disquiet about the possibilities and hazards of modern "Weltlichkeit."[113]

At the beginning of "Morality and Religion," Burckhardt sets the tone by quoting Machiavelli, who, speaking of the "irreligious Italians," declared: "we are individually highly developed; we have outgrown the limits of morality and religion which were natural to us in our undeveloped state."[114] Burckhardt offers historical factors to account for the emergence of the condition described by Machiavelli. With respect to the "cultivated natures" (*Gebildeten*), he emphasizes the secularizing influence of scholarly preoccupation with pagan antiquity. This preoccupation gave birth to new esteem for the imagination, new critical scholarship, heightened subjectivity, and decline in the belief of immortality.

In Burckhardt's view, the pagan conception of individual glory played a key role in the dissolution of Christian sensibilities. "After they [the educated] became familiar with antiquity they substituted for holiness – the Christian ideal of life – the cult of historical greatness."[115] In Burckhardt's judgment, this substitution brought a new prestige to creativity and individual expression, which he viewed as irreconcilable with the strictures of

Christian morality and community: "The fundamental vice of this character was at the same time a condition of its greatness, namely excessive individualism." Burckhardt characteristically historicizes the whole process, claiming that such "individual development did not come about . . . through personal fault, but rather through a world-historical decree (*weltgeschichtlichen Ratschluß*)."[116]

Captivated by the rediscovery of pagan antiquity, "the more cultivated natures" found their religious instincts attenuated by a new ethos of scholarly activity and artistic production:

> If unbelief in this respect made such progress among the more highly cultivated natures, the reasons lay partly in the fact that the great earthly tasks of discovering the world and representing it in word and form absorbed most of their higher spiritual faculties. We have already spoken of the inevitable worldliness (*notwendigen Weltlichkeit*) of the Renaissance. But this investigation and this art were necessarily accompanied by a general spirit of doubt and questioning.[117]

The humanists' individuality, skepticism, and scholarly activity led to subjectivity in religious matters and weakened their desire for other-worldly salvation. "These modern men," Burckhardt notes,

> were born with the same religious instincts as other medieval Europeans. But their powerful individuality made them in religion . . . altogether subjective. . . . The need of salvation thus becomes felt more and more dimly, while the ambition and the intellectual activity of the present either shut out altogether every thought of a world to come, or else caused it to assume a poetic instead of a dogmatic form.[118]

Under the section heading the "intellectual activity of the present," Burckhardt includes the "embarrassment of theology by philology." He also makes reference to the "newly born science of historical investigation," and suggests that at this time "some timid attempts at biblical criticism" were begun. The (modern) theological implications of such criticism were voiced by Pius II, whom Burckhardt cites as remarking that "even if Christianity were not confirmed by miracles, it ought still to be accepted on account of its morality."[119] In the same paragraph, Burckhardt gives dramatic narratives of two heretics, Giorgio da Novara and Gabriele da Salò, who denied the divinity of Christ on historical grounds and were persecuted by Dominican Inquisitors.[120] Finally, Burckhardt suggests that the beginnings of "humanistic rationalism" could be observed in the Italian Protestant heresy of Socinianism; "theism or deism, call it what you will," he writes, "[The Socinian heresy] wiped away the Christian element out of religion, without either seeking or finding any other substitute for the feelings to rest upon."[121]

Indeed, in Burckhardt's eyes something entirely novel and secular first emerged from the "critical spirit of the Italian." This new "Weltlichkeit" brought with it an impulse toward scholarly investigation, in general, and historical investigation, in particular, which had important consequences for the determination of religious truth-claims. "This secular spirit," writes Burckhardt in perhaps his most self-descriptive passage,

> was . . . earnest, and was ennobled by art and poetry. It is a lofty neces-
> sity of the modern spirit (*eine erhabene Notwendigkeit des modernen
> Geistes*) that this attitude, once gained, can never again be lost, that an
> irresistible impulse forces us to the investigation of men and things, and
> that we must hold this inquiry to be our proper end and destiny. How
> soon and by what paths this search will lead us back to God, and in what
> ways the religious temper of the individual will be affected by it, are ques-
> tions which cannot be met by a general answer.[122]

Nonetheless, despite such admiration, Burckhardt often voices equivo-
cal feelings about the "irresistible impulse" driving the modern secular
scholar. In passages echoing Burckhardt's own youthful *Weltschmerz*, he
suggests that many irreligious humanists were overcome by an insistent
fatalism. "Skepticism," he notes, "obtained in many cases a complete
mastery over the Italians . . . [and] their belief in God began to waver, and
their view of the government of the world became fatalistic."[123] Considering the problem of evil, Burckhardt writes that "the humanists seldom get
beyond a cold and resigned consideration of the prevalent violence and
misrule." Such resignation, in Burckhardt's eyes, accounted for the prolif-
eration of treatises on fate and for a more general preoccupation with
fortune. Finally, like Burckhardt himself, many humanists continued to
believe in providence after their apostasy; yet Burckhardt claims that "providence . . . is only brought up because the writers would still be ashamed
of undisguised fatalism, or the avowal of their ignorance or of useless
complaints."[124]

*   *   *

In the preceding passages, I do not intend to suggest that Burckhardt deliberately embedded a personal allegory in his *Renaissance*. However sugges-
tive such a claim might be, there is no concrete evidence to support it,
although there is none that would cause one categorically to deny it either.
I do contend, however, that Burckhardt's subjective experience of his own
religious crisis and its psychological and intellectual aftermath in the 1840s
and 1850s have a strong correlative relationship to the way he depicted the
birth of the modern secular scholar. The pattern of his own experience –
the encounter with de Wette's historical criticism, subsequent apostasy,
skepticism, the turn to historical study at Berlin, lingering fatalism, and a

wavering belief in providence – is remarkably similar to his conception of the nascent secularism among Italian humanists in the fourteenth and fifteenth centuries. In short, I suggest that Burckhardt's religious experience played a crucial, insight-bequeathing role in his representation of the Renaissance as a crucial "transitional period" in the making of modern Western society.

In making this claim, I am not reducing Burckhardt's thesis to mere subjective fabrication. To the contrary, along with many others, I contend that despite empirical adjustments and necessary qualifications Burckhardt's idea of the Renaissance, in general, and his notion of the modern secular individual, in particular, remains persuasive. And in fact his work is still quite often the starting point for much contemporary scholarship on the Renaissance, whether one agrees or disagrees with it. "Our conception of the Renaissance is Jacob Burckhardt's creation," Karl Brandi once noted.[125] "Burckhardt all but single-handedly created the picture of that age of cultural flowering known to modern scholarship," claims Hayden White.[126] Such claims make clear the magnitude of Burckhardt's achievement. It is my intent to point out the subjective origins of Burckhardt's interest in and interpretation of the secularizing tendencies of the Italian humanists. Burckhardt's achievement – or at least important aspects of it – can be traced neither to his general erudition nor to the studious data-gathering of a "detached" historian in search of objectivity. Rather, one must look to the *inspired* vision – the "inner necessity" – of a former theology student and an apostate pastor's son.

Finally, given Burckhardt's lifelong respect for the idea of tradition and his refusal to make a loud, public break with the Church (as Nietzsche later did), it is interesting to note that Burckhardt often remarked on the residual elements of religion that persisted, often gracefully so, in the Italian humanists despite their ostensible secularity. "It is probable," he observes (or perhaps intuits), "that most of them wavered inwardly between incredulity and a remnant of the faith they were brought up in, and outwardly held for prudential reasons to the church."[127] In some cases, the ruins of their former faith coalesced into new virtues:

> The highly gifted man of that day thought to find it ["a bulwark against evil"] in the sentiment of honor. This is that enigmatic mixture of conscience and egotism that often survives in the modern man after he has lost, whether by his own fault or not, faith, love, and hope. . . . All the noble elements that are left in the wreck of a character may gather around it, and from this fountain may draw new strength.[128]

Burckhardt even claims that "closer investigation often reveals to us that underneath this outward [secular] shell much genuine religion could still survive."[129] In his lectures, Burckhardt later raised this phenomenon to a historical principle: "At the critical moment of a people's spiritual development, a religion imprints upon it a mark which it will never cease to bear. . . . Just as great forests grow once, but never rise again . . . both individuals and peoples possess or inherit certain things in their youth or never."[130]

Burckhardt, the Fall, and Modernity

A similar religious residuum may be observed in Burckhardt himself.

As I discussed earlier, persistence-of-religion theses have been employed to understand nineteenth-century secular intellectual life. Such interpretations often reflect the notion that secular, progressive conceptions of history proceeded from a substratum of preexisting Christian eschatological thought patterns. As I have noted already, Burckhardt does not fit this model. For Burckhardt, history offered no progressive patterns, no redemptive hope whatsoever. Against prevailing tendencies, Burckhardt maintained that he did not depict progress, but simply "man, suffering, striving, doing, as he is and was and ever shall be. Hence our study will . . . be pathological in kind."[131]

Burckhardt's "static," "anthropological," and "pessimistic" modes of inquiry foreshadow late nineteenth- and twentieth-century concerns occasioned especially by Europe's 1914–45 crises and, in their wake, the widespread collapse of the "project of modernity" in existentialist and now postmodernist ideas.[132] Yet despite its present-day relevance, Burckhardt's antimodernism (to settle on one term) owes its existence to the persistence of a premodern theological idea – not to the Christian *eschaton* refracted through modernity, but, as I have noted, to the idea of original sin.

Disregarding the theological origins of Burckhardt's antimodernism, recent scholars have settled on the opinion that it stemmed from an intellectual debt to Arthur Schopenhauer.[133] The most thorough pessimist of the early nineteenth century, Schopenhauer would appear a likely influence on Burckhardt. In his correspondence with Nietzsche, Burckhardt himself often referred to Schopenhauer as "the philosopher."[134] Reflecting the "Schopenhauer thesis," Hayden White claims that Schopenhauer's philosophy was Burckhardt's "starting point," and that both Richard Wagner and Burckhardt "remained Schopenhauer's devotees to the end."[135] Among others, White argues that Burckhardt's Schopenhauerian pessimism yielded a politically indifferent and ironic form of historical contemplation. In criticizing Burckhardt on this point, White attacks an ironic way of thinking that he sees as endemic among modern historians. He calls upon historians to reject Burckhardtian irony and "will to view history from an anti-Ironic perspective."[136]

Although I sympathize in part with White's criticism of Burckhardt's "ironic vision," his analysis of the origins of Burckhardt's pessimism is historically incorrect. Burckhardt did not mention Schopenhauer until 1870, when he was fifty-three years old.[137] His historical imagination had assumed its hallmark pessimistic character long before this. To be sure, strong affinities between the two thinkers are undeniable, but Schopenhauer exercised no formative influence on Burckhardt. Scholarship that holds otherwise rests on a *post hoc ergo propter hoc* fallacy that obscures both deeper and more immediate sources of Burckhardt's pessimism.

Rooted in Basel's conservative, religious heritage, Burckhardt's pessimism has in fact a profoundly Christian – and explicitly premodern Christian – pedigree. It may be described as a secularized continuation of the idea of original sin, an abiding attachment to the orthodox world of his father. Burckhardt does not stress the ontological basis of this idea – human guilt and sin-consciousness – but rather its social consequences – the notion, as Linwood Urban states, that all human thought and action stem from "an inherited, bruised, and damaged nature that has distorted and perverted their wills and desires."[138] That progressive, bourgeois, educated Europeans of the nineteenth century would find such a doctrine unsavory is evident. Burckhardt's partial retention of it thus presents an interesting historical problem.

Examining the theological background of Burckhardt's pessimism and "ironic vision" allows for a more insightful cultural contextualization than White's formalist, literary critical approach provides. Moreover, unlike White, I do not see Burckhardt's pessimism as inherently problematic, conducive only to a politics of indifference and cynicism.[139] In fact, I shall argue for the positive moral content of Burckhardt's historical imagination. The residuum of original sin furnished Burckhardt with a social and anthropological realism and intellectual modesty in stark contrast to his more visionary and epistemologically self-assured contemporaries, such as Feuerbach, Marx, Comte, Spencer, and many others.[140]

In 1918, the University of Basel commemorated the deceased Burckhardt by celebrating the hundredth anniversary of his birth. For the occasion, a former student, Arnold von Salis, gave a speech in which he recounted a humorous story of Burckhardt exclaiming "the earth is a vale of tears" after observing a fish whose gills were made inoperative by parasites. Salis used the anecdote to illustrate Burckhardt's "thoroughly pessimistic attitude" (*pessimistische Grundstimmung*), which he contrasted to the optimizing and teleologizing tendencies of modern theology. Optimism and teleology baffled Burckhardt. "They [modern theologians] don't get anywhere," Salis quoted Burckhardt, "by putting teleology in their assessment of the world. I would rather hold on to the Christian doctrine of the world as a vale of tears."[141] "Es ist eine böse Welt" and "o vanitatus vanitatum vanitas" were among Burckhardt's favorite expressions.[142]

Burckhardt believed that the nineteenth century was awash with cheap optimism, an uncritical confidence in progressive forces reshaping history. He could not accept this optimism, convinced that progress was defined by political and economic leaders, who, despite allegiance to such ideals as popular sovereignty and social reform, were ultimately concupiscent human beings, inclined to the abuse of power. His judgments of contemporary political developments were made from this critical perspective. For instance, deeply disturbed by the outbreak of the Franco-Prussian war, Burckhardt commented:

> Such events demonstrate repeatedly on what hollowed-out ground we stand. But the reasons for this lie much deeper than one thinks: they are connected to the freedom swindle (*Freiheitsschwindel*), with Rousseau's ideas of the goodness of human nature. To be sure, Christianity has often made its doctrine of the corruptibility of the human heart unsavory, but it nonetheless rests on more profound insight into human nature.[143]

The case of Bismarck was no anomaly in Burckhardt's eyes; he saw Prussia's power politics and bureaucratic authoritarianism as representative of more general modernizing trends. These trends included political nationalism, laissez-faire capitalism, militarism at home, and imperialism abroad. Burckhardt was most alarmed that the modern state defined its progressive aspirations in a cultural situation unchecked by a skeptical attitude toward human nature. For Burckhardt, this betokened a disastrous future open to "terribles simplificateurs," who might descend on the culture of Old Europe and destroy it.[144]

The idea of progress itself, defined by material gain and political success, Burckhardt thought inherently dangerous. He traced the roots of this "doctrine" to the Enlightenment, the French Revolution, and, in particular, to the "absurd" Rousseau.[145] European intellectuals who bought into Rousseauean premises forfeited a critical stance toward the wiles of human egotism. "We cannot share even that invitingly optimistic view," Burckhardt warned his students, "according to which society came into being first, and the state arose as its protector. . . . Human nature is not like that."[146]

Burckhardt was equally critical of modern Christianity's embrace of progress. By adapting itself to progressive ideologies, Christianity had compromised its pessimistic appraisal of human nature. "The only conceivable salvation," Burckhardt commented to a friend in 1871, "would be for this insane optimism . . . to disappear from people's brains. But then our present-day Christianity is not up to the task; it has gone in for and got mixed up with optimism for the last two hundred years. A change will and must come, but after God knows how much suffering."[147] Lecturing to a predominantly Christian audience at Basel, Burckhardt lambasted the association of the present with cumulative historical progress, calling "progress" that "most ridiculous vanity, as if the world were marching toward a perfection of mind or even morality."[148]

> There is nothing more un-Christian than to promise as a virtue a lasting reign, a material divine reward here below. . . . It would be a horrible sight if, as a result of the consistent reward of good and punishment of evil on the earth, all men were to behave well with an ulterior motive, for they would continue to be evil men and to nourish evil in their hearts. The time might come when men pray Heaven for a little impunity for evildoers, simply in order that they might show their real nature once more. There is enough hypocrisy in the world as it is.[149]

Burckhardt held nostalgically to the ethos of premodern Christian pessimism with its conception of the world as a "vale of tears." This outlook contained in his judgment a sad, true wisdom, not present in the dominant political and intellectual tendencies of his time. Burckhardt's latent retention of this Christian pessimism helps to account for his critical and lonely perspectives on otherwise celebrated developments, such as the idea of progress and nationalism. Most notably, however, Burckhardt embraced a very unmodern mindfulness of human epistemological limitations. Skeptical of triumphal portrayals of human collective scientific achievement, Burckhardt concentrated instead on the manifold inanities and uncertainties besetting the individual knower. Indeed, in Burckhardt's view, near-Pascalian notions of "inconstancy, boredom, and anxiety" determined to a large degree why, how, and to what ends various forms of knowledge arose. In deliberate reaction to widespread scholarly confidence in nonpartisanship and *Wissenschaft*, Burckhardt described his mode of inquiry as essentially subjective and *unwissenschaftlich*.[150]

Burckhardt's epistemological modesty bore directly on his related judgments on the character of historical knowledge, on teleology in history, and on contemporary European historical developments. In attempting to elucidate this nexus of interrelated topics, I argue throughout that Burckhardt's vale-of-tears skepticism afforded him a politically valuable social and anthropological realism, atypical during a time of widespread confidence in science and utopian social formulae. On this point, I concur with Friedrich Meinecke and Reinhold Niebuhr, who regarded Burckhardt as one of the most farsighted nineteenth-century observers of the totalitarian potential within modern liberal political culture.[151] However, I shall also make clear the limitations and problems of Burckhardtian realism.

Burckhardt's youthful contempt for Hegelian historical optimism remained constant throughout his adult life. "My advice to you," he warned a young student in 1856, is that Hegel is "a dead stock, let him lie where he is."[152] When in 1878 a Hegelian pastor was elected *Antistes* in Basel, Burckhardt opined that he had little sympathy for a theological reformer "occupying a pulpit and even performing rituals in the meaning of which he does not believe!"[153] "The thought of a higher world plan . . . is cold comfort," Burckhardt told his students, for "every successful act of violence is a scandal, that is, a bad example. The only lesson to be drawn from an evil deed successfully perpetuated by the stronger party [e.g., Prussia] is not to set more value on earthly life than it deserves."[154]

Indeed, throughout his lectures, the notes of which are entitled straightforwardly *Über das Studium der Geschichte*, Burckhardt reprehended teleological approaches to history in general and Hegelian versions in particular. He disdained Hegel's conflation of historical and philosophical ways of knowing. The true historical knower in Burckhardt's judgment was necessarily restricted to "observing" (*wahrnehmen*) "transverse sections" (*Querdurchschnitte*) of the past; he or she did not have access to "historical laws" or "historical principles."

> We shall confine ourselves to observation, taking transverse sections of history in as many directions as possible. Above all, we have nothing to do with the philosophy of history. The philosophy of history is a centaur, a contradiction in terms, for history coordinates, and hence is unphilosophical, while philosophy subordinates, and hence is unhistorical.[155]

"Hegel," according to Burckhardt, "develops the fundamental idea that history is the record of the process by which mind becomes aware of its own progress toward freedom. . . . We are not [however] privy to the purposes of eternal wisdom: they are beyond our ken."[156]

Against the Hegelian grain, Burckhardt made clear that his conception of historical knowledge was fundamentally "unsystematic" and "unscientific (*unwissenschaftlich*)." "Our train of thought lays no claim to system."[157] "Of all scholarly disciplines history is the most *unwissenschaftlich*, because it possesses or can possess least of all an assured, approved method of selection."[158] Burckhardt repeatedly called attention to the role played by subjective experience and individual fancy in the formation of historical knowledge. Almost nonexistent in Hegel's scheme, the idiosyncratic individual – "suffering, striving, doing" – was regarded by Burckhardt not only as the proper subject of historical inquiry but also as the recognized maker of (inevitably fallible) historical knowledge. "Nor can *we* ever rid ourselves of the views of *our own time* and personality, and here, perhaps, is the worst enemy of knowledge. The clearest proof of it is this: as soon as history approaches our century and our worthy selves we find everything more 'interesting'; in actual fact it is we who are more 'interested.' "[159] On an even more skeptical note, Burckhardt called "our historical pictures . . . for the most part, pure constructions, . . . mere reflections of ourselves."[160] Consistently, in the preface to *Constantin*, Burckhardt made clear the "highly subjective selection" of material that "lack[s] virtually any reduction to system."[161] The avowed subjectivity of his *Renaissance* has already been discussed.

Relinquishing the possibility of detecting a *telos* in history or of attaining absolute objectivity, Burckhardt still deemed historical inquiry an indispensable component of human education. History's aims, however, should be "essentially propaedeutic,"[162] resulting only in the attainment of "true skepticism" and "wisdom."[163] "True skepticism," he opined, "has its indisputable place in the world where beginnings and end are not known, and the middle is in constant flux."[164] Acquiring this skepticism was a difficult enterprise, however, requiring one in some sense to relinquish the very self that, in another aspect, was the unavoidable starting point for historical investigation: "If history is ever to solve even an infinitesimal part of the great and grievous riddle of life, we must quit the regions of personal and temporal foreboding for a sphere in which our view is not forthwith dimmed by self."[165] Burckhardt regarded such efforts not only a "duty" but a "supreme need": "it is our freedom in the very awareness of universal bondage and the stream of necessities."[166] "Therewith," he stated, "the saying *Historia vitae magistra* takes on a higher yet a humbler sense. We wish experience to make us, not shrewder (for next time), but wiser (for ever)."[167] Yet with characteristic pessimism, Burckhardt added that "few are the contemporaries who can attain an Archimedean point outside events, and are able to 'overcome in the spirit.' Nor is the satisfaction of those who do so, perhaps, very great."[168]

Burckhardt regarded nationalism as ruinous to sound historical judgment, noting that "true knowledge finds its chief rival in our preoccupation with the history of our own country." Such a preoccupation posed problems because it produced an "optical illusion" potentially "injurious to others" and "intimately interwoven with our fears and desires."[169] In Burckhardt's eyes, it was a matter of course that recent German military victories under Bismarck would detrimentally affect German historiography. "The interpretation of the facts," he told a friend in 1872, "is going through a complete and thorough transformation, and one will [only] have to wait some years before the history of the world, beginning with Adam, has been painted in victorious German colors and oriented towards 1870 and 1871."[170] Importantly, Burckhardt did not see the German political scene as an anomalous development but rather as one disquietingly congenial to pervasive nationalist and revolutionary trends stemming from the French Revolution: "the very same tempest that has shaken humanity since 1789 bears us [in 1871] onward, too."[171]

Nowhere are Burckhardt's remarks more characteristically pessimistic than in his declamations against the European civilization that had come into existence after the French Revolution. Echoing an earlier contempt of the "spirit of 1789" among Basler pietists and clergymen, Burckhardt bemoaned many contemporary ideas and events. In his view, an Enlightenment-derived "essentially materialistic explanation of the world and equally irreligious doctrine of man's nature" was on a fateful collision course with "the age-old sacramental foundations of existence which had been riveted fast in the Middle Ages."[172] Moreover, nationalist sentiment, state centralization, industrial expansion, secularizing processes, and above all the "spirit of eternal revision" – that "profound principle of the revolution, one which differentiates it from all earlier such events" – had led to a "colossal problem of existence" (grosse Daseinsfrage) and to the "uncertainty of each individual's fate."[173]

The idée force behind "the revolutionary age" – the title he gave to his lectures on the modern period – was the "alleged goodness of human nature" formulated by Enlightenment theorists. In deriding this view, Burckhardt made manifest the tenacity of his inherited religious sensibilities. He could not accept the notion that change inspired by new social idealism ipso facto meant (teleological) human improvement. He sermonized:

> The driving force in all this is a great *optimistic will* which has suffused the times since the middle of the eighteenth century. The premise is the *goodness* of human nature. . . . That optimistic will hopes that changes will bring about an increasing and definitive well-being and in every crisis believes it to be quite at hand. . . . But the overwhelming majority of the desires are *material* in nature, no matter how they may disguise themselves as ideal. . . . Yet material desires are in themselves absolutely insatiable, and even if they were continually gratified then they would be all the more insatiable.[174]

Skeptical of human nature, Burckhardt scrutinized the putatively liberal rhetorical milieu for masked powers that might manipulate optimistic aspirations for sinister purposes. He found many. Perhaps his greatest concern though was the "lawless centralization" of state power.[175] The modern democratic nation-state in his eyes had retained the potential for a "sultanic despotism." Such phenomena as the coerced secularization of church property and wars for "national necessity" instanced for Burckhardt the subtle ways in which despotic behavior could coexist with the modern state. The concept of equality too, Burckhardt regarded with skepticism, arguing that it easily

> turns into abdication of the individual, because the more universal any possession is, the fewer individual defenders it finds. Once the people have

become accustomed to the state as the sole guardian of rights and public welfare even the will to decentralization no longer helps. . . . Despite all the talk about freedom, people and government demand unlimited state power internally.[176]

The natural outcome of this mentality, according to Burckhardt, was the specter of a new Caesarism. Since "public benefit" and "public opinion" cannot be realized collectively, "the people" must look to the state as "benevolent father." Burckhardt saw Napoleon, Bismarck, and Frederick the Great as prototypical examples of modern "sultans" at ease operating within a republican rhetorical environment. Frederick's characterization of himself as "the first servant of the state," Burckhardt remarked, led to "the concentration of all forces for war and readiness for war [and] . . . an inevitable and permanent dictatorship."[177] Burckhardt made clear, finally, that the concept of property had outlasted all other principles and values, and in the hands of the "all-powerful state" had become coterminous with the principle of "the nation." This portended militarism, the suppression of difference, and the ruthless imperialist agglomeration of lands.

Simply put, Burckhardt did not celebrate the intellectual and political realities that had come into existence after the French Revolution. Nationalist and revolutionary energies, combined with rampant commercialism, betokened for him a future "accelerated by nationalist wars and deadly industrial competition."[178] The individual was at risk of being subsumed by the state, which in turn might succumb to rule by "terribles simplificateurs." "It has long been clear to me," Burckhardt wrote his friend von Preen in 1882,

> that the world is moving toward the alternative between complete democracy and absolute, lawless despotism, and the latter would certainly not be run by the dynasties, who are too soft-hearted, but by supposedly republican Military Commanders. Only people do not like to imagine a world whose rulers utterly ignore law, prosperity, enriching work, and industry, credit, etc., and who would rule with utter brutality. But those are the people into whose hands the world is being driven.[179]

Conclusion: "Filius Antistitis," the Ironic, Ascetic Prophet

In light of World War I and Europe's subsequent descent into totalitarianism, many of Burckhardt's statements seem amazingly prescient. A remorseful Friedrich Meinecke, writing in 1946, asserted that Ranke and the "German School" neither knew nor anticipated the sunless side of history experienced in the 1930s and 1940s. "In our own times," Meinecke stated, "we have more or less experienced that future which Burckhardt painted untiringly during the seventies and eighties of the last century."[180]

Similarly, Karl Barth, Reinhold Niebuhr, and other neo-orthodox theologians have recognized in Burckhardt a voice of prudence and social realism in a period dangerously adrift in nationalism, state expansionism, and facile intellectual idealisms.[181] "Though he [Burckhardt] had little understanding for the positive [in bourgeois society]," wrote Niebuhr,

> no one predicted the modern totalitarian state more accurately. . . . He believed that modern tyrants would use methods which even the most terrible despots of the past would not have had the heart to use. . . . Burckhardt even predicted fairly accurately to what degree liberal culture in totalitarian countries would capitulate to tyranny through failure to understand the enemy.[182]

It is beyond the scope of the present study to offer a philosophical or theological justification of Burckhardt's pessimism, which I have historically interpreted as a residual form of the theological idea, original sin. My primary aim has been to point out the deep-seated cultural and biographical sources for the peculiar persistence of this pessimistic doctrine in Burckhardt's thinking. The idea of an innately sinful nature has been one of the most unpopular and consciously rejected aspects of Christian theology in the modern period;[183] there is indeed something profoundly disturbing and paradoxical about a doctrinal position that regards evil and sin as inevitable but also hold humans responsible for actions prompted by their ineluctable state.[184] Nonetheless I am persuaded that the moral and political judgments derived from such a skeptical evaluation of human nature often prove – as the case of Burckhardt aptly demonstrates – more profound and realistic than judgments that do not recognize this premise.[185] Consequently, I oppose the opinions of those, such as Hayden White, who argue that Burckhardt's pessimism "separated [him] from any relevance to the social and cultural problems of [his] . . . own time and place."[186] With Meinecke and the neo-orthodox camp, I hold that Burckhardt's thought still offers a powerful critique of nationalism, totalitarianism, and a variety of other ideological excesses. "Burckhardtian realism" provides insight into the complexity, pettiness, and self-interest that regrettably characterize the human condition. Burckhardt recognized that professions of ideals (e.g., "progress," "God," "the nation," "Absolute Spirit," "equality") frequently conceal more limited selfish interests, and that the expressed pursuit of justice may in fact mask a ruthless exercise of power. In other words, attentiveness to the "factions and forces" in both the intellectual and political sphere, and a mindfulness of the potentially disastrous unintended consequences of even the best moral aspirations, comprise the central feature of Burckhardt's sermonizing against modernity.

Burckhardt's teaching has practical political implications, and stands against the mistaken notion that devoting oneself exclusively to determining and proclaiming "the right thing to do" can produce sufficient political resolutions. This mistaken notion, in fact, is actually more likely to render one powerless in the actual course of events, and it may – in the event that the proclamation is widely heeded – prove destructive, abolishing the necessary balance of powers and unleashing potent fanaticisms. The effective resolution of conflicts takes into consideration the ever-shifting equilibrium of power interests and regards each solution as indeterminate and provisional; the creative work of moral inquiry and social analysis must always begin anew. Finally, since those who control moral and political discourse would be, in Burckhardt's view, most prone to mask interests and abuse power, honest assessments of situations would be more likely discovered by listening to those who have experienced injustice and repression.

*   *   *

Yet, finally, I am forced to make a sharp distinction between (a) Burckhardt, the producer of morally valuable texts, and (b) Burckhardt, the detached, ironic personality. As I have indicated, I am sympathetic to the former. I conclude with concerns about the latter.

Despite the manifest insight of his historical judgments, Burckhardt to a certain degree voluntarily abdicated the sphere of political and moral action. This assessment resembles many previous critiques of Burckhardt.[187] Yet I differ from Hayden White and others, for I argue that Burckhardt abdicated *despite* sound moral-historical judgment and *not because* of rooted flaws in his judgment that somehow compelled him to withdraw. Instead of moral engagement, Burckhardt opted for an ambiguous, problematically apolitical, ironic and aesthetic form of historical contemplation.[188] He withdrew into a world of private aestheticism, self-satisfied in his own *Bildung*, skeptical both of premodern dogmatic claims (Christianity) and of modern secular ones (progress, rationality, the state, the nation, etc.) Revealingly, Burckhardt described his withdrawal as a form of asceticism.[189]

A model for his withdrawal, strangely enough, was the Christian anchoritic monks who lived during the Roman Empire. While bemoaning the institutional triumph of Christianity in his *Constantin*, Burckhardt nevertheless singled out and praised the anchorites, those "crushed spirits" and "towering personalities" driven by "spiritual forces" into the desert where they "waged their struggles with God apart from the world."[190] "It is in the nature of man," Burckhardt wrote, when he feels lost in the large and busy external world, that he should seek to find his proper self in solitude. And the more deeply he has felt the inward cleavage and rending, the more absolute is the solitude required.... Every earthly consideration vanishes and the recluse becomes an ascetic, partly to do penance, partly to owe the world without nothing more than the barest existence, but partly also to keep the soul capable of constant intercourse with the sublime.[191]

Beginning in the 1840s, Burckhardt often referred to himself as a "hermit," one out of place in "the clutches of this miserable world." He expressed his principal desire as "satisfy[ing] my soul's thirst for beauty before I leave this world."[192] "It is a curious feeling," he told his friend Hermann Schauenburg in 1848, "to have done with world, and to ask for nothing more but a place in the sun, in which to hatch out plans that no one bothers about in the end."[193] Still, "there are moments," he noted in another letter, "when I believe in some future miracle that would reconcile me to the things around me.... And yet – (for me) – it is impossible. The people that can overcome the world are those who either (1) through Christian love or (2) through ambition, are joined to the world. And those two things I do not possess."[194]

Burckhardt's retreat from "the world" was accompanied by an intense longing for the culture and history of Italy. Planning a trip to Italy in 1846, he commented to a friend of "hav[ing] secretly fallen out with it ["this wretched age"] entirely, and for that reason am escaping from it to the beautiful, lazy south, where history is dead, and I, who am so tired of the present, will be refreshed by the thrill of antiquity as by some wonderful and peaceful tomb."[195] Italy offered Burckhardt the consoling ideal of a serene and petrified past ripe for private enjoyment and contemplation. In northern Europe, and especially in Basel, Burckhardt felt constrained, discontented with the Philistine surroundings and the "shitting piety" (*Frommscheisserei*).[196] Early on, he purposed to live in Basel nothing more than "a life of polite reserve."[197] During his brief time in Zurich after 1855, Burckhardt delighted in living "incognito," for "in Basel I have to keep up appearances and ... lose a lot of time with people."[198] Only in Italy – both the real Italy and his somewhat fanciful conception of it – did Burckhardt find genuine ascetic (and aesthetic) escape: "there will always be some place open to me here [in Italy], where I can make a room for myself and spin myself in a chrysalis."[199]

Linked with the anchoritic impulse, an unmistakable apolitical mood characterized Burckhardt's attitude. His correspondence makes clear that he desired nothing less than complete political withdrawal: "Yes, I want to get away from them all, from radicals, the communists, the industrialists, the intellectuals, the pretentious, the reasoners, the abstract, the absolute, the philosophers, the sophists, the State, fanatics, the idealists, the 'ist' and 'isms' of every kind."[200] He sought instead historical meditation as a way to cultivate his own garden, to enhance his private self; "personality is, after all," he told a student, "the highest thing there is."[201] Such a preoccupation with cultural grooming, analyzed insightfully by W. H. Bruford in his work on the German tradition of *Bildung*, indeed presents many problematic ethical and political shortcomings – an apolitical aestheticizing of self and world with disquietingly elitist and illiberal associations.[202] And Burckhardt confirms the picture: an apolitical and ironic detachment made up a central feature of his *Weltanschauung* and self-understanding. "Where politics are concerned," Burckhardt opined, "I am obliged to keep to myself as I despise all parties: I know them all and belong to none."[203] "States are not built by men like me. . . . I can do nothing more with society as a whole; my attitude towards it is *willy-nilly ironical*."[204] Thus, driven like the anchorites into the wilderness, Burckhardt detached himself from "this wretched age" – from modernity.[205]

What distinguishes Burckhardt from the anchorites is of course his pervasive incredulity – toward premodern religious beliefs, modern liberal theology, not to mention modern intellectual systems and progressive politics. He did not withdraw to contemplate the presence of a divinity or an ideal; his retreat was conditioned by the conviction of fundamental absence and uncertainty, tempered only by private nostalgia and delight in the aesthetic remains of Europe's dogmatic past. In short, he refused to believe in master narratives or metavocabularies, as we might say today. This refusal (symptomatic, paradoxically, of an inherited religious pessimism) fostered his peculiar case of temporal disaffection. In this regard, Burckhardt was the proto-postmodern ironist *par excellence*, seeking *ekstasis* in the purely private flight from the master narratives of his time.[206]

In the end, Burckhardt remained true to his vow of "honest heresy." His rejection of Christian orthodoxy (his father), liberal theology (de Wette), and modern philosophy (Hegel) placed him in a singular and negative position in relation to the dominant outlooks of his time. Indeed, his supreme discontent with the present cultural order compelled him to spurn putatively *a priori* claims of knowledge among theologians and philosophers alike. He settled instead for the "modest" knowledge of a historian.

Yet his *a priori* disavowal of the possibility of any *a priori* presented other problems – problems highlighted by Nietzsche's diatribe against historicism and irony in his *Vom Nutzen und Nachteil der Historie für das Leben*.[207] Indeed, it seems probable that Burckhardt's younger colleague at Basel had him in mind when he wrote this essay, although it is hard to discern precisely how Burckhardt would fit Nietzsche's various schemata therein. Surely, though, Burckhardt must have represented to Nietzsche both the glories and the dangers of "monumental" historiography, one so tied up in the cultural monuments of the past that the power of action in the present is diminished. Nietzsche's appeal at the end of the essay to "youth" and "life" may well be a reaction to and against his nonetheless deeply esteemed colleague. Burckhardt was, after all, the historian whom Nietzsche knew best. "Oversaturation with history," Nietzsche wrote, "leads an age to that dangerous mood of irony in regard to itself and subsequently into the even more dangerous mood of cynicism: in this mood, however, it develops more and more a prudent practical egoism through which the forces of life are paralyzed and at last destroyed."[208]

Nietzsche sent his essay to Burckhardt, seeking approval from the man he regarded as "our greatest teacher" and as "the greatest among living historians." In his response, Burckhardt dissimulated, opining that "my poor head has never been capable of reflecting, even at a distance, as you [Nietzsche] are able to do, upon the final causes, the aims, and the desirability of history." Burckhardt admitted, however, that Nietzsche had laid "right before our eyes: the antagonism between historical knowledge and the capacity to do or be." Burckhardt called this phenomenon a "tragic incongruity."[209]

*   *   *

The development of Burckhardt's thought has a profound – one is tempted to say symbolic – relationship to the secularizing and historicizing forces of modernity that he both experienced firsthand and attempted to interpret historically. My aim has been to make clear that his antimodernism did not originate within the cognitive possibilities of modernity; moreover, it is neither historically explicable as derivative from Schopenhauer nor as symptomatic of a more general *fin-de-siècle* disillusionment. Rather, Burckhardt's antimodernism reflects the *habitus* of premodern pessimistic theological views and the sensibilities toward culture that attend them. Such sensibilities are manifested in Basel's 1534 Confession, in the reactions of Basel's clergy to the French Revolution, in Burckhardt's father's catechism and sermons, in Burckhardt's own youthful *Totentanz* poems, and in his well-known declamations against modern "optimistic" theology and philosophy. Such vale-of-tears pessimism shadowed and shaped the type of historical imagination realizable by Burckhardt long after he forsook Christianity as a response to de Wette's criticism. In light of the recent ascendency of a cultural and epistemological milieu – the so-called postmodern condition – hailed increasingly by historians as Burckhardtian in ethos,[210] it is important to reflect on the origins and meaning of Burckhardt's intellect and his cultural productions. His thought – its irony, incredulity, promises, and problems – is rightly regarded as the mother of our own.

Abbreviations Used in Notes and Bibliography

AfKG	*Archiv für Kulturgeschichte*
AHR	*American Historical Review*
BJ	*Basler Jahrbuch*
BZ	*Basler Zeitschrift für Geschichte und Alterstumskunde*
ES	*European Studies*
ESR	*European Studies Review*
GW	*Gesammelte Werke*
HH	*On History and Historians*
HM	*History and Memory*
HT	*History and Theory*
HTR	*Harvard Theological Review*
HZ	*Historische Zeitschrift*
JAAR	*Journal of the American Academy of Religion*
JHI	*Journal of the History of Ideas*
JMH	*Journal of Modern History*
JR	*Journal of Religion*
JWCI	*Journal of the Warburg and Courtauld Institutes*
NGC	*New German Critique*
NTS	*New Testament Studies*
RH	*Reflections on History*
RP	*Review of Politics*
SdS	*Storia della Storiografia*
TS	*Theological Studies*
TZ	*Theologische Zeitschrift*

Notes

Introduction: History, Theology, and Modernity

1 See Joseph Margolis, *Historied Thought, Constructed World: A Conceptual Primer for the Turn of the Millennium* (Berkeley: University of California Press, 1995); Thomas Kuhn, *The Structure of Scientific Revolution*, 2nd ed. (Chicago: University of Chicago Press, 1970), 1–9; Pierre Manent, *The City of Man*, trans. Marc A. Lepain (Princeton: Princeton University Press, 1998), 11–49; and Leo Strauss, *Natural Right and History* (Chicago: University of Chicago Press, 1953), 9–34.

2 The problematic term "historicism" will be defined and discussed shortly.

3 See Konrad Jarausch, "The Institutionalization of History in Eighteenth-Century Germany," in Hans Erich Bödeker, Georg Iggers, Jonathan B. Knudsen, and Peter Hanns Reill, eds., *Aufklärung und Geschichte: Studien zur deutschen Geschichtswissenschaft im 18.Jahrhundert* (Göttingen: Vandenhoeck & Ruprecht, 1986), 31.

4 See Bödeker, et al., eds., *Aufklärung und Geschichte* (Göttingen: Vandenhoeck & Ruprecht, 1986); Peter Hanns Reill, *The German Enlightenment and the Rise of Historicism* (Berkeley and Los Angeles: University of California Press, 1975); Andreas Kraus, *Vernunft und Geschichte: Die Bedeutung der deutschen Akademien für die Entwicklung der Geschichtswissenschaft im späten 18.Jahrhundert* (Freiburg: Herder, 1963); Georg Iggers, *The German Conception of History: The National Tradition of Historical Thought from Herder to the Present* (Middletown, CT: Wesleyan University Press, 1983); Georg Iggers, "The University of Göttingen 1760–1800 and the Transformation of Historical Scholarship," *SdS* 2 (1982): 11–37; Jörn Rüsen, *Konfiguration des Historismus: Studien zur deutschen Wissenschaftskultur* (Frankfurt A. M.: Suhrkamp, 1993); and Ulrich Muhlack, *Geschichtswissenschaft im Humanismus und in der Aufklärung: Die Vorgeschichte des Historismus* (Munich: C. H. Beck, 1991).

5 Konrad Jarausch, "The Institutionalization of History in Eighteenth-Century Germany," in Bödeker, et al., eds., *Aufklärung und Geschichte*, 25ff. As Josef Engels notes, "The chair in history in the philosophical faculty . . . was until 1758 fully in the service of theology." Before history gained institutional autonomy, historical study was regarded as an "annex to theology" and as "preparation studies for theology." See Josef Engels, "Die deutschen Universitäten und die Geschichtswissenschaften," *HZ* 189 (1959): 223–378.

6 Jarausch, "The Institutionalization of History in Eighteenth-Century Germany," in Bödeker, et al., eds., *Aufklärung und Geschichte*, 46–8.

7 John Stroup, "Protestant Church Historians and the German Enlightenment," in Bödeker, et al., eds., *Aufklärung und Geschichte*, 171.

8 On "universal history" in the early modern period, see Adalbert Klempt, *Die Säkular-*

isierung der universal-historischen Auffassung im 16.und 17.Jahrhundert: Zum Wandel des Geschichtsdenkens im 16.und 17.Jahrhundert (Göttingen: Musterschmidt, 1960); Reill, *The German Enlightenment and the Rise of Historicism*, 1–8, 75ff; Ernst Breisach, *Historiography: Ancient, Medieval, and Modern* (Chicago: University of Chicago Press, 1983), 177–85; and Allan Megill, "Grand Narrative and the Discipline of History," in Frank Ankersmit and Hans Kellner, eds., *A New Philosophy of History* (Chicago: University of Chicago Press, 1995), 155–7.

9 Friedrich Meinecke, *Historism: The Rise of a New Historical Outlook*, trans. J. E. Anderson (New York: Herder and Herder, 1972), liv.

10 Ninian Smart, "Editorial Introduction," in Smart, et al., eds., *Nineteenth-Century Religious Thought in the West*, vol. 1 (Cambridge: Cambridge University Press, 1985), 11.

11 Ernst Cassirer, *The Philosophy of the Enlightenment*, trans. Fritz C. A. Koelln and James P. Pettegrove (Princeton: Princeton University Press, 1951), 134ff. Cf. Reill: "[The Aufklärers'] goal was to rescue religion not destroy it, through a transformation of its meaning and function. In doing so, they were forced to confront an ever-widening circle of historical, psychological, and philosophical problems." Reill, *The German Enlightenment and the Rise of Historicism*, 6.

12 Karl Löwith, *From Hegel to Nietzsche: The Revolution in Nineteenth-Century Thought*, trans. David E. Green (New York: Columbia University Press, 1964), 327–8.

13 Douglas J. Cremer, "Protestant Theology in Early Weimar Germany: Barth, Tillich, and Bultmann," *JHI* 56 (April, 1995): 289.

14 See Jörn Rüsen, "Historische Methode und religiöser Sinn – Vorüberlegungen zu einer Dialektik der Rationalisierung des historischen Denkens in der Moderne," in Wolfgang Küttler, Jörn Rüsen, Ernst Schulin, eds., *Geschichtsdiskurs: Anfänge modernen historischen Denkens*, vol. 2 (Frankfurt am Main: Fischer, 1994), 344–77. Also see Wolfgang Hardtwig, *Geschichtsschreibung zwischen Alteuropa und moderner Welt: Jacob Burckhardt in seiner Zeit* (Göttingen: Vandenhoeck & Ruprecht, 1974), 106. Cf. Franz Schnabel's chapter, "Der Weg der Verweltlichung," in his *Deutsche Geschichte im neunzehnten Jahrhundert: Die protestantischen Kirchen in Deutschland*, vol. 4 (Freiburg: Herder, 1965), 15–36.

15 M. H. Abrams, *Natural Supernaturalism: Tradition and Revolution in Romantic Literature* (New York: W. W. Norton, 1971), 65–6. Cf. George Steiner, *Real Presences* (Chicago: University of Chicago Press, 1989).

16 The historian John Gillis has recently criticized modern European historians for their preoccupation with "the project of modernity," which in his view has obscured many "nonmodern" aspects of modern European history, especially the continuance of religious thinking and activity. Writes Gillis: "One need only point to religion – an area largely neglected by modern historians – to see what benefits the abandonment of a priori notions of modernity might hold. . . . This recognition [of religion] offers us the opportunity to explore aspects of European history that have been treated only condescendingly as mere survivals. It may be that we end up questioning the distinction between the premodern and the modern that defines the way Europe has been approached." See John Gillis, "The Future of European History," *Perspectives: American Historical Association Newsletter*, 34 (1996): 6.

17 A notable exception is Frederick Gregory's *Nature Lost? Natural Science and the German Theological Traditions of the Nineteenth Century* (Cambridge: Harvard University Press, 1992). Further, John Toews's *Hegelianism: The Path toward Dialectical Humanism, 1805–1841* (Cambridge: Cambridge University Press, 1980) commendably examines a broad spectrum of (Right, Center, and Left) Hegelian theologians.

18 Wolfgang Hardtwig, ed., *Geschichtskultur und Wissenschaft* (Munich: Deutscher Taschenbuch Verlag, 1990), 15.

172

19 Carl Pletsch, *Young Nietzsche: Becoming a Genius* (New York: The Free Press, 1991), 165–6.

20 See the discussion of the "incomparable moral and spiritual influence of the *Pfarrhaus*" in Robert Minder, "Das Bild des Pfarrhaus in der deutschen Literatur von Jean Paul bis Gottfried Benn," in *Kultur und Literatur in Deutschland und Frankreich* (Frankfurt am main: Insel Verlag, 1962), 44–72.

   The phenomenon of apostasy was not German but European. Franklin L. Baumer notes that "conversions in reverse among the intelligentsia . . . were literally legion in the nineteenth century." Ernest Renan and George Eliot are two other well-known examples. See Franklin L. Baumer, *Religion and the Rise of Skepticism* (New York: Harcourt, Brace, & Co., 1960), 136–40.

21 Thomas Nipperdey, *Germany from Napoleon to Bismarck, 1800–1866*, trans. Daniel Nolan (Princeton: Princeton University Press, 1996), 466.

22 Owen Chadwick, *The Secularization of the European Mind in the Nineteenth Century* (Cambridge: Cambridge University Press, 1975).

23 I employ here and elsewhere the somewhat awkward phrase "his secularization" as shorthand to describe the complex of experiences that led Burckhardt to repudiate Christianity and adopt a more secular outlook.

24 Mircea Eliade, *The Sacred and the Profane*, trans. Willard R. Trask (New York: Harper & Row, 1957), 203–4.

25 See Jacob Burckhardt, *Briefe* I, ed. Max Burckhardt (Basel: Benno Schwabe & Co., 1952), 90. (Hereafter *Briefe*).

26 *Briefe* I, 84.

27 See "W. M. L. de Wette," *The Encyclopaedia Britannica: A Dictionary of Arts, Literature and General Information* (11th ed.), vol. 8 (Cambridge, 1910), 138.

28 Hans Frei, *The Eclipse of Biblical Narrative: A Study in Eighteenth and Nineteenth Century Hermeneutics* (New Haven: Yale University Press, 1974), 79.

29 The influence of pietism is discussed at various places in this study. For a definition and brief history, see F. Ernest Stoeffler, "Pietism," in Mircea Eliade, ed., *The Encyclopedia of Religion*, vol. 11 (New York: Macmilllan, 1987), 324–6. The classic history of pietism is still Albrecht Ritschl's *Geschichte des Pietismus*, 3 vols. (Bonn, 1880–1886). Also see F. Ernest Stoeffler, *German Pietism during the Eighteenth Century* (Leiden: E. J. Brill, 1973).

30 *Briefe* I, 101.

31 Friedrich Nietzsche, "The Uses and Disadvantages of History for Life" in *Untimely Meditations*, trans. R. J. Hollingdale (Cambridge: Cambridge University Press, 1983), 96–7.

32 Rudolf Bultmann called this tendency the "historical pantheism of liberal theology." See Rudolf Bultmann, *Die liberale Theologie und die jüngste theologische Bewegung* (1924).

33 On crisis thinking, see Allan Megill, *Prophets of Extremity: Nietzsche, Heidegger, Foucault, Derrida* (Berkeley: University of California Press, 1985); on the 1880–1920 period, see Charles R. Bambach, *Heidegger, Dilthey, and the Crisis of Historicism* (Ithaca: Cornell University Press, 1995).

34 Quoted in Van Austin Harvey, *The Historian and the Believer: The Morality of Historical Knowledge and Christian Belief* (London: SCM Press, 1967), 5.

35 Alister McGrath, *The Genesis of Doctrine: A Study in the Foundations of Doctrinal Criticism* (Oxford: Basil Blackwell, 1990), 85.

36 Thomas Willey, *Back to Kant: The Revival of Kantianism in German Social and Historical Thought, 1860–1914* (Detroit: Wayne State University Press, 1978).

37 Charles E. McClelland, *State, Society, and University in Germany, 1700–1914* (Cambridge: Cambridge University Press, 1980), 151ff; Thomas Nipperdey, *Deutsche Geschichte 1800–1866: Bürgerwelt und starker Staat* (Munich: C. H. Beck, 1983), 470–7.

38 *Briefe* III, 248.

39 Although I employ the term "premodern" here and elsewhere, I do so largely for the sake of semantic convenience. In fact, I hope this study suggests that there is often no neat dividing line between "the premodern" and "the modern."

40 The first title given to these posthumously published lectures was *Weltgeschichtliche Betrachtungen*. I have opted in this study for Peter Ganz's more recent employment of Burckhardt's original title – "Über das Studium der Geschichte." See Peter Ganz, ed., *Jacob Burckhardt: Über das Studium der Geschichte* (Munich: Verlag C. H. Beck, 1982).

41 The notion of historicism as a "last religion" was, to my knowledge, first put forth by Karl Löwith. See Karl Löwith, *Meaning in History: Theological Implications of the Philosophy of History* (Chicago: University of Chicago Press, 1949), 192. Also see Wolfgang Hardtwig, "Geschichtsreligion-Wissenschaft als Arbeit-Objektivität: Der Historismus in neuer Sicht," *HZ* 252 (1991): 1–32. Jörn Rüsen speaks of nineteenth-century historicism as "a form of rational religious worship." See Rüsen, "Historische Methode und religiöser Sinn," in Küttler, et al., eds., *Geschichtsdiskurs*, vol. 2, 365–7.

42 On the term "historicism," see Georg Iggers, "Historicism: The History and Meaning of the Term," *JHI* 56 (Spring 1995): 129–52; Georg Iggers, "Historicism," *Dictionary of the History of Ideas*, vol. 2 (New York, 1973), 456–64; Dwight E. Lee and Robert N. Beck, "The Meaning of Historicism," *AHR* 59 (1954): 568–77; Ernst Rothacker, "Das Wort Historismus," *Zeitschrift für deutsche Wortforschung* 16 (1960): 3–6; Otto Gerhard Oexle, " 'Historismus.' Überlegungen zur Geschichte des Phänomens und des Begriffs," *Jahrbuch der braunschweigischen wissenschaftlichen Gesellschaft* (1986): 119–55; Maurice Mandelbaum, *History, Man, and Reason: A Study in Nineteenth-Century Thought* (Baltimore: Johns Hopkins University Press, 1971), 41–140; Karl Mannheim, "Historismus," *Archiv für Sozialwissenschaft und Sozialpolitik* 52 (1924): 1–60; Herbert Schnädelbach, *Philosophy in Germany, 1831–1933*, trans. Eric Matthews (Cambridge: Cambridge University Press, 1984), 35–40; Harry Ritter, "Historicism, Historism," *Dictionary of Concepts in History* (Westport, CT: Greenwood, 1986), 183–7; Gunter Scholz, "Historismus," *Historische Wörterbuch der Philosophie*, vol. 3 (Basel: Schwabe, 1974); 1141–7; Hans-Georg Gadamer, "Historismus," *Religion in Geschichte und Gesellschaft*, vol. 3 (Tübingen: Mohr, 1959), 369–70; and F. R. Ankersmit, "Historicism: An Attempt at Synthesis," *HT* 34 (1995): 143–73.

43 Friedrich Meinecke, *Historism: The Rise of a New Historical Outlook*, trans. J. E. Anderson (New York: Herder and Herder, 1972). For a criticism of Meinecke's work, see Allan Megill, "Aesthetic Theory and Historical Consciousness in the Eighteenth Century," *HT* 17 (1978): 29–62.

44 For a "prophecy" about the future of historicism, see Margolis, *Historied Thought, Constructed World: A Conceptual Primer for the Turn of the Millennium* (Berkeley: University of California Press, 1995).

45 Karl Mannheim, *Essays on the Sociology of Knowledge*, ed., Paul Kecskemeti (New York: Oxford University Press, 1952), 85.

46 In concentrating on historicism in its German historical context, I dissociate my usage from two other important meanings of the term. The first was given by Karl Popper, who defined it as an attempt to formulate laws of historical development. Popper applied it, in particular, to Hegel and Marx and to their influence on twentieth-century totalitarianism. See Karl Popper, *The Poverty of Historicism* (London: Routledge, 1960).

I also distinguish my usage from the "New Historicism" discussion in the American humanities. In this discussion, which contains few references to older continental debates, historicism has come to signify the culturally constructed nature of reality and human subjectivity in opposition to theories of essentialism or foundationalism. See Paul Hamilton, *Historicism* (London: Routledge, 1996); H. A. Vesser, ed., *The New Historicism* (New York: Routledge, 1989); Brook Thomas, *The New Historicism and Other*

Old-Fashioned Topics (Princeton: Princeton University Press, 1991); and Paul Michael Lützeler, "Der postmoderne Neohistorismus in den amerikanischen Humanities," in Hart Eggert, et al., eds., *Geschichte als Literatur. Formen und Grenzen der Repräsentation von Vergangenheit* (Stuttgart, 1990), 67–76.

47 See Georg Iggers and George Powell, eds., *Leopold von Ranke and the Shaping of the Historical Discipline* (Syracuse, NY: Syracuse University Press, 1990), 5.

48 Iggers, "Historicism," *JHI* 56 (Spring 1995): 131–2, 142–51.

In the past several years, numerous books have appeared on the history and theory of German historiography and its relationship to historicism. Jörn Rüsen and the so-called Bielefeld School have been the chief agents in the production of this impressive body of scholarship. See Jörn Rüsen and Horst-Walter Blanke, eds., *Von der Aufklärung zum Historismus: Strukturwandel des historischen Denkens* (Paderborn, 1984); Jörn Rüsen and Friedrich Jaeger, *Geschichte des Historismus* (Stuttgart, 1990); Jörn Rüsen *Grundzüge des Historismus*, 3 vols. (Göttingen, 1983–9); Jörn Rüsen, *Konfiguration des Historismus: Studien zur deutschen Wissenschaftskultur* (Frankfurt am Main: Suhrkamp, 1993); Horst-Walter Blanke, *Historiographiegeschichte als Historik* (Stuttgart, 1991); Hans-Jürgen Pandel, *Historik und Didaktik* (Stuttgart, 1990).

For a criticism of the nationalistic excesses of nineteenth-century German historiography, see Georg Iggers, *The German Conception of History*. On the professionalization of German historiography, see W. Weber, *Priester der Clio: Historische-sozialwissenschaftliche Studien zur Herkunft und Karriere deutscher Historiker und zur Geschichte der Geschichtswissenschaft* (New York, 1984) and David A. J. Telman, "Clio Ascendant: The Historical Profession in Nineteenth-Century Germany," Ph.D. diss. (Cornell University, 1993).

49 Iggers, "Historicism," *JHI*, 56 (Spring 1995): 133–5, 137–42.

50 Ernst Troeltsch, *Protestantism and Progress: A Historical Study of the Relation of Protestantism to the Modern World*, trans. W. Montgomery (Beacon Press, 1966), 34.

51 Iggers also speaks of "classical historicism" as "optimistic historicist thought."

52 This is treated in chapter five. Although Burckhardt's well-known epistemological anti-idealism disqualifies him as an exemplary representative of historicism à la Ranke, his resistance to *a priori* (especially Hegelian) conceptions of history make him, nonetheless, a distinguished marginal figure in the tradition.

53 Annette Wittkau, *Historismus: Zur Geschichte des Begriffs und des Problems* (Göttingen: Vandenhoeck & Ruprecht, 1992); Charles R. Bambach, *Heidegger, Dilthey, and the Crisis of Historicism* (Ithaca: Cornell University Press, 1995); Otto Gerhard Oexle, " 'Historismus.' Überlegungen zur Geschichte des Phänomens und des Begriffs," *Jahrbuch der braunschweigischen wissenschaftlichen Gesellschaft* (1986): 119–55; and Wolfgang Hardtwig, "Geschichtsreligion-Wissenschaft als Arbeit-Objektivität: Der Historismus in neuer Sicht," *HZ* 252 (1991): 1–32.

54 Iggers, "Historicism," *JHI* 56 (Spring 1995): 142.

55 Bambach, *Heidegger, Dilthey, and the Crisis of Historicism*, 1–21.

56 Wittkau shows with commendable clarity the particular intensity with which theologians grappled with the problem of historicism. See Wittkau, *Historismus*, 116–9, 164–8. Wittkau notes that historicism as a theological problem had its roots in the *Leben-Jesu-Forschung* of the nineteenth-century – a scholarly tradition that came to an end with the publication of Albert Schweitzer's *Geschichte der Leben-Jesu-Forschung* (1906), a work in which, claims Alister McGrath, "the pseudo-historical theology of liberal Protestantism" was brought to a "final and most cruel exposure." See McGrath, *The Making of Modern German Christology: From the Enlightenment to Pannenberg* (Oxford: Basil Blackwell, 1986), 80. Cf. Michael Murrmann-Kahl, *Die entzauberte Heilsgeschichte: Der Historismus erobert die Theologie* (Gütersloh: Gütersloh Verlagshaus, 1992).

Martin Kähler's highly influential *Die sogennante historische Jesu und der geschichtliche, biblische Christus* (1892) also marks a turning point in the literature. Kähler criticized what he called nineteenth-century "Historizimus" for not recognizing the epistemological limitations placed on the historical knower. Ever since Kähler, notes James M. Robinson, "the problem of the historian's own historicity has become a [more] fundamental problem." See James M. Robinson, *The New Quest of the Historical Jesus* (Philadelphia: Fortress Press, 1983), 30ff.

In the early twentieth century a deluge of essays and books appeared by theologians on the problem of historicism, including Otto Kirn, *Glaube und Geschichte* (1900); Julius Käfton, *Dogmatik und Historismus* (1904); Ferdinand Jakob Schmidt, *Der Niedergang des Protestantismus* (1904); Ernst Troeltsch, "Die Krisis des Historismus," *Neue Rundschau* 33 (1922): 572–90; Ernst Troeltsch, *Historismus und seine Probleme* (1922); Ernst Troeltsch, *Historismus und seine Überwindung* (1932); Friedrich Gogarten, "Historismus," *Zwischen den Zeiten*, 8 (1924): 7–25; and Karl Heussi, *Die Krisis des Historismus* (1932).

Finally, the notion of the "crisis of historicism" is crucial for understanding the works of neo-orthodox theologians like Karl Barth, Emil Brunner, and Friedrich Gogarten. Brunner succinctly defined the situation confronting the neo-orthodox camp: "The attempt was made [in the nineteenth century] to retain the Absolute in a historical phenomenon, but it proved impossible to fence it off from the relativity of historical phenomena as such. It is only the latest phase of theology, known as the 'religious-historical,' which, in its most distinguished representative Troeltsch, has drawn out the consequences of historicism to its bitter end, and by doing so has done away with theology as such. It takes the modern, secular conception of history seriously. History is an endless flux, a continuum, and hence, relativity. In history there are no self-existent entities that can be isolated out." See Emil Brunner, *The Philosophy of Religion*, trans. A. J. D. Farrer and Bertram Lee Woolf (London, 1937), 47. On Barth's conception of history, see Barth, "The Christian Belief in Providence: The Doctrine of Providence, its Basis and Form," in C. T. McIntire, ed., *God, History, and Historians* (Oxford: Oxford University Press, 1977), 206–23. For a study of the category of history in the thought of Troeltsch and Barth, see Thomas W. Ogletree, *Christian Faith and History: A Critical Comparison of Ernst Troeltsch and Karl Barth* (New York: Abingdon Press, 1965).

57 This is the implication of Iggers's treatment of Troeltsch in *The German Conception of History*, 174ff.

58 Rüsen, "Historische Methode und religiöser Sinn," in Küttler, et al., eds., *Geschichtsdiskurs*, vol. 2, 351.

59 Hence the orthodox Kierkegaard spoke of the "Absolute Paradox: A Metaphysical Crochet." See Søren Kierkegaard, *Philosophical Fragments*, trans. David Swenson and Howard V. Hong (Princeton: Princeton University Press, 1967), 46–67.

60 On the Arian controversy, see Alister McGrath, *Christian Theology: An Introduction* (Oxford: Basil Blackwell, 1994), 18–20, 283–7.

61 This benchmark is still recognized by Protestants, Catholics, and Orthodox Christians alike.

62 Peter L. Berger defines a "plausibility structure" as the underlying institutional and cognitive conditions in societies that confer plausibility on certain beliefs, moralities, and ideas while rendering others untenable. See Peter L. Berger, *The Heretical Imperative: Contemporary Possibilities of Religious Affirmation* (Garden City, NY: Doubleday, 1979), 17ff. Cf. Peter L. Berger and Thomas Luckmann, *The Social Construction of Reality: A Treatise in the Sociology of Knowledge* (Garden City, NY: Doubleday, 1966).

63 See Roy A. Harrisville and Walter Sundberg, *The Bible in Modern Culture: Theology and Historical-Critical Method from Spinoza to Käsemann* (Grand Rapids, MI: Eerdmans, 1995), 25ff; Klaus Scholder, *Ursprünge und Probleme der Bibelkritik im 17.Jahrhundert*

(Munich: Kaiser, 1966); Henning Graf Reventlow, Walter Sparn, and John Woodbridge, eds., *Historische Kritik und biblische Kanon in der deutschen Aufklärung* (Wiesbaden, 1988). Also see the chapters "Heterodoxy," "The Rationalists," and "Richard Simon and Biblical Criticism" in Paul Hazard, *The European Mind, 1680–1715*, trans. J. Lewis May (London: Hollis and Carter, 1952), 80–98, 119–54, 180–97.

64 Frei, *Eclipse of Biblical Narrative*, 17.

65 Rüsen, "Historische Methode und religiöser Sinn," in Küttler, et al., eds., *Geschichtsdiskurs*, vol. 2, 357.

66 On premodern exegesis, see Frei, *Eclipse of Biblical Narrative*, 17–50.

67 Baumer, *Religion and the Rise of Skepticism*, 156.

68 Henry Sidgwick, "The Historical Method," *Mind: A Quarterly Review of Psychology and Philosophy* 11 (1886): 213–4.

69 McGrath, *The Genesis of Doctrine*, 81–5. For a sustained philosophical critique of historicism of the sort that I am suggesting here, see Leo Strauss, *Natural Right and History*, 9–34.

70 For a broad treatment of religion in nineteenth-century Europe, see Hugh McLeod, *Religion and the People of Western Europe, 1789–1970* (Oxford: Oxford University Press, 1981). Cf. James Hastings Nichols, *History of Christianity, 1650–1950, Secularization of the West* (New York: Ronald Press, 1956), 111ff, and Alec R. Vidler, *The Church in an Age of Revolution: 1789 to the Present Day* (New York: Penguin, 1961).

71 See Franz Schnabel, *Deutsche Geschichte im neunzehnten Jahrhundert: Die protestantischen Kirchen in Deutschland*, vol. 4; Hugh McLeod, ed., *European Religion in the Age of Great Cities, 1830–1930* (London: Routledge, 1995); and Owen Chadwick, *The Secularization of the European Mind in the Nineteenth Century*.

   For an introduction to the term "secularization" and its many uses, see James F. Childress and David B. Harned, eds., *Secularization and the Protestant Prospect* (Philadelphia: The Westminster Press, 1970); Bryan R. Wilson, "Secularization," in Mircea Eliade, ed., *Encyclopedia of Religion*, vol. 13 (New York: Macmillan, 1987), 159–65; David Martin, *A General Theory of Secularization* (New York: Harper & Row, 1978); "Säkularisation, Säkularisierung" in Otto Brunner, Werner Conze, Reinhart Koselleck, eds., *Geschichtliche Grundbegriffe*, vol. 5 (Stuttgart: Klett-Cotta, 1972), 789–829; "Säkularisation" in Josef Höfer and Karl Rahner, eds., *Lexikon für Theologie und Kirche* (Freiburg: Verlag Herder, 1964), 247–55; Steve Bruce, ed., *Religion and Modernization: Sociologists and Historians Debate the Secularization Thesis* (Oxford: Oxford University Press, 1992).

72 See James D. Hunter, "Conservative Protestantism," in Phillip E. Hammond, ed., *The Sacred in a Secular Age: Toward Revision in the Scientific Study of Religion* (Berkeley: University of California Press, 1985), 150; Peter L. Berger, *The Sacred Canopy: Elements of a Sociological Theory of Religion* (Garden City, NY: Doubleday, 1967), 111–3.

73 See Bryan Wilson, "Secularization: The Inherited Model," in Hammond, ed., *The Sacred in a Secular Age*, 16–7. I restrict my argument to European elite culture and especially to the public spheres of education, law, and politics. I recognize that religion per se has not been extinguished, and outside Europe, Christianity has become a leading world force. Some critics even speak of the "re-enchantment" of the world. See James T. Richardson, "Studies of Conversion: Secularization or Re-enchantment?" in Hammond, ed., *The Sacred in a Secular Age*, 104–21.

74 Berger, *The Sacred Canopy*, 112.

75 Schleiermacher, *Sämmtliche Werke* 1/2 (Berlin, 1836), 614, 617–8.

76 De Wette, *Über Religion und Theologie* (Berlin, 1815), 108.

77 Friedrich Paulsen, *The German Universities and University Study*, trans. Frank Thilly and William W. Elwang (New York: Charles Scribner's Sons, 1906), 233.

78 See W. Lexis, ed., *Die deutschen Universitäten* (Berlin, 1893), 126.

79 See the "dritte Tafel" in the appendices of Max Lenz, *Geschichte der königlichen Friedrich-Wilhelms-Universität zu Berlin*, vol. 3 (Halle, 1910).

80 On the importance of theology in medieval university life and culture, see Lowrie J. Daly, *The Medieval University* (New York, 1961), 102–7, 145–62.

81 See Schleiermacher, *Kurze Darstellung des theologischen Studiums* (Leipzig, 1810) and John M. Stroup, "The Idea of Theological Education at the University of Berlin: From Schleiermacher to Harnack," in Patrick Henry, ed., *Schools of Thought in the Christian Tradition* (Philadelphia: Fortress Press, 1984), 152–76.

82 J. H. Newman, *The Idea of a University* (San Francisco: Rinehart Press, 1960), 52–3. Interestingly, Newman wrote the following of history: "The evidence of History, I say, is invaluable in its place; but, if it assumes to be the sole means of gaining Religious Truth, it goes beyond its place. We are putting it to a larger office than it can undertake, if we countenance the usurpation; and we are turning a true guide and blessing into a source of inexplicable difficulty and interminable doubt." See p. 72.

83 On the emergence of the philosophical faculty in the nineteenth century, see Paulsen, *The German Universities*, 408ff.

84 Weber, *Priester der Clio*, 49.

85 Paulsen, *The German Universities*, 384.

86 See Stroup, "The Idea of Theological Education," in Henry, ed., *Schools of Thought in the Christian Tradition*, 165–6. Cf. Adolf Harnack, "Die Bedeutung der theologischen Fakultäten," *Preussische Jahrbücher* (March 1919): 362–74 and "Die Aufgabe der theologischen Fakultäten und die allgemeine Religiongeschichte" in Harnack, *Reden und Aufsätzen*, vol. 2 (Giesen, 1904), 161–87.

87 Paulsen, *The German Universities*, 384.

88 Paulsen, *The German Universities*, 238.

89 Berger, *The Heretical Imperative*, 18; Berger, *The Sacred Canopy*, 154–5.

90 Paulsen, *The German Universities*, 387.

91 Larry Shiner, "The Meanings of Secularization," in Childress and Harned, eds., *Secularization and the Protestant Prospect*, 38–9.

92 See Max Weber, *The Protestant Ethic and the Spirit of Capitalism*, trans. Talcott Parsons (New York: Charles Scribner's Sons, 1958); Philip Rieff, *The Triumph of the Therapeutic: Uses of Faith after Freud* (Chicago: University of Chicago Press, 1987). The view that Marxism was a secular form of Jewish-Christian messianic traditions is represented by a voluminous literature. For a summary and critique of this literature, see Norman Levine, "Humanism without Eschatology," *JHI* 33 (1972): 281–98.

93 Karl Löwith, *Meaning in History: Theological Implications of the Philosophy of History* (Chicago: University of Chicago Press, 1949), 19.

94 Löwith, *Meaning in History*, 191–203.

95 Blumenberg locates the birth of "the modern age" in two main early-modern experiences: (1) the advances in astronomy in the sixteenth and seventeenth centuries and (2) the "quarrel of the ancients and the moderns" in the late seventeenth century. See especially Part III, "The 'Trial' of Theoretical Curiosity," in Hans Blumenberg, *The Legitimacy of the Modern Age*, trans. Robert M. Wallace (Cambridge: MIT Press, 1983), 229ff. Blumenberg wrote the original version in 1966; it was emended in a second edition and published in three installments in 1973, 1974, and 1976.

96 Blumenberg, *The Legitimacy of the Modern Age*, 65.

97 For a summary of Blumenberg's critique of Löwith, see Robert M. Wallace, "Progress, Secularization, and Modernity: The Löwith-Blumenberg Debate," *NGC* 22 (1981): 63–80.

98 Martin Jay, "Blumenberg and Modernism: A Reflection on *The Legitimacy of the Modern Age*," in Martin Jay, *Fin-de-Siècle Socialism and Other Essays* (New York: Routledge, 1988), 163.

99 I refer the reader to Jacques Derrida's critique of the notion that past metaphysics can simply be overcome or transcended. The past is always disguised and embedded in the present. See Derrida, "The Ends of Man" in *Margins of Philosophy*, trans. Alan Bass (Chicago: University of Chicago Press, 1982), 109–36.

100 See Löwith's review of Blumenberg's book in the *Philosophische Rundschau*, 15 (1968): 195–201.

101 Even Blumenberg, it should be noted, admits a limited validity to the transposition thesis. See Blumenberg *Legitimacy of the Modern Age*, 30.

102 Michel Foucault, "Nietzsche, Genealogy, History," in Paul Rabinow, ed., *The Foucault Reader* (New York: Pantheon Books, 1984), 76–80.

Chapter One. W. M. L. de Wette: Enlightenment, Romanticism, and Biblical Criticism

1 See de Wette, *Theodore; or the Skeptic's Conversion*, vol. 1, trans. James F. Clarke (Boston, 1841). Quoted in translator's preface, vii. The name of the American theologian is not given.

2 H. Walker, "The University of Berlin," *The Christian Examiner* (November 1836): 220.

3 The following works of de Wette's were translated into English: *Theodore; or The Skeptic's Conversion*, 2 vols., trans. James F. Clarke (Boston, 1841); *Human Life; or Practical Ethics*, 2 vols., trans. Samuel Osgood (Boston, 1842); *Introduction to the Old Testament*, 2 vols., trans. Theodore Parker (Boston, 1843); *Introduction to the Canonical Books of the New Testament*, trans. Frederick Frothingham (Boston, 1858). De Wette's *Theodor* and *Human Life* were published in George Ripley's *Specimens of Foreign Literature* (Boston, 1838–42) as volumes X, XI, XII, XIII. Interestingly, de Wette was chosen over Schleiermacher to represent German theology. New Englanders were also familiar with de Wette through several journals: *The Christian Examiner*, *The Dial*, and *The Christian Review*. De Wette's stepson, Karl Beck, who had fled to Boston from Europe, helped establish the reputation of his stepfather. Samuel Osgood and Theodore Parker were the most ardent American popularizers of de Wette. See Samuel Osgood, "W. M. L. de Wette," *The Christian Examiner* (May 1838): 137–71. For Parker's debt to de Wette, see Perry Miller, "Theodore Parker: Apostasy within Liberalism," *HTR* 54 (1961): 275–95. For a general account of de Wette's influence in New England, see Siegfried B. Puknat, "De Wette in New England," *Proceedings of the American Philosophical Society* 102 (1958): 376–95.

4 B. Reicke, "W. M. L. de Wette's Contribution to Biblical Theology," *NTS* 29 (1984): 303.

5 Letter of January 18, 1835, in R. L. Rusk, ed., *Letters of Ralph Waldo Emerson*, vol. 1 (New York: Columbia University Press, 1939), 425.

6 John Rogerson, "Philosophy and the Rise of Biblical Criticism in England and Germany" in S. W. Sykes, ed., *England and Germany: Studies in Theological Diplomacy* (Frankfurt am main: Peter D. Lang, 1982), 79.

7 Rudolf Smend, *Deutsche Alttestamentler in Drei Jahrhunderten* (Göttingen: Vandenhoeck & Ruprecht, 1989), 38.

8 Carl Hinrichs has argued that de Wette played a major role in shaping Ranke's mature conception of history; see Carl Hinrichs, *Ranke und die Geschichtstheologie der Goethezeit* (Göttingen, 1958), 136ff.

9 Concerning Strauss and de Wette, see Horton Harris, *David Friedrich Strauss and his Theology* (Cambridge: Cambridge University Press, 1973), 34. I shall take up de Wette's positions vis-à-vis Strauss's in chapter three. On Bauer's debt to de Wette, see, for example, Bruno Bauer, *Kritik der Geschichte der Offenbarung* (Berlin, 1838), 107f.

10 See Rudolf Otto, *The Philosophy of Religion Based on Kant and Fries*, trans. E. B. Dicker (London, 1931).

11 Karl Barth, *Protestant Theology in the Nineteenth Century* (London: SCM Press, 1972), 482ff.

12 Ernst Staehelin, ed., *Dewettiana: Forschungen und Texte zu Wilhelm Martin Leberecht de Wette* (Basel: Helbing & Lichtenhahn, 1956), 115.

13 See especially John Rogerson, *Old Testament Criticism in the Nineteenth Century: England and Germany* (London: SPCK Press, 1984), 28ff, and Rudolf Smend, *Wilhelm Martin Leberecht de Wettes Arbeit am Alten und Neuen Testament* (Basel: Helbing & Lichtenhahn, 1958), 11–122.

14 Bernard M. G. Reardon, *Religion in the Age of Romanticism* (Cambridge: Cambridge University Press, 1985), 4.

15 M. H. Abrams, *Natural Supernaturalism* (New York: W. W. Norton, 1971), 66.

16 De Wette, *Theodore; or the Skeptic's Conversion*, vol. 1, trans. James F. Clarke (Boston, 1841), xxviii.

17 In making the distinction between internal and external approaches to intellectual history, and in attempting to combine them, I am well aware that I tread on a number of knotty theoretical issues. Sensitive to these issues, I would like to point out that I do not see such oppositions unproblematically. They are implicated in the larger issue of distinguishing between text and context in writing history – or in what Dominick LaCapra has called the "problem of textuality writ large." LaCapra writes: "For the historian, the very reconstruction of a 'context' or a 'reality' takes place on the basis of 'textualized' remainders of the past. The historian's position is not unique in that all definitions of reality are implicated in textual processes." See Dominick LaCapra, "Rethinking Intellectual History and Reading Texts," in *Modern European Intellectual History: Reappraisals and New Perspectives*, eds. Dominick LaCapra and Steven Kaplan (Ithaca: Cornell University Press, 1982). Cf. Hayden White, "The Context in the Text: Method and Ideology in Intellectual History" in Hayden White, ed., *The Content of the Form: Narrative Discourse and Historical Representation* (Baltimore: Johns Hopkins University Press, 1987), 185–213.

18 The most authoritative works to date providing biographical information about de Wette are by biblical scholars. See Adelbert Wiegand, *W. M. L. de Wette (1780–1849): Eine Säkularschrift* (Erfurt, 1879); Rudolf Smend, *Wilhelm Martin Leberecht de Wettes Arbeit am Alten und Neuen Testament* (Basel, 1958); Paul Handschin, *Wilhelm Martin Leberecht de Wette als Prediger und Schriftsteller* (Basel, 1858); John Rogerson, *W. M. L. de Wette: Founder of Modern Biblical Criticism* (Sheffield: JSOT Press, 1992).

19 Rogerson, *De Wette*, 14.

20 See Wiegand, *De Wette*, 8–10. De Wette seems to have met Goethe; he mentions an unsuccessful attempt to visit Goethe in a letter of 3 December 1819 to Schleiermacher. See Staehelin, *Dewettiana*, 92. On Weimar in the late eighteenth century, see W. H. Bruford, *Culture and Society in Classical Weimar* (Cambridge: Cambridge University Press, 1962) and Karl Heinz Hahn, *Goethe in Weimar: ein Kapital deutscher Kulturgeschichte* (Zurich, 1986).

21 Quoted in Wiegand, *De Wette*, 8.

22 Staehelin, *Dewettiana*, 183–4.

23 De Wette, *Über Religion und Theologie* (Berlin, 1815), 64. After de Wette's death, his books (along with those of a professor L. W. Hitzig) were sold at an auction. The auction list includes eighteen books by, or commentaries on, Herder. See Antiquar J. Meyri in Basel. Catalog No. 40. Auction on 31 July 1850; Basel Univ. Library, Falk. 3206 No. 8.12, 1850.

24 Wiegand, *De Wette*, 8–10. There is little evidence of de Wette's exact views on the French Revolution. However, in his novel *Theodor*, de Wette writes that "Theodor seized with

animation the political ideas set in circulation by the French Revolution, and joined to the philosophical study of morals and of religion, that of politics and natural law." See *Theodor* I, 20. Moreover, in light of some of de Wette's later political actions (especially during his years at Berlin) one can infer that the Revolution impressed him deeply, as it did many German intellectuals. For a broad treatment of this theme, see G. P. Gooch's classic *Germany and the French Revolution*, 2nd ed. (New York: Russell & Russell, 1966) and David Blackbourn, *The Long Nineteenth Century: A History of Germany, 1780–1918* (New York: Oxford University Press, 1998), 47–90.

25 Quoted in J. W. Rogerson, "Philosophy and the Rise of Biblical Criticism in England and Germany," in Sykes, ed., *England and Germany: Studies in Theological Diplomacy*, 63.

26 For more on Wellhausen, see Rogerson, *Old Testament Criticism*, 257ff.

27 In advancing this argument, I would like to acknowledge a debt to John Rogerson's article "Philosophy and the Rise of Biblical Criticism in England and Germany," in Sykes, ed., *England and Germany: Studies in Theological Diplomacy*, 63–79; to Rogerson's biography of de Wette; and to Rudolf Smend's article, "De Wette und das Verhältnis zwischen historischer Bibelkritik und philosophischem System im 19. Jahrhundert," *TZ* 14 (1957): 107–19.

28 Staehelin, *Dewettiana*, 11.

29 Rogerson, *De Wette*, 26.

30 See Nicholas Boyle, *Goethe: The Poet and the Age*, vol. 1. (Oxford: Oxford University Press, 1992), 389ff.

31 Rogerson, *De Wette*, 26–27. Cf. Karl Heussi, *Geschichte der theologischen Fakultät zu Jena* (Weimar, 1954), 202; Max Steinmetz, et al., eds., *Geschichte der Universität Jena: 1548/58–1958* (Jena: Ved Gustav Fischer, 1958), 246–9, 261–4.

32 Steinmetz, et al., eds., *Geschichte der Universität Jena*, 249.

33 See Max Wundt, *Die Philosophie an der Universität Jena: in ihrem geschichtlichen Verlaufe dargestellt* (Jena, 1932). For Hegel's early experiences in Jena, see H. S. Harris, *Hegel's Development, Night Thoughts (Jena 1801–1806)* (Oxford: Clarendon Press, 1983).

34 Quoted in James Sheehan, *German History, 1770–1866* (Oxford: Clarendon Press, 1989), 342.

35 Charles Taylor, *Hegel* (Cambridge: Cambridge University Press, 1975), 3–4.

36 Frederick Beiser, *The Fate of Reason: German Philosophy from Kant to Fichte* (Cambridge: Harvard University Press, 1987), 8.

37 Letter to Karl August Böttiger (1760–1835), 5 January 1806. Staehelin, *Dewettiana*, 64–5.

38 Heussi, *Geschichte der theologischen Fakultät zu Jena*, 211.

39 Immanuel Kant, *Der Streit der Fakultäten* (New York: Abaris Books, 1979), 36. This work contains a page-by-page English translation by Mary J. Gregor. I have cited the pagination of Kant's original publication, which Gregor also provides.

40 Kant, *Streit*, 28.

41 In many respects, Kant's views on religion differed little if at all from earlier eighteenth-century deist views, although Kant referred to himself strictly as a "theist." See Allen Wood, "Kant's Deism" in Philip J. Rossi and Michael Wren, eds., *Kant's Philosophy of Religion Reconsidered* (Bloomington and Indianapolis: Indiana University Press, 1991), 1–21. Cf. Allen Wood, *Kant's Moral Religion* (Ithaca: Cornell University Press, 1970) and *Kant's Rational Theology* (Ithaca: Cornell University Press, 1978).

42 Kant, *Streit*, 36–8.

43 Kant, *Streit*, 53 (translation modified).

44 See Steven Lestition, "Kant and the End of the Enlightenment in Prussia," *JMH* 65 (1993): 57ff.

45 Kant, *Streit*, 36. I shall touch on Kant's christology in chapter three when I discuss more specifically the background of de Wette's christology. On *Aufklärung* christology in general, see Alister E. McGrath, *The Making of Modern German Christology: From the Enlightenment to Pannenberg* (Oxford: Basil Blackwell, 1986), 9–31; Colin Brown, *Jesus in European Protestant Thought, 1778–1860* (Durham, NC: Labyrinth Press, 1985), 57–78.

46 Kant, *Streit*, 66–7 (translation modified). The distinction between the necessary truths of reason and the contingent truths of history by no means originates with Kant. As early as Aristotle's *Poetics*, a similar distinction is made: "Poetry is more philosophic and of more serious import than history; for poetry tends to deal with the general, while history is concerned with delimited particular facts." See *Aristotle's Poetics*, trans. H. Epps (Chapel Hill: University of North Carolina Press, 1942), 18. Deists and neologians in the eighteenth century pioneered this distinction afresh, and Kant derived much from their ideas. Also see Peter Hanns Reill, *The German Enlightenment and the Rise of Historicism* (Berkeley: University of California Press, 1975), 43–4.

47 De Wette, *Theodor, oder des Zweiflers Weihe: Bildungsgeschichte eines evangelischen Geistlichen*. 2 vols. (Berlin, 1822). While there are risks involved in using literature as a historical source, the parallels between life and book in the case of *Theodor* are so explicit that ignoring this material would be a great disservice in evaluating de Wette's early development.

48 See de Wette's introduction to *Theodore* (English translation), xxix.

49 Rogerson, *De Wette*, 31.

50 At the auction of de Wette's library, there were twenty-four books by Kant, fifty-seven about him, and a series of commentaries on his works. See Antiquar J. Meyri in Basel. Catalog No. 40. Auction on 31 July 1850; Basel Univ. Library, Falk. 3206 N.8.12, 1850. Noted in Rogerson, *De Wette*, 21–2.

51 Staehelin, *Dewettiana*, 11.

52 Quoted in Smend, *De Wette*, 14–5.

53 *Theodor* I, 18–9.

54 *Theodor* I, 27.

55 Staehelin, *Dewettiana*, 11; Rogerson, *De Wette*, 31.

56 *Theodor* I, 21.

57 *Theodor* I, 15; quoted in Rogerson, *De Wette*, 58.

58 *Theodor* I, 25.

59 Staehelin, *Dewettiana*, 184.

60 De Wette, *Über Religion und Theologie* (Berlin, 1815), 138.

61 De Wette, *Eine Idee über das Studium der Theologie* (1801), ed. A. Stieren (Lepizig, 1850).

62 *Theodor* I, 26–7.

63 *Theodor* I, 26.

64 *Theodor* I, 28.

65 Staehelin *Dewettiana*, 184.

66 See *Schellings Werke*, ed. Manfred. Schröter (Münich: Beck, 1927), III, 229–374, 375–507.

67 Richard Kroner, *Von Kant bis Hegel*, 2nd ed., vol. 2 (Tübingen, 1961), 46.

68 *Theodor* I, 65ff.

69 *Theodor* I, 77ff. Rogerson errs in stating that de Wette himself attended these lectures. In a letter of 13 March 1841, de Wette explicitly states that he did not attend Schelling's lectures. Of course, this does not alter the fact that de Wette read Schelling very seriously while at Jena. This de Wette does make clear. See Rogerson, *De Wette* 33; *Theodore* (English translation), xxx.

70 Rogerson, *De Wette*, 33.
71 For a more detailed discussion of Schelling's "Absolute" and its influence, see Andrew Bowie, *Schelling and Modern European Philosophy: An Introduction* (New York: Routledge, 1994).
72 *Schellings Werke* III, 297.
73 *Schellings Werke* III, 325; Rogerson, *De Wette*, 33.
74 Quoted in Sheehan, *German History*, 347.
75 *Schellings Werke* III, 425.
76 Rogerson, *De Wette*, 33.
77 *Theodor* I, 85.
78 Rogerson, *De Wette*, 34–5.
79 *Theodor* I, 87.
80 De Wette, *Theodore* (English translation), xxxi.
81 Besides Schelling, de Wette hints in one letter of having been greatly taken by Tieck and Wackenroder's *Phantasien über Kunst für Freunde der Kunst* (1799). Rogerson surmises that this work exerted considerable influence on de Wette's regard of art and myth. See Rogerson, *De Wette*, 35–7.
   For a broad historical treatment of the importance of myth for German culture during this time, see George Williamson, "The Longing for Myth in Germany: Culture, Religion, and Politics, 1790–1878," Ph.D. diss. (Yale University, 1996).
82 Toews, *Hegelianism*, 260.
83 Thomas Kuhn, *The Structure of Scientific Revolutions*, 2nd ed. (Chicago: University of Chicago Press, 1970).
84 De Wette, *Beiträge zur Einleitung in das Alte Testament* II (1807), 398–9; quoted in C. Hartlich and W. Sachs, *Der Ursprung des Mythosbegriffes in der modernen Bibelwissenschaft* (Tübingen, 1952), 94.
85 The "history question" implies actually two questions: (1) what elements in the Bible are truly historical instead of "mythical"? and (2) is the historical character of certain stories necessary for the establishment of doctrinal truth? The relationship between history and myth is treated in the present chapter. The question of history and doctrinal truth is treated more directly in chapter three.
86 Rogerson, *Old Testament Criticism*, 28. For more details on the state of Old Testament criticism in the late eighteenth and early nineteenth centuries, see Gottfried Hornig, *Die Anfänge der historische-kritische Theologie* (Göttingen: Vandenhoeck & Ruprecht, 1961); R. E. Clements, "The Study of the Old Testament," in Smart et al., eds., *Nineteenth-Century Religious Thought in the West*, vol. 3, 109–41; Emil G. Kraeling, *The Old Testament since the Reformation* (New York: Harper & Brothers, 1955); and C. Hartlich and W. Sachs, *Der Ursprung des Mythosbegriffes in der modernen Bibelwissenschaft* (Tübingen, 1952).
87 On neologians, see Emanuel Hirsch, *Geschichte der neuern evangelischen Theologie*, vol. 4 (Gütersloh: C. Bertelsmann Verlag, 1968), 2–121.
88 Hirsch, *Geschichte der neuern evangelischen Theologie*, vol. 4, 11.
89 Kraeling, *The Old Testament since the Reformation*, 43–58.
90 A. O. Doyson, "Theological Legacies of the Enlightenment: England and Germany," in Sykes, ed., *England and Germany: Studies in Theological Diplomacy*, 55ff.
91 See Hornig, *Anfänge der historische-kritischen Theologie*, 84.
92 See Clements, "The Study of the Old Testament," in Smart, et al., eds., *Nineteenth-Century Religious Thought in the West*, vol. 3, 111.
93 *Über Religion und Theologie*, 119.
94 Robert Lowth, *De sacra poesi Hebraeorum*, 1753. English translation by G. Gregory, *Lectures on the Sacred Poetry of the Hebrews*, 1847. For Lowth's importance in German

scholarship, see T. K. Cheyne, *Founders of Old Testament Criticism* (New York: Charles Scribner's Sons, 1893), 4.

95 I follow scholarly convention in using the term "mythical school"; it was not a term that the scholars under discussion applied to themselves. The term was coined by Hartlich and Sachs in their *Der Ursprung des Mythosbegriffes in der modernen Bibelwissenschaft* (1952), still the classic work on myth in late eighteenth- and early nineteenth-century biblical scholarship. Cf. Paul Barthel, *Interprétation du langage mythique et théologie biblique* (Leiden, 1967).

96 Rogerson, *Myth in Old Testament Interpretation*, 6.

97 Hartlich and Sachs, *Der Ursprung des Mythosbegriffes*, 20–87.

98 Clements, "The Study of the Old Testament," in Smart, et al., eds., *Nineteenth-Century Religious Thought in the West*, 112.

Because of his eclectic interests beyond Old Testament scholarship, I have omitted Herder from the discussion of the mythical school. However, there are many parallels between Herder and this school. Herder had personal contact with both Heyne and Eichhorn, and he cited Heyne's ideas on myth approvingly in his *Ideen zur Geschichte der Menschheit*, 1784–91. There are also numerous references to Herder in the works of Gabler and Bauer. What distinguishes Herder from the mythical school was that he did not share their desire to create a factual history based on the mythic material in the Old Testament. See Rogerson, *Myth in Old Testament Interpretation*, 1–5.

99 Rogerson, *Old Testament Criticism*, 28ff.

100 A notable exception is Rogerson's recent biography of de Wette.

101 *Eine Idee*, 19.

102 *Eine Idee*, 21.

103 The essay was written in preparation for a lectureship on the Old Testament. De Wette was rewarded with this teaching post in fall semester 1805 at the University of Jena. See Staehelin, *Dewettiana*, 11.

104 *Aufforderung*, 29.

105 *Aufforderung*, 28; quoted in Rogerson, *De Wette*, 47.

106 *Aufforderung*, 9.

107 It is revealing to compare de Wette's views on the Bible with a passage from Schelling's *Philosophie der Kunst*, where Schelling suggests that the mythology of ancient near Eastern peoples

> does indeed allow us to expect historical elements to play a part in it. Yet who can separate out individual elements in this divine whole without destroying the context of that whole? Just as this poetry, like a gentle fragrance, allows us to intuit nature through it, so also does it act as a kind of mist through which we recognize distant times in the primordial world.

Schelling also states that myths should be "viewed quite simply in and for themselves" and that by no means do they represent "merely an expedient prompted by the poverty of conceptual designations in general or by simple lack of knowledge of causal relationships." In short, both de Wette and Schelling argued that the proper *historical* understanding of the Old Testament depended on seeing it not negatively, as the work of deficient historians, but positively, as the religious expression of ancient myth–makers and storytellers. See F. W. J. Schelling, *The Philosophy of Art*, trans. Douglas W. Scott (Minneapolis: University of Minnesota Press, 1989), 50.

108 De Wette, *Dissertatio critica qua a prioribus Deuteronomium pentateuchi libris diversum alias cuiusdam recentioris auctoris opus esse monstratu* (1805). Reprinted in *Opuscula Theologica* (Berlin, 1830), 151–68. I am grateful for summaries of this work provided by Smend and Rogerson. See Smend, *De Wette*, 32–6; Rogerson, *De Wette*, 40–2.

109 *Dissertatio*, 151. De Wette was not the first to question Mosaic authorship; it had been

doubted as early as Spinoza. For a history of the scholarship on this issue, see Rogerson, *Old Testament Criticism*, 29ff.

110 *Dissertatio*, 164–5; Rogerson, *De Wette*, 41–2.

111 *Dissertatio*, 166–8.

112 Rogerson, *Old Testament Criticism*, 28f, 36.

113 R. E. Clements, "The Study of the Old Testament," in Smart, et al., eds., *Nineteenth–Century Religious Thought in the West*, 128ff.

114 Rogerson, *Old Testament Criticism*, 34.

115 Rogerson, *De Wette*, 58.

116 *Beiträge* I, 182; quoted in Rogerson, *De Wette*, 58.

117 See Rogerson, *Myth in Old Testament Interpretation*, 17.

118 *Beiträge* I, 6.

119 Rogerson, *De Wette*, 53.

120 See *Beitrage* II, 29ff; Rogerson, *De Wette*, 53–4.

121 *Beiträge* II, 52; quoted in Rogerson, *De Wette*, 54.

122 *Beiträge* II, 53.

123 *Beiträge* II, 398.

124 For details, see Rogerson, *Old Testament Criticism*, 50ff.

125 See Horton Harris, *The Tübingen School* (Oxford: Clarendon Press, 1975).

126 *Theodor* I, 59.

127 Letter to James Clarke, 13 March 1841. Reprinted in the preface to the American edition of *Theodore*, xxix. In this same letter de Wette also mentions Schleiermacher, who, in his *Reden* of 1799, had already emphasized feeling in religious matters. De Wette makes clear, however, that he did not agree until Fries had linked feeling and aesthetics in a more epistemologically sophisticated manner than had Schleiermacher. A fuller picture of the relationship between de Wette and Schleiermacher will be provided in chapter two.

128 See de Wette "Zum Andenken an J. F. Fries," in the appendix of E. L. T. Henke's *Jakob Friedrich Fries* (Leipzig, 1867), 284–5.

129 See de Wette, "Zum Andenken an J. F. Fries" in Henke, *Fries*; Staehelin, *Dewettiana*, 14.

130 On Herrnhuter, see "Herrnhut" in F. L. Cross and E. A. Livingstone, eds., *The Oxford Dictionary of the Christian Church*, 3rd. ed. (Oxford: Oxford University Press, 1997), 743. Fries was born in 1773 in Barby, Saxony, into a German Herrnhuter community. His father, Peter Fries, was active in the administrative hierarchy of the well-known pietist leader, Count Nicholas von Zinzendorf, and spent much time abroad. As a result, Fries and his siblings were sent at an early age to the boarding schools in Barby and nearby Niesky, the two educational centers of the isolated and self-contained Herrnhuter communities. In Niesky, Fries first heard of the critical philosophy of Kant from his teacher, Karl Bernhard Grave. Like Schleiermacher, who also grew up in a Herrn-huter community, Fries felt the need to escape what he deemed an intellectually and socially restraining environment. In 1795, he left Niesky in favor of a more secular education at the University of Leipzig. At first he intended to study law but soon changed over to philosophy, natural science, and mathematics. Completing his degree in 1797, he became a *Privatdozent* at the University of Jena. For further biographical information, see E. L. T. Henke, *Jakob Friedrich Fries* (Leipzig, 1867); Alexander P. D. Moutelatos, "Jakob Friedrich Fries," *The Encyclopedia of Philosophy*, vol. 3 (New York: Macmillan, 1967), 253–5; Frederick Gregory's introduction to J. F. Fries, *Knowledge, Belief, and Aesthetic Sense*, trans. Kent Richter (Cologne: Jürgen Dinter, 1989), 3–7.

131 Moutelatos, "Fries," *The Encyclopedia of Philosophy*, 253.

132 J. F. Fries, *Reinhold, Fichte, und Schelling*, 2nd edition of 1824. Reprinted in Fries, *Sämtliche Schriften*, vol. 24 (Aalen: Scientia Verlag, 1978), 31–359

133 See Fries, *Knowledge, Belief, and Aesthetic Sense*, 16. See also Frederick Gregory, "Die

Kritik von J. F. Fries an Schellings Naturphilosophie" *Sudhoffs Archiv* 66 (1983): 145–57.

134 In the early nineteenth century, *Ahnung* had the alternate spelling of *Ahndung*. When de Wette later employed this Friesian category, he generally spelled it without the "d." Thus, in order to avoid confusion, I have taken the liberty of consistently speaking of *Ahnung* (instead of *Ahndung*). Fries, however, spelled it with the "d."

135 I have chosen *Wissen, Glaube, Ahnung* as a representative work because it best illustrates Fries's continuation of the Kantian project and because it is in this work that Fries introduced the concept of *Ahnung*, "aesthetic sense." Later he published more systematic works. *Neue Kritik der Vernunft* was published in 1807. A revised version of this same work appeared in 1828 as *Neue oder Anthropologische Kritik der Vernunft*. De Wette's borrowing from Fries is most evident in *Über Religion und Theologie* (1815), which will be discussed in chapter two.

136 See Kent Richter's introduction to his translation of Fries, *Knowledge, Belief, and Aesthetic Sense*, 11. I have generally followed Richter's translations – "knowing," "belief," and "aesthetic sense." In many instances however – especially with the difficult word *Ahnung* – I have opted to leave the terms in the original German.

137 *Wissen, Glaube, Ahnung*, 61.

138 *Wissen, Glaube, Ahnung*, 111–2.

139 See Frederick Gregory, *Nature Lost? Natural Science and German Theological Traditions of the Nineteenth Century* (Cambridge: Harvard University Press, 1992), 20, 38–42. Cf. Ralph C. S. Walker, *The Coherence Theory of Truth: Realism, Anti–Realism, Idealism* (New York: Routledge, 1989).

140 Fries, *Wissen, Glaube, Ahnung*, 118; quoted in Gregory, *Nature Lost?*, 40.

141 Fries, *Wissen, Glaube, Ahnung*, 122; quoted in Gregory, *Nature Lost?*, 40.

142 Gregory, *Nature Lost?*, 40–1.

143 Fries, *Wissen, Glaube, Ahnung*, 122.

144 See W. Nieke, "Ahnung" in Joachim Ritter, ed., *Historisches Wörterbuch der Philosophie*, vol 1. (Basel and Stuttgart: Schwabe & Co. Verlag, 1971), 115–7. Nieke unfortunately does not provide a reference for the quotation from Kant. I believe that Kent Richter's translation of *Ahnung* as "aesthetic sense" best conveys Fries's meaning, for Fries often employed the word in association with emotions brought about by the experiences of beauty – especially natural beauty.

145 Fries, *Wissen, Glaube, Ahnung*, 173.

146 Fries, *Wissen, Glaube, Ahnung*, 173–4.

147 Fries, *Wissen, Glaube, Ahnung*, 176. For parallels with Schleiermacher conception of feeling (*Gefühl*), see Schleiermacher, *The Christian Faith*, eds. H. R. Mackintosh and J. S. Stewart (Edinburgh: T&T Clark, 1989), 131–41.

148 Fries, *Wissen, Glaube, Ahnung*, 176.

149 Fries, *Wissen, Glaube, Ahnung*, 177–8. There are manifest similarities between Fries's concept of *Ahnung* and Kant's notion of the sublime. See Paul Crowther, *The Kantian Sublime: From Morality to Art* (Oxford: Clarendon Press, 1989).

150 Fries, *Wissen, Glaube, Ahnung*, 181.

151 De Wette, "Zum Andenken an J. F. Fries," in Henke, *Fries*, 285.

152 De Wette, "Zum Andenken an J. F. Fries," in Henke, *Fries*, 277.

153 *Theodor* I, 84–5; quoted in Rogerson, *De Wette*, 78.

154 De Wette, *Beytrag zur Charakteristik des Hebräismus* (Heidelberg, 1807); De Wette, *Commentar über die Psalmen*, (Heidelberg, 1811).

155 See Rogerson, *De Wette*, 88–97.

156 De Wette, *Lehrbuch der christliche Dogmatik*, (Berlin, 1813), 9.

157 De Wette quoted in Rudolf Otto, *The Philosophy of Religion*, 185.

Chapter Two. De Wette and Schleiermacher at Berlin (1810–1819): Politics, History, and the Post-Enlightenment Transformation of Theology

1 Maurice Mandelbaum, *History, Man, and Reason: A Study in Nineteenth-Century Thought* (Baltimore: Johns Hopkins University Press, 1971), 29–30.

2 See Claude Welch, *Protestant Thought in the Nineteenth Century*, vol. 1 (New Haven: Yale University Press, 1972), 1ff; Karl Barth, *Protestant Theology in the Nineteenth Century* (London: SCM Press, 1972), 425ff.

3 Hans Frei, *The Eclipse of Biblical Narrative: A Study in Eighteenth- and Nineteenth-Century Hermeneutics* (New Haven: Yale University Press, 1972), 103–4, 233ff.

4 Welch, *Protestant Thought*, 45–8.

5 On these tendencies, see Mandelbaum, *History, Man, and Reason*, 31.

6 On the founding and importance of the University of Berlin, see Charles E. McClelland, " 'To Live for Science': Ideals and Realities at the University of Berlin," in Thomas Bender, ed., *The University and the City* (Oxford: Oxford University Press, 1988); Charles E. McClelland, *State, Society, and University in Germany, 1700–1914* (Cambridge: Cambridge University Press, 1980); Max Lenz, *Geschichte der Königlichen Friedrich-Wilhelms-Universität zu Berlin*, 5 vols. (Halle, 1910–1918); and Daniel Fallon, *The German University* (Boulder: Colorado Associated University Press, 1980).

7 On the conflict between rationalism and traditional religious thought in the eighteenth century, see Gerald R. Cragg, *Reason and Authority in the Eighteenth Century* (Cambridge: Cambridge University Press, 1964). On the nineteenth-century shape of this conflict, see Hans Rosenberg, "Theologischer Rationalismus und vormärzlicher Vulgärliberalismus" in *Politische Denkströmungen im deutschen Vormärz* (Göttingen: Vandenhoeck & Ruprecht, 1972), 18–50 and John Groh, *Nineteenth-Century German Protestantism* (Washington: University of America Press, 1982), 143ff.

8 The principles of the theology department were outlined in a memorandum Schleiermacher presented to the planning commission on 25 May 1810. He adhered to the traditional division of the theology faculty into four parts: exegetical, historical, dogmatic, and practical. He did not request a chair in practical theology, however, because he wanted to leave this function principally to the church. Eschewing strict specialization, each professor was to cover at least two disciplines. See Martin Redeker, *Schleiermacher: His Life and Thought*, trans. John Wallhauser (Philadelphia: Fortress Press, 1968), 98ff.

9 For an overview of the period, see James Sheehan, *German History, 1770–1866* (Oxford: Clarendon Press, 1989), 389–441.

10 For a demographic analysis of the "secular trend" in German higher learning at the beginning of the nineteenth century, see McClelland, *State, Society, and University*, 116–7.

11 Welch, *Protestant Thought*, 59.

12 Letter of 2 July 1816; Staehelin, *Dewettiana*, 77.

13 See Emil Brunner, *Die Mystik und das Wort: Der Gegensatz zwischen moderner Religionsauffassung und christliche Glauben dargestellt an der Theologie Schleiermacher*, 2nd ed. (Tübingen, 1928).

14 See B. A. Gerrish, *The Old Protestantism and the New* (Chicago: University of Chicago Press, 1982).

15 Quoted in B. A. Gerrish, *A Prince of the Church: Schleiermacher and the Beginnings of Modern Theology* (London: SCM Press, 1984), 6; Cf. Barth, *Protestant Theology in the Nineteenth Century*, 425ff.

16 B. A. Gerrish, "Friedrich Schleiermacher," in Smart et al., eds., *Nineteenth-Century Religious Thought in the West*, 123.

17 Wilhelm Dilthey, *Leben Schleiermachers*, vol. 1 (Berlin, 1870), 2.

18 Quoted in Sheehan, *German History*, 353.

19 Redeker, *Schleiermacher*, 11–37.

20 Gerrish, *The Old Protestantism and the New*, 179–95.

21 Schleiermacher, *Kurze Darstellung des theologischen Studiums* (Leipzig, 1810); quoted in Welch, *Protestant Thought*, 63.

22 Schleiermacher, *Sendschreiben an Dr. Lücke*, ed. Hermann Mulert (Giessen, 1908), 40; quoted in Welch, *Protestant Thought*, 63.

23 Gerrish, *Tradition and the Modern World*, 40–1.

24 The scope of my treatment of Schleiermacher here does not permit a fuller attempt to portray his thought. For an introduction to the very large Schleiermacher literature, see Terence Tice, *The Schleiermacher Bibliography* (Princeton: Princeton University Press, 1966) and Keith W. Clements, "Schleiermacher," in Alister McGrath, ed., *The Blackwell Encyclopedia of Modern Christian Thought* (Oxford: Basil Blackwell Press, 1993), 589–92.

25 Letter of 24 July 1810; Staehelin, *Dewettiana*, 68.

26 Letter of 26 September 1811; Staehelin, *Dewettiana*, 70–1; quoted and translated in Rogerson, *De Wette*, 90–1 (translation modified).

27 Rogerson, *De Wette*, 91.

28 De Wette wrote *Theodor* after his dismissal from Berlin. At this time, his relations with Schleiermacher were very cordial; Schleiermacher had even helped him financially. Consequently, I infer that the criticisms represented in *Theodor* stem from de Wette's attempt at an honest appraisal of Schleiermacher's theology and not from jealousy or malice – which perhaps cannot be said for some of his statements during his Berlin period.

29 *Theodor* I, 228f.

30 *Theodor* I, 229–30.

31 Rogerson, *De Wette*, 128.

32 *Theodor* I, 231.

33 Rogerson, *De Wette*, 129.

34 *Theodor* I, 164; Rogerson, *De Wette*, 128–30.

35 Rogerson, *De Wette*, 129.

36 *Theodor* I, 168.

37 See Friedrich Lücke, "Zur Erinnerung an D. Wilhelm Martin Leberecht de Wette," in *Theologische Studien und Kritiken* (1850), 502, and Rogerson, *De Wette*, 127.

38 For Schleiermacher's views on the church and for his role as preacher, see Redeker, *Schleiermacher*, 269–300.

39 De Wette's antipreaching stance seems to have been inspired by Schleiermacher's high public profile as preacher at Trinity church. De Wette later moderated his views considerably and even took a number of preaching assignments himself. In fact, after his dismissal from Berlin he considered accepting a preaching position at St. Katherine Church in Braunschwieg in 1821. He preached on numerous occasions in Basel. For a more extensive treatment of this theme, see Paul Handschin, *Wilhelm Martin Leberecht de Wette als Prediger und Schriftsteller* (Basel: Helbing & Lichtenhahn, 1957), 13–66.

40 See Rogerson, *De Wette*, 130–1; Staehelin, *Dewettiana*, 75. The senate waited two years after Fichte's death and convened on 13 March 1816.

41 Rogerson, *De Wette*, 131.

42 See Lenz, *Universität Berlin* I, 575.

43 Staehelin, *Dewettiana*, 76.

44 Lenz, *Universität Berlin* I, 573.

45 For more details, see Lenz, *Universität Berlin* I, 570–5. Hegel was at first offered the position but declined on account of having just accepted a position at Heidelberg. Two years

later (in 1818), however, he did come to Berlin. Fries moved from Heidelberg to Jena in 1816, where he spent the rest of his life.

46 Letter of 16 February 1813; Staehelin, *Dewettiana*, 72.

47 Rogerson, *De Wette*, 131.

48 See Edward A. Shils, "Centre and Periphery," in Shils, *Centre and Periphery: Essays in Macrosociology* (Chicago: University of Chicago Press, 1975). Writes Shils: "The power of the ruling class derives from its incumbency of certain key positions in the central institutional system. . . . Even where the ruling class is relatively segmental, there is, because of centralized control of appointments to the most crucial of the key positions or because of personal ties or because of overlapping personnel, some sense of affinity which, more or less, unites the different sectors of the elite." See p. 12. Although Shils refers mainly to political power, it does not belie his intent to transfer his ideas to the academic and intellectual realms.

Rudolf Otto notes that "when Hegel was appointed Professor at Berlin, the name of Fries was considered for the post. Possibly if Fries had been elected there might have been a Friesian epoch instead of a Hegelian. For the authority and environment of the chair did much to spread the Hegelian philosophy." See Rudolf Otto, *The Philosophy of Religion Based on Kant and Fries*, trans. E. B. Dicker (London, 1931), 26. Karl Barth makes a similar point, arguing that, given different circumstances, de Wette and Fries might have been the Bultmann and Heidegger of their times. See Barth, *Protestant Theology in the Nineteenth Century*, 490.

49 See Robert M. Bigler, *The Politics of German Protestantism: The Rise of the Protestant Church Elite in Prussia, 1815–1848* (Berkeley: University of California Press, 1972), 3ff. On Schleiermacher's very involved political activity during this time, see Jerry F. Dawson, *Friedrich Schleiermacher: The Evolution of a Nationalist* (Austin: University of Texas Press, 1966), 68ff.

50 Rogerson, *De Wette*, 149.

51 Dedication reprinted in Staehelin, *Dewettiana*, 78–80.

52 Staehelin, *Dewettiana*, 79.

53 Letter of 26 May 1817; Staehelin, *Dewettiana*, 81.

54 Letter of 5 July 1817; Staehelin, *Dewettiana*, 82.

55 Staehelin, *Dewettiana*, 83.

56 Rogerson, *De Wette*, 87.

57 Letter of 19 July 1817; Staehelin, *Dewettiana*, 82.

58 Redeker, *Schleiermacher*, 94.

59 See Thomas Willey, *Back to Kant: The Revival of Kantianism in German Social Science and Historical Thought, 1860–1914* (Detroit: Wayne State University Press, 1978).

60 An opinion shared by de Wette's main commentators, including John Rogerson, Rudolf Smend, Rudolf Otto, and Karl Barth.

61 *Über Religion und Theologie*, 2.

62 *Über Religion und Theologie*, 4–5.

63 *Über Religion und Theologie*, 6.

64 See Rogerson, *De Wette*, 98.

65 *Über Religion und Theologie*, 10.

66 *Über Religion und Theologie*, 11.

67 *Über Religion und Theologie*, 12; quoted and translated in Rogerson, *De Wette*, 99 (translation modified).

68 *Über Religion und Theologie*, 18.

69 See Rogerson, *De Wette*, 100–1.

70 *Über Religion und Theologie*, 31.

71 *Über Religion und Theologie*, 32.

72 *Über Religion und Theologie*, 33; quoted and translated in Rogerson, *De Wette*, 102 (translation modified).

73 Rogerson, *De Wette*, 102.

74 *Über Religion und Theologie*, 62.

75 See Rogerson, *De Wette*, 106.

76 *Über Religion und Theologie*, 65; quoted and translated in Rogerson, *De Wette*, 107 (translation modified).

77 *Über Religion und Theologie*, 76–84.

78 *Über Religion und Theologie*, 88–90; Rogerson, *De Wette*, 109–10.

79 *Über Religion und Theologie*, 91.

80 *Über Religion und Theologie*, 91–2. I truncate a discussion of de Wette's conception of Christ here because I focus on it at length in chapter three, where I treat it in a broader context of early nineteenth-century German christology.

81 *Über Religion und Theologie*, 101.

82 *Über Religion und Theologie*, 106.

83 *Über Religion und Theologie*, 107.

84 *Über Religion und Theologie*, 108.

85 *Über Religion und Theologie*, 110.

86 *Über Religion und Theologie*, 116–9.

87 *Über Religion und Theologie*, 119.

88 *Über Religion und Theologie*, 120.

89 *Über Religion und Theologie*, 123.

90 *Über Religion und Theologie*, 140.

91 De Wette's critique of Schleiermacher is very similar to that of F. C. Baur. Baur argued that theology and christology must proceed *von unten* (historically) instead of *von oben* (dogmatically). See Welch, *Protestant Theology*, 157. Also see the treatment of Baur in Horton Harris, *The Tübingen School* (Oxford: Clarendon Press, 1975).

92 *Über Religion und Theologie*, 144. "Anthropologically grounded" is shorthand for de Wette's Friesian epistemology and implies cognitive categories (*Wissen, Glaube, Ahnung*) that exist in the human mind prior to the historical shaping of human nature and religious expression.

93 *Über Religion und Theologie*, 144–5.

94 See Rogerson, *De Wette*, 86ff.

95 *Über Religion und Theologie*, 146.

96 *Über Religion und Theologie*, 157.

97 *Über Religion und Theologie*, 177.

98 *Über Religion und Theologie*, 198.

99 *Über Religion und Theologie*, 255.

100 For an interpretation of the political meaning of theological literature in *Vormärz* Germany, see Marilyn Massey, *Christ Unmasked: The Meaning of* The Life of Jesus *in German Politics* (Chapel Hill: University of North Carolina Press, 1983), 6ff.

101 Sheehan, *German History*, 401–4. De Wette was deeply disturbed by the new confederation and expressed his views in an anonymously published work, *Die neue Kirche oder Verstand und Glaube in Bunde* (Berlin, 1815), in which he argued that a pure Protestantism can only be led by a Protestant (i.e., Prussian) German nation. In de Wette's eyes, political entanglement with the Catholic Habsburgs would only dilute Protestant freedom and hinder its expression in national life. De Wette's authorship was never detected and therefore this book did not play a role in his dismissal from Berlin. See Rogerson, *De Wette*, 121–4.

102 Hegel and Metternich quoted in Sheehan, *German History*, 392.

103 Sheehan, *German History*, 405–6.

104 Fries interpreted the French Revolution as the political expression of the ideas of intellectual freedom that he extolled. In 1816, he had published his *Ethik*, an explicitly political work, in which he stressed the ideal of individual liberty and political equality as a consequence of the Kantian doctrine of the dignity of human beings. At the Wartburg festival, Fries delivered a speech and was even rumored to have participated in a book-burning. Hegel later accused Fries of being a "ringleader" of those "self-styled 'philosophers.'" Moreover, Hegel referred to Fries's Wartburg speech as "the quintessence of shallow thinking . . . , a broth of heart, friendship, and inspiration." See G. W. F. Hegel, *The Philosophy of Right*, trans. T. M. Knox (Oxford: Clarendon Press, 1952), 5–6. In 1819, Prussian officials suspended Fries from his position at Jena. This marked his permanent estrangement from participation in active political and philosophical debates. Although he was reinstated in 1824, his philosophical chair was taken away. He remained in Jena until his death in 1843 and was allowed to teach mathematics, astronomy, physics, and psychology.

105 Bigler, *Politics of German Protestantism*, 79.

106 See Otto Hintze, "Das preussische Staatsministerium im 19. Jahrhundert" in Hintze, *Gesammelte Abhandlungen*, vol. 3 (Göttingen, 1962–67), 530ff.

107 Bigler, *Politics of German Protestantism*, 48.

108 Bigler, *Politics of German Protestantism*, 21–3. Cf. Erich Foerster, *Die Entstehung der Preussischen Landeskirche*, vol. 1 (Tübingen, 1905), 172ff, and Fritz Fischer, *Ludwig Nicolovius: Rokoko, Reform, Restauration* (Stuttgart, 1939).

109 Neander (1789–1850) specialized in church history.

110 Bigler, *Politics of German Protestantism*, 66–7. See also F. W. Kantzenbach, ed., *Baron H. E. Kottwitz und die Erweckungsbewegung in Schlesien, Berlin, und Pommern* (Ulm, 1963).

111 Memorandum included in O. Dibelius, *Das königliche Predigerseminar zu Wittenberg, 1817–1917* (Berlin-Lichterfeld, 1917), 30–1; quoted in Rogerson, *De Wette*, 147.

112 Rogerson, *De Wette*, 147.

113 Letter of 11 May 1817; Staehelin, *Dewettiana*, 81.

114 Subsequent government records reveal that Schleiermacher's actions were under close surveillance at the time. See Lenz, *Universität Berlin* II, 62.

115 See Staehelin, *Dewettiana*, 81

116 De Wette's first wife, Eberhardine Boye (b. 1775) died on 18 February 1806, just over one year after their marriage. In 1809, he married Henriette Beck, the widow of a businessman from Mannheim.

117 Lenz, *Universität Berlin* II, 70.

118 Sheehan, *German History*, 407.

119 Sheehan, *German History*, 408. Also see E. R. Huber, ed., *Dokumente zur deutschen Verfassungsgeschichte*, vol. 1 (Stuttgart, 1956–57), 90ff.
    A separate proclamation issued in Prussia stated: "The federated governments oblige themselves to remove from universities those teachers who have obviously demonstrated their incapacity to fill their office by demonstrable deviation from their duty, or transgressing against the limits of their profession, or misusing their proper influence on the young, or spreading harmful theories inimical to the public order and peace or destructive to existing political institutions." Quoted in McClelland, *State, Society, and University in Germany*, 218–9.

120 Bigler, *Politics of German Protestantism*, 43.

121 See Rogerson, *De Wette*, 151. Plehwe had a "discussion group" of sorts called the "blue pleasure" (*blaue Vergnügen*) that met to discuss cultural and political issues. Prussian officials regarded it as a seedbed for spreading demagogic ideas. See H. Münebeck, "Siegmund Peter Martin und Hans Rudolf von Plehwe, zwei Vertreter des deutschen

Einheitsgedanken von 1806–1820," in *Quellen und Darstellungen zur Geschichte der Burschenschaft und der deutschen Einheitsbewegung* (Heidelberg, 1911), 151–94. De Wette seems to have visited only once; see Staehelin, *Dewettiana*, 87.

122 Lenz, *Universität Berlin* II, 65.

123 See Rogerson, *De Wette*, 152, and Lenz, "Zur Entlassung de Wettes," in Adolf Harnack, ed., *Philotesia* (Berlin, 1907), 337–88. This article contains all the important documents related to de Wette's dismissal. In an attempt to clear his name, de Wette was given permission to publish a small collection of important documents. See De Wette, *Aktensammlung über die Entlassung des Professors D. de Wette vom theologischen Lehramt zu Berlin, Zur Berichtung des öffentlichen Urtheil von ihm selbst herausgegeben* (Leipzig, 1820).

124 Letter of 20 July 1819; Staehelin, *Dewettiana*, 87.

125 Letter of 31 March 1819; Staehelin, *Dewettiana*, 86.

126 Letter of 31 March 1819; Staehelin, *Dewettiana*, 86.

127 Bigler, *Politics of German Protestantism*, 45.

128 Lenz, "Zur Entlassung De Wettes," 367.

129 See De Wette, *Aktensammlung*, 16–20.

130 Lenz, "Zur Entlassung De Wettes," 373.

131 Letter of 7 November 1819; Staehelin, *Dewettiana*, 91. The events of 1819 seem to have caused Schleiermacher to feel a genuine concern for de Wette's plight. From this time on, their correspondence is very cordial; Schleiermacher even later visited de Wette once at his new post in Basel.

132 Rogerson treats de Wette's time in Weimar. See Rogerson, *De Wette*, 161–89.

133 Some of these circumstances will be taken up in chapter four.

134 Bigler, *Politics of German Protestantism*, 67.

135 Hegel's condemnation of de Wette brought him into conflict with Schleiermacher. See Lenz, *Universität Berlin* II, 97–8; Staehelin, *Dewettiana*, 92.

136 Paul Burckhardt, *Die Geschichte der Stadt Basel* (Basel, 1942), 152.

Chapter Three. De Wette, D. F. Strauss, and the New *Christusbild*

1 See John Toews, *Hegelianism: The Path toward Dialectical Humanism* (Cambridge: Cambridge University Press, 1980), 255ff.

2 For reasons that will become clear later, I here emphasize the *figural dimension* of pre-Enlightenment interpretation because this is often overlooked and the situation before the Enlightenment caricatured as a mindless literalism. Complex, imaginative varieties of figural, allegorical, tropological, and anagogical readings of the Bible were as central to precritical biblical interpretation as were the literal readings. Saint Augustine, for instance, noted that "there is no prohibition against such [more "spiritual"] exegesis, provided that we also believe in the truth of the story as a faithful record of historical fact." See Augustine, *The City of God*, trans. Henry Bettenson (New York: Penguin Books, 1972), 525. Also see Karlfried Froelich, "Always to Keep the Literal Sense in Holy Scripture Means to Kill One's Soul" in Earl Miner, ed., *Literary Uses of Typology from the Late Middle Ages to the Present* (Princeton: Princeton University Press, 1977), 20–48.

3 Alister McGrath, *The Making of Modern German Christology: From the Enlightenment to Pannenberg* (Oxford: Basil Blackwell, 1986), 10–2.

4 Spinoza, *Tractatus theologico-politicus* 4, in *Works*, trans. R. H. M. Elwes, vol. 1 (New York, 1951), 61.

5 McGrath, *Modern German Christology*, 12.

6 Quoted in Albert Schweitzer, *The Quest of the Historical Jesus: A Critical Study of Its Progress from Reimarus to Wrede*, trans. W. Montgomery (London, 1910), 16.

7 Claude Welch, *Protestant Thought in the Nineteenth Century*, vol. 1 (New Haven: Yale University Press, 1972), 145.

8 See J. C. O'Neill, "The Study of the New Testament," in Smart, et al., eds., *Nineteenth-Century Religious Thought in the West*, vol. 3, 143.

9 There were four editions of *Das Leben Jesu*. The first two appeared in 1835 and 1836, respectively. After Strauss's radicalism had cost him his position at Tübingen and denied him chances elsewhere, a much moderated third edition appeared in 1838. However, in the fourth edition (1840), after he had lost hope of obtaining an academic position, Strauss returned to the negative conclusions of the first two editions. See Horton Harris, *David Friedrich Strauss and His Theology* (Cambridge: Cambridge University Press, 1975), 41–57, 117–22.

10 See Rudolf Smend, "De Wette und das Verhältnis zwischen historischer Bibelkritik und philosophischem System im 19.Jahrhundert," *TZ* 14 (1958), 116–7.

11 For relations between Strauss and F. C. Baur, his teacher at Tübingen, see Harris, *David Friedrich Strauss*, 85–116.

12 See the preface to the American edition of *Theodore*, trans. James F. Clarke (1851), xxxviii.

13 I borrow the term from McGrath, *Modern German Christology*, 9. For an introduction to post-Enlightenment christology from a theological perspective, see Ernst-Heinz Amberg, *Christologie und Dogmatik: Untersuchung ihres Verhältnisses in der evangelischen Theologie der Gegenwart* (Göttingen, 1966). For a more historical perspective, see Colin Brown, *Jesus in European Protestant Thought* (Durham, NC: Labyrinth Press, 1985).

14 See Gotthelf Samuel Steinbart, *System der reinen Philosophie oder Glückseligkeitslehre des Christentums* (Züllichau, 1778); noted in McGrath, *Modern German Christology*, 12.

15 Henry Chadwick, ed., *Lessing's Theological Writings* (London, 1956), 53: "Zufällige Geschichtswahrheiten können der Beweis von notwendige Vernunftswahrheiten nie werden."

16 See Dietrich Ritschl, "Johann Salomo Semler: The Rise of the Historical-Critical Method in Eighteenth-Century Theology on the Continent," in Robert Mollenauer, ed., *Introduction to Modernity: A Symposium on Eighteenth-Century Thought* (Austin: University of Texas Press, 1965), 119–21.

17 McGrath, *Modern German Christology*, 13.

18 On biblical realism, see Hans Frei, *the Eclipse of Biblical Narrative: A Study in Eighteenth and Nineteenth Century Hermeneutics* (New Haven: Yale University Press, 1974) Cf. Erich Auerbach, *Mimesis: The Representation of Reality in Western Literature*, trans. Willard R. Trask (Princeton: Princeton University Press, 1953), 15, 48ff.

19 See C. Hartlich and W. Sachs, *Der Ursprung des Mythosbegriffes in der modernen Bibelwissenschaft* (Tübingen, 1952), 15, 59, 135 passim. The widely used German term for "history-likeness" was *Geschichtsähnlichkeit*.

20 Frei, *Eclipse of Biblical Narrative*, 10. When Frei speaks of "precritical analytic or interpretive procedures" he does not mean simply an acceptance of the Bible as historical fact. Rather, as indicated earlier, he points out that the Bible's historical character was an assumption that allowed for and even encouraged other forms of analysis – the dominant ones being allegorical, figural, or typological readings.

21 The whole is over 4,000 pages long. Schweitzer, *Historical Jesus*, 14.

22 A synopsis of Reimarus's views on Christ is found in Schweitzer, *Historical Jesus*, 13–26.

23 Schweitzer, *Historical Jesus*, 15.

24 McGrath, *German Christology*, 14.

25 Schweitzer, *Historical Jesus*, 16.

26 On this point, see Emil L. Fackenheim, "Immanuel Kant," in Smart, et al., eds., *Nineteenth-Century Religious Thought in the West*, vol. 1, 17–40.

27 Heinrich Heine, *Selected Works*, trans. and ed. Helen M. Mustard (New York: Random House, 1973), 365.

28 Welch, *Protestant Thought*, 89.

29 Quoted in B. A. Gerrish, "Friedrich Schleiermacher" in Smart, et al., eds., *Nineteenth-Century Religious Thought in the West*, vol. 1, 142.

30 Welch, *Protestant Theology*, 82.

31 Strauss, *Charakteristiken und Kritiken* (Leipzig, 1844), 41.

32 See Leander E. Keck's introduction to D. F. Strauss, *The Christ of Faith and the Jesus of History* (Philadelphia: Fortress Press, 1977), lii.

33 Welch, *Protestant Thought*, 105.

34 Toews, *Hegelianism*, 49.

35 Hegel, *Introduction to the Philosophy of History*, trans. Leo Rauch (Indianapolis: Hackett Publishing, 1988), 39.

36 Welch, *Protestant Thought*, 73. On Hegel in this regard, see Stephen D. Crites, "The Gospel According to Hegel," *JR* 46 (April 1966): 246–63.

37 Welch, *Protestant Thought*, 89.

38 Toews, *Hegelianism*, 65–6 (my emphasis).

39 Toews, *Hegelianism*, 67.

40 The most sustained criticism of Schleiermacher was written by Strauss after the posthumous publication of Schleiermacher's *Life of Jesus* in 1864. See D. F. Strauss, *The Christ of Faith and the Jesus of History*. The work's subtitle was "A Critique of Schleiermacher's *The Life of Jesus*." F. C. Baur had earlier argued that no relationship existed between Schleiermacher's Christ and the question of history. See Welch, *Protestant Thought*, 156–7.

41 Toews's *Hegelianism*, especially chapters 7–10, is by far the best treatment of this subject. Also see McGrath, *Modern German Christology*, 32–53, and the essays on Strauss, Baur, and Feuerbach that appear in Smart, et al., eds., *Nineteenth-Century Religious Thought in the West*, vol. 1, 215–329.

42 Although Marx was not very interested in theology, the works of Strauss, Feuerbach, and other Left Hegelians did create an intellectual situation that he found personally and politically useful. See Massey, *Christ Unmasked*, 3.

43 Toews, *Hegelianism*, 255.

44 On mid-nineteenth-century crises of faith, see Franklin L. Baumer, *Religion and the Rise of Skepticism* (New York: Harcourt, Brace, & Co., 1960), 128–86.

45 The role of de Wette as the principal transitional figure from eighteenth-century criticism to Strauss has, to my knowledge, only once before been suggested: see Hartlich and Sachs, *Der Ursprung des Mythosbegriffes*, 122ff.

46 Frei, *Eclipse of Biblical Narrative*, 64–5.

47 De Wette, of course, classified historical knowledge under the *Überzeugungsweise* of *Wissen*. See *Über Religion und Theologie*, 161.

48 *Über Religion und Theologie*, 154.

49 *Über Religion und Theologie*, 154–5.

50 To the best of my understanding, this was de Wette's intent with the words "symbol" and "myth," although absolute terminological precision does not exist in his writings.

51 *Beiträge* II, 407.

52 See *Commentatio de morte Jesu Christi expiatoria* in *Opuscula Theologica* (Berlin, 1830), 103, and Rogerson, *De Wette*, 120.

53 Rudolf Smend, *Wilhelm Martin Leberecht de Wettes Arbeit am Alten und am Neuen Testament* (Basel: Helbing & Lichtenhahn, 1958), 166–9.

54 Of course, de Wette meant things not apprehensible through *Wissen*.

55 See Paul Handschin, *Wilhelm Martin Leberecht de Wette als Prediger und Schriftsteller* (Basel: Helbing & Lichtenhahn, 1957), 60. Handschin argues that the words de Wette selected were deliberately ambiguous: "code words (*Chiffre*) allowed de Wette to preach so that orthodox parishioners would not be offended by what he said. But achieving this was only possible at the cost of a clear and and unambiguous message." In de Wette's defense, it should be noted that he was not trying so much to conceal anything as to find a mode of expression better suited to convey, in his eyes, a truer but nontraditional view of Christ while not causing unnecessary strife in the Church.

56 *Lehrbuch* I, 196–7.

57 *Lehrbuch* II, xii.

58 *Lehrbuch* II, 53; Rogerson, *De Wette*, 133.

59 *Lehrbuch* I, 212.

60 *Lehrbuch* II, 157.

61 *Über Religion und Theologie*, 150–1.

62 *Kurzgefasstes exegetisches Handbuch zum Neuen Testament* (Leipzig, 1836–1848).

63 *Über Religion und Theologie*, 151.

64 *Über Religion und Theologie*, 161.

65 *Über Religion und Theologie*, 161–2; quoted in Rogerson, *De Wette*, 112.

66 *Über Religion und Theologie*, 164.

67 *Über Religion und Theologie*, 162.

68 See the section devoted to *Über Religion und Theologie* in chapter two. *Über Religion und Theologie*, 163.

69 Letter of 17 December 1817. Henke, "Berliner Briefe," 104; quoted and translated in Rogerson, *De Wette*, 136–7. Rogerson argues that the writing of the *Christliche Sittenlehre* testifies to a "revolution" in de Wette's christology. I am inclined to think that this is perhaps slightly overstated, because de Wette's aesthetic understanding of Christ had already been adumbrated in previous works. However, from 1817 on, de Wette does pay more attention to the ethical implications of Christ and his legacy in the development of Christian history. One might say that, in de Wette's hands, the ethical and the aesthetic, though normally in conflict, were united in the person of Christ, and Christ inspired a similar reconciliation in humanity at large.

70 *Christliche Sittenlehre*, 3 vols. (Berlin: 1819, 1821, 1823).

71 Rogerson, *De Wette*, 144.

72 *Christliche Sittenlehre* I, 178; Rogerson, *De Wette*, 144.

73 *Theodor* II, 476.

74 *Theodor* II, 255.

75 De Wette's anti-Hegelianism seems to have been as much a personal as an intellectual matter. Hegel was the favored replacement over Fries for Fichte's vacated philosophy chair at Berlin. Hegel was also a vocal opponent of de Wette at the time of his dismissal from the University of Berlin. See "Dismissal from Berlin" in chapter two. De Wette's contempt for Hegel lasted throughout his life. "What is a physical persecution of Christian belief with fire and sword when compared to the destructive . . . Hegelian dialectic?" de Wette asked rhetorically in his *Kurze Erklärung der Offenbarung Johannis* (1848), vi–viii.

76 My usage of idealism is derived from Maurice Mandelbaum, who notes that "metaphysical idealists" in the early nineteenth century were "not dependent on revelation to apprehend the truth . . . [but found] man's own spiritual nature to be the fullest expression of that which is to be taken as basic in reality." See Maurice Mandelbaum, *History, Man, and Reason* (Baltimore: Johns Hopkins University Press, 1971), 6.

77 I borrow the term from John Toews. See Toews, *Hegelianism*, 66–7.

78 Frei, *Eclipse of Biblical Narrative*, 29–37.

79 The *protoevangelium* refers to the passage in Genesis 3:15, when God speaks to the

serpent: "I will put enmity between you and the woman, and between your offspring and hers; he will strike your head, and you will strike his heel." See *New Oxford Annotated Bible* (NRSV) (New York: Oxford University Press, 1991), 5 OT. The offspring of woman here was widely held to be the first scriptural reference of God's redemptive work through Christ.

80 Frei, *Eclipse of Biblical Narrative*, 37.

81 Frei sees this process culminating in Strauss.

82 The ambiguity and overlap in the terms figural, symbolic, typological, and allegorical is a vexing problem. For helpful discussions, see Northrop Frye, *Anatomy of Criticism* (Princeton: Princeton University Press, 1957), 71–130; Hazard Adams, *Philosophy of the Literary Symbolic* (Tallahassee: University Press of Florida, 1983); and Meir Sternberg, *The Poetics of Biblical Narrative: Ideological Literature and the Drama of Reading* (Bloomington: Indiana University Press, 1985).

83 For example, in his *Commentatio*, mentioned above, de Wette argued that the Old Testament was altogether devoid of allusions to the Christ of orthodox Christianity.

84 See letter of 17 December 1817. Henke, "Berliner Briefe," 104; quoted in Rogerson, *De Wette*, 137.

85 *Theodor* II, 476.

86 The early Strauss very much sought to interpret Christ's meaning in positive Hegelian terms. See Toews, *Hegelianism*, 255ff.

87 For an interesting essay on symbol and historical understanding, see Robert Hollander, "Typology and Secular Literature: Some Medieval Problems and Examples," in Earl Miner, ed., *Literary Uses of Typology from the Late Middle Ages to the Present* (Princeton: Princeton University Press, 1977), 3–19. Hollander writes that "what is asserted [in historical symbolism] is that y is the continuation of, the direct inheritor of, the essential characteristics of x. . . . The most important use of this [symbolism] is that both x and y are highly charged with some kind of significance, different from all others, and the focus of a unique historical process" (see pp. 5–6).

88 To grasp in more detail the theological basis of Hegel's work, see Hegel, *On Christianity: Early Theological Writings*, trans. T. M. Knox (New York: Harper & Brothers, 1948). Also see Toews's chapter, "Christian Religion and Hegelian Philosophy," in *Hegelianism*, 141–99.

89 Frei, *Eclipse of Biblical Narrative*, 37.

90 Harris, *Strauss and His Theology*, 32.

91 Letter of 2 June 1832; quoted in Harris, *Strauss and His Theology*, 32–3.

92 This point is recognized by biblical critics but is often overlooked by historians and philosophers, who have tended to read Strauss through an overdetermined Strauss-to-Feuerbach-to-Marx narrative – two examples of which are William J. Brazill, *The Young Hegelians* (New Haven: Yale University Press, 1970) and Harold Mah, *The End of Philosophy and the Origin of "Ideology": Karl Marx and the Crisis of the Young Hegelians* (Berkeley and Los Angeles: University of California Press, 1987). For the biblical-critical interpretation that I would like to emphasize, see Hartlich and Sachs, *Der Ursprung des Mythosbegriffes*, 122ff, who argue for the "independence of *Das Leben Jesu*'s critical positions from specific premises of Hegelian philosophy."

93 David Friedrich Strauss, *The Life of Jesus Critically Examined*, trans. from the fourth edition by George Eliot. (Philadelphia: Fortress Press Reprint, 1972, of the 1892 edition), 50. This volume contains prefaces from all prior editions.

94 Strauss, *Life of Jesus*, 54.

95 Strauss, *Life of Jesus*, 55 (my emphasis).

96 Strauss, *Life of Jesus*, 59, 66, 69.

97 Strauss, *Life of Jesus*, 87.

98 While Strauss refers to *Über Religion und Theologie*, he fails to mention that de Wette

had recommended the application of "myth" to the Gospels as a programmatic possibility: "No other option is left for us than to view the Gospel stories . . . as the mythical view of a time after the origins of Christianity. The stories are certainly historical documents, not for primitive Christianity, but for a later period." Quoted also earlier in this chapter; see *Über Religion und Theologie*, 154.

99 Strauss, *Life of Jesus*, li.

100 Harris, *Strauss and His Theology*, 66.

101 Harris argues that the mildest reactions came from the "rationalists" – that is, from de Wette, H. E. G. Paulus, J. F. Röhr, and K. G. Bretschneider. But Harris errs in placing de Wette in the rationalist camp. Given de Wette's own distance from rationalism and the significance Strauss attributed to de Wette's reaction to *Das Leben Jesu*, it is fair to say that de Wette was indeed singular in this respect.

102 Strauss, *Life of Jesus*, lvi.

103 The authenticity of this Gospel – the contention that it was an eye-witness account by the apostle John – was the "central issue in the whole discussion." Harris asserts that it "was the one point that friend and foe alike were in agreement against him [Strauss], and one could even say that it was almost regarded as a test of one's orthodoxy." See Harris, *Strauss and his Theology*, 118. See also Schweitzer, *Historical Jesus*, 85ff.

104 Strauss, *Life of Jesus*, lvii. Strauss refers to de Wette's commentary on John: *Kurze Erklärung des Evangelium und der Briefe Johannes* (1837).

105 See Schweitzer, *Historical Jesus*, 66.

106 The distinction between "bodily" (the Synoptics) and "spiritual" (the Gospel of John) dates back to Clement of Alexandria. The distinction became a commonplace among eighteenth-century commentators. See J. C. O'Neill, "The Study of the New Testament," in Smart, et al., eds., *Nineteenth-Century Religious Thought in the West*, vol. 3, 143–78.

107 K. G. Bretschneider, *Probabilia de evangelii et epistolarum Ioannis apostoli indole et origine* (Leipzig, 1820). Bretschneider was not original in his criticism, though. The inauthenticity of John had been suggested in the eighteenth century. Bretschneider's strength lay in his ability to gather former criticisms and transform them into one coherent argument. See J. C. O'Neill, "The Study of the New Testament," in Smart, et al., eds., *Nineteenth-Century Religious Thought in the West*, vol. 3, 156.

108 For a more detailed commentary on de Wette's views on the Gospel of John, see Smend, *De Wette*, 153–6.

109 See *Theodore* (English translation), xxxviii. Cf. Bruno Bauer, *Die Posaune des Jüngsten Gericht über Hegel den Atheisten und Antichristen* (Leipzig, 1841).

110 Toews, *Hegelianism*, 231.

111 This was at least de Wette's criticism of those who interpreted Strauss in a radical fashion; however, de Wette is in fact ambiguous on the relationship between God and human consciousness. In many respects, I believe that Strauss precipitated in de Wette a conservative turn – at least in his language. Condoning neither Strauss nor his more radical followers, nor willing to embrace Christian orthodoxy, de Wette found himself in a truly singular position.

112 See *Kurzgefasstes exegetisches Handbuch zum Neuen Testament. I.1. Kurze Erklärung des Evangeliums Matthäi* (1836). In my exposition of this text, I recognize a debt to Rogerson, *De Wette*, 241ff.

113 *Matthäi*, vi; quoted in Rogerson, *De Wette*, 241.

114 *Matthäi*, vii; quoted in Rogerson, *De Wette*, 242.

115 *Matthäi*, vii.

116 *Kurzgefasstes exegetisches Handbuch zum Neuen Testament. I.3. Kurze Erklärung des Evangeliums und der Briefe Johannis* (Leipzig, 1837).

117 *Johannis*, 222. Strauss makes this claim in *Das Leben Jesu*. See *Life of Jesus*, lii.

118 *Johannis*, 223.

119 Rogerson, *De Wette*, 245.

120 Rogerson, *De Wette*, 245–6.

121 *Johannis*, 229.

122 *Johannis*, 230.

123 See Thomas Nipperdey, *Deutsche Geschichte, 1800–1866: Bürgerwelt und starker Staat* (Munich: C. H. Beck, 1983), 470–7; Charles E. McClelland, *State, Society, and University in Germany, 1700–1914* (Cambridge: Cambridge University Press, 1980), 151ff. Cf. R. Steven Turner," The Growth of Professorial Research in Prussia, 1818–1848 – Causes and Context," in Russel McCormmach, ed., *Historical Studies in the Physical Sciences*, vol. 3 (Philadelphia: University of Pennsylvania Press, 1971) 137–82 and "The Prussian Universities and the Research Imperative, 1806–1848," Ph.D. diss. (Princeton University, 1972).

124 Frei, *Eclipse of Biblical Narrative*, 233–4.

125 William Neil, "The Criticism and Theological Use of the Bible, 1700–1950," in S. L. Greenslade, ed., *The Cambridge History of the Bible: The West from the Reformation to the Present Day* (Cambridge: Cambridge University Press, 1963), 275.

126 F. C. Baur, *Kritische Untersuchungen über die kanonischen Evangelien* (Tübingen, 1847), 49; quoted in Harris, *Strauss and His Theology*, 71.

127 Toews, *Hegelianism*, 231.

128 *Evangelische Kirchenzeitung* (1836), 434; quoted in Harris, *Strauss and His Theology*, 78.

129 Letter of 12 July 1835; quoted in Harris, *Strauss and His Theology*, 59 (translation modified).

130 Letter of 5 December 1836; quoted in Harris, *Strauss and His Theology*, 82.

131 Harris, *Strauss and His Theology*, 77.

132 McClelland, *State, Society, and University in Germany*, 152, 160. For the influence of German universities on the development of American universities, see George Marsden, *The Soul of the American University* (New York: Oxford University Press, 1994), 101–2.

133 See Max Weber, "Science as a Vocation," in H. H. Gerth and C. Wright Mills, eds. and trans., *From Max Weber: Essays in Sociology* (New York: Oxford University Press, 1946).

134 Nipperdey, *Deutsche Geschichte*, 445.

135 Nipperdey, *Deutsche Geschichte*, 471.

136 McClelland, *State, Society, and University in Germany*, 172–3.

137 See, for example, de Wette's preface to Friedrich Lücke, *Dr. Strauss und die Züricher Kirche: eine Stimme aus Norddeutschland* (1839), 4.

138 Strauss, *Life of Jesus*, lii.

139 McClelland, *State, Society, and University in Germany*, 173.

140 Excerpted in Staehelin, *Dewettiana*, 89. The editors were Schleiermacher, Friedrich Lücke, and de Wette.

141 I am indebted to Frederick Gregory's application of this distinction to German theologians' relations to natural science in the late nineteenth century. See Frederick Gregory, *Nature Lost? Natural Science and German Theological Traditions of the Nineteenth Century* (Cambridge: Harvard University Press, 1992).

142 Gregory, *Nature Lost?*, 18–19. Cf. A. N. Prior, "The Correspondence Theory of Truth," *The Encyclopedia of Philosophy*, vol. 2. (New York: Macmillan Co. and Free Press, 1967), 223–32.

143 Jacob Moleschott, *Ursache und Wirkung in der Lehre vom Leben* (Giessen, 1867); quoted in Gregory, *Nature Lost?*, 19.

144 See Gregory, *Nature Lost?*, 19. Gregory cites Karl Popper, *Objective Knowledge: An Evolutionary Approach* (Oxford: Clarendon Press, 1983), 317, and Hilary Putnam "What Is Realism?" in Jarrett Leplin, ed., *Scientific Realism* (Berkeley: University of California Press, 1984), 140.

145 Gregory, *Nature Lost?*, 20. Cf. the discussion of positivism in Mandelbaum, *History, Man, and Reason*, 10–20.
146 Strauss, *Life of Jesus*, 88.
147 See Gregory, *Nature Lost?*, 20.
148 Fries, *Knowledge, Belief, and Aesthetic Sense*, ed. Frederick Gregory, trans. Kent Richter (Cologne: Dinter Verlag, 1989), 31; quoted in Gregory, *Nature Lost?*, 20.
149 Noted in Gregory, *Nature Lost?*, 20, 286 (n. 41).
150 Ralph C. S. Walker, *The Coherence Theory of Truth* (New York: Routledge, 1989), 2; quoted in Gregory, *Nature Lost?*, 21.
151 Strauss, *Life of Jesus*, 88.
152 *Der alte und der neue Glaube* in *Gesammelte Schriften*, VI, ed. Eduard Zeller (1876–78), 56; quoted in Harris, *Strauss and His Theology*, 239.
153 For my interpretation of de Wette here, I am indebted to Allan Megill's notion of "disciplinary objectivity." See Allan Megill, "Four Sense of Objectivity" in Megill, ed., *Rethinking Objectivity* (Durham, NC: Duke University Press, 1994), 5–7.
154 For this episode, see Harris, *Strauss and His Theology*, 123–33. Also see Gordon Craig, *The Triumph of Liberalism: Zurich in the Golden Age, 1830–1869* (New York: Macmillan, 1988), 139.
155 See de Wette's preface to Friedrich Lücke, *Dr. Strauss und die Züricher Kirche: eine Stimme aus Norddeutschland* (1839), 4.
156 Nipperdey, *Deutsche Geschichte*, 474–5.
157 See Johannes Tobias Beck, "Ueber die wissenschaftliche Behandlung der christlichen Lehre: Eine akademische Antrittsrede gehalten zu Basel den 7. November 1836" (Basel, 1836), 31–32. De Wette himself also delivered several rectorial addresses (see chapter four) addressing the faith-learning problem. Two others of relevance that I discovered in Basel are K. R. Hagenbach, "Über die Begriff und die Bedeutung der Wissenschaftlichkeit im Gebiete der Theologie" (Basel, 1830) and W. Hoffman, "Die Stellung der wissenschaftlichen Theologie zur gegenwärtigen Zeit: Eine Antritts-Vorlesung an der Universität Basel gehalten am 5. Mai 1843 von W. Hoffmann" (Basel, 1843).
158 Letter of 13 March 1829. See Peter Dietz, ed., "Briefe des Antistes Jakob Burckhardt an seinen Freund Johann Jakob Frei," *BZ* 53 (1954): 124.

Chapter Four. Basel, Burckhardt, and de Wette

1 *Briefe* VI, 235.
2 *Briefe* I, 86.
3 The office of "Antistes" corresponds to a *primus inter pares* ministerial post and dates back to the Reformation of the city in 1529; its first occupant was Johannes Oecolampadius. On the origins of the title, see "Antistes" in *Historische-biographische Lexicon der Schweiz*, vol. 1, 388f.

   Jakob Burckhardt was elected by the congregation on the first Monday of October, 1838. His inaugural address took place on Sunday, 25 November 1838. The first letter in which Burckhardt (the son) mentions his religious crisis and the influence of de Wette is dated 8 August 1838. See *Briefe* I, 83–7.

4 A notable exception is Werner Kaegi's massive, erudite, and rather hagiographical biography of Burckhardt, in which one chapter is devoted to Burckhardt's *Theologiestudium*. Kaegi concludes that Burckhardt's break with theology did not entail a break with the "deeper essence of Christianity" (*christlichen Wesen in seinen Tiefen*). Kaegi however does not define what he means by the "deeper essence of Christianity." Kaegi also drastically minimizes any potential conflict between father and son. See Werner Kaegi, *Jacob*

Burckhardt: Eine Biographie I (Basel: Benno Schwabe & Co., 1947), 150, 433–87 (hereafter, Kaegi).

Two other works should also be mentioned. The first is Alfred Martin, *Die Religion Jacob Burckhardts: Eine Studie zum Thema Humanismus und Christentum* (Munich: Erasmus-Verlag, 1947). Although Martin refers to de Wette and to Burckhardt's theological studies, his study is more an attempt to construct a systematic overview of Burckhardt's mature religious views drawn from various places in his *oeuvre*. Second, Ernst Walter Zeeden's article, "Die Auseinandersetzung des jungen Jacob Burckhardt mit Glaube und Christentum," *HZ* 178 (1954): 237–7, has proved insightful on several points. Because of its brevity, however, it raises more questions than it satisfactorily answers.

5 I make a distinction here between Burckhardt the "historian" and Burckhardt the "historical thinker." As a historian – primarily because of his *Renaissance* and his art guide, *Cicerone* – Burckhardt achieved considerable renown during the nineteenth century. As a "historical thinker," on the other hand, as someone who comments on the course and meaning of the historical process at large, Burckhardt's thought, as Alexander Dru rightly notes, "was slow to mature, slow to appear and slow to be understood." See Alexander Dru's introduction to Jacob Burckhardt, *Letters* (Westport, CT: Greenwood Press, 1955), 2 (hereafter, *Letters*). The turning point came when Burckhardt's nephew, Jacob Oeri, edited and published two of Burckhardt's works posthumously: his three-volume *Griechische Kulturgeschichte* (1902ff.) and *Weltgeschichtliche Betrachtungen* (1905). Most of Burckhardt's important letters did not surface until the 1920s. The first edition of his collected works appeared from 1929 to 1934.

The events of the second World War provided the final stage for Burckhardt's inclusion in the canon of modern historical thought. At this time, Burckhardt's prophecies and his contempt for politics – elements in his thought that had formerly been regarded as weaknesses – suddenly assumed profound significance. The most influential work written in this regard was Friedrich Meinecke's short essay on Ranke and Burckhardt, in which Meinecke conceded that Burckhardt after all was the more perceptive observer of historical events. See Friedrich Meinecke, "Ranke and Burckhardt," in Hans Kohn, ed., *German History: Some New German Views* (Boston: Beacon Press, 1954). For a recent treatment of this theme, see Felix Gilbert, *History: Politics or Culture? Reflections on Ranke and Burckhardt* (Princeton: Princeton University Press, 1990).

On the reception of Burckhardt, see Alexander Dru's very helpful introduction to Jacob Burckhardt, *Letters*, 1–34.

6 There are too many works dealing with Burckhardt's studies at Berlin to list individually. See Werner Kaegi, "Jacob Burckhardt und seine Berliner Lehrer," *Schweizerische Beiträge zur allgemeinen Geschichte* 7 (1949): 101–16. For a more recent view, see Felix Gilbert, "Jacob Burckhardt's Student Years: The Road to Cultural History," *JHI* 47 (1986): 249–74.

7 Karl Löwith also discusses Burckhardt in theological terms. See Löwith, *Jacob Burckhardt: Der Mensch inmitten der Geschichte* (Stuttgart: Kohlhammer, 1966). Also see his chapter on Burckhardt in *Meaning in History* (Chicago: University of Chicago Press, 1949). Löwith's philosophical analyses have proved illuminating on many points; however, his level of generality and his omission of many concrete aspects of Burckhardt's life render his discussion of Burckhardt vague and unsatisfactory from a historian's standpoint.

8 The connections between Burckhardt neo-orthodoxy, and anti- or postmodernism will be discussed in chapter five.

9 I borrow this term from Karl Barth. It will be developed later in the chapter. See quote from Barth in Kaegi I, 148.

10 For my understanding of Basel, I benefited greatly from the publications of, and a generous correspondence with, Lionel Gossman of Princeton University.

The widespread characterization of Basel as "das fromme Basel" dates from the influence of pietism in the eighteenth century. Some of the most informative treatments of Basel's history are Alfred Berchtold, *Bâle et L'Europe: une histoire culturelle* (Lausanne: Payot, 1990); Edgar Bonjour, *Die Universität Basel, 1460–1960* (Basel: Helbing & Lichtenhahn, 1971); Paul Burckhardt, *Geschichte der Stadt Basel von der Zeit der Reformation bis zur Gegenwart* (Basel: Helbing & Lichtenhahn, 1967); Lukas Burckhardt, René L. Frey, Georg Kreis, and Gerhard Schmid, eds., *Das polititische System Basel Stadt: Geschichte, Strukturen, Institutionen, Politikbereiche* (Basel: Helbing & Lichtenhahn, 1984); Lionel Gossman, "Basle, Bachofen and the Critique of Modernity in the Second Half of the Nineteenth Century," *JWCI* 74 (1986): 136–85; Lionel Gossman, "The 'Two Cultures' in Nineteenth-Century Basel: Between the French '*Encyclopédie*' and German Neohumanism," *European Studies* 20 (1990): 95–133; Hans R. Guggisberg, *Basel in the Sixteenth Century: Aspects of the City Republic before, during, and after the Reformation* (St. Louis: Center for Reformation Research, 1982); Hans Kohn, *Nationalism and Liberty: The Swiss Example* (New York: Macmillan, 1956); René Teutenberg, *Basler Geschichte* (Basel: Christoph Merian Verlag, 1986); Lionel Gossman, "Basel" in Nicolas Bouvier, Gordon Craig, and Lionel Gossman (with an introduction by Carl Schorske), *Geneva, Zurich, Basel: History, Culture, and National Identity* (Princeton: Princeton University Press, 1994), 65–98. (I shall refer to the latter hereafter as Gossman, "Basel.")

11 Eric Hobsbawm, *Nations and Nationalism since 1780: Programme, Myth, Reality* (Cambridge: Cambridge University Press, 1990), 41. Basel experienced a rather "precocious" social modernization; in fact, one could say that the *Ancien Régime* in Basel was even bourgeois, not aristocratic. Because of the political activity of the so-called *Herrenzünfte* ("gentlemen's guilds"), aristocratic nobles gradually were deprived of their power during the course of the sixteenth century. The bishop of Basel was later opposed and driven from the city when the Reformation came in 1529. Afterwards, the city emerged as a "patriciate," rule by an economic elite. The economic elite in Basel quite often intermarried, however, and one may speak of the establishment of an ersatz-aristocracy, where the money of several important families – namely the Bachofens, the Burckhardts, the Battiers, the Bernoullis, the De Baarys, the La Rouches, the Le Grandes, the Passavants, the Paravincinis, the Sarasinis, and the von der Mühls – dominated political decision making. See Gossman, "Basel," 67–8; Guggisberg, *Basel in the Sixteenth Century*, 3–8.

12 P. Burckhardt, *Geschichte der Stadt Basel*, 92.

13 There were, however, two notable "enlightened" exceptions to this rule: the francophile theorist of the Helvetic Republic, Peter Ochs (1752–21) and the professor Isaak Iselin (1728–82). In 1783, there was a public outcry to prevent the printing of the works of Voltaire in Basel. See Wernle, *Der schweizerische Protestantismus* III, 50.

14 For a more detailed discussion of the political and economic reasons for Basel's conservatism, see Gossman, "Basel," 65–94.

15 In 1795, the population numbered 15,720; in 1847, it had risen to only 25,787. See Philipp Sarasin, "Basel-Zur Sozialgeschichte der Stadt Bachofens" in *Johann Jakob Bachofen (1815–1887): Eine Begleitpublikation zur Austellung im Historischen Museum Basel* (Basel, 1987), 28.

16 Gossman, "Basle, Bachofen . . . ," *JWCI* 74 (1986): 136.

17 The first Confession was compiled by Oswald Myconius (1488–1552) on the basis of a shorter formula by Oecolampadius in 1531. Its theological standpoints represent an attempt to synthesize the views of Luther and Zwingli. For the original, see H. A. Niemeyer, *Collectio Confessionum in ecclesiis reformatis publicatarum* (Leipzig, 1840),

78–122. For an English trans., see A. C. Cochrane, *Reformed Confessions of the Sixteenth Century* (1966), 89–111. The Confession was read publicly annually and until 1826 all citizens were obliged to swear loyalty to it.

18 A classic example of the uses of the local past by later generations of Baslers can be found in the writings of Burckhardt's own father. See Jakob Burckhardt (Obersthelfer), *Kurze Geschichte der Reformation in Basel* (Basel, 1818), 96. I shall provide a closer examination of this book later in this chapter.

For another example of how nineteenth-century figures turned to Basel's past, see Lionel Gossman, "The Boundaries of the City: A Nineteenth-Century Essay on 'The Limits of Historical Knowledge,'" *HT* (1986): 33–51. Especially note Gossman's discussion of Wilhelm Vischer's rhetorical use of the legacy of Erasmus to advocate limits for historical knowledge. By doing this, Vischer implicitly criticized the nationalistic and hubristic trends of Prussian historiography. Vischer was a professor of history at Basel and a friend of Jacob Burckhardt.

19 Guggisberg, *Basel in the Sixteenth Century*, 11–2. Guggisberg writes that it was "amazing that the general urge to reach these aims [the deepening of the understanding of Christian ethics] did not lead to disputes among the scholars in which Origen would have been played off against Tertullian, or Plato against Aristotle and the Evangelists. The Basel humanists always tended toward a harmonization of the Greek tradition of 'philosophia' with the Hebrew-Christian heritage of 'revelatio.'" Guggisberg too perhaps has idealized the humanist heritage; however, it was exactly such a tendency toward idealization that played an important role among eighteenth- and nineteenth-century scholars and pastors in Basel.

20 For various European manifestations of humanism and their (often complex) relations to Christianity, see P. O. Kristeller, "The Moral Thought of Renaissance Humanism" in *Renaissance Thought and the Arts: Collected Essays by P. O. Kristeller*, expanded ed. (Princeton: Princeton University Press, 1990). Also see Donald R. Kelly, *Renaissance Humanism* (Boston: Twayne Publishers, 1991).

21 See Werner Kaegi, "Humanistische Kontinuität im konfessionellen Zeitalter," *Historische Meditationen* (Basel: Benno Schwabe & Co., 1994), 149ff.

22 Two other important figures for "moderate orthodoxy" were Jean-Alphonse Turrettini of Geneva and Jean-Frédéric Osterwald of Neuchâtel (one speaks of a "Helvetic triumvirate"). See Hagenbach, *Die theologische Schule Basels*, 36ff.

23 P. Burckhardt, *Geschichte der Stadt Basel*, 90.

24 Werenfels's favorite maxim was: "Hic liber est, in quo sua quaerit dogmata quisque / Invenit et partier dogmata quisque sua" (In this book everyone seeks his point of view / and everyone can find his point of view in it).

25 Berchtold, *Bâle et L'Europe* II, 457.

26 Practical considerations prevent a longer discussion of Werenfels here. Although his importance is widely recognized in general commentaries on the period, there is surprisingly no detailed work on his influence. Kaegi emphasizes the connection between Werenfels and the theology of Burckhardt's father. See Kaegi I, 148–9. Werenfels was the son of the professor and *Antistes* Peter Werenfels. He studied in Belgium, Holland, Germany, and Paris. From 1685 to 1740, he held numerous chairs at the University of Basel, including ones in Greek, rhetoric, dogmatics, and the Old and New Testament. Werenfels's major works are contained in *Opuscula theologica, philosophica et philologica*, 3 vols. (Basel, 1782). See also his collection of sermons, *Sermons sur des verités importantes de la religion* (Basel, 1715). Cf. Paul Wernle, *Der schweizerische Protestantismus im 18.Jahrhundert* I, (Basel, 1923); Andreas Staehelin, *Professoren der Universität Basel aus Fünf Jahrhunderten* (Basel: Friedrich Reinhardt, 1959), 86–7; Karl Barth, "Samuel Werenfels (1657–1740) und die Theologie seiner Zeit," *Evangelische Theologie* 3 (1936): 180–203; Eberhard Vischer, *Werenfelsiana* (Basel, 1935). A detailed study of Werenfels's

thought would provide a particularly interesting perspective on the view of the eighteenth century, characterized by Peter Gay as "the rise of modern paganism."

27 Bonjour, *Die Universität Basel*, 301–3. In 1860, Hagenbach, a native Basler educated at Berlin, criticized one of his predecessors, Emanuel Merian (1765–1829), on the following grounds: "He had unquestionably great learning in languages, mathematics, physics, and also an unmistakable philosophical acumen. *What he lacked, however, was a thorough formation in Wissenschaft in the German sense of the word and method*" (my emphasis). Hagenbach's words could be taken as a typical judgment of scholars schooled in German *Wissenschaft* on their eighteenth-century predecessors. See Hagenbach, *Die theologische Schule Basels*, 56.

28 Hagenbach, *Die theologische Schule Basels*, 50.

29 Bonjour writes: "In the central questions of dogma, the official *vernünftige Orthodoxie* did not recognize tolerance and demonstrated its orthodoxy by the sharp judgment of the modern biblical critic (i.e., Wettstein)." See Bonjour, *Die Universität Basel*, 302. Concerning the theological milieu of eighteenth-century Basel, Hagenbach writes: "We are not allowed to call this direction rationalist, nor can we call it neologist and heterodox. The men that we are observing remained attached to ecclesiastical orthodoxy in its main points; and if they deviated from this slightly, they were hardly aware of doing so. It did not occur to them to stand on any other ground than on that which the Protestant, reformed church was built, namely on the ground that the holy scripture, Old and New Testament, was the revealed Word of God." See K. R. Hagenbach, *Die theologische Schule Basels*, 36f. For the Wettstein affair, see K. R. Hagenbach, *J. J. Wettstein, der Kritiker und seine Gegner* (Leipzig, 1839).

30 Hagenbach, *Die theologische Schule Basels*, 51.

31 P. Burckhardt, *Geschichte der Stadt Basel*, 92.

32 Four of the brothers of Burckhardt's father also became pastors. There were also numerous "Burckhardt" pastors (distant relatives) in the eighteenth and nineteenth centuries in Basel. See Kaegi I, 49ff. See Urs Burckhardt and Rudolf Suter, *(Basel): Streiflichter auf Geschichte und Persönlichkeiten des Basler Geschlechts Burckhardt* (Basel: Buchverlag Basler Zeitung, 1990).

33 Muttenz lay on the outskirts of Basel.

34 Wernle, *Der schweizerische Protestantismus* I, 326.

35 For a detailed profile of d'Annoni and his influence in Basel, see Wernle, *Der schweizerische Protestantismus* I, 325–56.

36 Kaegi I, 84.

37 On Zinzendorf, see "Zinzendorf" in Cross and Livingstone, eds., *The Oxford Dictionary of the Christian Church*, 3rd ed. (1997), 1781–2.

38 Wernle, *Der schweizerische Protestantismus* I, 370.

39 See "Beilage V" in Hagenbach, *Die theologische Schule Basels*, 68. The poem dates from 1741.

40 Overall, the problem of separatism was rather mild in Basel. Vocal separatists were asked to leave the city. If they refused or if they later returned, they were subject to public pillory, but this seldom occurred in the eighteenth century. See Wernle, *Der schweizerische Protestantismus* I, 349ff.

41 See Max Geiger, "Basel, Christentumsgesellschaft" in G. Krause and Gerhard Müller, eds., *Theologische Realenzyklopädie*, vol. 5 (Berlin: de Gruyter, 1980), 276–8.

42 Ernst Staehelin, ed., *Die Christentumsgesellschaft in der Zeit von der Erweckung bis zur Gegenwart: Texte aus Briefen, Protokollen und Publikationen* I (Basel: Friedrich Reinhardt, 1974), 3.

43 Kaegi I, 88.

44 Quoted in K. R. Hagenbach, *Die Kirche des achzehnten und neunzehnten Jahrhunderts in ihrer geschichtlichen Entwicklung* I (Leipzig, 1871), 382.

45 Staehelin, ed., *Die Christentumsgesellschaft* I, 3.

46 For a more detailed survey of the broader influence of the *Christentumsgesellschaft*, see Wernle, *Der schweizerische Protestantismus* III, 28–62.

47 *Berlinischen Monatsschrift* (June, 1784). Quoted in Staehelin, ed., *Die Christentumsgesellschaft* I, 222. Kant's essay "Was ist Aufklärung?" appeared in this publication in December of the same year. The editors were Friedrich Gedike and Johann Erich Biester.

48 P. Burckhardt, *Geschichte der Stadt Basel*, 91.

49 Johann Wernhard Herzog, *Athenae raurica sive Catalogus Professorum academiae Basiliensis ab a. MCCCLX ad annum MDCCLXXVIII. cum brevi singulorum biographia* (Basel, 1778). Herzog too was deeply influenced by Werenfels's theology. He served as president of both the *Christentumsgesellschaft* and the *Bibelgesellschaft*, as well as rector of the university on five occasions. He taught at the University of Basel from 1765 until 1813. See Staehelin, ed., *Die Christentumsgesellschaft* I, 40.

50 Wernle, *Der schweizerische Protestantismus* III, 463.

51 On the philosophes' understanding of history and their desire to free it from "the parochialism of Christian scholars and from theological presuppositions," see Peter Gay, *The Enlightenment: An Interpretation: The Rise of Modern Paganism* I (London: Weidenfeld and Nicolson, 1966), 31ff.

52 Gossman, "Basel," 67. The Helvetic period refers to the short-lived (1798–1803) republic created in Switzerland by France. The period witnessed the separation of church and state in Basel. Except for a few supporters of the French Revolution, most of Basel's citizens, including Burckhardt's grandfather, regarded this time as wholly unfortunate and the republic as an imperialistic imposition. See Kaegi I, 93.

53 Quoted in Kaegi I, 91.

54 See P. Burckhardt, *Geschichte der Stadt Basel*, 155.

55 Cochrane, *Reformed Confessions of the Sixteenth Century*, 102.

56 Letter from July of 1798. Quoted in Kaegi I, 91.

57 Hagenbach, *Die Kirche des achtzehnten und neunzehnten Jahrhunderts* II, 479. For a detailed account of the background of de Wette's coming to Basel, see Ernst Jenny, "Wie de Wette nach Basel kam," *BJ* 41 (1941): 51–78.

58 Berchtold, *Bâle et L'Europe* II, 485.

59 Andreas Staehelin, *Geschichte der Universität Basel, 1818–1835* (Basel: Helbing & Lichtenhahn, 1959), 34.

60 Stein to Wolleb, 31 July 1821. Staehelin, *Dewettiana*, 104. Exactly how Stein and Wolleb knew one another is unknown.

61 Staehelin, *Dewettiana*, 101–2; quoted in Rogerson, *De Wette*, 181–2.

62 Staehelin, *Dewettiana*, 104.

63 Letter reprinted in Staehelin, *Dewettiana*, 99–100.

64 Georg Friedrich Creuzer (1771–1858); Karl Daub (1765–1836); Christian Schwarz (1766–1837). See Staehelin, *Dewettiana*, 102–4. See Rogerson, *De Wette*, 182.

65 Letter of 15 July 1821. Staehelin, *Dewettiana*, 102–3.

66 Letter of 16 July 1821. Staehelin, *Dewettiana*, 103.

67 See Rogerson, *De Wette*, 182 and A. Staehelin, *Geschichte der Universität Basel, 1818–1835*, 34.

68 For the chosen excerpts, see Staatsarchiv Basel, Erziehungsakten, Y8; noted in Rogerson, *De Wette*, 182.

69 Rogerson, *De Wette*, 182.

70 A. Staehelin, *Geschichte der Universität Basel, 1818–1835*, 34.

71 Jenny, "Wie de Wette nach Basel kam," *BJ* 41 (1941): 61.

72 Erziehungsakten: Staatsarchiv Basel, Y8; Staehelin, *Dewettiana*, 111–2.

73 See the copy of his acceptance letter in Staehelin, *Dewettiana*, 116. De Wette had initial reservations about swearing an oath to the Basel Confession. He expressed his fear to his

former teacher, J. P. Gabler, who replied that "you need not fear the Basel Confession; it is the shortest and most proper. Hopefully, however, the pledge will not command what one is supposed to believe, but only that one should not teach contrary to it [the Confession]." Letter of 4 February 1822; quoted in Staehelin, *Dewettiana*, 115–6.

On 9 March 1822, de Wette signed a statement promising that to "the young theology students entrusted to his teaching" he would teach "nothing but the pure, uncorrupted Protestant doctrine of human salvation as it is given in . . . the Holy Scriptures, Old and New Testaments, and in our Basel Confession." See Erziehungsakten: Staatsarchiv Basel, Y8.

74 See his rectorial address of 1829: De Wette, *Von der Stellung der Wissenschaft im Gemeinwesen* (Basel, 1829).

75 Rogerson, *De Wette*, 191ff.

76 Original in De Wette Nachlaß, University of Basel. Copy in Handschin, *De Wette als Prediger und Schriftsteller*, 322–6. Also see Rogerson, *De Wette*, 191–2.

77 See *Von der Prüfung der Geister* (Basel Univ. Library, FZ 201 no. 5, 1822) 17; Rogerson, *De Wette*, 193.

78 Vinet to pastor Louis Leresche (1796–1865), 2 October 1822. Staehelin, *Dewettiana*, 123–4. For Vinet's efforts on behalf of de Wette and for his role within in Basel's religious community, see Berchtold, *Bâle et L'Europe* II, 459–61; Hagenbach, *Die theologische Schule Basels*, 58.

79 Rogerson, *De Wette*, 193–4.

80 Buxtorf, professor of Old Testament, was seventy-five; Merian, professor of New Testament, was approaching sixty.

81 For de Wette's reforms, see Universitätsarchiv: Staatsarchiv Basel, Y15, "Protokolle der Sitzungen der theologischen Fakultät von 1744–1923," 55–7; noted in Rogerson, *De Wette*, 196.

82 Interestingly, de Wette also at this time attempted to have the Education Committee offer J. F. Fries a position in Basel's philosophical faculty. Because of his role in the *Burschenschaften* activities, Fries had been suspended from his teaching post at Jena in 1819. An offer was actually extended to Fries, but he decided against it because of the meager salary. At the time, the Weimar government supported Fries financially and he was soon allowed to teach again in 1824. Fries's decision against Basel seems to have caused a small disturbance in the Fries–de Wette relationship. See Rogerson, *De Wette*, 195; Staehelin, *Dewettiana*, 122.

83 On Hagenbach, see Staehelin, *Dewettiana*, 127; Kaegi I, 433–40.

84 The two *Dozenten* were J. J. Staehelin (1797–75) and Johann Georg Müller (1800–75). De Wette and Hagenbach had a heavy hand in their selection. See A. Staehelin, *Geschichte der Universität Basel, 1818–1835*, 36–41.

85 J. Bachman, *Ernst Wilhelm Hengstenberg: Sein Leben und Wirken*, vol. 1 (Gütersloh, 1879), 124ff; quoted in Rogerson, *De Wette*, 208 and Lenz, *Universität Berlin* II, 330–1.

86 On Spittler, see Gustav Adolf Wanner, "Christian Friedrich Spittler" in Rudolf Stier and René Teuteberg, eds., *Der Reformation verpflichtet: Gestalten und Gestalter in Stadt und Landschaft Basel aus fünf Jahrhunderten* (Basel: Christoph Merian Verlag, 1979), 85–9.

87 Rogerson, *De Wette*, 212ff.

88 Spittler to de Wette, 29 September 1825. Staehelin, *Dewettiana*, 140.

89 De Wette to Spittler, 3 October 1825. Staehelin, *Dewettiana*, 140–1.

90 Spittler to de Wette, 11 November 1825. Staehelin, *Dewettiana*, 141. Ultimately the two men met in person, discussed their differences, and worked out a more amicable relationship. However, those associated with the Basler Mission remained persistently skeptical of de Wette's theological program and his influence on university students. See Rogerson, *De Wette*, 212–4.

91 For more on these events, see P. Burckhardt, *Geschichte der Stadt Basel*, 159ff.

92 Ernst Jospeh Gustav de Valentini, ed., *Der graue Mann*, no. 42. (Nürnberg, 1833). See reprint of incriminating passages in Staehelin, *Dewettiana*, 161–2.
93 Jung had also come from northern Germany.
94 Rogerson, *De Wette*, 238–9.
95 De Wette, *Über den Angriff des grauen Mannes gegen Lehrer der hiesigen Universität* (Basel Univ. Library, Hagb 1742 no. 5, 1834).
96 A. Staehelin, *Geschichte der Universität Basel, 1818–1835*, 147.
97 Rogerson, *De Wette*, 238.
98 Letter of 13 January 1831. Staehelin, *Dewettiana*, 151. Also see P. Burckhardt, *Geschichte der Stadt Basel*, 215f.
99 De Wette, "Einige Betrachtungen über den Geist unserer Zeit, Academische Rede am 12 September 1834 gehalten" (Basel Univ. Library, Falk. 3190 No. 19, 1834), 21.
100 "Einige Betrachtungen über den Geist unserer Zeit," 24–5.
101 "Einige Betrachtungen über den Geist unserer Zeit," 1.
102 A. Staehelin, *Geschichte der Universität Basel, 1818–1835*, 148.
103 Bonjour, *Die Universität Basel*, 372.
104 See de Wette, *Über Religion und Theologie*, 255.
105 For details, see the chapter "Erste Kindheit" in Kaegi I, 3–23.
106 Until 1978 only a few letters from Burckhardt to his father were known to exist, when more were discovered in the archives of the Oeri family (relatives of Burckhardt). However, the newly discovered letters only go up to 1838 (the year of Burckhardt's apostasy). Based on Burckhardt's own statements in a letter to Paul Heyse, all later correspondence was presumably burned. See letter of 23 January 1859, *Briefe* IV, 36. Also see Heinrich Oeri-Schenk and Max Burckhardt, "Aus Jacob Burckhardts Jugendzeit: Ein Nachtrag zu seiner Bildungsgeschichte," *BZ* 82 (1982): 133–5.
107 Kaegi I, 151.
108 Note that Kaegi was not in possession of the letters discovered in 1978. Moreover, Kaegi does not probe the implications of several letters, which were available to him, that *would* suggest alienation between father and son.
109 For the influence of Erasmus and Werenfels's views on Burckhardt (Sr.), see Kaegi I, 128.
110 Letter of 8 May 1807; Staehelin, *Dewettiana*, 65–6.
111 Quoted in Kaegi I, 131.
112 Kaegi I, 128–31.
113 Kaegi I, 131.
114 Kaegi I, 138–9. See Jakob Burckhardt, "Nachricht über die öffentlichen Kinderlehren im Münster, 1. August 1816" (Handschriftenabteilung, Univ. Library Basel, Falk. 3165 N57, 1816).
115 Kaegi I, 137–8.
116 Kaegi I, 138.
117 Jakob Burckhardt (Sr.), *Kurze Geschichte der Reformation in Basel* (Basel Univ. Library, Falk. 851 No. 1, 1818), 2.
118 Burckhardt (Sr.), *Kurze Geschichte der Reformation in Basel*, 96.
119 "Rede gehalten im Münster am Reformations-Feste der Kinder, Sonntages den 10 Januar 1819 von Jakob Burckhardt, Obersthelfer" (Basel Univ. Library, Falk. 3203 No. 21, 1819).
120 See Jakob Burckhardt (Sr.), *Lehrbuch des christlichen Religionsunterrichtes für die Kirchen des Kantons Basel, Zum Gebrauch für die Kinderlehre und für den Confirmationsunterricht* (Basel Univ. Library, Ki Ar A VI 13, 1832).
121 II Timothy 1:13–4 (New Oxford Annotated Bible).
122 Kaegi I, 148. Kaegi quotes from a small unpublished and undated writing by Barth:

"Bemerkungen zu des Archdiacon J. Burckhardts Lehrbuch des christlichen Religionunterrichts."

123 Kaegi I, 148–9.

124 Burckhardt (Sr.), *Lehrbuch des christlichen Religions-unterrichtes*, 2.

125 Kaegi I, 145.

126 Burckhardt (Sr.), *Lehrbuch des christlichen Religions-unterrichtes*, 22. There are four sections that deal with sin and human nature: "VII Von dem Menschen"; "VIII Von dem Sündefalle"; "XIV Von der Sünde"; and "XV Von den Strafen der Sünde." See pp. 20–9.

127 Burckhardt (Sr.), *Lehrbuch des christlichen Religions-unterrichtes*, 22.

128 Burckhardt (Sr.), *Lehrbuch des christlichen Religions-unterrichtes*, 21.

129 Kaegi I, 147, 150.

130 Burckhardt (Sr.), *Lehrbuch des christlichen Religions-unterrichtes*, 31–2. Seven sections in the catechism deal with the nature of Christ: "XVII Von Jesu Christo, dem Sohne Gottes, unserem Erlöser"; "XVIII Von der Menschenwerdung des Sohnes Gottes"; "XIV Von der Lehre dem Wandel des Sohnes Gottes auf Erden"; "XX Von dem Leiden und Sterben unsers Erlösers"; "XXI Von der Auferstehung unseres Herrn"; "XXII Von der Himmelfahrt unsers Erlösers"; and "XXIII Von der Wiederkunft Christi zum Gerichte." See pp. 31–45.

131 For details on his election to *Antistes*, see "Acta über die Erwählung des Antistes Jacob Burckhardts, 1838" (Handschriftenabteilung, Basel Univ. Library, Mscr. Ki Ar 21, 1838).

132 Ibid.

133 "The saying is sure: If anyone aspires to the office of Bishop, he desires a noble task." I Timothy 3:1 (New Oxford Annotated Bible).

134 "Predigt über die Worte I Timotheum 3,1. gehalten bei seinem Amtsantritte Sonntags den 25. November 1838 in der Münsterkirche von Jakob Burckhardt, Pfarrer der Münstergemeinde und Antistes." (Basel Univ. Library, Falk. 3203 No. 36, 1838).

135 Ibid., 9.

136 Ibid., 21.

137 Susanna Maria Burckhardt-Schorndorff died on 17 March 1830, an event that Jacob Burckhardt later described as giving him an "impression of the great frailty and uncertainty of all earthly things." Kaegi I, 21.

138 Letter of 31 December 1832; translated into English from a German translation by Heinrich Oeri-Schenk and Max Burckhardt. Quoted in Oeri-Schenk and Burckhardt, "Aus Jacob Burckhardts Jugendzeit," 102.

139 Letter of 13 March 1829. See Peter Dietz, ed., "Briefe des Antistes Jakob Burckhardt an seinen Freund Johann Jakob Frei," *BZ* 53 (1954): 124.

140 Letter of 13 March 1829. Dietz, ed., "Briefe des Antistes Jakob Burckhardt," 124. Unfortunately, there are only a few scattered comments where Burckhardt (Sr.) explicitly comments on de Wette. Consequently, it is impossible to give a satisfactory account of his reaction to de Wette's coming to teach in Basel. Overall, it seems safe to say that he was skeptical of de Wette's beliefs, but felt that de Wette's learning, especially in ancient languages, had much to offer theology students at Basel.

141 Letter of 16 September 1830. Dietz, ed., "Briefe des Antistes Jakob Burckhardt," 137.

142 Letter of 13 September 1829. Dietz, ed., "Briefe des Antistes Jakob Burckhardt," 125–6.

143 Kaegi I, 151. In many respects, Burckhardt (Sr.) fits Karl Barth's description of the "Basler theologian," as someone who is conservative in all essentials, but devoted to a little freethinking and willing to attribute most disagreements to a dispute about words. See Karl Barth, *Protestant Theology in the Nineteenth Century* (London: SCM Press, 1972), 145; noted in Gossman, "Basel," 93–4.

144 *Briefe* II, 62; *Letters*, 89. Beyschlag (1823–76), educated in Berlin, served as a pastor in Trier and later as theology professor in Halle.

145 *Briefe* II, 172; *Letters*, 94.

146 *Briefe* V, 96; *Letters*, 139. The precise nature of Burckhardt's religious views perplexed many of his rather pious students at Basel. One student (later a theologian), Karl Frey, commented: "I remember that on 30 July 1912 the question about Jacob Burckhardt's atheism seized me, and I became powerless. I also remember that Rudolf Oeri . . . once said that Anna Freyvogel and other young women would often argue about whether Burckhardt believed in God or not. Clearly, this man's [religious] views were very important to us." See Elisabeth Pistor-Frey and Ernst Ziegler, "Karl Frey, ein Schüler Jacob Burckhardts," *BZ* 70 (1970): 190.

147 On this theme, see Owen Chadwick's chapter "History and the Secular" in *The Secularization of the European Mind*, 189–228. I also refer the reader to my introduction for an elaboration of this point.

148 Kaegi I, 445.

149 Burckhardt took the following courses from Hagenbach: summer semester (1837): *Kirchengeschichte* (II); winter semester (1837/38): *Kirchengeschichte* (I), *Patristicum*, Theological Encyclopedia; summer semester (1838): *Dogmengeschichte*, *Patristicum*; winter semester (1838/39): *Dogmengeschichte*, Calvin's Institutes; summer semester (1839): *Patristicum*. Hagenbach lectures on *Kirchengeschichte* and *Dogmeneschichte* were later published and went through several editions. See Hagenbach, *Kirchengeschichte von der ältesten Zeit bis zum 19. Jahrhundert*, 1834–92, and *Lehrbuch der Dogmengeschichte*, 1840–88. In his later lectures, Hegenbach extolled de Wette, comparing him to Schleiermacher and emphasizing his role as the bearer of German *Wissenschaft* to the Swiss churches. See especially Hagenbach, *Die Kirche des achtzehnten und neunzehnten Jahrhunderts* II, 479ff.

150 Jacob-Burckhardt-Archiv, Staatsarchiv Basel, 13a.

151 Based on Burckhardt's *Nachschriften* as quoted by Kaegi I, 443 (my emphasis).

152 See Arnold von Salis, "Zum hundertsten Geburtstag Jakob Burckhardt: Erinnerungen eines alten Schülers," *BJ* (1918): 288.

153 For Kaegi's discussion of Hagenbach, see Kaegi I, 435ff.

154 Kaegi I, 449.

155 For a complete listing of the lectures that Burckhardt attended during his *Theologiestudium* at Basel, see Otto Markwart, *Jacob Burckhardt: Persönlichkeit und Jugendjahre* (Basel, 1920), 396–7. Unfortunately, only Burckhardt's *Nachschriften* to de Wette's courses on Isaiah and Proverbs have survived. See Jacob-Burckhardt-Archiv, Staatsarchiv Basel, 207, 12f and 13f; Kaegi I, 449–53.

156 Riggenbach, initially attracted by Hegel's philosophy, came to a rather moderate, even conservative, standpoint later in his life and served as professor of systematic theology at Basel from 1851 to 1890. See Andreas Staehelin, ed., *Professoren der Universität Basel aus fünf Jahrhunderten* (Basel, 1960), 156–7.

157 *Briefe* I, 84; *Letters*, 36. When Nietzsche read D. F. Strauss as a young theology student at Bonn in 1864, he, strikingly similar to Burckhardt, confided to a friend that "if you give up Christ you have to give up God too." See Paul Deussen, *Erinnerungen an Friedrich Nietzsche* (Leipzig, 1901), 20. The following year Nietzsche refused communion on Easter and abandoned theology.

158 *Briefe* I, 84; *Letters*, 35.

159 "Filius Antistitis, einem gescheuten Kopf," wrote Hagenbach of Burckhardt in a letter in 1845 after hearing the young Burckhardt lecture on the art works in the city's cathedral. Cited in Kaegi I, 445.

160 *Briefe* I, 85; *Letters*, 36.

161 *Briefe* I, 101; *Letters*, 43 (translation modified).

162 *Briefe* I, 86; *Letters*, 37 (translation modified).

163 *Briefe* I, 84; *Letters*, 35–6 (translation modified).

164 *Briefe* I, 123; *Letters*, 46. Heinrich Schreiber (1792–1872) was a respected scholar in Freiburg for whom Burckhardt had conducted research in Basel's archives. Schreiber began his career as a Catholic theologian but because of deist tendencies was moved over to the philosophical faculty, where he lectured in history. In several letters Burckhardt indicates that Schreiber played an important role in inspiring him to seek his new vocation in history. See *Letters*, 8f, 45ff, 49ff.

165 *Briefe* I, 91.

166 Letter of 1 December 1839. *Briefe* I, 130; *Letters*, 47–8.

167 After his studies in Basel and Berlin, Biedermann became a pastor in Basel and then a professor in Zurich. He was deeply involved in the struggle between "positive" and "free-thinking" (*freisinnig*) Christianity in the Swiss church, insisting, on the one hand, on the necessity of complete scholarly freedom, but, on the other, on the possibility that liberals and conservatives could coexist in the church and proclaim the same Gospel. Biedermann's principal works are *Die freie Theologie oder Philosophie und Christentum im Streit und Frieden* (1844), *Unsere junghegelsche Weltanschauung oder der sogenannte neuste Pantheismus* (1849), *Christliche Dogmatik* (1869), and *Ausgewählte Vorträge und Aufsätze* (1884–5). He and Burckhardt seem to have had little or no contact after their university days. Given Burckhardt's later reactions to liberal theology and its optimism, one can only assume that he would have regarded Biedermann as a typically modern theologian. For more on Biedermann, see Claude Welch, *Protestant Thought in the Nineteenth Century* (New Haven: Yale University Press, 1972), 160ff.

168 See statements for example in *Briefe* I, 83f, 90f.

169 Kaegi I, 485.

170 Kaegi I, 482–7.

171 *Briefe* I, 113; *Letters*, 44 (translation modified).

172 *Briefe* I, 118. In all likelihood with Biedermann in mind, Burckhardt wrote Kinkel on 20 August 1843. In this letter he speaks of the "fanaticism of systems" and writes: "There is no fanaticism like that of a system, because [adherents to the system] feel pity toward all those who stand outside it. I have suffered under such people and experienced myself how this fanaticism insinuated itself into daily life and destroyed one personal relationship after another. To put it succinctly: . . . [adherents to the system] reason that I have come to this and that position in this manner. You do the same or else we are no longer intellectual comrades and our friendship has come to an end." See *Briefe* II, 30; Kaegi II, 16.

173 Letter of 8 September 1839. *Briefe* I, 122–3; *Letters*, 46. By this time, Burckhardt had resolved to change over to history. Significantly, Burckhardt adds in this letter that a "Dr. Gelzer, who has recently advised me concerning my studies, called to my attention how positive it is for me . . . [and my future historical studies] that I have previously studied theology (if I am not mistaken I believe he is himself a deserter of theology)." Johann Heinrich Gelzer (1813–89) was a *Dozent* at Basel, though originally from Schaffhausen. Burckhardt attended his course on German history in the spring semester of 1839. See *Briefe* I, 301.

Compare Burckhardt's statements in the earlier-cited letter to the following in an autobiographical sketch written near the end of his life: "He [Burckhardt] never regretted or saw as lost time his pursuit of theology under professors like de Wette and Hagenbach. Rather, he held it as a desirable preparation . . . [for] historical scholarship." Interestingly, in this very brief "Lebensabriß" de Wette and Hagenbach are the only professors of Burckhardt's mentioned besides Leopold von Ranke and Franz Kugler at Berlin. See Kaegi I, 433.

174 *Briefe* I, 85–6; *Letters*, 37.

175 *Briefe* I, 114; *Letters*, 45.

176 Kaegi writes that "the odd and indicative thing about this [Burckhardt's religious] crisis

is that it was not a question of actual Christianity. To be sure, it concerned Christian doctrine, the concept of revelation, practical ecclesiastical matters, and theological learning. But it was not about the message of Christ itself. The actual crisis of Christendom, which is said to have culminated with Nietzsche, does not take place in the biography of Jacob Burckhardt." See Kaegi I, 481. For Kaegi, the "message of Christ" seems to be something rather self-explanatory.

Kaegi also writes that Burckhardt's "break" was not with "the deepest essence of Christianty" and that "despite everything [he remained] the child of his parents. And one should guard against falsely dramatizing his relationship with them as one of antagonism." Kaegi I, 151.

177 Letter of 29 May 1839. *Briefe* I, 112; *Letters*, 44.
178 Letter of 29 May 1839. *Briefe* I, 112–3; *Letters*, 45.
179 *Briefe* I, 152. Burckhardt wrote this letter in English.
180 *Briefe* I, 123. Burckhardt refers to a public Latin disputation in Basel, which his father also attended.
181 Letter of 10 April 1839. *Briefe* I, 106.
182 Letter of 6 October 1838. *Briefe* I, 87.
183 Hayden White, *Metahistory: The Historical Imagination in Nineteenth-Century Europe* (Baltimore: Johns Hopkins University Press, 1973), 163ff; Peter Ganz, "Jacob Burckhardt: Wissenschaft-Geschichte-Literatur" in H. R. Guggisberg, ed., *Umgang mit Jacob Burckhardt* (Basel: Schwabe, 1994), 32f.
184 *Letters*, 125–6.
185 *Briefe* II, 26.
186 *Letters*, 129.
187 *Briefe* II, 62; *Letters*, 89.
188 *Briefe* II, 61; *Letters*, 88.

Chapter Five. History without Centaurs

1 Franz Overbeck, *Werke und Nachlaß*, vol. 4, ed. Barbara von Reibnitz et al. (Stuttgart: J. B. Metzler, 1995), 297.
2 Overbeck, *Werke und Nachlaß*, vol. 4, 118–9.
3 Overbeck refers principally to Burckhardt's *Die Zeit Constantins des Grossen* and his *Renaissance*. See Overbeck, *Werke und Nachlaß*, vol. 4, 297.
4 Karl Löwith, *Meaning in History* (Chicago: University of Chicago Press, 1949) 2. This point will be developed in what follows. I also refer the reader to the section in my introduction entitled "Secularization, Modernity, and Theology."
5 On the history of this doctrine, see "Original Sin" in Cross and Livingstone, eds., *The Oxford Dictionary of the Christian Church* (3rd ed.), 1195–7, and Linwood Urban, *A Short History of Christian Thought* (New York: Oxford University Press, 1995), 125–55. For one of its classic Protestant formulations, see John Calvin, *Institutes of the Christian Religion*, ed. John T. McNeill, trans. Ford Lewis Battles (Philadelphia: Westminster Press, 1960), 241–88.
6 See Jacob Burckhardt, *Die Gedichte*, ed. K. E. Hoffmann (Basel, 1926).
   "Nach dem Weltgericht," penned on 7 May 1835, gives an example of Burckhardt's adolescent apocalyptic imagination. One stanza reads: "Dort sinkt die letzte Sonn ins Nichts hinab / Und durch den Himmel dröhnt der Posaunen Schall / zum letzten Mal–Gott hat gerichtet, / feiert den letzten, den größten Sabbath."
   The "dance of death" theme is most noticeable in his "Zu einem Totentanz" cycle, which consists of the following: "1. Prolog," "2. Der Tod zur Welt," "3. Der Tod zum

Bettler," "4. Der Tod zur Hirten," and "5. Gott zum Tod." Burckhardt ends the "Prolog" with the following lines: "Was die Welt uns immer möge schenken, / Noch schöner ist des Himmels ew'ges Licht. / Drum laßt uns zu den stillen Gräbern gehen, / Das Leben durch das Sterben zu verstehen."

Kaegi discusses Burckhardt's early preoccupation with the Last Judgment and the "dance of death" in "Die Idee der Vergänglichkeit in der Jugendgeschichte Jacob Burckhardts," *BZ* 42 (1942): 209–43. Also see Kaegi I, 27ff. On Basel's renowned *Totentanz*, see chapter nine, "La mort à Bâle," and chapter ten, "Vergänglichkeit," in Berchtold, *Bâle et L'Europe* I, 142–78. Berchtold suggests that the prominence of death imagery in Basel helps account for the pessimistic undercurrent in the thought of many of Basel's modern sons, including Johann Peter Hebel, Arnold Böcklin, Johann Jakob Bachofen, Burckhardt, and Karl Barth.

7 *On History and Historians*, trans. Harry Zohn (New York: Harper & Row, 1958), 65 (hereafter, *HH*); Cf. *Historische Fragmente*, ed. Emil Dürr (Nördlingen: Franz Greno, 1988), 87–8.

8 *Reflections on History*, trans. M. D. Hottinger (Indianapolis: Liberty Fund, 1973), 33 (hereafter *RH*).

9 *RH*, 104.

10 See Hans R. Guggisberg, ed., *Umgang mit Jacob Burckhardt: Zwölf Studien* (Basel: Schwabe & Co., 1994), 8.

11 Jörn Rüsen, "Jacob Burckhardt: Political Standpoint and Historical Insight on the Border of Postmodernism," *HT* 24 (1985): 235–46.

12 See especially the essays by Peter Ganz, Wolfgang Hardtwig, Ernst Schulin, and Niklaus Röthlin in Guggisberg, ed., *Umgang mit Jacob Burckhardt*, 11–78, 87–100, 117–34, 159–90.

13 *Briefe* I, 86.

14 *Briefe* II, 26.

15 James L. Sheehan's phrase in *German History, 1770–1866* (Oxford: Clarendon Press, 1989), 543.

16 To be sure, there are many differences among these critics. However, their inclination to interpret modern forms of thought as transpositions of previous forms unifies them. See Karl Löwith, *Meaning in History*; M. H. Abrams, *Natural Supernaturalism* (New York: W. W. Norton, 1971); Carl L. Becker, *The Heavenly City of the Eighteenth-Century Philosophers* (New Haven: Yale University Press, 1932); Carl L. Becker, "Progress," *The Encyclopedia of the Social Sciences*, vol. 12 (1934): 495–9; Ronald S. Crane, "Anglican Apologetics and the Idea of Progress, 1699–1745," *Modern Philology* 31 (1934): 273–306; Ernest Lee Tuveson, *Millennium and Utopia: A Study in the Background of the Idea of Progress* (New York: Harper & Row, 1949).

For an intellectual history of Christian eschatology, see Norman Cohn, *The Pursuit of the Millennium* (London, 1957).

17 Antoine-Nicolas de Condorcet, *Sketch for a Historical Picture of the Progress of the Human Mind*, trans. June Barraclough (1955); See also Peter Gay, *The Enlightenment: The Science of Freedom* (New York: W. W. Norton, 1969), 98–125, 529–52, and Maurice Mandelbaum, *History, Man and Reason* (Baltimore: Johns Hopkins University Press, 1971), 51ff.

18 On the Romantics, see especially Abrams, *Natural Supernaturalism* (New York: W. W. Norton, 1971), 197–252.

19 On Ranke and Hegel's conceptions of history, see Georg Iggers, *The German Conception of History* (Middletown, CT: Wesleyan University Press, 1983), 63ff.

20 This point is forcefully made by C. T. McIntire in his introduction to C. T. McIntire, ed., *God, History, and Historians: Modern Christian Views of History* (Oxford: Oxford University Press, 1977), 10–4. Ernst Troeltsch noted that the "myth of the Fall and the

curse upon the world has practically ceased to have any influence [on modern civiliza-
tion] . . ." See Troeltsch, *Protestantism and Progress*, 77–8.

21 Besides Burckhardt, there is the similar case of Arthur Schopenhauer. Yet I believe that
Schopenhauer's pessimism is best accounted for by complex psychological factors and by
the influence of eastern religions, and not by the residue of explicitly Christian theological ideas. See Richard Taylor, "Arthur Schopenhauer" in Smart, et al., eds., *Nineteenth-
Century Religious Thought in the West*, 157–80. Cf. Rüdiger Safranski, *Schopenhauer
and the Wild Years of Philosophy*, trans. Ewald Osers (London: Weidenfeld and
Nicolson, 1989).

It is often erroneously assumed that Schopenhauer was the source of Burckhardt's
pessimism. The popularity of this interpretation arises from several occasions on which
Burckhardt referred to Schopenhauer as "the philosopher." However, Burckhardt himself
was not deeply influenced by Schopenhauer, but rather found in him only a kindred spirit.
Burckhardt does not mention Schopenhauer until 1870. See *Briefe* V, 327. I shall return
to this issue later in the chapter.

22 *Briefe* I, 139.

23 Letter of 15 January 1840. *Letters*, 49; *Briefe* I, 131–2 (translation modified).

24 He also wrote of "mein Beruf zur Geschichte." See *Briefe* I, 233, 234; II, 26. Before
leaving for Berlin, Burckhardt told Schreiber that he hoped to find his new "Lebensbes-
timmung in der Geschichtsforschung." See *Briefe* I, 122.

Burckhardt's understanding of his scholarly calling parallels, I believe, a similar understanding held by Max Weber. See Harvey Goldman, *Max Weber and Thomas Mann:
Calling and the Shaping of the Self* (Berkeley and Los Angeles: University of California
Press, 1988). Goldman argues that a secularized form of calling provided Weber with a
"foundation of a conception of self and meaning" and gave him "hope against the threat
of purposelessness, directionlessness, and the meaningless of death in a civilization . . .
unable to draw on more traditional solutions." See pp. 19, 109–12.

25 Burckhardt spent the summer semester of 1841 at Bonn conducting research.

26 I use the adjective "historicist" here to denote a near religious quest brought to
the historical discipline. For this usage I am indebted to Wolfgang Hardtwig,
"Geschichtsreligion-Wissenschaft als Arbeit-Objektivität: Der Historismus in neuer
Sicht," *HZ* 252 (1991): 1–32.

27 For the courses that Burckhardt attended in Berlin, see Markwart, *Jacob Burckhardt*,
399–400. On Burckhardt's student years at Berlin, see Felix Gilbert, "Jacob Burckhardt's
Student Years: The Road to Cultural History," *JHI* (1986): 249–74.

28 It is my assumption that the search for meaning is an irreducible feature of human con-
sciousness involving not just cognition but also emotion, will, and experience. For my
understanding of this category I am indebted to Robert Wuthnow, *Meaning and Moral
Order: Explorations in Cultural Analysis* (Berkeley and Los Angeles: University of
California Press, 1987). Also see Peter Berger's chapter, "Religion and World-
Construction," in *The Sacred Canopy* (Garden City, NY: Doubleday, 1969), 3–28.

29 On the character of historical knowledge at Berlin during this period, see Iggers, *The
German Conception of History*, 63–89.

30 Rüsen, "Historische Methode und religiöser Sinn," in Küttler et al., eds., *Geschichtsdiskurs*, vol. 2, 344ff.

31 Weber lucidly states the conflict: "And finally, science (*Wissenschaft*) as a way to God?
. . . That science today is irreligious no one will doubt in his innermost being, even if he
will not admit it to himself. Redemption from the rationalism and intellectualism of
science is the fundamental presupposition of living in union with the divine." See Max
Weber, "Science as a Vocation," in H. H. Gerth and C. Wright Mills, eds., *From Max
Weber: Essays in Sociology* (New York: Oxford University Press, 1946), 142.

32 Hardtwig similarly interprets the "callings" of many nineteenth-century German his-

torians. See Hardtwig, "Geschichtsreligion-Wissenschaft als Arbeit-Objektivität: Der Historismus in neuer Sicht," *HZ* 252 (1991): 1–32.

33 *Letters*, 54; *Briefe* I, 146.

34 *Letters*, 72, 75; *Briefe* I, 203.

35 *Letters*, 47; *Briefe* I, 124. Burckhardt cryptically alludes to Revelation 10:10: "So I [John] took the little scroll from the hand of the angel and ate it; it was sweet as honey in my mouth, but when I had eaten it, my stomach was made bitter." See *New Oxford Annotated Bible* (NRSV) (New York: Oxford University Press, 1991), 374 NT.

36 *Letters*, 72; *Briefe* I, 203–4.

37 See *Briefe* I, 86, 98, 130. On the distinction between "artistic melancholy" and "religious melancholy," see Julius H. Rubin's chapter "The Protestant Ethic and the Melancholy Spirit," in his *Religious Melancholy and Protestant Experience in America* (New York: Oxford University Press, 1994), 3–41. Note that Burckhardt's religious melancholy does not seem to be anxiety brought about by fear of damnation, as described by Robert Burton in his *Anatomy of Melancholy* (1621); rather, it was a certain world-weariness and a feeling of crisis after spiritual conversion (in Burckhardt's case a "de-conversion"). Both these aspects of religious melancholy are also mentioned by Burton. See Rubin's summary of Burton's views in *Religious Melancholy*, 5. The literature on melancholy is large and growing. See Stanley W. Jackson, *Melancholia and Depression, from Hippocratic Times to Modern Times* (New Haven: Yale University Press, 1986); Wolf Lepenies, *Melancholy and Society*, trans. Jeremy Gaines and Doris Jones (Cambridge, MA: Harvard University Press, 1992); Ludwig Völker, ed., *Komm, heilige Melancholie: Eine Anthologie deutscher Melancholie-Gedichte* (Stuttgart: Reclam, 1983).

38 *Briefe* I, 131.

39 *Letters*, 40; *Briefe* I, 97. On the theme of *Weltschmerz* in Romantic and post-Romantic German literature, see William Rose, *From Goethe to Byron: The Development of "Weltschmerz" in German Literature* (London: Routledge, 1924).

40 *Letters*, 55; *Briefe* I, 155–6.

41 *Letters*, 39; *Briefe* I, 92.

42 Exactly when Burckhardt read Goethe's *Faust* is unknown, but the lasting impression it made is unmistakable. For a listing of Burckhardt's many references to Goethe, see Burckhardt, *Briefe: Gesamtregister*, ed. Max Burckhardt (Basel: Schwabe & Co., 1994), 36.

43 *Letters*, 116; *Briefe* III, 228–9.

44 *Letters*, 48; *Briefe* I, 130–1 (translation modified).

45 See "Heilmittel," in *Deutsches Wörterbuch von Jacob und Wilhelm Grimm*, vol. 10, ed. Moriz Heyne (Munich: Deutscher Taschenbuch Verlag, 1984), 54.

46 *Letters*, 53–4; *Briefe* I, 145.

47 *Letters*, 73; *Briefe* I, 204–5.

48 Tension between the *a posteriori* views of the "Historical School" and the *a priori* views among idealist philosophers (mostly Hegelians) had dominated discussion about the nature of history at Berlin for several decades before Burckhardt's arrival. See Iggers, *The German Conception of History*, 65ff. On Ranke's influence on Burckhardt, see Gilbert, *History: Politics or Culture?*, 93ff.

49 The Prussian authorities invited Schelling to Berlin in 1841 to counterbalance the powerful influence of the radical Left Hegelians. Schelling died there in 1846. On Schelling at Berlin, see Lenz, *Universität Berlin* III, 42–9.

50 See especially E. H. Gombrich, *In Search of Cultural History* (Oxford: Clarendon Press, 1969). Cf. William Kerrigan and Gordon Braden, *The Idea of the Renaissance* (Baltimore: Johns Hopkins University Press, 1989), 3–35.

51 On metaphysical idealism and historical knowledge, see Mandelbaum, *History, Man, and Reason*, 6ff.

52 *Briefe* I, 117.
53 *Letters* 53; *Briefe* I, 145, 313. The "post-Hegelians" he refers to were Georg Andreas Gabler, Karl Friedrich Werder, Johannes Friedrich Leopold George, Leopold von Henning, Karl Ludwig Michelet, and Karl Althaus. See Lenz, *Universität Berlin* II, 200ff; *Briefe* I, 342. Interestingly, Burckhardt also heard the young J. G. Droysen on the subject and noted that "in ten years time he will be numbered among the great."

Burckhardt had also encountered Hegelian philosophy in a course at Basel entitled "The History of Modern Philosophy since Descartes" taught by the philosophy professor Friedrich Fischer, a committed Aristotelian. The course ended with brief lectures on Fichte, Schelling, and Hegel. See Kaegi I, 464ff.
54 *Letters*, 74; *Briefe* I, 206. Karl Fresenius (1819–76) studied natural science and philosophy. He taught first in Weinheim and later in Eisenach. See *Briefe* I, 331, 365.
55 *Letters*, 74; *Briefe* I, 206 (emphasis added).
56 *Letters*, 74; *Briefe* I, 206–7 (translation modified).
57 *Letters*, 73; *Briefe* I, 204 (translation modified). Burckhardt's appeal to the sources (*Quelle*) and his repudiation of an *a priori* standpoint are both foundational rhetorical moves in the history of the legitimation of the historical discipline. See Allan Megill and Donald N. McCloskey, "The Rhetoric of History," in John S. Nelson, Allan Megill, and Donald N. McCloskey, eds., *The Rhetoric of the Human Sciences: Language and Argument in Scholarship and Public Affairs* (Madison: University of Wisconsin Press, 1987), 221–5.
58 *Letters*, 74–5; *Briefe* I, 208.
59 *Letters*, 71–2; *Briefe* I, 202–3.
60 *Letters*, 89; *Briefe* II, 61–2 (translation modified). Burckhardt's post-crisis conception of Christ borders on what McGrath calls the "exemplarist" theory – although there is also a strong (de Wette-inspired?) aesthetic understanding as well. See McGrath, *Modern German Christology*, 13ff.
61 For Burckhardt's reactions to Bauer's appointment to Bonn (1839) and Strauss's to Zurich (1839), see chapter four.
62 *Letters*, 94; *Briefe* II, 172 (translation modified).
63 *Letters*, 88; *Briefe* II, 60–1.
64 *Letters*. 88; *Briefe* II, 61 (Burckhardt's emphasis).
65 *RH*, 72; *GW* IV, 28.
66 The notion of "symbolic universe" is taken from Peter L. Berger and Thomas Luckmann, *The Social Construction of Reality* (Garden City, NY: Doubleday, 1966).
67 *Briefe* I, 170–1.
68 *GW* IV, 114–5.
69 *Briefe* V, 97. Burckhardt writes in his lecture notes: "And yet one has an inkling that all poetry and spiritual matters have passed through the temple and were once in the service of the holy." See *GW* IV, 77. Writes Burckhardt to a friend in 1855: "When we give up a connection to the sublime and eternal we are surely lost and caught up in the wheels of the present time." See *Briefe* III, 227.
70 *Briefe* II, 61.
71 See *Briefe* I, 90; *GW* I, ix, xi, 182. Moreover, Burckhardt told the theologian Arnold von Salis that "what you say about a transitional period is experienced by all educated people." See *Briefe* V, 158.
72 On Kinkel, see *Neue Deutsche Biographie*, vol. 11 (Berlin, 1977), 623–4.
73 Kaegi II, 118; *Briefe* I, 202, 226, 234.
74 Gottfried Kinkel, *Selbstbiographie, 1838–1948*, ed. Richard Sander (Bonn, 1931), 29.
75 Kaegi II, 118.
76 See *Briefe* I, 226; *Briefe* II, 171.
77 Kinkel's political radicalism disturbed the more conservative Burckhardt and resulted in

the termination of their friendship. Yet Kinkel's influence on Burckhardt proved lasting. Their relationship has received little scholarly attention. See Kaegi II, 116ff.

78 *Briefe* I, 226.

79 *Letters*, 94; *Briefe* II, 171–2 (translation modified). In all likelihood Burckhardt wrote this while living under the roof of his *orthodox* father.

80 Kaegi II, 118.

Before the appearance of *Constantin*, Burckhardt published several minor works, including *Die Kunstwerke der belgischen Städte* (1842); *Conrad von Hochstaden, Erzbischof von Kölln, 1238–1261* (1843); and *Über die vorgotischen Kirchen am Nieder-rhein* (1843). He also wrote and did editorial work for Franz Kugler's famous *Geschichte der Malerei* and *Handbuch der Kunstgeschichte* (1846–7).

Interestingly, in 1846 Burckhardt wrote a little-known "trial run" of his *Constantin*: "Die Alemannen und ihre Bekehrung zum Christentum," *Neujahrsblatt für Basels Jugend* (1846). In this thirty-two-page article, Burckhardt portrays the religion of the pagan "Alemannen" as "pleasant and humane" and he has little positive to say about their christianization. See Kaegi II, 372–5.

81 Both Overbeck and Kaegi have made this observation. Kaegi has argued that this one book embodied "all the tensions of Burckhardt's early existence." See Kaegi III, 377; Overbeck, *Werke und Nachlaß*, vol. 4, 297.

82 *RH*, 249; *GW* IV, 139 (translation modified).

83 *GW* I, 105.

One might ask why Burckhardt did not write about Christ and the earlier apostolic period. I believe he did not do so for three reasons. First, he seems to have felt that de Wette and other modern theologians had decisively (and negatively) settled the christological question. Second, attempting to write a profane history of Christ and the apostolic Church might have jeopardized his professional standing, not to mention his comfortable social status in Basel. Finally, since he respected the *pneuma* of Christ, at least from a historico-psychological point of view, the historicization of Christianity as an institution and as an orthodoxy proved a more logical endeavor. Burckhardt had much respect for the writings of the French scholar, Ernest Renan, who did attempt to historicize and humanize Christ and the apostles in his *Vie de Jésus* (1863).

84 Overbeck, *Werke und Nachlaß*, vol. 4, 297. Peter Gay writes that Burckhardt's *Constantin* was "a final reckoning with Christianity, a personal debate with a personal adversary. It stands against piety, edification, and hypocrisy. It is the last reverberation of a private struggle that Burckhardt fought out years before in his correspondence and in family discussions." Gay, *Style in History* (New York: Basic Books, 1974), 166.

85 *Constantine*, 12; *GW* I, 107.

86 *Constantine*, 131; *GW* I, 112 (translation modified).

87 *Constantine*, 283; *GW* I, 262.

88 *Constantine*, 68; *GW* I, 50.

89 On this point, Overbeck later commented that "one can leave the abstract controversy about Constantine's stance toward Christianity to pastors. Burckhardt was the first [scholar] to start asking the right questions." See Overbeck, *Werke und Nachlaß*, vol. 4, 298.

90 *Constantine*, 301; *GW* I, 281.

91 *Constantine*, 292; *GW* I, 271.

92 *Constantine*, 214; *GW* I, 193.

93 *Constantine*, 11; *GW* I, x (my emphasis). It was on this point in particular that Burckhardt saw himself as making a break with previous scholarship – whether "edifying" or secular. He felt that his predecessors had attributed too much inevitability or "triumph" to Christianity – even Gibbon, whose *Decline and Fall of the Roman Empire* Burckhardt criticized as being "outdated." See *Briefe* I, 234, 354.

94 *Constantine*, 214; *GW* I, 193.
95 *Constantine*, 257; *GW* I, 236.
96 *Constantine*, 308; *GW* I, 281.
97 *Constantine*, 243; *GW* I, 222.
98 *Constantine*, 371; *GW* I, 350–1.
99 Jacob Burckhardt, *The Cicerone: An Art Guide to Painting in Italy for the Use of Travelers and Students*, trans. A. H. Clough (New York: Charles Scribner's Sons, 1908), 9–10.
100 *Constantine*, 312–3; *GW* I, 291–2 (translation modified).
101 *Zeitschrift für lutherische Theologie* (1856): 755. For a more detailed treatment of the reception of *Constantin*, see Kaegi III, 415–21.
102 On this point, see especially Peter Ganz, "Jacob Burckhardts *Kultur der Renaissance in Italien*: Handwerk und Methode," *Deutsche Vierteljahrsschrift für Literaturwissenschaft und Geistesgeschichte* 62 (1988), 24–59. In 1847, Burckhardt thought that he might devote his career to producing a multivolume work on the Middle Ages (See *Briefe* III, 5, 94). The plan never came to fruition. Still, twenty-five years later he stated that he had once thought of his *Constantin* as the first book of a "cultural history of the Middle Ages, in which the Renaissance would be the conclusion." See *Briefe* V, 225f.
103 *GW* III, 89.
104 *Renaissance*, 289; *GW* III, 289; Kaegi III, 743.
105 Overbeck, *Werke und Nachlaß*, vol. 4, 297.
106 *GW* III, 1.
107 *Letters*, 125; *Briefe* IV, 53.
108 *Letters*, 126–7; *Briefe* IV, 76.
109 *Letters*, 134; *Briefe* V, 74 (translation modified).
110 For example, see Wallace Ferguson, *The Renaissance in Historical Thought* (Cambridge: Riverside Press, 1948), 179–88.
111 See *GW* III, xvii–xix.
112 Burckhardt does not use the terms "Säkularisierung" or "Verweltlichung." He describes Renaissance scholars as "weltlich" and their era as one of "Weltlichkeit." See "Weltlichkeit" in Alfred Götze, ed., *Deutsches Wörterbuch von Jacob und Wilhelm Grimm*, vol. 28 (Munich: Deutscher Taschenbuch Verlag, 1984), 1641–3.
113 On Burckhardt's predecessors, see Ferguson, *The Renaissance in Historical Thought*, 67–72, 87–98. Bayle and Voltaire had admired the secular qualities of the Renaissance, but neither writer linked the secular with the birth of the modern in a coherent historical synthesis.
114 *Renaissance*, 272; *GW* III, 292.
115 *Renaissance*, 272; *GW* III, 292–3.
116 *Renaissance*, 289; *GW* III, 311 (translation modified). Burckhardt's phraseology is revealing. With "weltgeschichtlichen Ratschluß," he alludes to the German expression "Gottes Ratschluß," which is the idiomatic equivalent of the English expression "the ways of the Lord." Historical causality displaces divine causality.
117 *Renaissance*, 346; *GW* III, 379 (translation modified).
118 *Renaissance*, 313; *GW* III, 338.
119 Cf. Kant, *Religion innerhalb der Grenzen der blossen Vernunft* (1793).
120 *Renaissance*, 320; *GW* III, 346.
121 *Renaissance*, 349–50; *GW* III, 384.
122 *Renaissance*, 314; *GW* III, 339 (translation modified).
123 *Renaissance*, 313; *GW* III, 338.
124 *Renaissance*, 321; *GW* III, 347–8. Burckhardt refers the reader to such works as Bracciolini Poggio, *de miseriis humanae conditionis*, and Giovano Pontano, *de fortuna*.
125 See W. Goetz, ed., *Propyläen Weltgeschichte* 4 (Berlin, 1932), 157.
126 Hayden White, *Metahistory*, 236.

127 *Renaissance*, 320; *GW* III, 346.

128 *Renaissance*, 273; *GW* III, 293.

129 *Renaissance*, 313; *GW* III, 338–9.

130 *RH*, 144–5; *GW* IV, 74 (translation modified).

131 *RH*, 34; *GW* IV, 3.

132 "Static," "anthropological," and "pessimistic" are adjectives commonly employed to describe Burckhardt's historiography.

133 See Felix Gilbert, *History: Politics or Culture?* (Princeton, NJ: Princeton University Press, 1990), 73; Hayden White, *Metahistory* (Baltimore: Johns Hopkins University Press, 1973), 237ff; Karl Löwith, *Burckhardt* (Stuttgart: Kohlhammer, 1966), 12.

134 *Letters*, 147, 170.

135 White, *Metahistory*, 238.

136 White, *Metahistory*, 434.

137 See *Briefe* V, 327. Presumably Burckhardt read Schopenhauer some time before 1870, but there is no evidence in his correspondence that suggests this.

138 Linwood Urban, *A Short History of Christian Thought* (New York: Oxford University Press, 1995), 127.

139 White, *Metahistory*, 263–4.

140 Marx is the contemporary who provides the strongest contrast. See Martin Warnke, "Jacob Burckhardt and Karl Marx" in Guggisberg, ed., *Umgang mit Jacob Burckhardt*, 135–58. I am grateful to Johannes Mikuteit of the University of Freiburg for calling my attention more closely to the contrast between Marx and Burckhardt.

141 Salis, "Zum hundertsten Geburtstag Jakob Burckhardts: Errinnerungen eines alten Schülers," *BJ* (1918): 273.

142 Kaegi, "Die Idee der Vergänglichkeit in der Jugendgeschichte Jacob Burckhardts," *BZ* 42 (1942): 209, 228.

143 Quoted in Arnold von Salis, "Zum hundertsten Geburtstag Jakob Burckhardts" *BJ* (1918): 294.

144 *Briefe* IX, 203.

145 *RH*, 61; *GW* IV, 21.

146 *RH*, 62; *GW* IV, 22.

147 *Letters*, 147–8; *Briefe* V, 130.

148 *RH*, 323; *GW* IV, 185.

149 *RH*, 332–3; *GW* IV, 191 (translation modified).

150 On Burckhardt's rhetorical use of "Unwissenschaftlichkeit," see Peter Ganz, "Jacob Burckhardt: Wissenschaft, Geschichte, Literatur," in Guggisberg, ed., *Umgang mit Jacob Burckhardt*, 11–35. For a more typical nineteenth-century valuation of the scientific quality of historical inquiry, see Fustel de Coulanges, "The Ethos of a Scientific Historian," in Fritz Stern, ed., *The Varieties of History from Voltaire to the Present* (New York: Vintage Books, 1973), 178–90.

151 Friedrich Meinecke, "Ranke and Burckhardt" in Hans Kohn, ed., *German History: Some New German Views* (Boston: Beacon Press, 1954); Reinhold Niebuhr, "The Historian as Prophet," *The Nation* 156 (April 1943): 530–1.

152 *Letters*, 122; *Briefe* III, 248 (translation modified).

153 *Letters*, 177; *Briefe* VI, 235–6.

154 *RH*, 219–20; *GW* IV, 120.

155 *RH*, 32; *GW* IV, 1–2. In what follows, I quote from Burckhardt's *GW*, although I have frequently consulted Peter Ganz's more recent edition of Burckhardt's lectures. See Peter Ganz, ed., *Jacob Burckhardt: Über das Studium der Geschichte* (Munich: C. H. Beck, 1982).

156 *RH*, 33; *GW* IV, 2.

157 *RH*, 35; *GW* IV 3.

158 *HH*, 163; *Historische Fragmente*, 210.

159 *RH*, 41; *GW* IV, 7 (Burckhardt's emphasis).

160 *RH*, 35; *GW* IV, 4.

161 *Constantine* (Eng. trans.), 10, 11.

162 *Letters*, 158; *Briefe* V, 222.

163 *RH*, 40, 340; *GW* IV, 7, 196.

164 *RH*, 40; *GW* IV, 7.

165 *RH*, 41; *GW* IV, 8.

166 *RH*, 40; *GW* IV, 7.

167 *RH*, 39; *GW* IV, 7.

168 *RH*, 37; *GW* IV, 5.

169 *RH*, 41–42; *GW* IV, 8–9 (translation modified).

170 *Letters*, 157; *Briefe* V, 184 (translation modified).

171 *HH*, 225; *Historische Fragmente*, 289. Cf. *Jacob Burckhardts Vorlesungen über die Geschichte des Revolutionszeitalters in den Nachschriften seiner Zuhörer* (Basel: Schwabe & Co., 1974), 13ff.

172 *HH*, 241, 253; *Historische Fragmente*, 310, 324.

173 *HH*, 218ff; *Historische Fragmente*, 279ff.

174 *HH*, 230; *Historische Fragmente*, 296–7 (Burckhardt's emphasis).

175 *HH*, 219; *Historische Fragmente*, 281.

176 *HH*, 218–9; *Historische Fragmente*, 281–2.

177 *HH*, 237–8; *Historische Fragmente*, 305.

178 *HH*, 231; *Historische Fragmente*, 297.

179 *Letters*, 207; *Briefe* VIII, 31–2.

180 Meinecke, "Ranke and Burckhardt," 146–8.

181 See Karl Barth, *Kirchliche Dogmatik* (Zurich, 1932ff), III / 1, 382; III / 2, 3, 25; III / 4, 446; IV / 2, 125. Barth admired Burckhardt's prescient understanding of the twentieth-century "crisis of humanism" and his willingness to speak of the "pathological" aspects of history. See also Robert Lovin, *Reinhold Niebuhr and Christian Realism* (Cambridge: Cambridge University Press, 1995). I use the term "social realism" in a similar fashion to Lovin's "Christian realism": realism recognizes that the articulation of moral ideals can never completely overcome the stubborn realities of self-interest and subsequent unexpected distortions. See especially p. 11.

182 Reinhold Niebuhr, "The Historian as Prophet," *The Nation* 156 (April 1943): 530.

183 Urban, *A Short History of Christian Thought*, 125f.

184 The failure of rationalist thought to understand this idea is often recognized and even cherished by Christian thinkers. Pascal writes: "For it is beyond doubt that there is nothing which more shocks our reason than to say that the sin of the first man has rendered guilty those who, being so removed from its source, seem incapable of participating in it. . . . Certainly nothing offends us more rudely than this doctrine, and yet without this mystery, the most incomprehensible of all, we are incomprehensible to ourselves." Quoted in Reinhold Niebuhr, *The Nature and Destiny of Man*, vol. 1 (New York: Charles Scribner's Sons, 1964), 243.

185 Cf. Jean Bethke Elshtain, *Augustine and the Limits of Politics* (Notre Dame: University of Notre Dame Press, 1995).

186 White, *Metahistory*, 236.

187 See White, *Metahistory* and Johannes Wenzel, *Jacob Burckhardt in der Krise seiner Zeit* (Berlin, 1967). Jörn Rüsen also mentions this problem in "Jacob Burckhardt: Political Standpoint and Historical Insight on the Border of Postmodernism," *HT* 24 (1985): 235–6.

188 A cultural critique originating from the aesthete's "inwardness protected by power," notes Rüsen referring to Thomas Mann's famous formulation, "is a hidden ally of the disaster

it laments." See Rüsen, "Jacob Burckhardt: Political Standpoint and Historical Insight on the Border of Postmodernism," 246. Cf. Thomas Mann, *Reflections of a Nonpolitical Man*, trans. Walter D. Morris (New York: Frederick Ungar Publishing Co., 1983).

189 See *Letters*, 104, 106, 108, 157.
190 *Constantine*, 324; *GW* I, 302–3.
191 *Constantine*, 323–4; *GW* I, 302–3. The section is entitled "Die Anfechtungen der Einsiedler."
192 See *Letters*, 104, 105, 108; *Briefe* III, 54, 58, 125.
193 *Letters*, 106; *Briefe* III, 104.
194 *Letters*, 105; *Briefe* III, 54.
195 *Letters*, 96; *Briefe* II, 209.
196 *Briefe* II, 193.
197 *Letters*, 83; *Briefe* II, 34.
198 *Letters*, 113; *Briefe* III, 217.
199 *Letters*, 113; *Briefe* III, 173. Burckhardt made ten lengthy trips to Italy. On his experiences there, see the relevant sections in Kaegi's biography. Burckhardt's attitude toward Italy reflects a general fascination of many German youths with the Mediterranean South in general and Italy in particular. Cf. Johann Wolfgang Goethe, *Italian Journey*, trans. W. H. Auden and Elizabeth Mayer (San Francisco: North Point Press, 1982) and Eberhard Haufe, ed., *Deutsche Briefe aus Italien von Winckelmann bis Gregorovius* (Leipzig: Koehler & Amelang, 1965).
200 *Letters*, 96; *Briefe* II, 209.
201 *Letters*, 123. Cf. Goethe's statement: "Personality is the greatest joy of the children of this earth"; quoted in Hajo Holborn, *A History of Modern Germany, 1648–1840* (Princeton, NJ: Princeton University Press, 1964), 478.
202 W. H. Bruford, *The German Tradition of Self-Cultivation: Bildung from Humboldt to Thomas Mann* (New York: Cambridge, 1975).
203 *Letters*, 83, 86–7; *Briefe* II, 34, 52–3.
204 *Letters*, 96; *Briefe* II, 209 (my emphasis).
205 *Letters*, 96; *Briefe* II, 209.
206 Cf. Richard Rorty's definition of an ironist in *Contingency, Irony, and Solidarity* (Cambridge: Cambridge University Press, 1989), 73ff; Jean-François Lyotard, *The Postmodern Condition: A Report on Knowledge*, trans. Geoff Bennington and Brian Massumi (Minneapolis: University of Minnesota Press, 1979). For a discussion of postmodern irony and its political problems, see Michael Roth, "The Ironist's Cage," in Roth, *The Ironist's Cage* (New York: Columbia University Press, 1995), 148–62.
207 Friedrich Nietzsche, "The Uses and Disadvantages of History for Life" in *Untimely Meditations*, trans. R. J. Hollingdale (Cambridge: Cambridge University Press, 1983).
208 Nietzsche, "The Uses and Disadvantages of History for Life," 83.
209 *Letters*, 158–9; *Briefe* V, 222–3.
210 Rüsen, "Jacob Burckhardt: Political Standpoint and Historical Insight on the Border of Postmodernism," *HT* 24 (1985): 235–46. F. R. Ankersmit has recently spoken of Burckhardt's "proto-postmodernism." See his "Historicism: An Attempt at Synthesis," *HT* 34 (1995), 153. Also see F. R. Ankersmit, "Historiography and Postmodernism," *HT* 28 (1989): 141.

Bibliography

For a bibliography that covers de Wette's minor works as well as the secondary literature on de Wette by biblical scholars, see John Rogerson, *W. M. L. de Wette: Founder of Modern Biblical Criticism: An Intellectual Biography* (Sheffield: JSOT Press, 1992), 272–306. A more comprehensive guide to the German scholarship on Burckhardt may be found in Wolfgang Hardtwig, *Geschichtsschreibung zwischen Alteuropa und moderner Welt: Jacob Burckhardt in seiner Zeit* (Göttingen: Vandenhoeck & Ruprecht, 1974), 384–405. Also of relevance to this study is the compilation of works on theology and history done by Robert North. See Robert North, "Bibliography of Works in Theology and History," *History and Theory* 12 (1973): 55–144.

Primary Sources

Burckhardt, Jacob. *Gesammelte Werke*. 10 vols. Basel: Benno Schwabe & Co., 1955–9.
———. *Briefe*. 10 vols. Edited by Max Burckhardt. Basel: Benno Schwabe & Co., 1949–94.
———. *Jacob Burckhardt: Vorträge, 1844–1887*. Edited by Emil Dürr. Basel: Benno Schwabe & Co., 1918.
———. *Historische Fragmente aus dem Nachlaß gesammelt von Emil Dürr*. Nördlingen: F. Greno, 1988.
———. *Jacob Burckhardts Vorlesung über die Geschichte des Revolutionszeitalters in den Nachschriften seiner Zuhörer*. Edited by Ernst Ziegler. Basel: Benno Schwabe & Co., 1974.
———. *Über das Studium der Geschichte*. Edited by Peter Ganz. Munich: C. H. Beck, 1982.
———. *Die Gedichte*. Basel, 1926.
———. *The Age of Constantine the Great*. Translated by Moses Hadas. Berkeley: University of California Press, 1949.

——. *The Cicerone: An Art Guide to Painting in Italy for the Use of Travelers and Students*. Translated by A. H. Clough. New York: Charles Scribner's Sons, 1908.

——. *The Altarpiece in Renaissance Italy*. Edited and translated by Peter Humfrey. Cambridge: Cambridge University Press, 1988.

——. *The Civilization of the Renaissance in Italy* Translated by S. G. C. Middlemore. London: Penguin Books, 1990.

——. *On History and Historians*. Translated by Harry Zohn with an introduction by H. R. Trevor-Roper. New York: Harper & Row, 1958.

——. *Force and Freedom: Reflections on History*. Translated and edited by James Nichols. New York: Pantheon Books, 1943.

——. *The Letters of Jacob Burckhardt*. Translated and edited by Alexander Dru. New Westport, CT: Greenwood Press, 1955.

——. *History of Greek Culture*. Translated by Palmer Hilty. New York: Frederick Ungar, 1963.

——. *Reflections on History*. Translated by M. D. Hottinger. Indianapolis: Liberty Press, 1979.

——. *The Architecture of the Italian Renaissance*. Translated by James Palmes. Revised and edited by Peter Murray. Chicago: University of Chicago Press, 1985.

*   *   *

Burckhardt, Jakob (Sr.). *Kurze Geschichte der Reformation in Basel*. Basel, 1818.

——. "Rede gehalten im Münster am Reformations-feste der Kinder, Sonntag den 10. Januar 1819, von Jakob Burckhardt (Obersthelfer)." Basel, 1819.

——. *Lehrbuch der christlichen Religionsunterrichtes für die Kirchen des Kantons Basel: Zum Gebrauche für die Kinderlehre und die Konfirmationsunterricht*. Basel, 1832.

——. "Predigt über die Worte 1 Timotheum 3,1. gehalten bei seinem Amtsantritte, Sonntags den 25. November 1838, in der Münsterkirche von Jakob Burckhardt." Basel, 1838.

*   *   *

De Wette, W. M. L. *Eine Idee über das Studium der Theologie* (1801). Edited by A. Stieren. Leipzig, 1850.

——. *Dissertatio critica qua a prioribus Deuteronomium pentateuchi libris diversum alias cuiusdam recentioris auctoris opus esse monstratur* (1805). Reprinted in *Opuscula Theologica*. Berlin, 1830.

——. *Aufforderung zum Studium der hebräischen Sprache und Literatur; zur Eröffnung seiner Vorlesungen*. Jena and Leipzig, 1805.

——. *Beiträge zur Einleitung in das Alte Testament*. 2 vols. Halle, 1806–7.

——. *Beytrag zur Charakteristik des Hebraismus*. Heidelberg, 1807.

De Wette, W. M. L. *Commentar über die Psalmen*. Heidelberg, 1811 (2nd ed., 1823; 3rd ed., 1829; 4th ed., 1836).

———. *Commentatio De Morte Jesu Christi Expiatoria* (1813). Reprinted in *Opuscula Theologica*. Berlin, 1830.

———. *Lehrbuch der christliche Dogmatik in ihrer historischen Entwicklung dargestellt*. I. *Biblische Dogmatik Alten und Neuen Testaments oder kritische Darstellung der Religionslehre des Hebraismus, des Judentums und Urchristenthums: Zum Gebrauch akademischer Vorlesungen*. Berlin, 1813. (2nd ed., 1818; 3rd ed., 1831). II. *Dogmatik der evangelische-lutherischen Kirche nach den symbolischen Büchern und die ältern Dogmatikern*. Berlin, 1816 (2nd. ed., 1821; 3rd ed., 1839).

———. *Die neue Kirche oder Verstand und Glaube im Bunde*. Berlin, 1815.

———. *Über Religion und Theologie: Erläuterung zu seinem Lehrbuche über Dogmatik*. Berlin, 1815 (2nd ed., 1822).

———. *Lehrbuch der historisch-kritischen Einleitung in die Bibel Alten und Neuen Testaments*. I. *Die Einleitung in das Alte Testament enthaltend*. Berlin, 1817 (2nd ed., 1822; 3rd ed., 1829; 4th ed., 1833; 5th ed., 1840; 6th ed., 1844). II. *Einleitung in das Neue Testament enthaltend*. Berlin, 1826 (2nd ed., 1830; 3rd ed., 1834; 4th ed., 1842; 5th ed., 1848).

———. *Christliche Sittenlehre*. 3 vols. Berlin, 1819–23.

———. *Aktensammlung über die Entlassung des Professors D. de Wette vom theologischen Lehramt zu Berlin: Zur Berichtigung des öffentlichen Urteils von ihm selbst herausgegeben*. Leipzig, 1820.

———. *Theodor, oder des Zweiflers Weihe: Bildungsgeschichte eines evangelischen Geistlichen*. 2 vols. Berlin, 1822 (2nd ed., 1828).

———. *Vorlesungen über die Sittenlehre*. 2 vols. Berlin, 1822–3.

———. "Von der Prüfung der Geister." Basel, 1822.

———. *Über die Religion: ihr Wesen, ihre Erscheinungsformen und ihren Einfluß auf das Leben*. Berlin, 1827.

———. *Heinrich Melchthal oder Bildung und Gemeingeist: eine belehrende Geschichte*. 2 vols. Berlin, 1829.

———. "Von der Stellung der Wissenschaft im Gemeinwesen." Basel, 1829.

———. *Lehrbuch der christlichen Sittenlehre und der Geschichte derselben*. Berlin, 1833.

———. *Über den Angriff des grauen Mannes gegen Lehrer der hiesigen Universität*. Basel, 1834.

———. "Einige Betrachtungen über den Geist unserer Zeit, Academische Rede am 12 September 1834 gehalten." Basel, 1834.

———. "Rede der öffentlichen Feier der Wiederherstellung der Universität am 1. October 1835 im Chor der Münster-Kirche, gehalten von W. M. L. de Wette, Dr. und Professor der Theologie, d.Z. Rector." Basel, 1835.

———. *Kurzgefasstes exegetisches Handbuch zum Neuen Testament*. Mutliple vols. and eds. Leipzig, 1836–48.

———. *Das Wesen des christlichen Glaubens vom Standpunkte des Glaubens*. Basel, 1845.

———. *Dewettiana: Forschungen und Texte zu Wilhelm Martin Leberecht De*

Wettes Leben und Werk. Edited by Ernst Staehelin. Basel: Helbing & Lichtenhan, 1956.

———. *Theodore; or, the Skeptic's Conversion*. Translated by James F. Clarke. Boston, 1841.

———. *Historico-Critical Introduction to the Canonical Books of the New Testament*. 2 vols. Translated by Theodore Parker. Boston, 1843.

———. *Human Life; or Practical Ethics*. Translated by Samuel Osgood. 2 vols. Boston, 1856.

———. *A Critical and Historical Introduction to the Canonical Scriptures of the Old Testament*. Translated by Frederick Frothingham. Boston, 1858.

Secondary Sources

Abrams, M. H. *Natural Supernaturalism: Tradition and Revolution in Romantic Literature*. New York: W. W. Norton, 1971.

Adams, Hazard. *Philosophy of the Literary Symbolic*. Tallahassee: University Press of Florida, 1983.

Amberg, Ernst-Heinz. *Christologie und Dogmatik: Untersuchung ihres Verhältnisses in der evangelischen Theologie der Gegenwart*. Göttingen, 1966.

Angermeier, Heinz. "Ranke und Burckhardt." *AfKG* 69 (1987): 407–52.

Ankersmit, F. R. "Historiography and Postmodernism." *HT* 28 (1989): 137–53.

———. "Historicism: An Attempt at Synthesis." *HT* 34 (1995): 143–73.

Ankersmit, F. R. and Hans Kellner, eds. *A New Philosophy of History*. Chicago: University of Chicago Press, 1995.

Antoni, Carlo. *From History to Sociology: The Transition in German Historical Thinking*. Translated by Hayden White. Detroit: Wayne State University, 1959.

Auerbach, Erich. *Mimesis: The Representation of Reality in Western Literature*. Translated by Willard R. Trask. Princeton, NJ: Princeton University Press, 1953.

Bambach, Charles R. *Heidegger, Dilthey, and the Crisis of Historicism*. Ithaca, NY: Cornell University Press, 1995.

Baron, Hans. *Burckhardt and the Renaissance: One Hundred Years After*. Lawrence: University of Kansas Press, 1960.

Barth, Karl. *Protestant Theology in the Nineteenth Century: Its Background and History*. Translated by John Bowden. London: SCM Press, 1972.

Barthel, Paul. *Interprétation du langage mythique et théologie biblique*. Leiden, 1967.

Bauer, Bruno. *Kritik der Geschichte der Offenbarung*. Berlin, 1938.

———. *Die Posaune des Jüngsten Gericht über Hegel den Atheisten und Antichristen*. Leipzig, 1841.

Baumer, Franklin L. *Religion and the Rise of Skepticism*. New York: Harcourt, Brace, 1960.

———. *Modern European Thought: Continuity and Change, 1600–1959*. New York: Macmillan, 1977.

Beck, Johannes Tobias. "Ueber die Wissenschaftliche Behandlung der christlichen Lehre: Eine akademische Antrittsrede gehalten zu Basel den 7. November 1836." Basel, 1836.

Becker, Carl L. *The Heavenly City of the Eighteenth-Century Philosophers.* New Haven, CT: Yale University Press, 1932.

Beiser, Frederick C. *The Fate of Reason: German Philosophy from Kant to Fichte.* Cambridge, MA: Harvard University Press, 1987.

———. *Enlightenment, Revolution, and Romanticism: The Genesis of Modern German Political Thought, 1790–1800.* Cambridge: Harvard University Press, 1992.

Berchtold, Alfred. *Bâle et L'Europe: Une Historie culturelle.* 2 vols. Lausanne: Payot, 1990.

Berger, Peter. *The Sacred Canopy: Elements of a Sociological Theory of Religion.* Garden City, NY: Doubleday, 1969.

———. *A Rumor of Angels: Modern Society and the Rediscovery of the Supernatural.* Garden City, NY: Doubleday, 1969.

———. *The Heretical Imperative: Contemporary Possibilities of Religious Affirmation.* Garden City, NY: Doubleday, 1979.

Berger, Peter and Thomas Luckmann. *The Social Construction of Reality.* Garden City, NY: Doubleday, 1966.

Bergmann, Peter. *Nietzsche: The Last Antipolitical German.* Bloomington and Indianapolis: Indiana University Press, 1987.

Berlin, Isaiah. *Vico and Herder: Two Studies in the History of Ideas.* London: Hogarth Press, 1976.

Bigler, Robert M. *The Politics of German Protestanism: The Rise of the Protestant Church Elite, 1815–1848.* Berkeley and Los Angeles: University of California Press, 1975.

Blackbourn, David. *The Long Nineteenth Century: A History of Germany, 1780–1918.* New York: Oxford University Press, 1998.

Blanke, Horst-Walter. *Historiographiegeschichte als Historik.* Stuttgart: Frommann-Holzboog 1991.

Blanke, Horst-Walter and Jörn Rüsen, eds. *Von Aufklärung zum Historismus: Zum Strukturwandel des historischen Denkens.* Paderborn: Ferdinand Schöningh, 1984.

Blanke, Horst-Walter Dirk Fleischer, and Jörn Rüsen. "History in History Lectures: The German Tradition of *Historik.*" HT 23 (1984): 331–56.

Blumenberg, Hans. *Work on Myth.* Translated by Robert M. Wallace. Cambridge, MA: MIT Press, 1985.

———. *The Legitimacy of the Modern Age.* Translated by Robert M. Wallace. Cambridge, MA: MIT Press, 1983.

———. *Säkularisierung und Selbstbehauptung.* Frankfurt am Main: Suhrkamp, 1974.

Bödeker, Hans Erich, Georg Iggers, Jonathan B. Knudsen, and Peter Hanns Reill, eds. *Aufklärung und Geschichte: Studien zur deutschen Geschichtswissenshaft im 18. Jahrhundert.* Göttingen: Vandenhoeck & Ruprecht, 1986.

Boerling-Brodeck, Yvonne, ed. *Die Skizzenbücher Jacob Burckhardts.* Vol. 2, Beiträge zu Jacob Burckhardt. Basel: Schwabe & Co., 1994.

Bonjour, Edgar. *Die Universität Basel: von den Anfängen bis zur Gegenwart, 1460–1960*. Basel, 1971.

Bouvier, Nicolas, Gordon Craig, and Lionel Gossman, with an Introduction by Carl Schorske. *Geneva, Zurich, Basel: History, Culture, and National Identity*. Princeton, NJ: Princeton University Press, 1994.

Bowie, Andrew. *Schelling and Modern European Philosophy: An Introduction*. New York: Routledge, 1993.

Brazill, William J. *The Young Hegelians*. New Haven, CT: Yale University Press, 1970.

Breen, Quirinus. *Christianity and Humanism*. Grand Rapids, MI: Eerdmans, 1968.

Breisach, Ernst. *Historiography: Ancient, Medieval, and Modern*. Chicago: University of Chicago Press, 1983.

Brown, Colin. *Jesus in European Protestant Thought, 1778–1860*. Durham, NC: Labyrinth Press, 1985.

Bruce, Steve, ed. *Religion and Modernization: Sociologists and Historians Debate the Secularization Thesis*. Oxford: Oxford University Press, 1992.

———. *Religion in the Modern World: From Cathedrals to Cults*. Oxford: Oxford University Press, 1996.

Bruford, W. H. *Culture and Society in Classical Weimar, 1775–1806*. Cambridge: Cambridge University Press, 1962.

———. *The German Tradition of Self-Cultivation: Bildung from Humboldt to Thomas Mann*. Cambridge: Cambridge University Press, 1975.

Brunner, Emil. *Die Mystik und das Wort: Der Gegensatz zwischen moderner Religionsauffasung und christliche Glauben dargestellt an der Theologie Schleiermacher*. 2nd ed. Tübingen, 1928.

———. *The Philosophy of Religion*. Translated by A. J. D. Farrer and Bertram Lee Woolf. London, 1937.

Bubner, Rüdiger. *Modern German Philosophy*. Translated by Eric Mathews. Cambridge: Cambridge University Press, 1981.

Buckley, Michael J. *At the Origins of Modern Atheism*. New Haven, CT: Yale University Press, 1987.

Burckhardt, Paul. *Geschichte der Stadt Basel: von der Zeit der Reformation bis zur Gegenwart*. Basel: Helbing & Lichtenhahn, 1957.

Burckhardt, Abel T. *Johann Rudolf Burckhardt: eine Pfarrergestalt aus dem alten Basel, seine Frömmigkeit und sein Wirken, sein Familieleben und die religiösen Verhältnisse seiner Zeit*. Basel, 1944.

Burckhardt, Lukas, René L. Frey, Georg Kreis, and Gerhard Schmid, eds. *Das polititische System Basel Stadt: Geschichte, Strukturen, Institutionen, Politikbereiche*. Basel: Helbing & Lichtenhahn, 1984.

Burckhardt, Urs and Rudolf Stuer. *(Basel): Streiflichter auf Geschichte und Persönlichkeiten des Basler Geschlechts Burckhardt*. Basel: Buchandlung Basler Zeitung, 1990.

Burke, Peter. *The Italian Renaissance: Culture and Society in Italy*. Princeton, NJ: Princeton University Press, 1986.

Butler, E. M. *The Tyranny of Greece over Germany*. Boston: Beacon Press, 1958.

Cassirer, Ernst. *The Philosophy of the Enlightenment*. Translated by Fritz C. A.

Koelln and James P. Pettegrove. Princeton, NJ: Princeton University Press, 1951.

Chadwick, Owen. *The Secularization of the European Mind in the Nineteenth Century.* Cambridge: Cambridge University Press, 1975.

Chai, Leon. *Aestheticism: The Religion of Art in Post-Romantic Literature.* New York: Columbia University Press, 1990.

Cheyne, T. K. *Founders of Old Testament Criticism.* New York: Charles Scribner's Sons, 1893.

Childress, James F., and David B. Harned, eds. *Secularization and the Protestant Prospect.* Philadelphia: Westminster Press, 1970.

Chytry, Josef. *The Aesthetic State: A Quest in Modern German Thought.* Berkeley and Los Angeles: University of California Press, 1989.

Clayton, John Powell, ed. *Ernst Troeltsch and the Future of Theology.* Cambridge: Cambridge University Press, 1976.

Cohn, Norman. *The Pursuit of the Millennium.* London, 1957.

Collingwood, R. G. *The Idea of History.* Oxford: Oxford University Press, 1956.

Conger, Yves. *A History of Theology.* Translated by Hunter Guthrie. Garden City, NY: Doubleday, 1968.

Cocks, Geoffrey and Konrad Jarausch, eds. *German Professions 1800–1950.* New York: Oxford University Press, 1990.

Cosslett, Tess. *Science and Religion in the Nineteenth Century.* Cambridge: Cambridge University Press, 1984.

Cragg, Gerald. *Reason and Authority in the Eighteenth Century.* Cambridge: Cambridge University Press, 1964.

Craig, Gordon. *The Triumph of Liberalism: Zurich in the Golden Age, 1830–1869.* New York: Charles Scribner's Sons, 1988.

Cremer, Douglas J. "Protestant Theology in Early Weimar Germany: Barth, Tillich, and Bultmann." *JHI* 56 (April, 1995): 289–307.

Crites, Stephen D. "The Gospel According to Hegel." *JR* 46 (April, 1966): 246–63.

Croce, Benedetto. *History as the Story of Liberty.* Translated by Sylvia Sprigge. London, 1941.

Cromwell, Richard S. *David Friedrich Strauss and His Place in Modern Thought.* Fair Lawn, NJ: R. E. Burdick, 1974.

Crouter, Richard. "Hegel and Schleiermacher at Berlin: A Many-Sided Debate," *JAAR* 48 (1980): 19–43.

Crowther, Paul. *The Kantian Sublime: From Morality to Art.* Oxford: Clarendon Press, 1989.

D'Amico, Robert. *Historicism and Knowledge.* New York: Routledge, 1989.

D'Arcy, M. C. *The Sense of History: Secular and Sacred.* London: Faber and Faber, 1959.

Dawson, Jerry F. *Friedrich Schleiermacher: The Evolution of a Nationalist.* Austin: University of Texas Press, 1966.

Dibelius, O. *Das Königliche Predigerseminar zu Wittenberg, 1817–1917.* Berlin: Lichterfeld, 1917.

Dickey, Laurence. *Hegel: Religion, Economics, and the Politics of the Spirit, 1770–1807.* Cambridge: Cambridge University Press, 1987.

Dilthey, Wilhelm. *Leben Schleiermachers.* Vol. 1. Berlin, 1870.

———. "Das achtzehnte Jahrhundert und die historische Welt." *Gesammelte Schriften*. Vol. 3. Leipzig and Berlin: Teubner, 1927.

Droysen, Johann Gustav. *Outline of the Principles of History*. Translated by Elisha Benjamin Andrews. Boston, 1893.

Duray, John. *Critics of the Bible, 1724–1873*. Cambridge: Cambridge University Press, 1989.

Dürr, Emil. *Jacob Burckhardt als politischer Publizist*. Zurich, 1937.

Eliade, Mircea. *The Sacred and the Profane*. Translated by Willard R. Trask. New York: Harper & Row, 1957.

Elshtain, Jean Bethke. *Augustine and the Limits of Politics*. Notre Dame: University of Notre Dame Press, 1995.

Engell, James. *The Creative Imagination: Enlightenment to Romanticism*. Cambridge: Harvard University Press, 1981.

Engels, Josef. "Die deutschen Universitäten und die Geschichtswissenschaften." *HZ* 189 (1959): 223–378.

Fackenheim, Emil L. *The Religious Dimension in Hegel's Thought*. Bloomington: Indiana University Press, 1967.

Fallon, Daniel. *The German University*. Boulder: Colorado Associated University Press, 1980.

Ferguson, Wallace K. *The Renaissance in Historical Thought*. Cambridge, MA: Houghton Mifflin, 1948.

Fest, Joachim. *Wege zur Geschichte: Über Theodor Mommsen, Jakob Burckhardt, und Golo Mann*. Zurich: Marsee Verlag, 1992.

Findlay, M. I. "Myth, Memory, and History." *HT* 4 (1965): 281–302.

Fischer, Fritz. *Ludwig Nicolovius: Rokoko, Reform, Restauration*. Stuttgart, 1939.

Foerster, Erich. *Die Entstehung der preußischen Landeskirche*. 2 vols. Tübingen, 1905.

Foucault, Michel, "Nietzsche, Genealogy, History." In *The Foucault Reader*, ed. Paul Rabinow. New York: Pantheon Books, 1984.

Frei, Hans. *The Eclipse of Biblical Narrative: A Study in Eighteenth and Nineteenth Century Hermeneutics*. New Haven, CT: Yale University Press, 1974.

———. *Types of Christian Theology*. Edited by George Hunsinger and William C. Placher. New Haven, CT: Yale University Press, 1992.

———. *Theology and Narrative*. Oxford: Oxford University Press, 1993.

Fries, Jakob Friedrich. *Sämtliche Schriften*. 8 vols. Aalen: Scientia Verlag, 1968.

———. *Knowledge, Belief, and Aesthetic Sense*. Translated by Kent Richter and edited by Frederick Gregory. Cologne: Jürgen Dinter, 1989.

Frye, Northrop. *Anatomy of Criticism*. Princeton, NJ: Princeton University Press, 1957.

Fuller, Daniel. "The Fundamental Presupposition of the Historical Method. *TZ* 24 (1968): 93–101.

Ganz, Peter. "Jacob Burckhardts Kultur der Renaissance in Italien: Handwerk und Methode." *Deutsche Vierteljahrschrift für Literaturwissenschaft und Geistesgeschichte* 62 (1988): 24–59.

Garland, H. B. *Lessing: Founder of Modern German Literature*. London: Macmillan, 1962.

Gass, Alfred Lukas. *Die Dichtung im Leben und Werk Jacob Burckhardts*. Bern: Francke, 1967.

Gauchet, Marcel. *The Disenchantment of the World: A Political History of Religion*. Translated by Oscar Bruge with an Introduction by Charles Taylor. Princeton, NJ: Princeton University Press, 1997.

Gay, Peter. *The Enlightenment: An Interpretation*. 2nd ed. 2 vols. New York: Knopf, 1967, 1969.

———. *Style in History*. New York: Basic Books, 1974.

Geertz, Clifford. *The Interpretation of Cultures*. New York: Basic Books, 1973.

Gerrish, B. A. *The Old Protestantism and the New: Essays on the Reformation Heritage*. Edinburgh: T. & T. Clark, 1982.

———. *A Prince of the Church: Schleiermacher and the Beginnings of Modern Theology*. London: SCM, 1984.

Gerth, H. H. and C. Wright Mills, eds. *From Max Weber: Essays in Sociology*. New York: Oxford University Press, 1946.

Gil, Thomas. *Kritik der Geschichtsphilosophie: L. Ranke, J. Burckhardt, and H. Freyers Problematisierung der klassischen Geschichtsphilosophie*. Stuttgart, 1993.

Gilbert, Felix. "Jacob Burckhardt's Student Years: The Road to Cultural History." *JHI* 47 (1986): 249–74.

———. *History: Politics or Culture? Reflections on Ranke and Burckhardt*. Princeton, NJ: Princeton University Press, 1990.

Gillis, John. "The Future of European History." *Perspectives: American Historical Association Newsletter* 34 (1996): 1, 4–6.

Goldman, Harvey. *Max Weber and Thomas Mann: Calling and the Shaping of the Self*. Berkeley and Los Angeles: University of California Press, 1988.

Gombrich, E. H. *In Search of Cultural History*. Oxford: Clarendon Press, 1969.

Gooch, G. P. *Germany and the French Revolution*. 2nd ed. New York: Russell & Russell, 1966.

———. *History and Historians in the Nineteenth Century*. Boston: Beacon Press, 1959.

Gossman, Lionel. "Basle, Bachofen and the Critique of Modernity in the Second Half of the Nineteenth Century." *JWCI* 74 (1986): 136–85.

———. "The Boundaries of the City: A Nineteenth Century Essay on the Limits of Historical Knowledge." *HT* 25 (1986): 33–51.

———. "Antimodernism in Nineteenth-Century Basel: Franz Overbeck's Antitheology and J. J. Bachofen's Antiphilology." *Interpretation* 16 (1989): 359–89.

———. *Between History and Literature*. Cambridge, MA: Harvard University Press, 1990.

———. "The 'Two Cultures' in Nineteenth-Century Basel: Between the French 'Encyclopédie' and German Neohumanism." *ES* 20 (1990): 95–133.

Greenslade, S. L., ed. *The Cambridge History of the Bible: The West from the Reformation to the Present Day*. Vol. 3. Cambridge: Cambridge University Press, 1963.

Gregory, Frederick. "Die Kritik von J. F. Fries an Schellings Naturphilosophie." *Sudhoffs Archiv* 66 (1983): 145–57.

————. "Kant, Schelling, and the Administration of Science in the Romantic Era." *Osiris* 5 (1989): 17–35.

————. *Nature Lost? Natural Science and the German Theological Traditions of the Nineteenth Century.* Cambridge, MA: Harvard University Press, 1992.

Greschat, Martin, ed. *Theologen des Protestantismus im 19. und 20. Jahrhundert.* 2 vols. Stuttgart: Kohlhammer, 1978.

Griffin, David Ray and Joseph C. Hough, eds. *Theology and the University: Essays in Honor of John B. Cobb, Jr.* Albany: State University of New York Press, 1991.

Groh, John E. *Nineteenth-Century German Protestantism.* Washington: University Press of America, 1982.

Gross, David. "Jacob Burckhardt and the Critique of Mass Society." *ESR* 8 (1978): 393–410.

Grunwald, Albert. "Jacob Burckhardts Stellung zur Religion." Ph.D. diss., University of Toronto, 1938.

Guggisberg, Hans R. "Der amerikanische Nachruhm Jacob Burckhardts." *Schweizer Monatshefte* 44 (1964): 747–53.

————. *Basel in the Sixteenth Century: Aspects of the City Republic before, during, and after the Reformation.* St. Louis: Center for Reformation Research, 1982.

————, ed. *Umgang mit Jacob Burckhardt: Zwölf Studien.* Vol. 1, Beiträge zu Jacob Burckhardt. Basel: Schwabe & Co., 1994.

Hagenbach, K. R. *Wilhelm Martin Leberecht de Wette: eine academische Gedächtnisrede.* Leipzig, 1850.

————. *Die theologische Schule Basels und ihre Lehrer von Stiftung bis zu de Wettes Tod 1849.* Basel, 1860.

Hahn, Karl Heinz. *Goethe in Weimar: ein Kapital deutscher Kulturgeshichte.* Zurich, 1986.

Hall, John, ed. *Rediscoveries.* Oxford: Clarendon Press, 1986.

Hamilton, Paul. *Historicism.* New York: Routledge, 1996.

Hammond, Phillip E., ed. *The Sacred in a Secular Age: Toward Revision in the Scientific Study of Religion.* Berkeley: University of California Press, 1985.

Handschin, Paul. *Wilhelm Martin Leberecht de Wette als Prediger und Shriftsteller.* Basel: Helbing & Lichtenhahn, 1958.

Hardtwig, Wolfgang. *Geschichtsschreibung zwischen Alteuropa und moderner Welt: Jacob Burckhardt in seiner Zeit.* Göttingen: Vandenhoeck & Ruprecht, 1974.

————, ed. *Über das Studium der Geschichte.* Munich: Deutscher Taschenbuch Verlag, 1990.

————. *Geschichtskultur und Wissenschaft.* Munich: Deutscher Taschenbuch Verlag, 1990.

————. "Geschichtsreligion-Wissenschaft als Arbeit- Objektivität: Der Historismus in neuer Sicht." *HZ* 252 (1991): 1–32.

Harris, Horton. *David Friedrich Strauss and His Theology.* Cambridge: Cambridge University Press, 1973.

————. *The Tübingen School.* Oxford: Clarendon Press, 1975.

Harris, H. S. *Hegel's Development: Night Thoughts (Jena 1801–1806)*. Oxford: Clarendon Press, 1983.

Harrisville, Roy A. and Walter Sundberg. *The Bible in Modern Culture: Theology and Historical-Critical Method from Spinoza to Käsemann*. Grand Rapids, MI: Eerdmans, 1995.

Hartlich, C. and W. Sachs. *Der Ursprung des Mythosbegriffes in der modernen Bibelwissenschaft*. Tübingen, 1952.

Harvey, Van Austin. *The Historian and the Believer: The Morality of Historical Knowledge and Christian Belief*. London: SCM Press, 1967.

Haufe, Eberhard von, ed. *Deutsche Briefe aus Italien von Winckelmann bis Gregorovius*. Leipzig: Koehler & Amelang, 1965.

Hazard, Paul. *The European Mind, 1680–1715*. Translated by J. Lewis May. London: Hollis and Carter, 1952.

Heftrich, Eckhard. *Hegel und Jacob Burckhardt: Zur Krisis des geschichtlichen Bewußtsein*. Frankfurt and Main: Vittorio Klostermann, 1967.

Hegel, G. W. F. *On Christianity: Early Theological Writings*. Translated by T. M. Knox. New York: Harper and Brothers, 1948.

———. *The Philosophy of Right*. Translated by T. M. Knox. Oxford: Clarendon Press, 1952.

———. *The Essential Writings*. Translated and edited by Frederick G. Weiss. New York: Harper & Row, 1974.

———. *Introduction to the Philosophy of History*. Translated and edited by Leo Rausch. Indianapolis and Cambridge: Hackett, 1988.

Heller, Erich. *The Disinherited Mind*. London: Bowes and Bowes, 1975.

Henke, E. L. T. *Jakob Friedrich Fries*. Leipzig, 1867.

Henry, Patrick, ed. *Schools of Thought in the Christian Tradition*. Philadelphia: Fortress Press, 1984.

Heussi, Karl. *Geschichte der theologischen Fakultät zur Jena*. Weimar, 1954.

Hinde, John. "Jacob Burckhardt's Political Thought." *JHI* 53 (1992): 425–36.

———. "Jacob Burckhardt and Art History: Two New Interpretations." *SdS* 26 (1994): 119–23.

Hinrichs, Carl. *Ranke und die Geschichtstheologie der Goethezeit*. Göttingen, 1954.

Hintze, Otto. *Gesammelte Abhandlungen*. Göttingen, 1962–67.

Hirsch, Emanuel. *Geschichte der neuern evangelischen Theologie*. 5 vols. Gütersloh, 1968.

Hodgsen, Peter C. *The Formation of Historical Theology: A Study of Ferdinand Christian Baur*. New York: Harper & Row, 1966.

Holborn, Hajo. "Der deutsche Idealismus in sozialgeschichtlicher Beleuchtung." *HZ* 174 (1952): 359–84.

———. *A History of Modern Germany, 1648–1840*. Princeton, NJ: Princeton University Press, 1969.

———. *History and the Humanities*. Garden City, NY: Doubleday, 1972.

Holly, Michael Ann. "Cultural History as a Work of Art: Jacob Burckhardt and Henry Adams." *Style* 22 (Summer 1988): 209–18.

Hope, Nicholas. *German and Scandinavian Protestantism, 1700–1918*. Oxford: Clarendon Press, 1995.

Hornig, Gottfried. *Die Anfänge der historisch-kritischen Theologie: Johann Salomo Semlers Schriftsverständis und seine Stellung zu Luther.* Göttingen: Vandenhoeck & Ruprecht, 1961.

Huber, E. R., ed. *Dokumente zur deutschen Verfassungsgeschichte.* Vol. 1. Stuttgart, 1956–57.

Iggers, Georg. *New Directions in European Historiography.* Middletown, CT: Wesleyan University Press, 1975.

———. "The University of Göttingen 1760–1800 and the Transformation of Historical Scholarship." *SdS* 2 (1982): 11–37.

———. *The German Conception of History: The National Tradition of Historical Thought from Herder to the Present.* Rev. ed. Middletown, CT: Wesleyan University Press, 1983.

Iggers, Georg and George Powell, eds. *Leopold von Ranke and the Shaping of the Historical Discipline.* Syracuse, NY: Syracuse University Press, 1990.

Iggers, Georg, Friedrich Jaeger, and Jörn Rüsen. *Geschichte des Historismus.* Munich: C. H. Beck, 1992.

Iggers, Georg. "Historicism: The History and Meaning of the Term." *JHI* 56 (Spring 1995): 129–52.

Jahnke, H. N. and M. Otte, eds. *Epistemological and Social Problems of the Sciences in the Early Nineteenth Century.* Boston: D. Reidel, 1981.

Janssen, E. M. *Jacob Burckhardt und die Renaissance.* Assen, Netherlands: van Gorcum, 1970.

Jay, Martin. *Fin-de-Siècle Socialism and Other Essays.* New York: Routledge, 1988.

Jenny, Ernst. "Wie de Wette nach Basel kam." *BJ* (1941): 51–78.

———. "Basel zur Biedermeierzeit." *BJ* (1949): 21–58.

Joël, Karl. *Jacob Burckhardt als Geschichtsphilosoph.* Basel, 1918.

Jones, Howard M. *Revolution and Romanticism.* Cambridge, MA: Harvard University Press, 1974.

Kaegi, Werner. "Die Idee der Vergänglichkeit in der Jugendgeschichte Jacob Burckhardts." *BZ* 42 (1942): 209–43.

———. *Jacob Burckhardt: Eine Biographie.* 7 vols. Basel: Benno Schwabe & Co., 1947–82.

———. "Jacob Burckhardt und seine Berliner Lehrer," *Schweizerische Beiträge zur Allgemeine Geschichte* 7 (1949): 101–16.

———. *Historische Meditationen.* Basel: Benno Schwabe and Co., 1994.

Kahan, Alan S. *Aristocratic Liberalism: The Social and Political Thought of Jacob Burckhardt, John Stuart Mill, and Alexis de Tocqueville.* New York: Oxford University Press, 1992.

Kant, Immanuel. *The Conflict of the Faculties.* Translated by Mary J. Gregor. New York: Abaris Books, 1979.

———. *Religion within the Limits of Reason Alone.* Translated by Theodore H. Greene and Hoyt H. Hudson. New York: Harper & Row, 1960.

Katzenbach, F. W. *Baron H. E. Kottwiz und die Erweckungsbewegung in Schlesien, Berlin, und Pommern.* Ulm, 1963.

Kerrigan, William and Gordon Braden. *The Idea of the Renaissance.* Baltimore: Johns Hopkins University Press, 1989.

Kinkel, Gottfried. *Selbstbiographie*. Edited by Richard Sander. Bonn, 1931.

Klaus, Fritz. *Basel-Landschaft in Historischen Dokumente*. 2 vols. Liestal, 1983.

Kocka, Jürgen and Werner Conze, eds. *Bildungsbürgertum im 19. Jahrhundert (Teil I): Bildungssystem und Professionalisierung in internationalen Vergleichen*. Stuttgart: Klett-Cotta, 1985.

———, eds. *Bildungsbürgertum im 19. Jahrhundert (Teil IV): Politischer Einfluß und gesellschaftliche Formation*. Stuttgart: Klett-Cotta, 1989.

Kohn, Hans, ed. *Nationalism and Liberty: The Swiss Example*. New York: Macmillan, 1956.

———. *German History: Some New German Views*. Translated by Herbert Brown. Boston: Beacon Press, 1971.

Köhnke, Klaus Christian. *The Rise of Neo-Kantianism: German Academic Philosophy between Idealism and Positivism*. Cambridge: Cambridge University Press, 1991.

Kraeling, Emil G. *The Old Testament since the Reformation*. New York: Harper & Brothers, 1955.

Kraus, Andreas. *Vernunft und Geschichte: Die Bedeutung der deutschen Akademien für die Entwicklung der Gerchichtswissenschaft im späten 18. Jahrhundert*. Freiburg: Herder, 1963.

Krieger, Leonard. *The German Idea of Freedom*. Boston: Beacon Press, 1957.

Kristeller, Paul Oskar. *Renaissance Thought and the Arts*. Exp. ed. Princeton, NJ: Princeton University Press, 1990.

Kuhn, Thomas. *The Stucture of Scientific Revolution*. 2nd ed. Chicago: University of Chicago Press, 1970.

Kümmel, Werner Georg. *The New Testament: The History of the Investigation of its Problems*. Translated by S. McLean Gilmour and Howard C. Kee. New York: Abingdon Press, 1970.

Küttler, Wolfgang, Jörn Rüsen, and Ernst Schulin, eds. *Geschichtsdiskurs: Anfänge modernen historischen Denkens*. Vol 2. Frankfurt am Main: Fischer, 1994.

LaCapra, Dominick and Steven Kaplan, eds. *Modern European Intellectual History: Reappraisals and New Perspectives*. Ithaca, NY: Cornell University Press, 1982.

Langner, Albrecht, ed. *Säkularisation und Säkularisierung im 19.Jahrhundert*. Paderborn: Ferdinand Schöningh, 1978.

Lassman, Peter, Irving Velody, and Herminio Martins, eds. *Max Weber's "Science as a Vocation."* London: Unwin Hyman, 1989.

Latourette, Kenneth Scott. *Christianity in a Revolutionary Age: A History of Christianity in the Nineteenth and Twentieth Centuries*. 5 vols. Grand Rapids, MI: Zondervan, 1969.

Lawler, Edwina. *David Friedrich Strauss and His Critics: The Life of Jesus Debate in Early Nineteenth-Century German Journals*. New York: Peter Lang, 1986.

Lee, Dwight E. and Robert N. Beck. "The Meaning of Historicism." *AHR* 59 (1954): 568–77.

Lenz, Max. "Zur Entlassung de Wettes," in *Philotesia*, ed. Adolf Harnack, 337–388. Berlin, 1907.

———. *Geschichte der königlichen Wilhelms-Universität zu Berlin*. 5 vols. Leipzig, 1910.

Lestition, Steven. "Kant and the End of the Enlightenment in Prussia." *JMH* 65 (1993): 57–112.

Lexis, W., ed. *Die deutschen Universitäten*. Vol. 1. Berlin, 1893.

Loewenich, Walter. "Jacob Burckhardt und die Kirchengeschichte." *Zeitwende* 18 (1946/47): 199–212.

Löwith, Karl. "Burckhardts Stellung zu Hegels Gesichtsphilosophie." *Deutsche Vierteljahrsschrift für Literaturwissenschaft und Geisteswissenschaft* 6 (1928): 702–41.

———. *Meaning in History: Theological Implications of the Philosophy of History*. Chicago: University of Chicago Press, 1949.

———. *From Hegel to Nietzsche: The Revolution in Nineteenth-Century Thought*. Translated by David Green. New York: Columbia University Press, 1964.

———. *Jacob Burckhardt: Der Mensch inmitten Der Geschichte*. Stuttgart: Kohlhammer, 1966.

Lücke, Friedrich. *W. M. L. de Wette*. Hamburg, 1850.

Luckmann, Thomas. *The Invisible Religion: The Problem of Religion in Modern Society*. New York: Macmillan, 1967.

Lyotard, Jean-François. *The Postmodern Condition: A Report on Knowledge*. Translated by Geoff Bennington and Brian Massumi with a foreword by Frederic Jameson. Minneapolis: University of Minnesota Press, 1979.

Macintosh, H. R. *Types of Modern Theology: Schleiermacher to Barth*. London: Collins, 1964.

MacIntyre, Alasdair. *Three Rival Forms of Moral Inquiry*. Notre Dame, IN: University of Notre Dame Press, 1990.

Maclean, Michael J. "Johann Gustav Droysen and the Development of Historical Hermeneutics." *HT* 21 (1982): 347–65.

Mah, Harold. *The End of Philosophy and the Origin of "Ideology": Karl Marx and the Crisis of the Young Hegelians*. Berkeley and Los Angeles: University of California Press, 1987.

Mali, Joseph. "Jacob Burckhardt: Myth, History, and Mythistory." *HM* 3 (Spring 1991): 86–118.

Mandelbaum, Maurice. *History, Man, and Reason: A Study in Nineteenth Century Thought*. Baltimore: Johns Hopkins University Press, 1971.

———. *The Anatomy of Historical Knowledge*. Baltimore: Johns Hopkins University Press, 1977.

Manent, Pierre. *The City of Man*. Translated by Marc A. LePain with a foreword by Jean Bethke Elshtain. Princeton, NJ: Princeton University Press, 1998.

Mannheim, Karl. "Historismus." *Archiv für Sozialwissenschaft und Sozialpolitik* 52 (1924): 1–60.

———. *Essays on the Sociology of Knowledge*. Edited by Paul Kecskemeti. New York: Oxford University Press, 1952.

Margolis, Joseph. *Historied Thought, Constructed World: A Conceptual Primer for the Turn of the Millennium*. Berkeley: University of California Press, 1995.

Marsden, George. *The Soul of the American University*. New York: Oxford University Press, 1994.

Martin, Alfred. *Die Religion Jacob Burckhardts*. Munich: Erasmus-Verlag, 1947.

Martin, Alfred. *Nietzsche und Burckhardt: Zwei geistige Welten im Dialog*. Munich: Erasmus-Verlag, 1947.

Martin, David. *A General Theory of Secularization*. New York: Harper & Row, 1978.

Marx, Werner. *The Philosophy of F. W. J. Schelling: History, System, and Freedom*. Bloomington: Indiana University Press, 1984.

Massey, M. C. "The Literature of Young Germany and D. F. Strauss's Life of Jesus." *JR* 59 (1979): 298–323.

———. *Christ Unmasked: The Meaning of the* Life of Jesus *in German Politics*. Chapel Hill: University of North Carolina Press, 1983.

Mayer, Arno. *The Persistence of the Old Regime*. London: Croom Helm, 1981.

McClelland, Charles E. *State, Society, and University in Germany, 1700–1914*. Cambridge: Cambridge University Press, 1980.

———. " 'To Live for Science': Ideals and Realities at the University of Berlin. In *The University and the City*, ed. Thomas Bender. Oxford: Oxford University Press, 1988.

McGrath, Alister. *The Making of Modern German Christology: From the Enlightenment to Pannenberg*. Oxford: Basil Blackwell, 1986.

———. *The Genesis of Doctrine: A Study in the Foundations of Doctrinal Criticism*. Oxford: Basil Blackwell, 1990.

———, ed. *The Blackwell Encyclopedia of Modern Christian Thought*. Oxford: Basil Blackwell, 1993.

———. *Christian Theology: An Introduction*. Oxford: Basil Blackwell, 1994.

McIntire, C. T., ed. *God, History, and Historians: Modern Christian Views of History*. New York: Oxford University Press, 1977.

McLeod, Hugh. *Religion and the People of Western Europe, 1789–1970*. Oxford: Oxford University Press, 1981.

Megill, Allan. "Aesthetic Theory and Historical Consciousness in the Eighteenth Century." *HT* 17 (1978): 29–62.

———. *Prophets of Extremity: Nietzsche, Heidegger, Foucault, Derrida*. Berkeley: University of California Press, 1985.

———, ed. *Rethinking Objectivity*. Durham, NC: Duke University Press, 1994.

Meinecke, Friedrich. *Historism: The Rise of a New Historical Outlook*. Translated by J. E. Anderson. New York: Herder and Herder, 1972.

Melzer, Arthur M., Jerry Weinberger, and M. Richard Zinman, eds. *History and the Idea of Progress*. Ithaca: Cornell University Press, 1995.

Michaelson, Gordon E. *Lessing's "Ugly Ditch": A Study of Theology and History*. University Park: Pennsylvania State University Press, 1985.

Mildenberger, Friedrich. *Geschichte der deutschen evangelischen Theologie im 19. und 20.Jahrhundert*. Stuttgart: Kohlhammer, 1981.

Miller, Perry. "Theodore Parker: Apostasy within Liberalism." *HTR* 54 (1961): 275–95.

Minder, Robert. *Kultur und Literatur in Deutschland und Frankreich*. Frankfurt am Main, 1962.

Momigliano, Arnaldo. *Historicism Revisited*. Amsterdam: North Holland Publising Co., 1974.

————. *Essays in Ancient and Modern Historiography*. Oxford: Basil Blackwell, 1977.

Mommsen, Wolfgang J. "Jacob Burckhardt – Defender of Culture and Prophet of Doom." *Government and Opposition* 18 (Autumn 1983): 458–75.

Muhlack, Ulrich. *Geschichtswissenschaft im Humanismus und in der Aufklärung: Die Vorgeschichte des Historismus*. Munich: C. H. Beck, 1991.

Murrmann-Kahl, Michael. *Die enzauberte Heilsgeschichte: Der Historismus erobert die Theologie*. Gütersloh, 1992.

Neff, Emery. *The Poetry of History: The Contribution of Literary Scholarship to the Writing of History since Voltaire*. New York: Columbia University Press, 1947.

Nelson, John S., Allan Megill, and Donald N. McCloskey, eds. *The Rhetoric of the Human Sciences: Language and Argument in Scholarship and Public Affairs*. Madison: University of Wisconsin Press, 1987.

Nelson, Leonard. *Progress and Regress in Philosophy from Hume and Kant to Hegel and Fries*. 2 vols. Edited by Julius Kraft. Translated by Humphrey Palmer. Oxford: Basil Blackwell, 1970.

Nelson, N. "Individualism as a Criterion of the Renaissance." *Journal of English and Germanic Philology* 32 (1933): 316–34.

Neumann, Carl. *Jacob Burckhardt*. Munich, 1927.

Newman, J. H. *The Idea of a University*. San Francisco: Rinehart Press, 1960.

Nichols, James Hastings. *History of Christianity, 1650–1950, Secularization of the West*. New York: Ronald Press, 1956.

Nietzsche, Friedrich. *Untimely Meditations*. Translated by R. J. Hollingdale. Cambridge: Cambridge University Press, 1983.

————. *Selected Letters*. Translated by A. N. Ludovici. London: Soho, 1985.

————. *Selected Letters*. Translated and edited by Christopher Middleton. Chicago: University of Chicago Press, 1969.

————. *Sämtliche Werke*. 15 vols. Munich: Deutscher Taschenbuch Verlag, 1980.

Nipperdey, Thomas. *Deutsche Geschichte, 1800–1866: Bürgerwelt und starker Staat*. Munich: C. H. Beck, 1983.

————. *Germany from Napoleon to Bismarch, 1800–1866*. Translated by Daniel Nolan. Princeton, NJ: Princeton University Press, 1996.

Noll, Thomas. *Vom Gluck des Gelehrten: Versuch über Jacob Burckhardt*. Göttingen, 1997.

North, Robert. "Bibliography of Works in Theology and History." *HT* 12 (1973): 55–140.

Novak, Kurt. *Geschichte des Christentums in Deutschland: Religion, Politik und Gesellschaft vom Ende der Aufklärung bis zur Mitte des 20.Jahrhunderts*. Munich: C. H. Beck, 1995.

Novick, Peter. *That Noble Dream: The "Objectivity Question" and the American Historical Profession*. Cambridge: Cambridge University Press, 1988.

Ogletree, Thomas W. *Christian Faith and History: A Critical Comparison of Ernst Troeltsch and Karl Barth*. New York: Abingdon Press, 1967.

Osgood, Samuel. "De Wette's Views of Religion and Theology." *The Christian Examiner* (1838): 137–71.

Otto, Rudolf. *The Philosophy of Religion Based on Kant and Fries.* Translated by E. B. Dicker. London, 1931.

Overbeck, Franz. *Werke und Nachlaß: Kirchenlexicon Texte, Ausgewählte Artikel A-I.* Vol. 4. Edited by Barbara von Reibnitz et al. Stuttgart: J. B. Metzler, 1995.

Pandel, Hans-Jürgen. *Historik und Didaktik.* Stuttgart, 1990.

Pannenberg, Wolfhart. *Theology and the Philosophy of Science.* Translated by Francis McDonagh. Philadelphia: Westminster Press, 1976.

Paul, Jean-Marie. *D. F. Strauss (1808–1874) et son époche.* Paris: Société les Belles Lettre, 1982.

Paulsen, Friedrich. *Geschichte des gelehrten Unterrichts auf den deutschen Schulen und Universitäten.* Leipzig, 1885.

———. *The German Universities and University Study.* Translated by William W. Elwang. New York: Charles Scribner's Sons, 1906.

Peacocke, A. R., ed. *The Sciences and Theology in the Twentieth Century.* Notre Dame, IN: University of Notre Dame Press, 1981.

Pelikan, Jaroslav. *Historical Theology: Continuity and Change in Christian Doctrine.* Philadelphia: Westminster Press, 1971.

———. *From Luther to Kierkegaard: A Study in the History of Theology.* St. Louis, MO: Concordia Publishing House, 1950.

Pistor-Frey, Elizabeth and Ernst Ziegler. "Karl Frey, ein Schüler Jacob Burckhardt." *BZ* 70 (1970): 161–208.

Pletsch, Carl. *Young Nietzsche: Becoming a Genius.* New York: The Free Press, 1991.

Pfleiderer, Otto. *The Development of Theology in Germany since Kant and Its Progress in Great Britain since 1825.* Translated by J. Frederick Smith. London, 1890.

Pocock, J. G. A. "The Origins of Study of the Past: A Comparative Approach." *Comparative Studies in Society and History* 4 (1962): 209–46.

Poggi, Stefano and Maurizio Bossi, eds. *Romanticism in Science: Science in Europe, 1790–1840.* Dordrecht: Kluwer Academic Publishers, 1994.

Popper, Karl. *The Poverty of Historicism.* London: Routledge & Kegan Paul, 1960.

Puknat, Siegfried B. "De Wette in New England." *Proceedings of the American Philosophical Society* (1958): 376–95.

Ralph, Philip L. *The Renaissance in Perspective.* New York: St. Martin's Press, 1973.

Rand, Calvin G. "Two Meanings of Historicism in the Writings of Dilthey, Troeltsch, and Meinecke." *JHI* 25 (1964): 503–18.

Rathmann, Jänos. *Historizität in der deutschen Aufklärung.* Frankfurt am Main: Peter Lang, 1993.

Reardon, Bernard, ed. *Liberal Protestantism.* Stanford: Stanford University Press, 1968.

———. *Religion in the Age of Romanticism.* Cambridge: Cambridge University Press, 1985.

———. *Religious Thought in the Nineteenth Century.* Cambridge: Cambridge University Press, 1966.

Redeker, Martin. *Schleiermacher: His Life and Thought.* Translated by John Wallhauser. Philadelphia: Fortress Press, 1973.

Reicke, B. "W. M. L. de Wette's Contribution to Biblical Theology." *NTS* 29 (1982): 293–305.

Reill, Peter Hanns. "History and Hermeneutics in the *Aufklärung*: The Thought of Johann Christoph Gatterer." *JMH* 45 (1973): 24–51.

———. *The German Enlightenment and the Rise of Historicism*. Berkeley and Los Angeles: University of California Press, 1975.

Reimarus, Hermann Samuel. *Reimarus Fragments*. Translated by Ralph S. Fraser and edited by Charles H. Talbert. Philadelphia: Fortress Press, 1970.

Reventlow, Henning Graf. *The Authority of the Bible and the Rise of the Modern World*. Translated by John Bowden. London: SCM Press, 1984.

Reventlow, Henning Graf, Walter Sparn, and John Woodbridge, eds. *Historische Kritik und biblischer Kanon in der deutschen Aufklärung*. Wiesbaden: Harrassowitz, 1988.

Riesterer, Berthold P. *Karl Löwith's View of History: A Critical Appraisal of Historicism*. The Hague: Martinus Nijhoff, 1969.

Ringer, Fritz. *The Decline of the German Mandarins: The German Academic Community, 1890–1933*. Cambridge, MA: Harvard University Press, 1969.

Ritschl, Dietrich. "Johann Salomo Semler: The Rise of the Historical-Critical Method in Eighteenth-Century Theology on the Continent." In *Introduction to Modernity: A Symposium on Eighteenth-Century Thought*, ed. Robert Mollenauer, 109–33. Austin: University of Texas Press, 1965.

Ritter, Joachim. *Historisches Wörterbuch der Philosophie*. 8 vols. Basel/Stuttgart: Benno Schwabe & Co., 1971.

Roberts, David D. *Benedetto Croce and the Uses of Historicism*. Berkeley: University of California Press, 1987.

Robinson, James M. *A New Quest of the Historical Jesus and Other Essays*. Philadelphia: Fortress Press, 1983.

Rogerson, John W. *Myth in Old Testament Interpretation*. Berlin: De Gruyter, 1974.

———. *Old Testament Criticism in the Nineteenth Century*. London: SPCK Press, 1984.

———. *W. M. L. de Wette: Founder of Modern Biblical Criticism: An Intellectual Biography*. Sheffield: JSOT Press, 1992.

Rorty, Richard. *Contingency, Irony, Solidarity*. Cambridge: Cambridge University Press, 1989.

Rose, William. *From Goethe to Byron: The Development of "Weltschmerz" in German Literature*. London, 1924.

Rosenberg, Hans. *Politische Denkströmungen im deutschen Vormärz*. Göttingen: Vandenhoeck & Ruprecht, 1972.

Rossi, Philip J. and Michael Wren, eds. *Kant's Philosophy of Religion Reconsidered*. Bloomington and Indianapolis: Indiana University Press, 1991.

Rossi, Roberto. *Nietzsche e Burckhardt*. Genova: Tilgher, 1987.

Roth, Michael. *Rediscovering History: Culture, Politics and the Psyche*. Stanford, CA: Stanford University Press, 1994.

Röthlin, Niklaus, "Burckhardts Stellung in der Kulturgeschichtsschreibung des 19.Jahrhundert." *AfKG* 69 (1987): 389–406.

Rüsen, Jörn. *Grundzüge des Historismus*. 3 vols. Göttingen, 1983–89.

Rüsen, Jörn. "Jacob Burckhardt: Political Standpoint and the Historical Insight on the Border of Post-Modernism." *HT* 24 (1985): 235–46.

———. *Zeit und Sinn: Strategien historischen Denkens*. Frankfurt am main: Fischer Taschenbuch Verlag, 1990.

———. *Konfiguration des Historismus: Studien zur deutschen Wissenschaftskultur*. Frankfurt am main: Suhrkamp, 1993.

Rüsen, Jörn and Friedrich Jaeger. *Geschichte des Historismus*. Stuttgart, 1990.

Rust, Eric C. *The Christian Understanding of History*. London, 1946.

———. *Towards a Theological Understanding of History*. New York: Oxford University Press, 1963.

Safranski, Rüdiger. *Schopenhauer and the Wild Years of Philosophy*. Translated by Ewald Osers. London: Weidenfeld and Nicolson, 1989.

Salin, Edgar. *Burckhardt und Nietzsche*. Heidelberg: Rowohlt, 1948.

Sax, Benjamin C. "State and Culture in the Thought of Jacob Burckhardt." *Annals of Scholarship* 3 (March 1986): 1–36.

Scheider, Wolfgang, "Religion in the History of the Modern World: A German Perspective." *ESR* 12 (July 1982): 289–99.

Schelling, F. W. J. *Schellings Werke*. Edited by Manfred Schröter. Vol. 3. Munich: Beck und R. Oldenbourg, 1927.

———. *The Philosophy of Art*. Translated by Douglas W. Scott. Minneapolis: University of Minnesota Press, 1989.

Schenk, H. G. *The Mind of the European Romantics*. New York: Doubleday, 1969.

Schleiermacher, Friedrich. *The Christian Faith*. Edited and Translated from the 2nd edition by H. R. Mackintosh and J. S. Stewart. Edinburgh: T.& T. Clark, 1989.

———. *On Religion: Speeches to Its Cultured Despisers*. Translated by John Oman with an introduction by Rudolf Otto. New York: Harper & Row, 1958.

———. *The Life of Jesus*. Translated by S. MacLean Gilmour. Philadelphia: Fortress Press, 1975.

———. "Reflections Concerning the Nature and Function of Universities." Translated by Gerhard E. Spiegler. *The Christian Scholar* 48 (1965): 139–57.

Schlink, Wilhelm. *Jacob Burckhardt und die Kunsterwartung im Vormärz*. Wiesbaden: F. Steiner, 1982.

Schmidt, Ferdinand Jakob. *Der Niedergang des Protestantismus*. Berlin, 1904.

Schmidt, Martin, ed. *Kirchen und Liberalismus im 19.Jahrhundert*. Göttingen: Vandenhoeck & Ruprecht, 1976.

Schnabel, Franz. *Deutsche Geschichte im neunzehnten Jahrhundert: (Band 4) Die religiösen Kräfte*. 2nd ed. Freiburg: Herder Verlag, 1951.

Schnädelbach, Herbert. *Philosophy in Germany, 1831–1933*. Translated by Eric Matthews. Cambridge: Cambridge University Press, 1984.

Scholder, Klaus. *Ursprünge und Problem der Bibelkritik im 17.Jahrhundert*. Munich: Kaiser, 1966.

Schorske, Carl. "Science as a Vocation in Burckhardt's Basel." In *The University and the City: From Medieval Origins to the Present*, ed. Thomas Bender. New York, 1988.

Schulenburg, Werner von der. *Der junge Burckhardt*. Stuttgart-Zurich: Montana Verlag A. G., 1926.

Schulin, Ernst. *Burckhardts Drei Potenzen*. Heidelberg: Carl Winter-Universitätsverlag, 1983.

Schweitzer, Albert. *The Quest of the Historical Jesus: A Critical Study of Its Progress from Reimarus to Wrede*. Translated by W. Montgomery. London, 1910.

Shaffer, E. S. *"Kubla Khan" and The Fall of Jerusalem: The Mythological School in Biblical Criticism and Secular Literature, 1770–1880*. Cambridge: Cambridge University Press, 1975.

Sheehan, James. *German Liberalism in the Nineteenth Century*. Chicago: University of Chicago Press, 1978.

———. *German History, 1770–1866*. Oxford: Clarendon Press, 1989.

Shils, Edward. *Center and Periphery: Essays in Macrosociology*. Chicago: University of Chicago Press, 1975.

Siebart, Irmgard. *Jacob Burckhardt: Studien zur Kunst- und Kulturgeschichtsschreibung*. Basel: Benno Schwabe, 1991.

Sigurdson, Richard F. "Jacob Burckhardt: The Cultural Historian as Political Thinker." *RP* 52 (1990): 417–40.

Smart, Ninian, John Clayton, Steven Katz, and Patrick Sherry, eds. *Nineteenth Century Religious Thought in the West*. 3 vols. Cambridge: Cambridge University Press, 1985.

Smend, Rudolf. "De Wette und das Verhältnis zwischen historischer Bibelkritik und philosophischem System im 19.Jahrhundert." *TZ* 14 (1957): 107–19.

———. *Wilhelm Martin Leberecht De Wettes Arbeit am Alten und Neuen Testament*. Basel, 1958.

———. *Deutsche Altestestamentler in Drei Jahrhunderten*. Göttingen: Vandenhoeck & Ruprecht, 1989.

Southard, Robert. "Theology in Droysen's Early Political Historiography: Free Will, Necessity, and the Historian." *HT* 18 (1979): 378–96.

Spohn, Willfried. "Protestantism, Secularization, and Politics in Nineteenth-Century Germany." In *Render unto Caesar: The Religious Sphere in World Politics*, eds. Sabrina Petra Ramet and Donald W. Treadgold, 173–89. Washington: American University Press, 1995.

Stadelmann, Rudolf. "Jacob Burckhardts Weltgeschichtliche Betrachtungen." *HZ* 169 (1949): 31–72.

Stähelin, Rudolf. *W. M. L. de Wette nach seiner theologische Wirksamkeit und Bedeutung*. Basel, 1880.

Staehelin, Ernst. *Dewettiana: Forschungen und Texte zu Wilhelm Martin Leberecht de Wette*. Basel: Helbing & Lichtenhahn, 1956.

———. "Kleine Dewettiana." *TZ* 13 (1957): 33–41.

———. *Professoren der Universität Basel aus Fünf Jahrhunderten*. Basel: Friedrich Reinhardt, 1959.

———, ed. *Die Christentumsgesellschaft in der Zeit von der Erweckung bis zur Gegenwart: Texte aus Briefen, Protokollen, Publikationen*. 2 vols. Basel: Friedrich Renhardt Verlag, 1974.

Staehelin, Felix. "Erinnerungen an Jacob Burckhardt." *BJ* 46 (1946): 117–23.

Staehelin, Andreas. *Geschichte der Universität Basel*. 3 vols. Basel: Helbing & Lichtenhahn, 1959.

Steiner, George. *Real Presences*. Chicago: University of Chicago Press, 1989.

Stern, Fritz. *The Politics of Cultural Despair: A Study in the Rise of the Germanic Ideology*. Berkeley and Los Angeles: University of California Press, 1961.

———, ed. *Varieties of History from Voltaire to the Present*. New York: Vintage Books, 1956.

Sternberg, Meir. *The Poetics of Biblical Narrative: Ideological Literature and the Drama of Reading*. Bloomington: Indiana University Press, 1985.

Stoeffler, F. Ernest. *German Pietism during the Eighteenth Century*. Leiden: E. J. Brill, 1973.

Stone, Laurence. *The University in Society*. Vol. 2. Princeton, NJ: Princeton University Press, 1974.

Strauss, D. F. *Charakteristiken und Kritiken*. Leipzig, 1844.

———. *The Life of Jesus: Critically Examined*. Translated from the 4th edition by George Eliot. London: Chapman Brothers, 1846.

———. *The Christ of Faith and the Jesus of History*. Translated and edited by Leander E. Keck. Philadelphia: Fortress Press, 1977.

———. *The Old Faith and the New*. Translated by Mathilde Blind with notes and an introduction by G. A. Wells. Amherst, MA: Prometheus Books, 1997.

Strauss, Leo. *Natural Right and History*. Chicago: University of Chicago Press, 1953.

Strich, Fritz. *Die Mythologie in der Deutschen Literatur von Klopstock bis Wagner*. 2 vols. Bern: Francke Verlag, 1970.

Suter, Rudolf and René Teuteberg, eds. *Der Reformation verpflichtet: Gestalten und Gestalter in Stadt und Landschaft Basel aus fünf Jahrhunderten*. Basel: Christian Merian Verlag, 1979.

Sykes, S. W., ed. *England and Germany: Studies in Theological Diplomacy*. Frankfurt am Main: Verlag Peter D. Lang, 1982.

Taylor, Charles. *Hegel*. Cambridge: Cambridge University Press, 1975.

Telman, David A. J. "Clio Ascendant: The Historical Profession in Nineteenth-Century Germany." Ph.D. diss., Cornell University, 1993.

Thomas, Brook. *The New Historicism and Other Old-Fashioned Topics*. Princeton: Princeton University Press, 1991.

Thomasius, G., I. A. Dorner, and A. E. Biedermann. *God and Incarnation in Mid-Nineteenth Century German Theology*. Translated and edited by Claude Welch. New York: Oxford University Press, 1965.

Thompson, James W. *A History of Historical Writing*: (vol. 2) *The Eighteenth and Nineteenth Centuries*. New York: Macmillan, 1942.

Tice, Terence. *The Schleiermacher Bibliography*. Princeton: Princeton University Press, 1966.

Tillich, Paul. *A History of Christian Thought*. New York: Simon & Schuster, 1967.

Toews, John. *Hegelianism: The Path toward Dialectical Humanism, 1805–1841*. Cambridge: Cambridge University Press, 1980.

Treitschke, Heinrich von. *Deutsche Geschichte im neunzehnten Jahrhundert*. 5 vols. Leipzig: S. Hirzel, 1879–94.

Trevor-Roper, H. R. *Historical Essays*. London: Macmillan Press, 1957.

Troeltsch, Ernst. *Die Bedeutung der Geschichte für die Weltanschauung*. Berlin, 1918.

———. "Die Krisis des Historismus." *Die neue Rundschau* 33 (1922): 572–90.

———. *Protestantism and Progress: A Historical Study of the Relation of Protestantism to the Modern World*. Translated by W. Montgomery. Boston: Beacon Press, 1966.

Turner, R. Steven. "The Growth of Professorial Research in Prussia, 1818–1848 – Causes and Context. In *Historical Studies in the Physical Sciences*, ed. Russel McCormmach. Vol. 3. Philadelphia: University of Pennsylvania Press, 1971.

———. "The Prussian Universities and the Research Imperative, 1806–1848." Ph.D. diss, Princeton University, 1972.

Tuveson, Ernest Lee. *Millennium and Utopia: A Study in the Background of the Idea of Progress*. New York: Harper & Row, 1949.

Urban, Linwood. *A Short History of Christian Thought*. Rev. ed. New York: Oxford University Press, 1995.

Van der Berg, Jan. "Vray piétisme: Die aufgeklärte Frömmigkeit des Basler Pfarrers Pierre Rogues." *Zwingliana* 16 (1983–85): 35–53.

Vesser, H. A., ed. *The New Historicism*. New York: Routledge, 1996.

Vidler, Alec R. *The Church in an Age of Revolution: 1789 to the Present Day*. New York: Penguin, 1961.

Vischer, Eberhard. "Die Lehrstühle und Unterricht an der theolog. Fakultät Basels seit der Reformation." In *Festschrift zur Feier des 450 jährigen Bestehens der Universität Basel*. Basel: Helbing & Lichtenhahn, 1905.

Walker, Ralph C. S. *The Coherence Theory of Truth: Realism, Anti-Realism, Idealism*. New York: Routledge, 1989.

Walker, H. "The University of Berlin." *The Christian Examiner* (November 1836): 213–23.

Wallace, Robert M. "Progress, Secularization, and Modernity: The Löwith-Blumenberg Debate." *NGC* 22 (1981): 63–80.

Weber, Wolfgang. *Priester der Clio: Historisch-sozialwissenschaftliche Studien zur Herkunft und Karriere deutscher Historiker und zur Geschichte der Geschichtswissenshaft*. Frankfurt am Main: Verlag Peter D. Lang, 1987.

Wehler, Hans-Ulrich. *Deutsche Historiker*. Göttingen: Vandenhoeck and Ruprecht, 1971–72.

Weintraub, Karl Joachim. *Visions of Culture*. Chicago: University of Chicago Press, 1966.

———. "Jacob Burckhardt: The Historian among the Philologists." *American Scholar* 57 (Spring 1988): 273–82.

Weiss, John. *Life and Correspondence of Theodore Parker*. New York: D. Appleton, 1864.

Welch, Claude. *Protestant Thought in the Nineteenth Century*. 2 vols. New Haven, CT: Yale University Press, 1972, 1985.

Wenzel, Johannes. *Jacob Burckhardt in der Krise seiner Zeit*. Berlin: Veb Deutscher Verlag der Wissenschaften, 1967.

Wernel, Paul. *Der Schweizerische Protestantismus im 18.Jahrhundert*. 3 vols. Tübingen, 1924.

White, Hayden. "The Burden of History." *HT* 5 (1966): 111–34.

———. *Metahistory: The Historical Imagination in Nineteenth-Century Europe*. Baltimore and London: Johns Hopkins University Press, 1973.

White, Hayden. *The Content of the Form: Narrative Discourse and Historical Representation.* Baltimore: Johns Hopkins University Press, 1987.

Wiegand, Adelbert. *W. M. L. de Wette 1780–1849: Eine Säkularschrift.* Erfurt, 1879.

Willey, Thomas. *Back to Kant: The Revival of Kantianism in German Social and Historical Thought, 1860–1914.* Detroit: Wayne State University Press, 1978.

Williamson, George. "The Longing for Myth in Germany: Culture, Religion, and Politics, 1790–1878," Ph.D. diss., Yale University, 1996.

Wittkau, Annette. *Historismus: Zur Geschichte des Begriffs und des Problems.* Göttingen: Vandenhoeck & Ruprecht, 1992.

Wood, Allen. *Kant's Moral Religion.* Ithaca: Cornell University Press, 1970.

Wundt, Max. *Die Philosophie an der Universität Jena in ihrem geschichtlichen Verlaufe dargestellt.* Jena, 1932.

Wuthnow, Robert. *Meaning and Moral Order: Explorations in Cultural Analysis.* Berkeley and Los Angeles: University of California Press, 1987.

Zeeden, Ernst Walter. "Der Historiker als Kritiker und Prophet." *Die Welt als Geschichte* 11 (1931): 154–73.

———. "Die Auseinandersetzung des jungen Jacob Burckhardt mit Glaube und Christentum." *HZ* 178 (1954): 493–514.

Index